Coding4Fun

10 .NET Programming Projects for Wiimote, World of Warcraft, YouTube, and More

Dan Fernandez & Brian Peek

O'REILLY®

BEIJING · CAMBRIDGE · FARNHAM · KÖLN · SEBASTOPOL · TAIPEI · TOKYO

Coding4Fun By Dan Fernandez and Brian Peek

Editors: **Laurel R. T. Ruma and John Osborn**

Production Editor: **Rachel Monaghan**

Production Services: **Newgen North America**

Copyeditor: **Genevieve d'Entremont**

Cover Designer: **Mark Paglietti**

Interior Designer: **Ron Bilodeau**

Published by O'Reilly Media, Inc., 1005 Gravenstein Highway North, Sebastopol, CA 95472.

O'Reilly books may be purchased for educational, business, or sales promotional use. Online editions are also available for most titles (*safari.oreilly.com*). For more information, contact our corporate/institutional sales department: 800.998.9938 or *corporate@oreilly.com*.

Print History: November 2008: First Edition
ISBN: 978-0-596-52074-8

[V]

Dedications

Dan Fernandez

To my mother, who always gave me the encouragement and support to succeed; to my father, for inspiring me to become who I am today; and to Angie, the love of my life and the woman of my dreams.

Brian Peek

In loving memory of my Dad. You left us too soon, and we all miss you.

To my Mom, for a lifetime of support, who remains strong and will make it through.

And to Michelle, my girlfriend and best friend, who went above and beyond to help us through it all, and who continues to make every day better.

Contents

Section 3 Hardware

Preface

Software development can take many forms. For many professional developers, this often involves the drudgery of implementing applications that query databases or build extensive reports. For students or hobbyists, software creation may take the form of simple exercises that return mundane sorted lists or draw a few images to the screen.

However, no matter what your skill level or career, building computer software can be a lot more entertaining and, at the same time, educational. Instead of dropping controls on forms and retrieving a customer's order, why not create a video game or drive a remote-controlled car using a Nintendo Wii Remote?

This is the whole concept behind *Coding4Fun*: building software that does fun and interesting things with your computer. In this book, we will take you through 10 different projects that, at the end, will give you something fun to play with, and something cool to impress your friends and family with. Here you will find full-on tutorials, diagrams, code snippets, photos, and everything you need to have fun with software development, and learn a few things in the process.

Do you want to interface your computer to external hardware and unique input devices? We have you covered. Do you want to build a video game that runs on your computer, Xbox 360, and Zune? You'll find it here. Do you want to use some of the popular social networking sites, such as YouTube and Twitter, in new and interesting ways? Keep reading. Want to query a database for your customer's last 10 orders? You're in the wrong place, bub.

Who This Book Is For

This book is aimed at a variety of computer users and software developers. If you are familiar with .NET development using C# or Visual Basic, you'll be able to conquer every project in this book. If you are a computer user who doesn't have a great handle on software development, there are several projects here you can tackle and complete without issues. Regardless of your development experience and skills, every chapter comes with a downloadable, complete application that you can immediately run and use if you wish to skip to the final product.

So don't be afraid if you don't have a PhD in computer science. No matter what your skill level is, we're confident there is a project in this book you will be able to accomplish, and many you'll be able to learn from to increase your knowledge and abilities—and have fun in the process!

What You Need to Use This Book

Every chapter has its own set of requirements and pieces it may need to work, but there are a few common pieces of software you should download and install in order to get started.

First, you will need some form of Visual Studio 2008 installed. If you are a professional developer, you may already have a version of Visual Studio installed on your computer. If you don't, or you're just starting out, don't sweat it: Visual Studio 2008 Express is available for free and is a simple download and install. Also note that Visual Studio 2008 Express installs side-by-side with Visual Studio 2005 (and Visual Studio 2005 Express) and will not cause any problems.

All Visual Studio 2008 Express editions can be found at *http://www.microsoft.com/Express/download*.

Visual Studio 2008 Express is broken up into several different versions, depending on the language you wish to use and the application you're looking to use. If you want to compile the C# versions of the code in these chapters, you should download and install Visual C# 2008 Express Edition. If you are more familiar with Visual Basic, you should download and install Visual Basic 2008 Express Edition. For the projects in this book that require web development, you will need to download and install Visual Web Developer 2008 Express Edition.

For the hardware chapters, it is also assumed you have some standard tools and parts, such as screwdrivers, hammers, pliers, a soldering iron, etc.

There are some chapters that do require some specialized components and software. Read through the next section to see what specific items are required to complete each project so you can get a head start before diving into the project you want to build. Each chapter will also explain the requirements in a bit more detail.

All of these projects were written and run using a Windows PC running Windows XP SP2 or higher and Windows Vista. If you have a Mac or some other operating system, you might be able to use virtual machine software (such as VMWare or Parallels) for some of these projects, but we can't guarantee you will be successful, and we won't be able to help you if you're not.

How This Book Is Organized

Section 1, Gaming

Chapter 1, *Alien Attack*

This chapter will teach you how to build a simple 2-D video game using XNA Game Studio. The game will be playable on a Windows computer capable of running DirectX9 with a video card that supports pixel shader 1.1 or higher, an Xbox 360, or a Microsoft Zune media player. To create this project you will need to download and install XNA Game Studio 3.0, which is a free Microsoft product. Obviously you will need an Xbox 360 or Zune if you wish to run the game on these devices; otherwise, the Windows version can be created and run with no additional hardware or software.

Chapter 2, *LEGO Soldier: A 2-D LEGO Side Scroller Popfly Game*

This chapter shows how to build LEGO Soldier, a 2-D Silverlight game built with Popfly, a free, Silverlight-based set of tools for building websites, mashups, and games. This chapter requires that you install the Silverlight runtime to work properly. To build custom LEGO designs, you will need to download and install LEGO's Digital Designer software.

Chapter 3, *Feed Reader: An In-Game RSS Reader for World of Warcraft*

This chapter walks through how to build Feed Reader, an in-game RSS Reader for *World of Warcraft*. To modify the add-on, it's recommended that you install Add-On Studio for *World of Warcraft* version 2.0. To use Feed Reader, you will need to install *World of Warcraft*.

Section 2, Software and Web

Chapter 4, *InnerTube: Download, Convert, and Sync YouTube Videos*

In this chapter, you will take a tour of InnerTube, an application that downloads, converts, and syncs YouTube videos. Although it is not required, InnerTube can sync videos with the following optional hardware devices: iPod, iPhone, or Zune.

Chapter 5, *PeerCast: Watch Videos on Your PC Anywhere in the World*

In this chapter, you will learn about PeerCast, an application that enables you to stream video from your home PC to another PC anywhere in the world. Since PeerCast communicates using the Peer Channel protocol, your Internet router must support the Peer Channel protocol.

Chapter 6, *TwitterVote*

In this chapter, you will create a web-based application that will allow you to create online polls using the Twitter service and then view its results in a bar graph. This application requires no additional hardware or software other than Visual Web Developer 2008 Express and the Silverlight runtime.

Chapter 7, *WHSMail: Outlook Webmail Add-in for Windows Home Server*

This chapter demonstrates how to build a website plugin for Windows Home Server that will allow you to view your Outlook message store from the Web at any time. To finish this project you will need a Windows Home Server (any product with Internet Information Services will allow you to run the app, but without full functionality).

Section 3, Hardware

Chapter 8, *Wiimote Controlled Car*

This chapter contains a step-by-step implementation of a Wii Remote (Wiimote) controlled car. In order to complete this project you will need:

- A Bluetooth-enabled PC

- Nintendo Wii Remote (Wiimote)

- Phidget Interface Kit 0/0/4 or 0/16/16 (and the Phidget API, downloadable for free)

- A remote-controlled car with "digital" inputs

- Soldering iron and solder

- Wire

Chapter 9, *Wiimote Whiteboard*

In this chapter, you will learn how to build an interactive whiteboard using a Wii Remote (Wiimote). To complete this project you will need:

- Nintendo Wii Remote (Wiimote)

- An infrared (IR) LED

- A normally open momentary switch

- AAA or AA battery

- A white-erase marker

- Soldering iron and solder

- Dremel tool

Chapter 10, *Animated Musical Holiday Lights*

In this chapter you will find directions for building an animated light show set to music, much like the famous holiday light show videos you may have seen on YouTube. To complete this chapter you will need:

- One or more Phidget Interface Kits 0/0/4 (each kit gives you four channels to control)
- The Phidget API (downloadable for free)
- Five 2-prong outdoor use extension cords per Interface Kit
- 14–16 gauge wire
- Two wire nuts that can handle 14–16 gauge wire per Interface Kit
- A project box of some sort that can hold the finished Interface Kit devices
- Strings of holiday lights
- External speakers or FM transmitter so the music can be heard

Conventions Used in This Book

The following typographical conventions are used in this book:

Italic

Introduces new terms and indicates URLs, commands, file extensions, filenames, directory or folder names, and UNC pathnames

`Constant width`

Indicates commands, options, switches, variables, attributes, keys, functions, types, classes, namespaces, methods, modules, properties, parameters, values, objects, events, event handlers, XML tags, HTML tags, macros, the contents of files, and the output from commands

`Constant width italic`

Shows text that should be replaced with user-supplied values

`Constant width bold`

Shows commands or other text that should be typed literally by the user

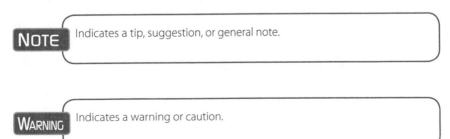

NOTE

Indicates a tip, suggestion, or general note.

WARNING

Indicates a warning or caution.

About the Code

For projects that require actual coding, you will find examples in both Visual Basic and C#, *except* for the chapter on XNA, which requires C#. All code was developed using a version of Visual Studio 2008 SP1 with .NET 3.5 SP1.

The .NET code and Visual Studio solution can be found for every chapter in this book at the book's website, located at *http://www.c4fbook.com/*. Many of these projects will continue to be updated after the book is published, so be sure to check the site for new and improved versions of the applications that include bug fixes and feature additions.

Using Code Examples

This book is here to help you get your job done. In general, you may use the code in this book in your programs and documentation. You do not need to contact us for permission, unless you're reproducing a significant portion of the code. For example, writing a program that uses several chunks of code from this book does not require permission. Selling or distributing a CD-ROM of examples from O'Reilly books *does* require permission. Answering a question by citing this book and quoting example code does not require permission. Incorporating a significant amount of example code from this book into your product's documentation *does* require permission.

We appreciate, but do not require, attribution. An attribution usually includes the title, author, publisher, and ISBN. For example: "*Coding4Fun* by Dan Fernandez and Brian Peek. Copyright 2009 Dan Fernandez and Brian Peek, 978-0-596-52074-8."

If you feel your use of code examples falls outside fair use or the permission given here, feel free to contact us at *permissions@oreilly.com*.

Comments and Questions

We have tested and verified the information in this book to the best of our ability, but you may find that features have changed or that we have made a mistake or two (shocking and hard to believe). Please let us know about any errors you find, as well as your suggestions for future editions by writing to:

> O'Reilly Media, Inc.
> 1005 Gravenstein Highway North
> Sebastopol, CA 95472
> 800-998-9938 (in the United States or Canada)
> 707-829-0515 (international or local)
> 707-829-0104 (fax)

We have a web page for this book where we list examples, figures, and any plans for future editions. You can access this information at:

>   *http://www.c4fbook.com/*

or

>   *http://www.oreilly.com/catalog/9780596520748*

You can also send messages electronically. To be put on the mailing list or request a catalog, send an email to:

>   *authors@c4fbook.com*

or

>   *info@oreilly.com*

To comment on the book, send an email to:

>   *authors@c4fbook.com*

or

>   *bookquestions@oreilly.com*

For more information about our books, conferences, Resource Centers, and the O'Reilly Network, see our website at:

>   *http://www.oreilly.com*

Safari® Books Online

 When you see a Safari® Books Online icon on the cover of your favorite technology book, that means the book is available online through the O'Reilly Network Safari Bookshelf.

Safari offers a solution that's better than e-books. It's a virtual library that lets you easily search thousands of top tech books, cut and paste code samples, download chapters, and find quick answers when you need the most accurate, current information. Try it for free at *http://safari.oreilly.com*.

Acknowledgments

As with any book, a ton of people were involved in making our ideas actually come together in the pile of bound paper you're holding in your hand (or reading off your computer monitor).

First, a huge amount of appreciation goes out to our editor, the lovely and talented Laurel Ruma, who put up with our silliness and kicked our butts into action when we needed it. You were absolutely fantastic to work with.

We also wish to thank the contributing authors to the book who took the time to write about their own projects, which made the concept even better.

Our technical reviewers also deserve a huge amount of praise. These chapters were very time-consuming to read through and test thoroughly. In many cases, hardware needed to be built by hand, code had to be tested in two languages, and projects needed to be retested as we refined certain portions. Thank you to Chris Charabaruk, Jenny Chowdhury, Andy Dunn, Micheal Eaton, Jake Good, Johnny Halife, Ed Kaim, Brian Keller, Mike Korcynksi, Michael Letterle, Gio Montrone, Adam Nathan, Scott C. Reynolds, Michael Sampson, Griffith Townsend, Dean Weber, Chris G. Williams, and Lou Vega for going above and beyond to make this book better.

From Dan Fernandez

Thanks to Brian Peek and Laurel Ruma for putting up with me. We laughed, we cried, we actually finished it!

Special thanks go out to my wife, Angie, who carried my bloodied, half-dead corpse across the finish line to complete this book. I couldn't have written this without your love, support, and guidance.

Many people helped shape this book, including, in no particular order, Adam Kinney for his WPF skills, Daniel Moth for helping me out of VB namespace hell, Rob Schlender for his assistance with the C4F P2P library, Brian Keller for his technical reviews and for helping co-create the Coding4Fun website in 2004, Clint Rutkas for keeping the site going on a regular basis, Gabor Ratky for AddOn Studio and his deep *Warcraft* expertise, Jeff Sandquist for his patience and wisdom, BassDrive.com for energizing me into the wee hours of the night, The Uldum Cabal for understanding my absence from *Warcraft*, Bambino for keeping me company, and of course to all of our loyal Coding4Fun readers and contributors.

From Brian Peek

First, thanks to Dan Fernandez for being great to work with and sharing a common sense of humor when things were difficult. Looking forward to the next one….

Thanks to Michelle Leavitt, my favorite, for being the single most supportive, loving, and caring person in my life. No matter how good or bad things are, you're always right there to make it better. Your boundless love and infinite encouragement makes me a better person. I love you, and nothing I could write in this paragraph could explain how much. Maaaaah!

Thanks to my mom for supporting me and all of my projects and endeavors, especially this one. Stay strong. It will all work out in time….

A big thank you to my friends Joey Buczek for providing all of the artwork and David Wallimann for providing all of the music and sound effects for the Alien Attack chapter. Be sure to check out their websites at *http://www.joeybphotography.com/* and *http://www.davidwallimann.com/* for some amazing photography, art, and music.

Thanks to Leslie Sanford (*http://www.lesliesanford.com/*) for providing the MIDI toolkit used in the Animated Musical Holiday Lights chapter.

And finally, huge thanks to all of my friends and family, in no particular order, who were amazingly supportive of me throughout my life: Mike Kilcullen, Matt Kennedy, Mark Zaugg (who remains both highly mellifluous and Canadian), Jonathan Goodyear, Gio Montrone (diamfh), Dave Bancroft, Patti Rossi, Arden Rauch, Robert Sharlet, Megan Potter, Mr. Beaver, and Mr. Turtley.

Section 1

Gaming

Alien Attack

AUTHOR	Brian Peek
DIFFICULTY	Medium
TIME REQUIRED	5 hours
COST	Windows—free; Xbox 360—cost of hardware, plus $99/year for XNA Creators Club membership (note that there are ways to get this for free, such as DreamSpark for student developers); Zune—cost of Zune device
SOFTWARE	Visual C# 2008 Express or any full edition of Visual Studio 2008 and XNA Game Studio 3.0
HARDWARE	Xbox 360 version requires an Xbox 360 with a hard drive; Zune version requires a Zune device
DOWNLOAD	*http://www.c4fbook.com/AlienAttack*

With the release of XNA Game Studio, Microsoft has brought homebrew game development to a new level. XNA provides an easy-to-use framework for developing games, and allows those games to be distributed and run not only on a PC, but also on the Xbox 360 and Zune. Additionally, because of a common framework and common development language, XNA provides for an almost perfect "write once and run everywhere" scenario. The code used for the Windows version will, in almost every case, compile and run on the Xbox 360 and Zune with few to no changes.

Overview

In this chapter, we walk through creating a very simple two-dimensional game using the XNA Framework that will run on a PC, Xbox 360, and Zune. We will discuss the concepts of 2-D graphics, sound, user input, and simple artificial intelligence (AI) while writing a clone of the arcade classic *Space Invaders* called Alien Attack, as shown in Figure 1-1.

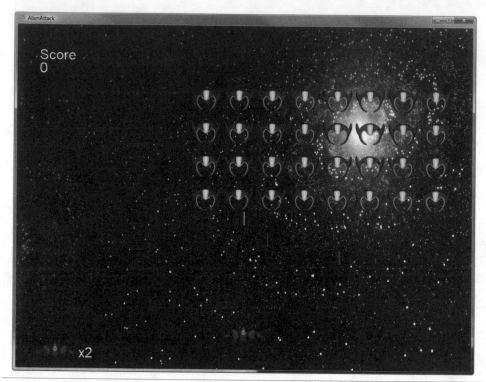

Figure 1-1. *Alien Attack*

As you build this game, keep in mind that it will be playable on all three supported platforms—Windows, Xbox 360, and Zune—using the same code base, as long as you write the code appropriately using compiler directives. Compiler directives can be used to block out portions of code depending on which version is being compiled. By default, Windows projects will define a symbol named *WINDOWS*, Xbox 360 projects will define a symbol named *XBOX*, and Zune projects will define a symbol named *ZUNE*. By using the `#if` compiler directives, we can make certain portions of code available to specific projects.

Setup

Ensure that you have Visual C# 2008 Express or Visual Studio 2008 already installed. With that complete, download the latest version of XNA Game Studio 3.0, located at *http://creators.xna.com/*. Install this package and when asked if you wish to open firewall ports for deployment to the Xbox 360, choose yes if you plan on doing development with the Xbox 360. This will set up everything XNA requires on your machine, and it will create several default templates for building XNA games in Visual Studio.

As always, the full source code for this project can be found on the book's website at *http://www.c4fbook.com/AlienAttack*. However, if you wish to build the game from scratch using the steps here, you will need the asset package (graphics, sounds, etc.) that the game uses. This will also be available at the website. Download, unzip, and have these asset files ready as the chapter progresses.

Windows Version

Let's start by building the Windows version of the game. In general, when building an XNA game, you will start by developing a Windows version of the game and then "port" that game to an Xbox 360 or Zune project. This is done simply to ease debugging and deployment over the course of development.

Start Visual C# 2008 Express or Visual Studio 2008, and create a new *Windows Game (3.0)* project named **AlienAttack** from the Visual C#→XNA Game Studio 3.0 project types, as shown in Figure 1-2.

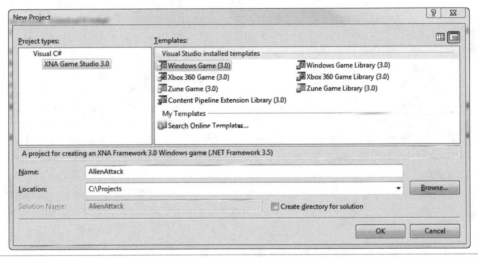

Figure 1-2. *Creating a Windows Game (3.0) project*

A default Windows Game project will be created. Go ahead and either press F5 or click Debug→Start Debugging to run the application. The game will run and you'll be presented with a window filled with the color CornflowerBlue. All you need to do is fill in, well, everything.

Start by renaming the *Game1.cs* file to *AlienAttackGame.cs*. The IDE will ask you if you wish to rename all project references to the new name. Select "Yes" when prompted.

If you look through this class, you will see the basic architecture of any XNA game. There are five methods you need to worry about as you progress. They are outlined in Table 1-1.

Table 1-1. *Base XNA methods*

METHOD	DESCRIPTION
Initialize	Set up anything related to your game that's not content-related.
LoadContent	Load sounds, music, graphics, fonts, or anything else.
UnloadContent	Unload anything that's not part of the ContentManager (see the "Code" section).
Update	Handle any game logic, such as reading the keyboard, controllers, moving sprites, etc.
Draw	Draw everything to the screen.

Let's discuss a few of these methods in detail.

LoadContent

This method is used to, as its name implies, load content. Content can be anything from graphics to sound, music to fonts, and anything else supported by the *Content Pipeline*. This may be called multiple times per game, whenever the system requires an asset that may no longer be in memory.

At its simplest, the *Content Pipeline* takes assets (graphics, sounds, fonts, etc.) included in your project and, at compile time, turns them into custom files that can be used directly by the XNA runtime on your PC, Xbox 360, or Zune device. This means you don't need to worry about writing custom image type converters, audio file importers, etc. You can just drag and drop your game assets directly to the *Content* folder in your game project, and the XNA framework will take care of the rest.

In this game, we will be using three types of content: graphics, sounds, and fonts. As we progress, we will discuss how these items are loaded, the objects that represent them, and how to use them.

In this method, you will see that a SpriteBatch object is created. A SpriteBatch, as its name implies, is used to draw a batch of sprites that all require the same parameters for drawing. We will see this object used later in our drawing methods.

Update

This method is used to update game logic. By default, it is called 60 times per second. This is where user input is handled, the positions of sprites are changed, AI is performed, and so on. Anything that doesn't require drawing is done in this method.

Draw

This method is where everything is drawn to the screen. By default, it is called 60 times per second on the PC and Xbox 360, and 30 times per second on the Zune. Note, however, that there is not necessarily a 1:1 calling of Update and Draw. For our 2-D game, we will be using the previously discussed SpriteBatch to draw our sprites to the screen at the positions calculated during our Update method.

Screens

This game will contain two "screens": the title screen and the game screen. To help separate out the logic for these two screens, you will create an interface named IScreen which will be implemented by two classes: TitleScreen and GameScreen. To start, create a new enumeration named GameState so you can later keep track of which screen you are currently displaying. This can be created above the AlienAttackGame class in the *AllienAttackGame.cs* file, as shown in Example 1-1.

Example 1-1. GameState enumeration

```
public enum GameState
{
    TitleScreen,
    GameScreen
};
```

Next, to keep things organized, start by creating a new folder in your project named *Screens*. You can do this by right-clicking on the project root in Solution Explorer and selecting Add→New Folder. Inside this folder, add a new Interface named IScreen. To do this, right-click on the *Screens* folder and select Add→New Item…, selecting Interface in the Templates pane, and then entering the filename *IScreen.cs*. Our title and game screens will implement this interface, which will provide a generic way to refer to the classes later on. The code for this interface is presented in Example 1-2.

Example 1-2. IScreen interface

```
using Microsoft.Xna.Framework;
using Microsoft.Xna.Framework.Graphics;

namespace AlienAttack
{
    public interface IScreen
    {
        GameState Update(GameTime gameTime);
        void Draw(GameTime gameTime, SpriteBatch spriteBatch);
    }
}
```

You should notice two methods that look very familiar: Update and Draw. The existing AlienAttackGame class also contains these two methods, albeit with slightly different signatures. These methods will be called on the screen object during the regular game's update and draw cycles. Essentially, you will pass off the updating and drawing work to these methods, depending on what screen is currently being displayed.

Title screen

The title screen will contain a pretty simple implementation. You need to show the title screen logo, a message to the user to press a button to start the game, and handle the user pressing that button.

Content. First, let's add our content for this screen. Create a new folder named *gfx* in the *Content* folder of the project. All game-related graphics will be stored in this directory. From the Windows game assets that were downloaded earlier, drag and drop *bgScreen.png* and *titleScreen.png* from the *gfx* folder into the Content Pipeline's *gfx* folder. Then, drag the *Arial.spritefont* file from the root directory into the root of the *Content* folder.

PNG files are simply graphics files like any other format, though this format allows for easy application of a transparency channel. This helps draw images without a background getting in the way.

The *SpriteFont* file is something special. XNA contains methods to draw text to the screen, but it needs a SpriteFont object to know how to render the font. *Arial.spritefont* is an XML file that defines the characteristics of the font. The *Content Pipeline* takes this XML file and, at compile time, creates a custom image file containing the alphanumeric characters requested in the font and style specified. Feel free to open the file to view its contents. All of its parameters are very well documented. You can also create your own *SpriteFont* file by right-clicking the *Content* folder, selecting Add→New Item, and then selecting Sprite Font.

Code. Now you can start writing the implementation of the title screen. Start by creating a new class in the previously created *Screens* folder named TitleScreen. This class must implement the previously created IScreen interface and provide code for its two methods, Update and Draw. The basic class format can be seen in Example 1-3.

Example 1-3. *TitleScreen base class*

```
using Microsoft.Xna.Framework;
using Microsoft.Xna.Framework.Graphics;
using Microsoft.Xna.Framework.Content;

namespace AlienAttack
{
    public class TitleScreen : IScreen
    {
        public TitleScreen(ContentManager contentManager)
        {
        }

        public GameState Update(GameTime gameTime)
```

```
        {
        }

        public void Draw(GameTime gameTime, SpriteBatch spriteBatch)
        {
        }
    }
}
```

Previously, you added three items to the content manager. To load them into the game, you need variables to hold them. The PNG files will map to Texture2D objects, and the font will map to a SpriteFont object when all is said and done. So, create three member variables to hold these items, as shown in Example 1-4.

Example 1-4. *TitleScreen member variables*

```
public class TitleScreen : IScreen
{
    private Texture2D titleScreen;
    private Texture2D bgScreen;
    private SpriteFont arialFont;
```

Next, you need to actually load the content into those variables. This is handled in the TitleScreen constructor. Create the constructor as shown in Example 1-5.

Example 1-5. *TitleScreen constructor*

```
public TitleScreen(ContentManager contentManager)
{
    titleScreen = contentManager.Load<Texture2D>("gfx\\titleScreen");
    bgScreen = contentManager.Load<Texture2D>("gfx\\bgScreen");
    arialFont = contentManager.Load<SpriteFont>("Arial");
}
```

As you can see, the constructor will expect a ContentManager object to be passed in. The ContentManager is what actually handles the loading of the pipeline-created content at runtime. The Load method is a generic method that must specify a type to load (in this case, Texture2D and SpriteFont), and whose first argument is a path to the content itself. By default, the content pipeline will place the content at the same path shown in the project, and it will give the content the same name as the filename but without the extension.

When this screen is created in the game engine, you will see where that Content Manager object comes from.

Now that the content is loaded, you can implement the Update and Draw methods. First, let's create the Update method as shown in Example 1-6.

Example 1-6. *Update method for TitleScreen class*

```
public GameState Update(GameTime gameTime)
{
    if(InputManager.ControlState.Start)
        return GameState.GameScreen;
    return GameState.TitleScreen;
}
```

This class simply uses the InputManager class (see the "InputManager" section next), and, if the Start button is pressed, returns the GameScreen element from the GameState enumeration, telling the main game engine that it should change to that state. Otherwise, it will continue to return the TitleScreen state.

Before getting to the InputManager class, let's write the Draw method and finish off the implementation of this class. This can be seen in Example 1-7.

Example 1-7. *Draw method for TitleScreen class*

```
public void Draw(GameTime gameTime, SpriteBatch spriteBatch)
{
    spriteBatch.Draw(bgScreen, Vector2.Zero, Color.White);
    spriteBatch.Draw(titleScreen, Vector2.Zero, Color.White);
#if WINDOWS
    spriteBatch.DrawString(arialFont, "Press Enter or Start to Play",
                        new Vector2(600, 680), Color.White);
#endif

#if XBOX
    spriteBatch.DrawString(arialFont, "Press Start to Play", new Vector2(600, 680),
                        Color.White);
#endif

#if ZUNE
    spriteBatch.DrawString(arialFont, "Press Play to Play", new Vector2(80, 290),
                        Color.White);
#endif
}
```

This method uses the SpriteBatch object discussed earlier to draw three things to the screen: a background image, then a title screen image, and finally the appropriate text at the bottom of the screen that explains how to start the game.

Each call to the Draw method of the SpriteBatch object requires a Texture2D object (which was loaded earlier), a position at which to draw it, and a color "tint" to give it. The first line of this method draws the background screen shown in Figure 1-3 at position (0, 0), which is what *Vector2.Zero* equates to, with a color tint of White (that is, no color).

Figure 1-3. *Background image*

The second line does the same thing, but this time draws the `titleScreen` logo image, shown in Figure 1-4, to the screen, layering it on top of the previous image.

Figure 1-4. *Title screen logo*

Since the title screen logo image is transparent in the right places, it will seamlessly overlay on top of the background stars.

Finally, it overlays the text as specified on the two layered images at various positions. You'll notice the use of our WINDOWS, XBOX, and ZUNE compiler directives here to draw different text to the screen at different locations depending on the platform you are compiling for. Since the Zune screen is so much smaller, you need to position it at a different location so it will fit on the screen correctly. All of this comes together to produce the screen shown in Figure 1-5.

Figure 1-5. Final title screen image

InputManager

Before continuing on, let's discuss the InputManager object mentioned earlier. This is a pretty simple helper class that manages input from the keyboard, Xbox 360 controller, or Zune device in one fell swoop. You will again be using the compiler directives to handle input devices for the correct platforms.

Create a new class named InputManager in the root of the project. This will be a public, static class, so be sure to change the class definition to include the public static keywords. Replace the "using" statements with the code in Example 1-8.

Example 1-8. *Using statements for InputManager class*

```
using Microsoft.Xna.Framework;
using Microsoft.Xna.Framework.Input;
```

At the top, before the class definition, create a struct named ControlState as shown in Example 1-9.

Example 1-9. *ControlState structure*

```
public struct ControlState
{
    public bool Left;
    public bool Right;
    public bool Start;
    public bool Quit;
    public bool Fire;
}
```

This struct contains the five input elements we care about for our game. The player ship can move left and right, and it can fire. At a global level, you can start the game or quit the game.

Next you will need to read the current keyboard and control pad states, and you will need to retain a reference to the previous frames states so that you can determine whether a button was newly pressed or is still held down from the previous frame. The main reason for this is that you want to fire only a single shot when the player fires, not one shot for every frame that they have the button held down.

Add the member variables as shown in Example 1-10.

Example 1-10. *InputManager member variables*

```
#if !ZUNE
    private static KeyboardState keyboardState, lastKeyboard;
#endif
    private static GamePadState gamePadState, lastGamePad;
    private static ControlState controlState;
```

Next, we create a method named Update that will be called once per frame by the game's Update method shown earlier. The code for the Update method can be seen in Example 1-11.

Example 1-11. *Update method for InputManager class*

```
public static void Update()
{
#if !ZUNE
    keyboardState = Keyboard.GetState();
#endif
```

```
        gamePadState = GamePad.GetState(PlayerIndex.One);

        controlState.Quit   = (gamePadState.Buttons.Back== ButtonState.Pressed);
        controlState.Start  = (gamePadState.Buttons.B    == ButtonState.Pressed);
        controlState.Left   = (gamePadState.DPad.Left    == ButtonState.Pressed);
        controlState.Right  = (gamePadState.DPad.Right   == ButtonState.Pressed);
        controlState.Fire   = (gamePadState.Buttons.B    == ButtonState.Pressed &&
                               lastGamePad.Buttons.B     == ButtonState.Released);

#if !ZUNE
        controlState.Quit   = (controlState.Quit    ||
                               keyboardState.IsKeyDown(Keys.Escape));
        controlState.Start  = (controlState.Start   ||
                               keyboardState.IsKeyDown(Keys.Enter) ||
                               gamePadState.IsButtonDown(Buttons.Start));
        controlState.Left   = (controlState.Left    ||
                               gamePadState.ThumbSticks.Left.X < -0.1f);
        controlState.Right  = (controlState.Right   ||
                               gamePadState.ThumbSticks.Left.X > 0.1f);
        controlState.Left   = (controlState.Left    ||
                               keyboardState.IsKeyDown(Keys.Left));
        controlState.Right  = (controlState.Right   ||
                               keyboardState.IsKeyDown(Keys.Right));
        controlState.Fire   = (controlState.Fire    ||
                               keyboardState.IsKeyDown(Keys.Space) &&
                               !lastKeyboard.IsKeyDown(Keys.Space));
#endif

        lastGamePad = gamePadState;

#if !ZUNE
        lastKeyboard = keyboardState;
#endif
    }
```

This code gets the state of the keyboard and the state of the first controller and stores it away. It then checks the various buttons using the `GamePadState` and `KeyboardState` objects, and assigns Boolean values to the `controlState` struct based on what is pressed and what is not. Finally, it stores the current values away to be used next frame to determine whether buttons are newly pressed or held down.

Also note that this class uses compiler directives to compile only certain sections for certain versions. The Zune has no keyboard, but does have its buttons mapped to the `GamePadState` object. The Xbox 360 does have a keyboard attachment for the controller (the *Chatpad* device), and its keys can be read like that of a normal PC keyboard.

Finally, you add a property to return the current value of the `controlState` member variable, as shown in Example 1-12.

Example 1-12. *ControlState property*

```
public static ControlState ControlState
{
    get { return controlState; }
}
```

Back to the Game

Now that we have a title screen object, its assets, and a way to manage input from the user, we can actually hook up the title screen and have it processed and drawn by the main game class.

Back in the `AlienAttackGame` class, add the member variables as shown in Example 1-13. Note the usage of the `#if` compiler directive to set the screen size differently on the Zune build.

Example 1-13. *AlienAttackGame member variables*

```
    private GameState gameState;
    private IScreen screen;
#if ZUNE
    public static int ScreenWidth = 240;
    public static int ScreenHeight = 320;
#else
    public static int ScreenWidth = 1024;
    public static int ScreenHeight = 768;
#endif
```

The `gameState` member will maintain the current state of the game (that is, what screen is being displayed), and the screen member will hold an instance of a class that implements the `IScreen` interface, namely our `TitleScreen` class and soon the `GameScreen` class.

`ScreenWidth` and `ScreenHeight` define the size of the screen on which you will be drawing the game. For the PC and Xbox 360 versions, this defaults to 1024x768 as shown. The Zune's native screen resolution is 240x320, and it is defaulted as such. Note that these are public, static variables so that they can be easily used by other parts of the game engine later on.

Next, you need to tell XNA that you want your game to run at the specified resolution. This can be done by setting the `PreferredBackBufferWidth` and `PreferredBack BufferHeight` properties on the `GraphicsDevice` object created in the constructor, as shown in Example 1-14.

Example 1-14. *Setting the screen size in AlienAttackGame constructor*

```
public AlienAttackGame()
{
    graphics = new GraphicsDeviceManager(this);

    // set our screen size based on the device
    graphics.PreferredBackBufferWidth = ScreenWidth;
    graphics.PreferredBackBufferHeight = ScreenHeight;

    Content.RootDirectory = "Content";
}
```

Now we use the Initialize method to instantiate the TitleScreen class and set up our initial game state, as shown in Example 1-15.

Example 1-15. *Initialize method*

```
protected override void Initialize()
{
    // create the title screen
    screen = new TitleScreen(this.Content);
    gameState = GameState.TitleScreen;

    base.Initialize();
}
```

Next, you need to tell the game's Update method to handle input from the user via the InputManager class that was just created, and then update the instance of the IScreen object (now holding an instance of our TitleScreen object). This is shown in Example 1-16, and it replaces the existing Update method in its entirety.

Example 1-16. *Update method*

```
protected override void Update(GameTime gameTime)
{
    // update the user input
    InputManager.Update();

    // Allows the game to exit
    if(InputManager.ControlState.Quit)
        this.Exit();

    // update the current screen
    GameState newState = screen.Update(gameTime);

    base.Update(gameTime);
}
```

Note that this method uses the `InputManager` to directly determine whether the "Quit" button is pressed and exits immediately if it is.

Finally, we need to draw our title screen in the `Draw` method of the `AlienAttackGame` class. This is shown in Example 1-17, and as before, replaces the entire `Draw` method.

Example 1-17. *Draw method*

```
protected override void Draw(GameTime gameTime)
{
    // open the spritebatch, draw the screen, close it up
    this.spriteBatch.Begin();
        screen.Draw(gameTime, this.spriteBatch);
    this.spriteBatch.End();
}
```

This method tells the sprite batch that a pile of sprites with the same parameters are coming with the `Begin` method, then hands over drawing to the screen object by calling its `Draw` method, and finally closes the sprite batch with the `End` method.

Seeing the Title Screen

With all of this in place, there is actually enough to see something on the screen for the first time. If you compile and run the application, you should see what appears in Figure 1-6.

Figure 1-6. *The title screen*

Game Screen

Now that we have the title screen done, we can begin implementing the actual game. To start, add a new class named GameScreen to the *Screens* folder. As with the TitleScreen class, GameScreen will also implement the IScreen interface and provide implementations for the Update and Draw methods. As with the title screen, the first thing to draw to the screen is the background star field. This code looks identical to the title screen class and is presented along with the base GameScreen class in Example 1-18.

Example 1-18. GameScreen base class implementation

```
using System.Collections.Generic;
using Microsoft.Xna.Framework;
using Microsoft.Xna.Framework.Graphics;
using Microsoft.Xna.Framework.Content;

namespace AlienAttack
{
    public class GameScreen : IScreen
    {
        private ContentManager contentManager;
        private Texture2D bgScreen;

        public GameScreen(ContentManager cm)
        {
            contentManager = cm;

            bgScreen = contentManager.Load<Texture2D>("gfx\\bgScreen");
        }

        public GameState Update(GameTime gameTime)
        {
            return GameState.GameScreen;
        }

        public void Draw(GameTime gameTime, SpriteBatch spriteBatch)
        {
            spriteBatch.Draw(bgScreen, Vector2.Zero, Color.White);
        }
    }
}
```

Adding GameScreen to the main game

Adding this class to the main game is quite simple. Back in the `AlienAttackGame` class, change the `Update` method as shown in Example 1-19. The new and modified lines of code are emphasized (and will be henceforth) to help them stand out.

Example 1-19. *Rewritten Update method*

```
protected override void Update(GameTime gameTime)
{
    // update the user input
    InputManager.Update();

    // Allows the game to exit
    if(InputManager.ControlState.Quit)
        this.Exit();

    // update the current screen
    GameState newState = screen.Update(gameTime);

    // if the screen returns a new state, change it here
    if(gameState != newState)
    {
        switch(newState)
        {
            case GameState.TitleScreen:
                screen = new TitleScreen(this.Content);
                break;
            case GameState.GameScreen:
                screen = new GameScreen(this.Content);
                break;
        }
        gameState = newState;
    }

    base.Update(gameTime);
}
```

In this changed method, we now grab the returned value from the screen's `Update` method. If it returns a state other than the one we are in, we create the screen that handles that new state and continue.

Sound engine

With the release of XNA 3.0 comes a brand-new sound API that is much simpler than the existing XACT API. The new sound library allows you to very easily play simple sound effects, which is all that is required for this game.

First, drag the *sfx* folder from the downloaded assets to the Content Pipeline. Then, create a new class named AudioManager in the root of the project. We will define an enumeration of the various sound effects that can be played, load them when the AudioManager class is instantiated, and then create a PlayCue method that will play the requested sound effect. All of this is shown in Example 1-20.

Example 1-20. *AudioManager class*

```
using Microsoft.Xna.Framework.Audio;
using Microsoft.Xna.Framework.Content;

namespace AlienAttack
{
    public class AudioManager
    {
        // the different fx that can be played
        public enum Cue
        {
            Theme,
            EnemyShot,
            PlayerShot,
            Explosion
        };

        // instances of the effects
        private SoundEffect theme;
        private SoundEffect enemyShot;
        private SoundEffect playerShot;
        private SoundEffect explosion;

        public AudioManager(ContentManager contentManager)
        {
            // load 'em up
            theme = contentManager.Load<SoundEffect>("sfx\\theme");
            enemyShot = contentManager.Load<SoundEffect>("sfx\\enemyShot");
            playerShot = contentManager.Load<SoundEffect>("sfx\\playerShot");
            explosion = contentManager.Load<SoundEffect>("sfx\\explosion");
        }

        public void PlayCue(Cue cue)
        {
            // play the effect requested
            switch(cue)
            {
                case Cue.Theme:
```

```
                    theme.Play();
                    break;
                case Cue.EnemyShot:
                    enemyShot.Play();
                    break;
                case Cue.PlayerShot:
                    playerShot.Play();
                    break;
                case Cue.Explosion:
                    explosion.Play();
                    break;
            }
        }
    }
}
```

Next, we can add the AudioManager to our AlienAttackGame class and make it available to all of our other classes by making it a static instance. Add a static member variable of type AudioManager to the AlienAttackGame class and then instantiate it in the Initialize method, as shown in Example 1-21.

Example 1-21. *AudioManager creation*

```
public static AudioManager AudioManager;

protected override void Initialize()
{
    // create the title screen
    screen = new TitleScreen(this.Content);
    gameState = GameState.TitleScreen;

    // create the audio helper
    AudioManager = new AudioManager(this.Content);

    base.Initialize();
}
```

This can be immediately used to play the background music for the game screen by adding a call to the PlayCue method in the GameScreen constructor, as shown in Example 1-22.

Example 1-22. *Play background music*

```
public GameScreen(ContentManager cm)
{
    contentManager = cm;
    AlienAttackGame.AudioManager.PlayCue(AudioManager.Cue.Theme);
```

```
        bgScreen = contentManager.Load<Texture2D>("gfx\\bgScreen");
    }
```

Player ship and sprites

The next thing we will add to the game screen is the player ship. This will appear at the bottom of the screen and can move left and right to the edges. To begin, drag the *player.png* file from the previously downloaded assets to the root of the *gfx* folder in the solution explorer. This will add it to the content pipeline, just like our previous images, and allow it to be used by the game directly.

A sprite is simply a graphical element drawn to the screen, and the player ship will be one of many sprites in our game. We will be drawing this player ship, the enemies, player shots, and enemy shots throughout the course of the game, so it makes sense to create a Sprite class from which these objects can inherit.

This object will allow you to easily load a single sprite image, provide a position for it on-screen, provide a velocity at which it will move for every frame, and a few extra properties to determine its width, height, and bounding box.

Create a new folder named *Sprites* in the project. In this folder, add a class named Sprite, and implement it as shown in Example 1-23.

Example 1-23. *Sprite class implementation*

```
using Microsoft.Xna.Framework;
using Microsoft.Xna.Framework.Content;
using Microsoft.Xna.Framework.Graphics;

namespace AlienAttack
{
    public abstract class Sprite
    {
        // all textures in animation set
        protected Texture2D[] spriteTextures;

        // current frame to draw
        protected int frameIndex;

        public ContentManager Content;
        public Vector2 Position;
        public Vector2 Velocity;

        // bounding box of image...used for collision detection
        private Rectangle boundingBox;

        public Sprite()
        {
```

```csharp
    }

    public Sprite(ContentManager contentManager)
    {
        this.Content = contentManager;
    }

    public Sprite(ContentManager contentManager, string contentName) :
        this(contentManager)
    {
        spriteTextures = new Texture2D[1];

        // load the image
        spriteTextures[0] = this.Content.Load<Texture2D>(contentName);
    }

    public virtual void Update(GameTime gameTime)
    {
        // move the sprite based on the provided velocity
        this.Position += this.Velocity;
    }

    public virtual void Draw(GameTime gameTime, SpriteBatch spriteBatch)
    {
        spriteBatch.Draw(spriteTextures[frameIndex], this.Position, Color.White);
    }

    public virtual int Width
    {
        get { return spriteTextures[0].Width; }
    }

    public virtual int Height
    {
        get { return spriteTextures[0].Height; }
    }

    public virtual Rectangle BoundingBox
    {
        get
        {
            // only need to assign this once
            if(boundingBox == Rectangle.Empty)
            {
                boundingBox.Width = this.Width;
```

```
            boundingBox.Height = this.Height;
        }
        boundingBox.X = (int)this.Position.X;
        boundingBox.Y = (int)this.Position.Y;

        return boundingBox;
    }
  }
 }
}
```

This class represents a very simple sprite. It has a position on-screen, a velocity at which it moves, a width, a height, and a bounding box based on where it is on the screen (see the later section "Collision detection and explosions"). Additionally, it contains an array of images named spriteTextures (Texture2D objects) to be loaded. These would be all the frames of animation required to draw the sprite to the screen. The frameIndex variable maintains the current frame to draw and will be updated by the derived sprites later on as required.

With the base class in place, we can now implement the player object, which will represent the player's ship on-screen.

Add a new class named Player to the sprites folder, and implement as shown in Example 1-24.

Example 1-24. *Player class implementation*

```
using Microsoft.Xna.Framework.Content;

namespace AlienAttack
{
    public class Player : Sprite
    {
        public Player(ContentManager contentManager) : base(contentManager,
                                                          "gfx\\player")
        {
            this.Position.X = AlienAttackGame.ScreenWidth/2 - this.Width/2;
#if ZUNE
            this.Position.Y = AlienAttackGame.ScreenHeight - 40;
#else
            this.Position.Y = AlienAttackGame.ScreenHeight - 100;
#endif
        }
    }
}
```

This class simply loads the content for the player (a single sprite frame), and sets its default position to the center of the screen near the bottom. The default Update and

Draw methods from the base Sprite class will be used to update and draw the sprite to the screen.

Back in the GameScreen class, we can create a new Player object, update it, and draw it. To do this, we will modify the GameScreen's member variables, constructor, and Update and Draw methods, and add a new method named MovePlayer, as shown in Example 1-25.

Example 1-25. *Adding Player to GameScreen*

```
private Player player;
private float PlayerVelocity = AlienAttackGame.ScreenWidth / 200.0f;

public GameScreen(ContentManager cm)
{
    contentManager = cm;
    AlienAttackGame.AudioManager.PlayCue(AudioManager.Cue.Theme);
    bgScreen = contentManager.Load<Texture2D>("gfx\\bgScreen");
    player = new Player(contentManager);
}

public GameState Update(GameTime gameTime)
{
    MovePlayer(gameTime);
    return GameState.GameScreen;
}

public void Draw(GameTime gameTime, SpriteBatch spriteBatch)
{
    spriteBatch.Draw(bgScreen, Vector2.Zero, Color.White);

    // draw the player
    if(player != null)
        player.Draw(gameTime, spriteBatch);
}

private void MovePlayer(GameTime gameTime)
{
    if(player != null)
    {
        // move left
        if(InputManager.ControlState.Left && player.Position.X > 0)
            player.Position.X -= PlayerVelocity;

        // move right
        if(InputManager.ControlState.Right &&
```

```
        player.Position.X + player.Width < AlienAttackGame.ScreenWidth)
    player.Position.X += PlayerVelocity;
    player.Update(gameTime);
}
    }
```

Note that the Update method uses the InputManager object we previously wrote to check the state of the Left and Right controls. If either is pressed, the player ship's position is moved either left or right as appropriate.

If you were to run the game at this point, you would hear the background music and should see the background and the lonely player ship at the bottom of the screen, which can move left and right via the arrow keys and gamepad. Not much of a game, but it's a good start.

Player shots

Now let's add the ability for the player to fire. First, let's add the content to the content pipeline. To do this, drag the *pshot* folder from the downloaded assets to the *gfx* directory in the project. This will add the directory and its contents—two image files that will be played as a short animation.

Next, we will create another object in the *Sprites* folder that inherits from the Sprite class named PlayerShot, as shown in Example 1-26.

Example 1-26. *PlayerShot class*

```
using Microsoft.Xna.Framework;
using Microsoft.Xna.Framework.Content;
using Microsoft.Xna.Framework.Graphics;

namespace AlienAttack
{
    public class PlayerShot : Sprite
    {
        // all frames of animation
        private double lastTime;

        public PlayerShot(ContentManager contentManager) : base(contentManager)
        {
            spriteTextures = new Texture2D[2];

            // load the frames
            for(int i = 0; i <= 1; i++)
                spriteTextures[i] =
                    contentManager.Load<Texture2D>("gfx\\pshot\\pshot_" + i);
        }
```

```
public override void Update(GameTime gameTime)
{
    // draw a new frame very 200ms...seems to be a good value
    if(gameTime.TotalGameTime.TotalMilliseconds - lastTime > 200)
    {
        // toggle between frames
        frameIndex = frameIndex == 0 ? 1 : 0;
        lastTime = gameTime.TotalGameTime.TotalMilliseconds;
    }

    this.Position.Y -= 5;
}
```

This class loads the two animation frames in the constructor and stores them away. The two frames are used to give the sprite a flashing effect as it travels up the screen. The Update method determines when 200 milliseconds have elapsed and, when it has, moves to the next frame to display. The base Sprite class handles the drawing.

Back in the GameScreen class, we can now allow the player to fire from the ship. Since many shots can appear on the screen at once, we will use a List object to store all instances of the player's shots currently on the screen. In the Update method we will call a new UpdatePlayerShots method, which will determine when the Fire button has been pressed and, if a specified time interval has elapsed (so we don't create a shot per frame), we will create a new PlayerShot object and add it to the list, as well as play the sound cue to go with it. Finally, the Update method will enumerate through all player shots, update their positions, and remove any that have gone off the top of the screen, and the Draw method will enumerate all shots and draw them to the screen. All of this can be seen in Example 1-27.

Example 1-27. *PlayerShot usage*

```
private List<PlayerShot> playerShots;
private double lastTime;

public GameScreen(ContentManager cm)
{
    contentManager = cm;
    AlienAttackGame.AudioManager.PlayCue(AudioManager.Cue.Theme);
    bgScreen = contentManager.Load<Texture2D>("gfx\\bgScreen");
    player = new Player(contentManager);

    playerShots = new List<PlayerShot>();
}
```

```
public GameState Update(GameTime gameTime)
{
    MovePlayer(gameTime);
    UpdatePlayerShots(gameTime);

    return GameState.GameScreen;
}

public void Draw(GameTime gameTime, SpriteBatch spriteBatch)
{
    spriteBatch.Draw(bgScreen, Vector2.Zero, Color.White);

    // draw the player
    if(player != null)
        player.Draw(gameTime, spriteBatch);

    // draw the player shots
    foreach(PlayerShot playerShot in playerShots)
        playerShot.Draw(gameTime, spriteBatch);
}

private void UpdatePlayerShots(GameTime gameTime)
{
    // if we are allowed to fire, add a shot to the list
    if(InputManager.ControlState.Fire &&
       gameTime.TotalGameTime.TotalMilliseconds - lastTime > 500)
    {
        // create a new shot over the ship
        PlayerShot ps = new PlayerShot(this.contentManager);
        ps.Position.X = (player.Position.X + player.Width/2) - ps.Width/2;
        ps.Position.Y = player.Position.Y - ps.Height;
        playerShots.Add(ps);
        lastTime = gameTime.TotalGameTime.TotalMilliseconds;
        AlienAttackGame.AudioManager.PlayCue(AudioManager.Cue.PlayerShot);
    }

    // enumerate the player shots on the screen
    for(int i = 0; i < playerShots.Count; i++)
    {
        PlayerShot playerShot = playerShots[i];

        playerShot.Update(gameTime);

        // if it's off the top of the screen, remove it from the list
        if(playerShot.Position.Y + playerShot.Height < 0)
```

```
            {
                playerShots.RemoveAt(i);
                playerShot = null;
            }
        }
    }
}
```

Running the game at this point will allow you to fire shots up the screen.

Scoring and lives remaining

Next, let's add the score display and the lives remaining icon at the lower left of the screen. For this, we will need our Arial font that we used earlier, but since it's already in the Content Pipeline, we do not need to add it again.

We will use the existing Arial SpriteFont to draw the score and number of lives remaining. Additionally, we will use our already created Player sprite to draw the ship icon to the left of the lives remaining. This can all be seen in Example 1-28.

Example 1-28. *Score and lives remaining*

```
private Player livesIcon;
private int score;
private int lives;
private SpriteFont arial;
private bool loseGame;

public GameScreen(ContentManager cm)
{
    contentManager = cm;
    AlienAttackGame.AudioManager.PlayCue(AudioManager.Cue.Theme);
    bgScreen = contentManager.Load<Texture2D>("gfx\\bgScreen");
    player = new Player(contentManager);

    playerShots = new List<PlayerShot>();

    arial = contentManager.Load<SpriteFont>("arial");

    // draw a lives status icon in the lower left
    livesIcon = new Player(contentManager);

#if ZUNE
    livesIcon.Position = new Vector2(0, AlienAttackGame.ScreenHeight-20);
#else
    livesIcon.Position = new Vector2(40, AlienAttackGame.ScreenHeight-60);
#endif
```

```
        lives = 2;
    }

    public void Draw(GameTime gameTime, SpriteBatch spriteBatch)
    {
        spriteBatch.Draw(bgScreen, Vector2.Zero, Color.White);

        // draw the player
        if(player != null)
            player.Draw(gameTime, spriteBatch);

        // draw the player shots
        foreach(PlayerShot playerShot in playerShots)
            playerShot.Draw(gameTime, spriteBatch);

#if ZUNE
        // draw the score
        spriteBatch.DrawString(arial, "Score", new Vector2(0, 0), Color.White);
        spriteBatch.DrawString(arial, score.ToString(), new Vector2(0, 20), Color.White);

        // draw the lives icon
        livesIcon.Draw(gameTime, spriteBatch);
        spriteBatch.DrawString(arial, "x" + lives.ToString(),
            new Vector2(livesIcon.Position.X + livesIcon.Width + 4,
                        livesIcon.Position.Y),
            Color.White);
#else
        // draw the score
        spriteBatch.DrawString(arial, "Score", new Vector2(50, 50), Color.White);
        spriteBatch.DrawString(arial, score.ToString(), new Vector2(50, 80),
            Color.White);

        // draw the lives icon
        livesIcon.Draw(gameTime, spriteBatch);
        spriteBatch.DrawString(arial, "x" + lives.ToString(),
            new Vector2(livesIcon.Position.X + livesIcon.Width + 4,
                        livesIcon.Position.Y+8),
            Color.White);
#endif
    }
```

If you run the project at this point, you should see a score and lives remaining display, and you should be able to shoot using either the space bar or the A button on the game pad.

Now we need enemies.

Enemies

Enemies are just another sprite in our game engine. We must first drag the content to the Content Pipeline for the enemy. In this case, drag the *enemy1* folder from the downloaded assets to the *gfx* folder in the project. Then, create a new class named Enemy in our *Sprites* folder. This class, as with all of our other sprites, will inherit from the base Sprite class. The implementation for this class looks very similar to that of our PlayerShot class. It will load all frames of animation, and change the animation frame index in the Update method. The animation simply moves forward through the animation set, and then backward. The implementation is shown in Example 1-29.

Example 1-29. Enemy class implementation

```
using Microsoft.Xna.Framework;
using Microsoft.Xna.Framework.Content;
using Microsoft.Xna.Framework.Graphics;

namespace AlienAttack
{
    public class Enemy : Sprite
    {
        // which direction are we moving through the animation set?
        private int direction = 1;

        double lastTime;

        public Enemy(ContentManager contentManager)
        {
            spriteTextures = new Texture2D[10];

            // load the spriteTextures
            for(int i = 0; i <= 9; i++)
                spriteTextures[i] =
                    contentManager.Load<Texture2D>("gfx\\enemy1\\enemy1_" + i);

            this.Velocity.X = 1;
        }

        public override void Update(GameTime gameTime)
        {
            // if we're at the end of the animation, reverse direction
            if(frameIndex == 9)
                direction = -1;

            // if we're at the start of the animation, reverse direction
            if(frameIndex == 0)
```

```
            direction = 1;

            // every 70ms, move to the next frame
            if(gameTime.TotalGameTime.TotalMilliseconds - lastTime > 70)
            {
                frameIndex += direction;
                lastTime = gameTime.TotalGameTime.TotalMilliseconds;
            }
        }
    }
}
```

EnemyGroup

As shown in the earlier game screenshot, the screen contains a grid of enemies that will move back and forth. In order to easily maintain this entire group, we will create another Sprite-based object named EnemyGroup. EnemyGroup will create the grid of enemies, move them around the screen, make them fire shots at the player, and handle collisions from the player shots.

Create a new class named EnemyGroup in the *Sprites* folder. As with all sprites, this will inherit from the base Sprite class. This won't be quite like the rest of the sprites we already created, but it allows us to take advantage of some of the inherent sprite functionality we've already written.

This class is a bit large, so I'm going to break it down a bit differently than the previous sections. For now, we are only going to worry about creating the grid of enemy sprites and moving them around the screen. First, let's set up the base class as shown in Example 1-30.

Example 1-30. *EnemyGroup base class*

```
using System;
using System.Collections.Generic;
using Microsoft.Xna.Framework;
using Microsoft.Xna.Framework.Content;
using Microsoft.Xna.Framework.Graphics;

namespace AlienAttack
{
    public class EnemyGroup : Sprite
    {
        // grid of enemies
        private Enemy[,] enemies;

        // width of single enemy
        private int enemyWidth;
```

```
#if ZUNE
        private const int EnemyRows = 4; // number of rows in grid
        private const int EnemyCols = 6; // number of cols in grid
        private const int EnemyVerticalJump = 3; // number of pixels to jump
                                        // vertically after hitting edge
        private const int EnemyStartPosition = 10; // vertical position of grid
        private const int ScreenEdge = 3; // virtual edge of screen to change dir
        private Vector2 EnemySpacing = new Vector2(2, 2); // space between sprites
        private const float EnemyVelocity = 0.5f; // speed at which grid moves per
                                        // frame
#else
        private const int EnemyRows = 4; // number of rows in grid
        private const int EnemyCols = 8; // number of cols in grid
        private const int EnemyVerticalJump = 10; // number of pixels to jump
                                        // vertically after hitting edge
        private const int EnemyStartPosition = 100; // vertical position of grid
        private const int ScreenEdge = 20; // virtual edge of screen to change dir
        private Vector2 EnemySpacing = new Vector2(4, 4); // space between sprites
        private const float EnemyVelocity = 1.5f; // speed at which grid moves per
                                        // frame
#endif
        public EnemyGroup(ContentManager contentManager) : base(contentManager)
        {
        }

        public override void Update(GameTime gameTime)
        {
        }

        public override void Draw(GameTime gameTime, SpriteBatch spriteBatch)
        {
        }
    }
}
```

All of those constant values will be used later as we progress though this class.

The constructor for this object will create and center our enemy grid on the screen, as shown in Example 1-31.

Example 1-31. *EnemyGroup constructor*

```
public EnemyGroup(ContentManager contentManager) : base(contentManager)
{
    enemies = new Enemy[EnemyRows,EnemyCols];

    // create a grid of enemies
    for(int y = 0; y < EnemyRows; y++)
    {
        for(int x = 0; x < EnemyCols; x++)
        {
            Enemy enemy = new Enemy(contentManager);
            enemy.Position.X = x * enemy.Width + EnemySpacing.X;
            enemy.Position.Y = y * enemy.Height + EnemySpacing.Y;
            enemies[y,x] = enemy;
        }
    }

    enemyWidth = enemies[0,0].Width;

    // position the grid centered at the vertical position specified above
    this.Position.X = AlienAttackGame.ScreenWidth/2 -
                        ((EnemyCols * (enemyWidth + EnemySpacing.X)) / 2);
    this.Position.Y = EnemyStartPosition;
    this.Velocity.X = EnemyVelocity;
}
```

The Update method shown in Example 1-32 will use a method we will write named
MoveEnemies to move the enemies left and right across the screen, dropping them a
few pixels when they hit the edge. We will also write a few helper methods to determine the leftmost and rightmost enemies still left in the grid so we know when the left
and right side of the grid hits the edges of the screen.

Example 1-32. *Update method for EnemyGroup class*

```
public override void Update(GameTime gameTime)
{
    MoveEnemies(gameTime);
}

private Enemy FindRightMostEnemy()
{
    // find the enemy in the right-most position in the grid
    for(int x = EnemyCols-1; x > -1; x--)
    {
        for(int y = 0; y < EnemyRows; y++)
        {
```

```
            if(enemies[y,x] != null)
                return enemies[y,x];
        }
    }
    return null;
}

private Enemy FindLeftMostEnemy()
{
    // find the enemy in the left-most position in the grid
    for(int x = 0; x < EnemyCols; x++)
    {
        for(int y = 0; y < EnemyRows; y++)
        {
            if(enemies[y,x] != null)
                return enemies[y,x];
        }
    }
    return null;
}

public bool AllDestroyed()
{
    // we won if we can't find any enemies at all
    return (FindLeftMostEnemy() == null);
}

private void MoveEnemies(GameTime gameTime)
{
    Enemy enemy = FindRightMostEnemy();

    // if the right-most enemy hit the screen edge, change directions
    if(enemy != null)
    {
        if(enemy.Position.X + enemy.Width > AlienAttackGame.ScreenWidth - ScreenEdge)
        {
            this.Position.Y += EnemyVerticalJump;
            this.Velocity.X = -EnemyVelocity;    // move left
        }
    }

    enemy = FindLeftMostEnemy();

    // if the left-most enemy hit the screen edge, change direction
    if(enemy != null)
```

```
    {
        if(enemy.Position.X < ScreenEdge)
        {
            this.Position.Y += EnemyVerticalJump;
            this.Velocity.X = EnemyVelocity;    // move right
        }
    }


    // update the positions of all enemies
    for(int y = 0; y < EnemyRows; y++)
    {
        for(int x = 0; x < EnemyCols; x++)
        {
            if(enemies[y,x] != null)
            {
                // X = position of the whole grid +
                // (X grid position * width of enemy) + padding
                // Y = position of the whole grid +
                // (Y grid position * width of enemy) + padding //
                enemies[y,x].Position.X =
                    (this.Position.X + (x * (enemyWidth + EnemySpacing.X)));
                enemies[y,x].Position.Y =
                    (this.Position.Y + (y * (enemyWidth + EnemySpacing.X)));
                enemies[y,x].Update(gameTime);
            }
        }
    }


    this.Position += this.Velocity;
}
```

The final methods will be used later, to determine when all enemies have been destroyed and to reset the board appropriately.

And finally, we will draw all enemies in the grid at their current positions, shown in Example 1-33.

Example 1-33. Draw method for EnemyGroup class

```
public override void Draw(GameTime gameTime, SpriteBatch spriteBatch)
{
    // draw all active enemies
    foreach(Enemy enemy in enemies)
    {
        if(enemy != null)
            enemy.Draw(gameTime, spriteBatch);
    }
}
```

Now we can hook up the EnemyGroup class in our GameScreen. We create an instance of the EnemyGroup in the constructor, update it in the Update method, and draw it in the Draw method as shown in Example 1-34.

Example 1-34. *Using EnemyGroup in GameScreen*

```
private EnemyGroup enemyGroup;

public GameScreen(ContentManager cm)
{
    contentManager = cm;
    AlienAttackGame.AudioManager.PlayCue(AudioManager.Cue.Theme);
    bgScreen = contentManager.Load<Texture2D>("gfx\\bgScreen");

    player = new Player(contentManager);

    playerShots = new List<PlayerShot>();

    arial = contentManager.Load<SpriteFont>("arial");

    // draw a lives status icon in the lower left
    livesIcon = new Player(contentManager);
#if ZUNE
    livesIcon.Position = new Vector2(0, AlienAttackGame.ScreenHeight-20);
#else
    livesIcon.Position = new Vector2(40, AlienAttackGame.ScreenHeight-60);
#endif

    enemyGroup = new EnemyGroup(contentManager);

    lives = 2;
}

public GameState Update(GameTime gameTime)
{
    MovePlayer(gameTime);
    HandlePlayerShots(gameTime);

    // as long as we're not in the lose state, update the enemies
    if(!loseGame)
        enemyGroup.Update(gameTime);

    return GameState.GameScreen;
```

```
    }

    public void Draw(GameTime gameTime, SpriteBatch spriteBatch)
    {
        spriteBatch.Draw(bgScreen, Vector2.Zero, Color.White);

        // draw the player
        if(player != null)
            player.Draw(gameTime, spriteBatch);

        // draw the enemy board
        enemyGroup.Draw(gameTime, spriteBatch);

        // draw the player shots
        foreach(PlayerShot playerShot in playerShots)
            playerShot.Draw(gameTime, spriteBatch);

        // draw the score
#if ZUNE
        spriteBatch.DrawString(arial, "Score", new Vector2(0, 0), Color.White);
        spriteBatch.DrawString(arial, score.ToString(), new Vector2(0, 30), Color.White);
#else
        spriteBatch.DrawString(arial, "Score", new Vector2(50, 50), Color.White);
        spriteBatch.DrawString(arial, score.ToString(), new Vector2(50, 80),
                               Color.White);
#endif

        // draw the lives icon
        livesIcon.Draw(gameTime, spriteBatch);
        spriteBatch.DrawString(arial, "x" + lives.ToString(),
            new Vector2(livesIcon.Position.X + livesIcon.Width + 4,
                        livesIcon.Position.Y + 8),
            Color.White);
    }
```

Running the game now will show the enemy grid moving left and right, and advancing down the screen after hitting the screen boundaries.

Next, you need the enemies to shoot at the player, or otherwise the game won't be very challenging. So, you need the opposite of the PlayerShot—the EnemyShot.

Drag the *eshot* folder into the *gfx* folder in the Content Pipeline so you have something to draw on the screen. These animation frames look just like the player shot, except they are pink.

Next, create a new class named EnemyShot in the *Sprites* folder. The code for this is almost identical to the PlayerShot class, except that it loads different content when created. The full class implementation can be found in Example 1-35.

Example 1-35. *EnemyShot class*

```
using System.Collections.Generic;
using Microsoft.Xna.Framework;
using Microsoft.Xna.Framework.Content;
using Microsoft.Xna.Framework.Graphics;

namespace AlienAttack
{
    public class EnemyShot : Sprite
    {
        double lastTime;

        public EnemyShot(ContentManager contentManager) : base(contentManager)
        {
            spriteTextures = new Texture2D[2];

            for(int i = 0; i <= 1; i++)
                spriteTextures[i] =
                    contentManager.Load<Texture2D>("gfx\\eshot\\eshot_" + i);

            this.Velocity.Y = 3;
        }

        public override void Update(GameTime gameTime)
        {
            if(gameTime.TotalGameTime.TotalMilliseconds - lastTime > 200)
            {
                frameIndex = frameIndex == 0 ? 1 : 0;
                lastTime = gameTime.TotalGameTime.TotalMilliseconds;
            }

            this.Position += this.Velocity;
        }
    }
}
```

Next, you need to actually drop the shot from the enemy toward the player. The easiest way to implement this is to create a random number generator and get a new value on every frame. When that value is above a certain threshold, you will create a new enemy shot on the screen and drop it toward the player.

Back in your EnemyGroup object, you will create a list to hold enemy shots currently on screen and set up the random number generator, as shown in Example 1-36.

Example 1-36. *EnemyGroup constructor with EnemyShot set up*

```
// all enemy shots
private List<EnemyShot> enemyShots;

private Random random;

public EnemyGroup(ContentManager contentManager) : base(contentManager)
{
    random = new Random();

    enemyShots = new List<EnemyShot>();

    enemies = new Enemy[EnemyRows,EnemyCols];

    // create a grid of enemies
    for(int y = 0; y < EnemyRows; y++)
    {
        for(int x = 0; x < EnemyCols; x++)
        {
            Enemy enemy = new Enemy(contentManager);
            enemy.Position.X = x * enemy.Width + EnemySpacing.X;
            enemy.Position.Y = y * enemy.Height + EnemySpacing.Y;
            enemies[y,x] = enemy;
        }
    }

    enemyWidth = enemies[0,0].Width;

    // position the grid centered at the vertical position specified above
    this.Position.X = AlienAttackGame.ScreenWidth/2 -
                        ((EnemyCols * (enemyWidth + EnemySpacing.X)) / 2);
    this.Position.Y = EnemyStartPosition;
    this.Velocity.X = EnemyVelocity;
}
```

In the Update method we will call a new method named EnemyFire that will grab a random value and then create an enemy shot under the selected enemy if the random value is above a certain threshold. The NextDouble method from the Random object will provide us with a decimal value between 0 and 1. We will check whether this value is above 0.99 and create a new enemy shot. It will also update all shots in the list to move them down the screen, removing any that have fallen off the bottom, as shown in Example 1-37.

Example 1-37. *Updated Update method*

```
public override void Update(GameTime gameTime)
{
    MoveEnemies(gameTime);
    EnemyFire(gameTime);
}

private void EnemyFire(GameTime gameTime)
{
    // at random times, drop an enemy shot
    if(random.NextDouble() > 0.99f)
    {
        int x, y;

        // find an enemy that hasn't been destroyed
        do
        {
            x = (int)(random.NextDouble() * EnemyCols);
            y = (int)(random.NextDouble() * EnemyRows);
        }
        while(enemies[y,x] == null);

        // create a shot for that enemy and add it to the list
        EnemyShot enemyShot = new EnemyShot(this.Content);
        enemyShot.Position = enemies[y,x].Position;
        enemyShot.Position.Y += enemies[y,x].Height;
        enemyShots.Add(enemyShot);

        AlienAttackGame.AudioManager.PlayCue(AudioManager.Cue.EnemyShot);
    }

    for(int i = 0; i < enemyShots.Count; i++)
    {
        // update all shots
        enemyShots[i].Update(gameTime);

        // remove those that are off the screen
        if(enemyShots[i].Position.Y > AlienAttackGame.ScreenHeight)
            enemyShots.RemoveAt(i);
    }
}
```

Our Draw method will enumerate the enemy shot list and draw all enemy shots to the screen. This can be seen in the updated code in Example 1-38.

Example 1-38. *Updated Draw method*

```
public override void Draw(GameTime gameTime, SpriteBatch spriteBatch)
{
    // draw all active enemies
    foreach(Enemy enemy in enemies)
    {
        if(enemy != null)
            enemy.Draw(gameTime, spriteBatch);
    }

    // draw all enemy shots
    foreach(EnemyShot enemyShot in enemyShots)
        enemyShot.Draw(gameTime, spriteBatch);
}
```

Finally, add a method named Reset that will clear the screen of all EnemyShot objects, as shown in Example 1-39.

Example 1-39. *Reset method*

```
public void Reset()
{
    enemyShots.Clear();
}
```

Running the game at this point will now show a pretty complete game. The player can move and fire, the enemies can move and fire, but you'll notice that shots will travel right through the player and the enemies. We now need to add collision detection and explosions.

Collision detection and explosions

Collision detection does exactly what it sounds like: it detects collisions. In our game, we need to know when a player bullet hits an enemy ship, when their bullets hit the player, and when an enemy and player collide.

There are a variety of methods to handle collision detection, but we will use one of the simplest of all since our game really doesn't require more: bounding-box collision detection.

The concept here is that each sprite on screen has an invisible border drawn around its outermost edges, as shown in Figure 1-7. If two of these borders intersect each other, as shown in Figure 1-8, we know the two objects touched each other and we respond appropriately.

Figure 1-7. *Bounding box around sprite*

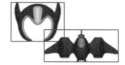

Figure 1-8. *Two bounding boxes intersecting*

The response will be an explosion at the site of the collision. So, before we implement the actual collision detection, let's set up our explosion animation.

First, drag the *explosion* folder from the downloaded assets to the *gfx* folder in the Content Pipeline. Then, create a new sprite named Explosion in the *Sprites* folder. This class will inherit from the base Sprite object and provide the usual loading and animation routines. The full class is shown in Example 1-40.

Example 1-40. *Explosion class*

```
using Microsoft.Xna.Framework;
using Microsoft.Xna.Framework.Content;
using Microsoft.Xna.Framework.Graphics;

namespace AlienAttack
{
    public class Explosion : Sprite
    {
        double lastTime;

        public Explosion(ContentManager contentManager)
        {
            spriteTextures = new Texture2D[10];

            for(int i = 0; i <= 9; i++)
                spriteTextures[i] =
                    contentManager.Load<Texture2D>("gfx\\explosion\\explosion_" + i);
        }

        public new bool Update(GameTime gameTime)
        {
            // if it's the final frame,
            // return true to let the other side know we're done
            if(frameIndex == 9)
```

```
            return true;

        // new frame every 70ms
        if(gameTime.TotalGameTime.TotalMilliseconds - lastTime > 70)
        {
            frameIndex++;
            lastTime = gameTime.TotalGameTime.TotalMilliseconds;
        }

        return false;
        }
    }
}
```

To actually handle collisions, we will rely on our EnemyGroup object, since it knows where all enemies and enemy shots are at any given time. Let's start with player shot and enemy collisions. We will pass all the player shots on-screen to a new method named HandlePlayerShotCollision. This will enumerate through all enemies left on the screen and determine whether their bounding boxes intersect with the player shots. If there is an intersection, it will drop an animation sprite at the appropriate position. This is all shown in Example 1-41.

Example 1-41. *HandlePlayerShotCollision method*

```
private List<Explosion> explosions;

public EnemyGroup(ContentManager contentManager) : base(contentManager)
{
    random = new Random();

    enemyShots = new List<EnemyShot>();

    enemies = new Enemy[EnemyRows,EnemyCols];

    explosions   = new List<Explosion>();

    // create a grid of enemies
    for(int y = 0; y < EnemyRows; y++)
    {
        for(int x = 0; x < EnemyCols; x++)
        {
            Enemy enemy = new Enemy(contentManager);
            enemy.Position.X = x * enemy.Width + EnemySpacing.X;
            enemy.Position.Y = y * enemy.Height + EnemySpacing.Y;
            enemies[y,x] = enemy;
        }
```

```
        }

        enemyWidth = enemies[0,0].Width;

        // position the grid centered at the vertical position specified above
        this.Position.X = AlienAttackGame.ScreenWidth/2 -
                            ((EnemyCols * (enemyWidth + EnemySpacing.X)) / 2);
        this.Position.Y = EnemyStartPosition;
        this.Velocity.X = EnemyVelocity;
    }

    public bool HandlePlayerShotCollision(PlayerShot playerShot)
    {
        for(int y = 0; y < EnemyRows; y++)
        {
            for(int x = 0; x < EnemyCols; x++)
            {
                // if a player shot hit an enemy, destroy the enemy
                if(enemies[y,x] != null && CheckCollision(playerShot, enemies[y,x]))
                {
                    Explosion explosion = new Explosion(this.Content);
                    explosion.Position = enemies[y,x].Position;
                    explosions.Add(explosion);
                    enemies[y,x] = null;
                    return true;
                }
            }
        }
        return false;
    }

    public bool CheckCollision(Sprite s1, Sprite s2)
    {
        // simple bounding box collision detection
        return s1.BoundingBox.Intersects(s2.BoundingBox);
    }
```

You will note that this method (and the next two) use the CheckCollision method shown in Example 1-41. This method uses the BoundingBox property we created on our Sprite object earlier, a .NET Rectangle object, and the Intersects method of that Rectangle object to determine whether the two bounding boxes intersect.

Next, let's write the enemy shot/player collision detection method, HandleEnemy ShotCollision. In this method, shown in Example 1-42, we enumerate all enemy shots on the screen and see if any of their bounding boxes intersect with the player ship's bounding box.

Example 1-42. *HandleEnemyShotCollision method*

```csharp
public bool HandleEnemyShotCollision(Player player)
{
    for(int i = 0; i < enemyShots.Count; i++)
    {
        // if an enemy shot hit the player, destroy the player
        if(CheckCollision(enemyShots[i], player))
        {
            enemyShots.RemoveAt(i);
            return true;
        }
    }
    return false;
}
```

And finally, we can write the HandleEnemyPlayerCollision method to determine whether any enemy remaining on-screen intersects with the player's ship, as shown in Example 1-43.

Example 1-43. *HandleEnemyPlayerCollision method*

```csharp
public bool HandleEnemyPlayerCollision(Player player)
{
    for(int y = 0; y < EnemyRows; y++)
    {
        for(int x = 0; x < EnemyCols; x++)
        {
            // if an enemy hit the player, destroy the enemy
            if(enemies[y,x] != null && CheckCollision(enemies[y,x], player))
            {
                Explosion explosion = new Explosion(this.Content);
                explosion.Position = enemies[y,x].Position;
                explosions.Add(explosion);
                enemies[y,x] = null;
                return true;
            }
        }
    }
    return false;
}
```

We also need to update and display the explosions list. Update the Update and Draw methods of EnemyGroup as shown in Example 1-44.

Example 1-44. *Updated Update and Draw methods*

```
public override void Update(GameTime gameTime)
{
    MoveEnemies(gameTime);
    EnemyFire(gameTime);

    for(int i = 0; i < explosions.Count; i++)
    {
        // update all explosions, remove those whose animations are over
        if(explosions[i].Update(gameTime))
            explosions.RemoveAt(i);
    }
}

public override void Draw(GameTime gameTime, SpriteBatch spriteBatch)
{
    // draw all active enemies
    foreach(Enemy enemy in enemies)
    {
        if(enemy != null)
            enemy.Draw(gameTime, spriteBatch);
    }

    // draw all enemy shots
    foreach(EnemyShot enemyShot in enemyShots)
        enemyShot.Draw(gameTime, spriteBatch);

    // draw all explosions
    foreach(Explosion explosion in explosions)
        explosion.Draw(gameTime, spriteBatch);
}
```

Now we can hook up these methods back in our GameScreen class and even handle scoring. The Update method handles the brunt of the work. Because this method is getting rather large, I'm going to break the following code sections up a bit so I can more easily explain what is happening, but remember that this is all sequential code from the one and only Update method.

First, we need a single member variable to hold an instance of the animation that shows the player ship exploding. To the other member variables, add the line shown in Example 1-45.

Example 1-45. *playerExplosion member variable*

```
private Explosion playerExplosion;
```

Now back to our Update method, shown in Example 1-46.

Example 1-46. *Update method, part 1*

```csharp
public GameState Update(GameTime gameTime)
{
    MovePlayer(gameTime);
    UpdatePlayerShots(gameTime);

    // as long as we're not in the lose state, update the enemies
    if(!loseGame)
        enemyGroup.Update(gameTime);

    HandleCollisions(gameTime);

    return GameState.GameScreen;
}

private void HandleCollisions(GameTime gameTime)
{
    // see if a player shot hit an enemy
    for(int i = 0; i < playerShots.Count; i++)
    {
        PlayerShot playerShot = playerShots[i];
        // check the shot and see if it it collided with an enemy
        if(playerShot != null &&
            enemyGroup.HandlePlayerShotCollision(playerShots[i]))
        {
            // remove the shot, add the score
            playerShots.RemoveAt(i);
            score += 100;
            AlienAttackGame.AudioManager.PlayCue(AudioManager.Cue.Explosion);
        }
    }

    // see if an enemy shot hit the player
    if(player != null && enemyGroup.HandleEnemyShotCollision(player))
    {
        // blow up the player
        playerExplosion = new Explosion(this.contentManager);
        playerExplosion.Position = player.Position;
        player = null;
        AlienAttackGame.AudioManager.PlayCue(AudioManager.Cue.Explosion);
    }

    // see if an enemy hit the player directly
```

```
if(player != null && enemyGroup.HandleEnemyPlayerCollision(player))
{
    // blow up the player
    playerExplosion = new Explosion(this.contentManager);
    playerExplosion.Position = player.Position;
    player = null;
    loseGame = true;
    AlienAttackGame.AudioManager.PlayCue(AudioManager.Cue.Explosion);
}

// if the player explosion animation is running, update it
if(playerExplosion != null)
{
    // if this is the last frame
    if(playerExplosion.Update(gameTime) && !loseGame)
    {
        // remove it
        playerExplosion = null;

        // we lose if we have no lives left
        if(lives == 0)
            loseGame = true;
        else
        {
            // subract 1 life and reset the board
            lives--;
            enemyGroup.Reset();
            playerShots.Clear();
            player = new Player(this.contentManager);
        }
    }
}
```

The emphasized code in this section calls out a new method named Handle
Collisions, which uses our collision detection routines in the EnemyGroup object to
determine if an enemy shot hit the player, or if an enemy hit the player directly. If it
has, it instantiates a new Explosion object and removes the player from the screen.
Note that in the case where the enemy hits the player directly, the game is automatically lost by setting the loseGame variable to true.

The final chunk updates the explosion animation for the destroyed player ship. If the
explosion has ended and the player has not lost the game, we check the lives counter.
If they have no lives left, they lose; otherwise, we subtract one from the lives counter,
reset the screen, and create a new player ship to display on the screen.

The final things to hook up are drawing the player explosion to the screen and drawing the win or lose text. The final Draw method looks like the code in Example 1-47.

Example 1-47. Final GameScreen Draw method

```
public void Draw(GameTime gameTime, SpriteBatch spriteBatch)
{
    spriteBatch.Draw(bgScreen, Vector2.Zero, Color.White);

    // draw the player
    if(player != null)
        player.Draw(gameTime, spriteBatch);

    // draw the enemy board
    enemyGroup.Draw(gameTime, spriteBatch);

    // draw the player shots
    foreach(PlayerShot playerShot in playerShots)
        playerShot.Draw(gameTime, spriteBatch);

    // draw the explosion
    if(playerExplosion != null)
        playerExplosion.Draw(gameTime, spriteBatch);

#if ZUNE
    // draw the score
    spriteBatch.DrawString(arial, "Score", new Vector2(0, 0), Color.White);
    spriteBatch.DrawString(arial, score.ToString(), new Vector2(0, 20), Color.White);

    // draw the lives icon
    livesIcon.Draw(gameTime, spriteBatch);
    spriteBatch.DrawString(arial, "x" + lives.ToString(),
                        new Vector2(livesIcon.Position.X + livesIcon.Width + 4,
                                    livesIcon.Position.Y),
                        Color.White);
#else
    // draw the score
    spriteBatch.DrawString(arial, "Score", new Vector2(50, 50), Color.White);
    spriteBatch.DrawString(arial, score.ToString(), new Vector2(50, 80),
                        Color.White);

    // draw the lives icon
    livesIcon.Draw(gameTime, spriteBatch);
    spriteBatch.DrawString(arial, "x" + lives.ToString(),
                        new Vector2(livesIcon.Position.X + livesIcon.Width + 4,
                                    livesIcon.Position.Y+8),
                        Color.White);
#endif
```

```
// draw the proper text, if required
if(enemyGroup.AllDestroyed())
{
    Vector2 size = arial.MeasureString("You win!");
    spriteBatch.DrawString(arial, "You win!",
                        new Vector2((AlienAttackGame.ScreenWidth - size.X) / 2,
                                    (AlienAttackGame.ScreenHeight - size.Y) / 2),
                        Color.Green);
}

if(loseGame)
{
    Vector2 size = arial.MeasureString("Game Over");
    spriteBatch.DrawString(arial, "Game Over",
                        new Vector2((AlienAttackGame.ScreenWidth - size.X) / 2,
                                    (AlienAttackGame.ScreenHeight - size.Y) / 2),
                        Color.Red);
}
}
```

The updated code here draws the playerExplosion sprite, and then, based on whether the enemy group is destroyed or the player has lost, draws the appropriate text to the center of the screen.

Running the Application

Running the game at this point should produce a fully working game! It's certainly not the most exciting game in the world, but it's a great start to building a game that is. Have at it!

Xbox 360 and Zune Support

If you have an Xbox 360 with a Creator's Club Account or a Microsoft Zune device, we can take this game to the next step and run it on either device.

Xbox 360

Creating the Xbox 360 version of this project is quite simple. By right-clicking on the *AlienAttack* project in the Solution Explorer, you should see an option labeled "Create Copy of Project for Xbox 360," as shown in Figure 1-9.

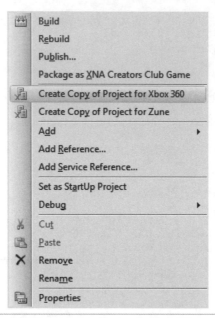

Figure 1-9. *Create Copy of Project for Xbox 360 menu item*

This will, as it says, create a brand-new project, link your existing code files and content, and put it in the same solution. If you build this new project, you will now have an Xbox 360 version ready to deploy to your console.

If you haven't already done so, you will need to install the XNA Game Studio Connect application on your Xbox 360 from the Games Marketplace. Once logged in with the Gamertag associated with your Creators Club Premium membership, enter the Games Marketplace area and select All Games→Browse→All Games→XNA Creators Club. From here, download the XNA Game Studio Connect application.

Next, you will have to connect the Xbox 360 to your PC. Run the XNA Game Studio Connect application on your Xbox 360. Run the XNA Game Studio Connect application on your Xbox 360 by navigating to the My Xbox channel→Game Library→Community Games→XNA Game Studio Connect.

When it starts, you will be presented with a screen that includes a 25-character connection key, as shown in Figure 1-10.

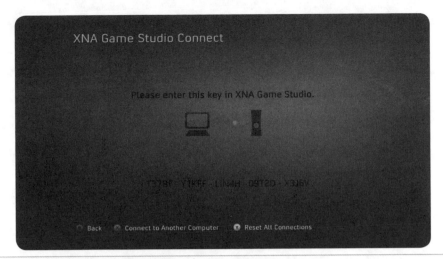

Figure 1-10. *XNA Game Studio Connect*

Back on the PC, start XNA Game Studio Device Center and click the Add Device button, as shown in Figure 1-11.

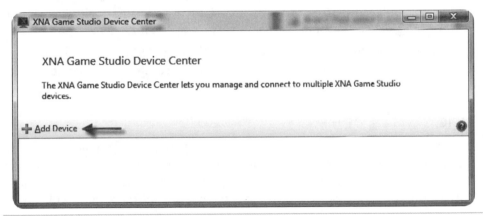

Figure 1-11. *XNA Game Studio Device Center*

Select the Xbox 360 as the device to connect to, as shown in Figure 1-12.

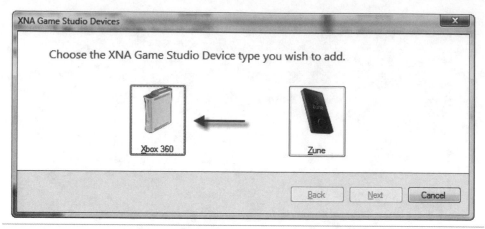

Figure 1-12. *Xbox 360 selection*

Give the Xbox 360 a name and click Next. Enter the connection key displayed on the Xbox 360 and click Next. The PC should find the Xbox 360 and connect. Click Finish to end adding the device.

Now, in Visual Studio, if you build and run the Xbox 360 project, it should deploy to the selected Xbox 360 and start. Later on, if you wish to run the game again, you will find it on the My Games section of the Games Library on your Xbox 360.

You can also debug this game as it is running on the Xbox 360 as though it were running on your PC. Breakpoints can be set, code can be set through, variables can be inspected, and so on.

Zune

Creating the Zune project is a bit more complex, but certainly not difficult. Because the graphics need to be reformatted to fit the 240x320 resolution screen, we need to recreate our Content Pipeline. The easiest way to handle this is to start a new instance of Visual Studio and create a new Zune game project, as shown in Figure 1-13.

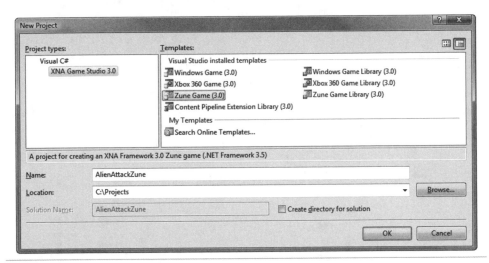

Figure 1-13. *Create new Zune game project*

Name the project `AlienAttackZune` and save it to a new, separate directory from the Windows and Xbox 360 versions.

Next, drag all of the downloaded assets from the Zune folder to the Content Pipeline. Finally, we need to add all of the code. Create a *Sprites* folder and a *Screens* folder to match the previous project.

Visual Studio has a feature where you can link files to a project instead of including them directly. Right-click on the root of the project and choose Add→Existing Item.... Browse to the root of the Windows project, select all .cs files, and then click Add As Link, as shown in Figure 1-14.

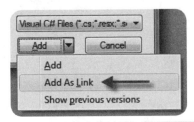

Figure 1-14. *Add As Link menu item*

This will add the code files as a link instead of copying them to the new project directly. Next, do the same with the .cs files located in the *Sprites* and *Screens* folder.

Now that the project is complete, we need to set up our Zune device. First, ensure you are running Zune firmware version 3.0 or greater. To view the Zune's firmware version, select settings→about→zune. If it is a version earlier than 3.0, you will need to update the Zune.

If you do not have the Zune software installed on your computer, you can download it from *http://www.zune.net/setup*. Connect the Zune to your PC using the USB cable, start the Zune software, and select Settings→General→Check for Updates, as shown in Figure 1-15.

Figure 1-15. *Check for Zune updates*

The latest version will be downloaded and installed automatically.

Next, we need to add the Zune device as a deployable device. Ensure the Zune is connected to the PC, start XNA Game Studio Device Center, and click the Add Device button. Choose the Zune as the device type you wish to add and click Next. You will be presented with a list of Zune devices connected to the PC. Select the one you wish to add and click the Next button. This will add the device.

Back in Visual Studio, run the Zune project and it will be automatically built, deployed, and run on the Zune device. As with the Xbox 360 and PC versions, the Zune-compatible version can also be debugged in Visual Studio while it is running on the device.

Final Thoughts

That was a lot of work, but we have Alien Attack running on Windows, Xbox 360, and the Zune with very few changes between the versions. As you can see, XNA is a pretty powerful library that allows you to create games that cross platforms with little effort. Take what we've done here and add some new rules, new enemies, or create a brand-new game!

AUTHOR	Dan Fernandez
DIFFICULTY	Beginner
TIME REQUIRED	6–9 hours
COST	Free
SOFTWARE	Silverlight 1.0, LEGO Digital Designer (*http://ldd.lego.com/*), and Paint.NET (*http://www.getpaint.net/*) or image editing equivalent
HARDWARE	None
DOWNLOAD	*http://www.popfly.com/users/Dan/LEGOSoldier*

In LEGO Soldier, you play a specially trained soldier sent to stop a rogue government laboratory from conducting genetic cloning experiments deep under the earth's surface. The lab is run by a nefarious scientist known only as the "Blind Scientist."

If you choose to accept this mission, you will use Popfly (*http://www.popfly.com/*), a website that allows users to create games, web mashups, and web pages right inside a web browser. We will be using the Popfly Game Creator portion of Popfly to create LEGO Soldier. Popfly Game Creator provides an easy-to-use drag-and-drop interface for creating simple games with minimal effort.

Overview

In the game, you play a soldier driving a LEGO car with hydraulics that you can use to crush enemies ranging from gun-wielding security guards to mindless zombies, as shown in Figure 2-1.

Figure 2-1. *The main actor that you play*

As you explore the underground cavern, you'll learn to use environmental objects, such as a catapult to jump over obstacles, or blow up enemies using powder kegs, as shown in Figure 2-2.

Figure 2-2. *Blowing up skeletons using powder kegs*

You can also easily publish your game to Facebook so your friends can challenge each other to defeat the evil Blind Scientist, as shown in Figure 2-3.

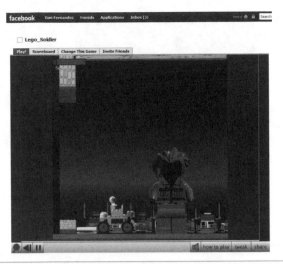

Figure 2-3. *Publish your games directly to Facebook*

Popfly Game Creator Terms

Before we get started, let's review some of the Popfly Game Creator terms we'll need to know in order to build a game, including:

Scene

A scene is where you lay out your game's user interface. For LEGO Soldier, we'll build one long game scene.

Viewport

A viewport enables you to limit the portion of the scene that is visible at any time. We'll turn a viewport on for LEGO Soldier so that the entire scene isn't shown at once, and just the viewport portion is visible.

Actor

Actors represent graphical elements in a game scene. Although technically you can put non-actor Silverlight elements into a scene, like a `TextBlock` control, actors are special in that they can have behaviors. Some actors in LEGO Soldier include the scene background, our Main actor, walls, enemies, and anything else in our game.

Behaviors

Behaviors are the brains, or logic, of an actor or scene. For example, you can define a motion behavior for how an actor should move.

Properties

The properties pane is where you change the attributes of an actor or scene. For example, you can set the opacity of an actor to any value between 0 and 1 to represent how translucent you would want the actor to appear, with 0 being invisible and 1 being fully visible.

Game Screen

This is where you can build custom properties for your game as well as upload game assets, such as images, sounds, and video.

Building LEGO Soldier Step-by-Step

Now that we've defined the key terms, let's go through how you can build the LEGO Soldier game step-by-step. Here are the steps we'll take:

1. Building the Popfly game

2. Designing custom actors

3. Designing the scene

4. Building scene behaviors

5. Adding brains to actors with behaviors

6. Publishing your game to Facebook

Building the Popfly Game

The first thing we need to do is to build the game. To do that, go to *www.popfly.com* and select "Create a Game." You will need to either log in with an existing Popfly user ID or create a new user ID if you have never used Popfly before.

After logging in, you'll be taken to the Popfly Game Creator, which will prompt you with a "Create a New Game" wizard, as shown in Figure 2-4 and select the "…or start from scratch" option.

Figure 2-4. *Create a New Game menu*

At this point, we've built an empty game shell. Save the empty game by clicking the Save button in the top-right corner, and give your project a name like *LEGOSoldier*.

Designing Custom Actors

Although Popfly ships with hundreds of built-in actors, because we're building a LEGO game, we obviously need to build custom LEGO actors. Popfly enables anyone to upload and contribute custom actors into their actor repository, which is what we'll do for our LEGO models. Your graphic design skills may be awesome, but some of us need more help, so we'll use LEGO's free Digital Designer application, which enables you to build 3D LEGO models in a drag-and-drop environment. Digital Designer also has a large user community where users upload and share their own custom LEGO models. For LEGO Soldier, we'll download and customize several user-created LEGO models for a LEGO tower, a lab, and more.

To build our custom actors, we need to do a couple of things:

1. Design a LEGO model using LEGO Digital Designer

2. Export one or more screenshots of the LEGO model we want to use

3. Trim any extra whitespace in the image

4. Upload the image to Popfly

5. Build some very basic XAML to hold the image

6. Build a new actor in Popfly

Designing a LEGO Model Using LEGO Digital Designer

To build our Main actor model, open up LEGO Digital Designer, select Choose Free Build, and expand the Brick Palette, which contains the list of available LEGOs. Now that the designer is open, you can begin building LEGO models by dragging-and-dropping bricks onto the design grid. Figure 2-5 shows the final actor design of the Main actor in LEGO soldier. This was built by simply snapping together LEGO bricks piece-by-piece onto the design surface.

Figure 2-5. *Building a custom model using LEGO Digital Designer*

Exporting a LEGO Model

For our Main actor, once you're finished designing a model in Digital Designer, rotate it so it appears as a flat, 2-D image, and then click Toolbox→Take a Screenshot to export a screenshot of the model exactly as it appears on-screen. Digital Designer screenshots use the transparent Portable Network Graphics (PNG) file format. All screenshots are saved to the current user's *Pictures* directory with the filename *LDDScreenshot1. png*, with additional screenshots being numbered 2, 3, 4, and so on.

Cropping out Empty Space

When Digital Designer takes a screenshot, it will create the image based on the size of the application window, For example, if the window is sized to 1280x1024, the image will have those same dimensions. This means that there will be a big chunk of empty (transparent) space that we don't need, and we should use image-editing software to remove it.

To remove the extra space, we'll use Paint.NET, available at *http://www.getpaint.net/*, a free, easy-to-use image-editing tool. In Paint.NET, open the screenshot and select just the LEGO model by using the Rectangle Select tool. With just the model selected, click the "Crop to Selection" menu option, as shown in Figure 2-6. This will remove all the additional extra space from the image, making it smaller and easier to work with when building our actor. Make sure to save the newly trimmed image with a better name, such as *MainCharacter.png*.

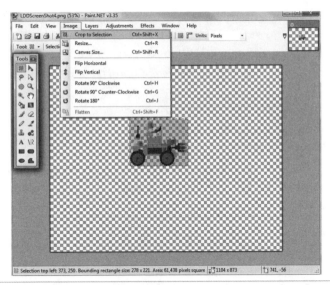

Figure 2-6. *Removing extra whitespace from the screenshot using Paint.NET*

Upload Images to Popfly

Now that we're done editing our image, let's upload it to Popfly. To do that, switch back to the Popfly game you created in "Building the Popfly game." Next, select the Game menu option, and under the "Add a file from..." text, select "your computer" to upload the image from your computer. Click Browse... to navigate to the *MainCharacter.png* file you previously created, as shown in Figure 2-7.

Figure 2-7. *Uploading images to Popfly from the Game menu*

When you upload an image to Popfly, the image will be saved using the following convention:

http://www.popfly.com/users/<UserName>/<ProjectName>/<ImageName>.png

For example, for a user named Dan, the *MainCharacter.png* image will be uploaded to:

http://www.popfly.com/users/Dan/LegoSoldier/MainCharacter.png

Rather than typing out the full qualified image URL, you should use a built-in Popfly shortcut to reference images using the $base$ token.

Using the $base$ token, we can reference the same image from inside Popfly with *$base$/MainCharacter.png*, which translates to the fully qualified URL.

Why Using $base$ Is a Good Practice

The reason why **$base$** is the preferred mechanism for referencing game assets (images, sound files, etc.) revolves around Popfly's **Rip** feature. **Rip** enables a Popfly user to create a personal copy of another user's project.

Let's say we have two Popfly users, Angie and Dan. Angie has built and shared a Popfly game and Dan has ripped (copied) her game. If Angie has built her game using fully qualified paths, such as ***www.popfly.com/users/Angie/MyProject/img1.png***, when Dan rips her project, Dan's new project will contain hardcoded links to Angie's project files (for example, ***Angie/MyProject/img1.png***). This is bad because if Angie deletes ***img1*** or replaces it with something completely different, Dan's game is essentially broken.

If, instead of using the fully qualified path, Angie uses **$base$** for her image (***$base$/img1.png***), when Dan rips her project this time, Popfly will create local copies of those images for Dan—for example, ***Dan/RippedProject/img1.png***. Since the image is now a local copy, if Angie deletes or replaces ***img1.png***, it will no longer break Dan's ripped project.

Building an Actor in the Actor Designer

Now that we've sliced our images, switch back to Popfly and select the Actors icon to go to the Actor designer. Click New to create a new actor, as shown in Figure 2-8.

Figure 2-8. *The New actor menu option*

Let's quickly examine the pieces of the Actor designer, as shown in Figure 2-9:

1. Actor List: This is the list of actors you have defined in your game.

2. States: This is where you can create or view the different states for an actor. Each State is listed vertically.

3. Appearance: This is where you define the appearance of the currently selected state.

4. Behaviors: Behaviors are the brains that will control what your actor does.

5. Properties: Properties are a way to store game or actor variables, such as the current score or a player's health.

6. Export: This enables you to share actors you've built with the community.

7. Preview: This shows the current actor's appearance.

8. Collision Edges: This is used for when actors collide with one another. You can set the actor's collision edges by dragging the red collision border to build custom edges. You can also turn off the Solid option, which means that the actor won't fire collision events. This is handy if you're creating actors for a scene background, such as a city skyline or clouds, and you don't actually want your actor to collide with these parts of the background image.

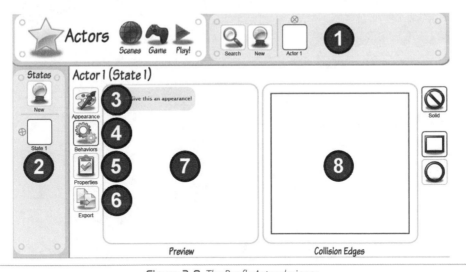

Figure 2-9. *The Popfly Actor designer*

To define the appearance of our Main actor, click the Appearance button (#3 on Figure 2-9), and then click the "Switch to XAML" button. Underneath the covers, an actor is made up of Silverlight XAML. To define the XAML for the Main actor, define the height, width, and the image for the actor, as shown in Example 2-1.

Example 2-1. *Basic XAML to hold an Image control*

```
<!-- XAML for Main actor -->
<Canvas xmlns="http://schemas.microsoft.com/winfx/2006/xaml/presentation"
    Width="419" Height="336">
<Image Width="419" Height="336" Source="$base$/MainCharacter.png" />
</Canvas>
```

Copy and paste this XAML into the XAML definition textbox, as shown in Figure 2-10.

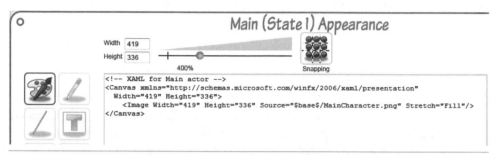

Figure 2-10. *Setting the XAML that defines the appearance for the Main actor*

Save the XAML and exit the screen. Finally, let's update the actor name for our actor to something more intuitive. Click on the actor name to change its name from "Actor1" to "Main".

When you are done, your completed Main actor should look like Figure 2-11.

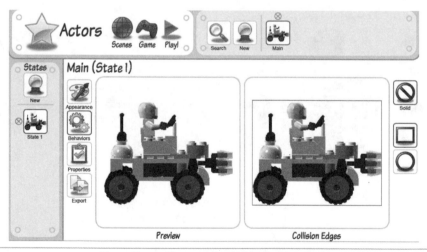

Figure 2-11. *The completed UI for the Main actor*

Adding a Health Bar and a Scoreboard

Remember that each visual element in the game is an actor, and so we will also need to create a new actor to display the health bar and the game's current score. Many games have the concept of a health bar, in which the bar is reduced by a particular amount when an actor gets hit or attacked, rather than have the actor die.

Like we did previously when creating the Main actor, create a new actor and name it HealthBar. Next, click the "Switch to XAML" button to switch to the XAML view, and copy and paste the XAML from Example 2-2 into the TextBlock control. When you switch back to the Design view, the rendered actor should look like Figure 2-12.

Example 2-2. *XAML markup for defining a health bar and scoreboard*

```
<Canvas xmlns:x="http://schemas.microsoft.com/winfx/2006/xaml"
  Width="100" Height="35" x:Name="HealthBar">
  <Rectangle Width="100" Height="20" Fill="Gray" Stroke="Black"
    RadiusX="2" RadiusY="2" Canvas.ZIndex="1"/>
  <Rectangle Width="100" Height="20" Name="HealthValue" Fill="Green"
    Stroke="Black" RadiusX="2" RadiusY="2" Canvas.ZIndex="2"/>
  <TextBlock Width="50" Height="20" Text="Score:" FontFamily="Trebuchet MS"
    FontWeight="Bold" Foreground="LightBlue" Canvas.Left="9" Canvas.Top="20"/>
  <TextBlock Width="30" Height="20" Name="ScoreValue" Text="0"
    Foreground="LightBlue" FontFamily="Trebuchet MS" FontWeight="Bold"
    Canvas.Top="20" Canvas.Left="60" TextWrapping="Wrap"/>
</Canvas>
```

Let's quickly walk through the code in Example 2-2. Inside the Canvas control we define gray and green Rectangle controls that are placed on top of each other. The reason we stack the Rectangle controls on top of one another is that when the Main actor gets injured, we will shrink the green rectangle's width to reveal the empty gray rectangle, as shown in Figure 2-13. We also define two TextBlock controls: one that is a label for the score, and another to hold the actual value for the score. We'll show how to dynamically update the health bar later in this chapter in the "Building the HealthBar Behaviors" section.

Figure 2-12. *The health bar and scoreboard actor appearance*

Figure 2-13. *The health bar set with a smaller width reveals the gray rectangle*

Importing Actors

To save you time and energy, rather than going through the process of building and importing additional LEGO actors, you can instead import LEGO actors tagged with "LEGOSoldier" that have been built for the finished game. Each of the LEGO actors was built using the same exact steps in "Designing Custom Actors."

To add the actors, click on the Search button, type in "LEGOSoldier" as the search term, and then click on each of the five actor results to add them to the game, as shown in Figure 2-14.

Figure 2-14. *Adding prebuilt LEGOSoldier actors*

In addition to LEGO actors, we also want to add some of Popfly's built-in actors for our background and game environment. The names of the built-in actors are listed next and pictured in Figure 2-15. To add each actor, simply search on the actor's name, click on it, and add it to the game. From left-to-right, the actor's names are Stone Block, Cave, Dark Room, Dirt Block, Rock-Horizontal, Sign – Up, Sign – Right, Barrel, and Catapult.

Figure 2-15. *Import built-in Popfly actors*

Now that we've chosen all of our actors, let's switch over to the scene designer and lay out the actors for our game.

Designing the Main Scene

Now that we added all of the actors, let's use them to build the game scene. As we explained earlier, a scene is where you design a game's user interface. Let's examine the parts of the scene designer in Figure 2-16.

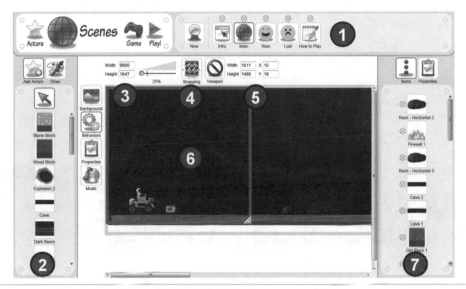

Figure 2-16. *Popfly Game Creator scene designer*

1. Scene list: By default, when you create a Popfly game, it will create the following scenes:

   a. Intro: The splash screen for a game before it starts

   b. Main: The first scene that will load after the intro screen

   c. Won: The scene when you win the game

   d. Lost: The scene when you lose the game

   e. How to Play: The scene where you explain how to play the game

2. Actor list: This is the list of actors that have been added to the current game. From here, you can click and drag an actor onto the scene designer.

3. Scene size: This is where you can set the width, height, and zoom of the scene. You should use the zooming tool to zoom in and out of longer scenes.

4. Snapping: This enables you to easily align actors in a scene horizontally and vertically. You can toggle this off if you want free-form drag-and-drop support of actors.

5. Viewport: A viewport enables you to visually limit the portion of the scene that is visible at any time. It is represented by the blue square in the scene designer.

6. Scene Designer: This is the drag-and-drop surface where you add actors.

7. Actor Scene list: Unlike the actor list, this list represents each instance of an actor in the current scene. If there are five actor skeletons in a scene, each skeleton will be listed separately.

Designing the Main Scene

The Main scene for our game will be a left-to-right scroller that goes through a multi-level cave. Along the way, we'll add the LEGO tower, guards, zombies, powder kegs, and more, all on the way to meet the "boss" of the game, the Blind Scientist. You can see the full scene zoomed out in Figure 2-17.

Figure 2-17. *The completed design for the Main scene*

Now that you've seen what the completed scene looks like, let's show how to build it step-by-step. The first thing we need to do is to click the Viewport button (located at #5 in Figure 2-16) to turn on a viewport for the scene. Next, we will set the dimensions of our scene:

Scene dimensions
Width: 9900, Height: 1650

Viewport dimensions
Width: 1600, Height: 1650, X: 0, Y: 0

This will create a long, horizontal scene and a viewport displaying only one portion of the scene at a time. The X and Y values for the viewport represent the location of the starting viewport, and since our side-scroller moves from left to right, these will be 0,0.

Adding the Two Cave Background Actor Files

Now, we need to add two background actors tiled as the background for the game. The background will consist of two stretched-out Cave actors as the background. To add an actor to a scene, simply click and drag the actor from the actor list (#2 in Figure 2-16) and drag it onto the design surface (#6 in Figure 2-16).

 If you're having trouble positioning the actors, you may want to turn off the snapping feature (#4 in Figure 2-16) so you can free-form place actors in a scene. You should also use the zoom-in/zoom-out feature regularly (#3 in Figure 2-16) to easily navigate large scenes like this one.

When you place the Cave actor, blue resizing bars will appear that show you the width and height of the actor. For the Cave background, have the background start in the upper-left corner at "0,0" and stretch it to a width of 4950 and a height of 1650.

Figure 2-18 shows the zoomed-out scene designer with the resized Cave actor background.

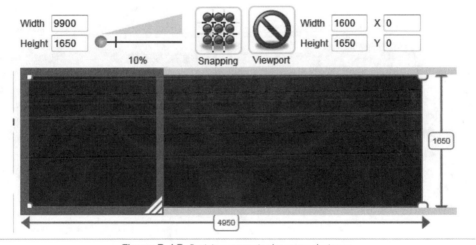

Figure 2-18. *Resizing actors in the scene designer*

Tiling the Background

Once you have an actor exactly where you want it, you can tile the actor, which will copy the actor, including its width and height dimensions, and tile it directly to the right of an actor. To do this, make sure you have the Cave actor selected, and use Ctrl-C to copy and Ctrl-V to paste the actor. The newly copied actor will automatically be aligned and tiled directly to the right of the first actor, as shown in Figure 2-19.

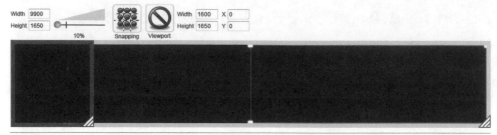

Figure 2-19. *Use copy and paste to automatically tile actors*

Tiling the Ground Floor

Now that we've built the background, let's build a floor for our scene by dragging a Dirt Block actor, setting its dimensions to a width of 4950 and height of 55.

Place the stretched Dirt Block tile in the bottom left-hand corner of the scene, as shown in Figure 2-20. Like we did earlier with the Cave block, we will also tile the Dirt Block by using Ctrl-C and Ctrl-V to paste the second Dirt Block actor to the right of the first actor. At this point, both the Cave background tiles should have a Dirt Block floor along the bottom.

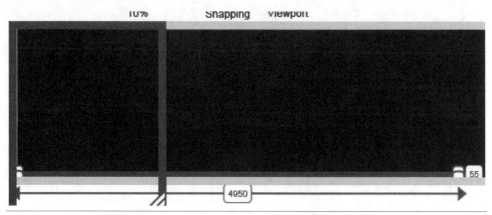

Figure 2-20. *Dirt Block actor stretched out along the bottom of the scene*

Designing the First Half of the Scene

The first half of our scene will include the Main actor, some enemy actors, and some background/scenery actors, as shown in Figure 2-21. We'll go through adding each of these actors step-by-step, but when you're building this scene, the exact positioning of the actors doesn't matter. Feel free to experiment with the background, actors, and positioning as you're building.

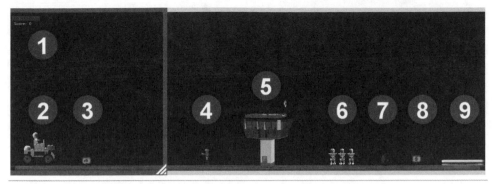

Figure 2-21. *The actors to add for the first half of the scene*

As you can see in Figure 2-21, we've added a number of actors with corresponding numbers. These include:

1. HealthBar. This displays the current health of your Main actor and the score for the game. Resize this actor to a width of 300 and a height of 100.

2. Main Actor. This is the Main actor we built. You do not need to resize this actor.

3. Sign-Right Arrow. A visual guide for new players that indicates they should continue moving to the right. Resize this actor to a width of 100 and a height of 100.

4. LEGO Security Guy. This is the first enemy players will encounter that can shoot projectiles at the player. You do not need to resize this actor.

5. LEGO Tower. A tower that looks like a security checkpoint. Resize this actor to a width of 600 and a height of 700.

6. Three LEGO Skeletons. These are slow-moving enemy actors. You do not need to resize this actor.

7. Rock-Horizontal. A solid rock that players must jump over. Resize this actor to a width of 130 and a height of 130.

8. Sign-Up Arrow. A visual guide that indicates the player should go upward when the player first encounters the Catapult actor. Resize this actor to a width of 100 and a height of 100.

9. Catapult. When jumped on, the Catapult will launch the actor into the air. Resize this actor to a width of 270 and a height of 50.

Designing the Second Half of Our Scene

The second half of our scene includes multiple levels, powder kegs, and the laboratory of the final boss, the Blind Scientist, as shown in Figure 2-22.

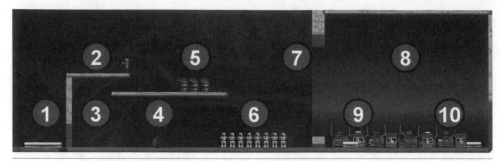

Figure 2-22. *The actors to add to the second half of the scene*

Just like we did with the first half, we're also adding a number of actors to the second half of the scene, shown with their corresponding numbers in Figure 2-22. These actors include:

1. Catapult. This is actually the catapult from the first half of the scene and is included here so that the continuation between the first and second halves of the scene are clear.

2. Horizontal Stone block and Security actor. This is a raised platform that players will have to use the Catapult actor to reach. On top of the platform is the Security actor. Resize the Stone block actor to a width of 750 and a height of 50, and keep the Security actor size as-is.

3. A tall stone block to block the player from moving to the right. Players will need to use the Catapult to jump onto the platform. Resize this actor to a width of 50 and a height of 830.

4. Rock – Horizontal. Just like in the first half of the scene, we'll place a solid rock that players must jump over. Since this rock will be the same height and width as the previous rock actor (#7 from Figure 2-21), you can select the first rock and hit Ctrl-C and Ctrl-V to copy and paste the actor with the same dimensions.

5. Stone Block and Barrels. This Stone Block is placed in about the middle of the scene height-wise and sized to a width of 1350 and a height of 50. The three Barrel actors represent powder kegs that, when pushed off the Stone Block by players, will land on the Skeletons below and blow them up. Resize the Barrel actor to a width of 120 and a height of 165, and copy and paste the barrels so that there are three barrels on this platform.

6. Eight LEGO Skeletons. Place a few of the Skeleton actors underneath the platform (#5) so that barrels knocked off the platform will land on top of these enemies.

7. Two Stone Blocks. These actors form a sort of doorway that separates the Cave from the laboratory. The top stone block is sized to a width of 150 and a height of 450. The bottom stone block is sized to a width of 150 and a height of 125.

8. Dark Room, top and right Stone Block walls. This is the laboratory where you will fight the final boss, the Blind Scientist. To give the laboratory a different look and feel from the cave, we'll use the Dark Room actor to cover the entire room, including behind the laboratory door (#7). Resize the Dark Room actor to width=2050, height=1625. We'll also want to add a ceiling and a right wall using two Stone Block actors. Resize the ceiling Stone Block actor to width=1950 and height=50, and resize the right wall actor to be width=75, height=1650.

9. Two LEGO Labs and Catapult. In our game, you cannot shoot or run over the Blind Scientist (he'll grow four times his size when you first collide with him), but instead you must use the Catapult actor in his laboratory to land on top of his head. To give the laboratory a lab-like feeling, we'll use two tiled LEGO Lab actors. Resize one of the actors to width=780, height=280, and copy and paste to tile a second LEGO Lab actor to the right of it. Since the Blind Scientist is going to grow in size, we'll need to add small Catapults so that players can launch themselves into the air to land on the boss's head. Add a Catapult to the left side of the LEGO Lab actor, and resize it to width=185, height=60.

10. Blind Scientist and Catapult. Place the Blind Scientist actor in the center of the laboratory without resizing him, and place another Catapult on the far right side of the laboratory. Resize the right Catapult actor to the same dimensions as the Catapult in #9.

At this point, we've designed the entire Main scene, which now should look like the completed scene we saw in Figure 2-17. The next step in building our game is to add properties that store the Main actor's health and the game's score.

Building Game Properties

For LEGO Soldier, we want to store the current game's score and the current health of the Main actor in the game's properties. Since the Score property is created automatically when you first create your game, the only property we need to add is Health. To do this, switch to the Game tab and click "Add a Property" to add the Health property with a default value of 100, as shown in Figure 2-23. You will also want to make sure the "higher score is better" button is selected so that Popfly's achievements feature will automatically know how to rank the game's score.

Figure 2-23. *Adding a Health property for the Health bar*

Building Behaviors

With our game properties defined, we now need to add behaviors to our actors. Behaviors are the "brain" of an actor, controlling what the actor can and cannot do, such as move, run, and jump. Behaviors can also be event-based, such as adding points to a score when a monster is killed.

Let's examine the types of behaviors you can add to an actor, as shown in Figure 2-24.

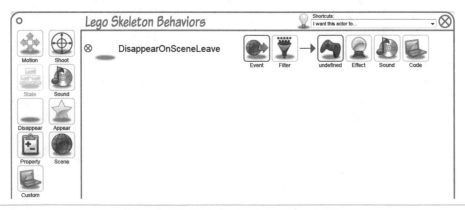

Figure 2-24. *The behavior designer for an actor*

1. Shortcuts: Shortcuts are like macros that add multiple behaviors for common tasks. For example, rather than defining individual motion behaviors for moving left, right, and jumping, you can add the run and jump behaviors by pressing the "run and jump by pressing keys" shortcut.

2. Behavior List: When you add a behavior, it is added to the behavior list.

3. Motion: This enables you to specify an actor's motion. We will use this extensively for our actors.

4. Shoot: As the name implies, this behavior enables you to shoot a projectile—for example, a bullet—from an actor. We will use this for gun-wielding actors.

5. State: This behavior enables you to switch the states for an actor. This is useful for actors that have two states, a left-facing and right-facing state, that you could switch depending on whether a user presses the left or right arrow key.

6. Sound: This behavior enables you to play a sound based on a particular event.

7. Disappear: This behavior controls the visibility of an actor. For example, when a bullet hits an enemy actor, you would want the enemy to disappear.

8. Appear: This is the opposite of the disappear behavior in that it can cause an actor to become visible.

9. Property: This behavior is used when you want to update a property, such as increasing a score by one point for every enemy you kill.

10. Scene: This behavior is used when you want to change the current scene of the game—say, when loading the second scene after completing the first scene in a game.

11. Custom: This behavior is used to define custom code to execute for an actor.

 NOTE At the time of this writing, Popfly only supports JavaScript custom code. The Popfly team is looking to support Silverlight 2 languages in the future, but the exact details are still up in the air.

Figure 2-25 shows a newly created motion behavior. From left to right, you'll see:

- The behavior name, "Motion1"
- The event that will trigger when the behavior will execute
- The event filter that can be used to filter when the event should execute
- The actual behavior, which in this case is a motion behavior
- A sound effect to play when the behavior executes
- A code button that can be used to add custom code

Motion1

Event   Filter   Motion Sound   Code

Figure 2-25. *A newly added motion behavior*

We will create a number of behaviors for each of the actors in LEGO Soldier, and so the key thing to remember is that we need to define:

- The event that indicates when the behavior will execute
- The behavior or action to take when the event is triggered

Renaming Behaviors

To rename a behavior, click on the current behavior name, which will convert the name into an editable text box control as shown in Figure 2-26.

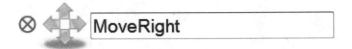

MoveRight

Figure 2-26. *Renaming a behavior*

Building the Main Scene Behaviors

The first set of behaviors we're going to build are for the Main scene. We want the Main scene Viewport to follow our Main actor, so that the Main actor is always visible.

Using Shortcuts to Build the Main Scene Behaviors

Starting from the scene designer, click on the Behaviors button (see Figure 2-16), which should take you to the Main Scene Behaviors window, as shown in Figure 2-27. From here, expand the Shortcuts drop-down list in the top-right corner, and select the option to "have a viewport following Main 1". This shortcut makes it so that the scene's Viewport (the visible part of the scene) will now follow our Main actor, so if he goes right, the Viewport also will scroll right and we can discover new parts of the scene.

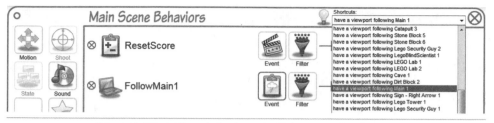

Figure 2-27. *Adding a behavior to the Main scene using shortcuts*

Building a Property Change Behavior to Reset the Health Property

For our scene, we want to build a property change behavior that will reset the Health-Bar property that we defined earlier in the "Building Game Properties" section. To do this, click the property icon on the left to add a new property behavior (see Figure 2-28).

Figure 2-28. *Creating a property change behavior*

We want to reset the HealthBar property to 100 when the game loads. Because Popfly Game Creator will, by default, fire the event when the scene loads, we do not need to change when the event should reset the score. To set the HealthBar to 100, click the property button, select the Health property, select the "Set it to:" radio button, and enter a value of 100, as shown in Figure 2-29.

Figure 2-29. *Resetting the health property to 100 when the scene loads*

Creating a Custom Code Behavior

The final behavior we need to add to our scene is a custom code behavior that causes the HealthBar actor to scroll with our viewport. To build this behavior, click the Custom button in the Main scene behavior, which will add a behavior to the list of Main scene behaviors (Figure 2-30).

Figure 2-30. *Creating a custom code behavior for the Main scene*

Click on the Event button and set the event to be a property change event that will fire the event any time the value of X changes, as shown in Figure 2-31. This event will fire whenever the Main actor moves along the X axis.

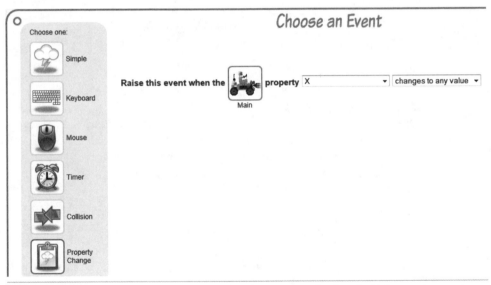

Figure 2-31. *Setting the property change event to fire custom code when the Main actor moves along the X axis*

Now that we have set when the event will fire, we now need to set the code that will execute when the event fires. To do that, click the Code button shown in Figure 2-30 and add the JavaScript code in Example 2-3.

Example 2-3. *Code to automatically scroll the HealthBar actor*

```
//Code modified from: http://www.popfly.com/users/nick-potter/U-Boot%20Treasure%20
Hunt

// Get the location of the viewport
var viewportX = Game.CurrentScene.GetValue("X");

//if the viewport is negative, set the healthbar location to zero
if(viewportX < 0)
{
  viewportX = 0;
}

// Get a reference to the healthBar actor and set the value
var healthBar = Game.CurrentScene.GetActor("HealthBar 1");
healthBar.SetValue("X",viewportX);
```

The first thing we do in this code is get the X-axis value for the Viewport using built-in Popfly JavaScript functions. Next, we make sure the Viewport isn't negative, and then get a reference to the "HealthBar 1" actor instance and update its position along the X axis based on the position of the Viewport. In other words, our "HealthBar 1" actor will continually move to keep itself visible in the Viewport. If the Main actor scrolls the Viewport to x=100, "HealthBar 1" will also move to x=100.

> **NOTE**
> Underneath the covers, the graphical IDE features of Popfly are really just calling JavaScript functions defined in the Popfly Game Creator API. This means that you as a developer can also build custom code behaviors that use the Game Creator API. For additional information on the Popfly Game Creator API, visit *http://www.popflywiki.com/GameCreatorAPI.ashx*.

Adding Main Actor Behaviors Using Shortcuts

In the previous step we added behaviors for how a *scene* will behave; now we'll next add behaviors for how each *actor* should behave, starting with our Main actor. To set an actor's behavior, switch back to the Actor designer, select the Main actor, and click the Behaviors button. The first set of behaviors we will add for the Main actor will be to move left, move right, and jump. The easiest way to do this is to use the shortcut "run and jump by pressing keys (side view)", as shown in Figure 2-32.

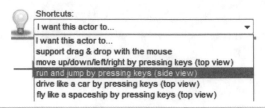

Figure 2-32. Adding running and jumping behaviors to the Main actor using Shortcuts

You'll see that a number of behaviors will be automatically added to the Main actor, as shown in Figure 2-33.

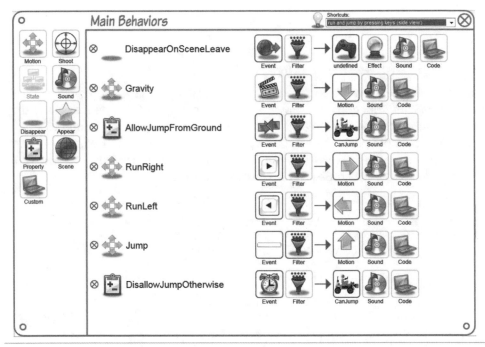

Figure 2-33. The list of newly added behaviors for the Main actor

Let's quickly explain what these behaviors do:

DisappearOnSceneLeave
> This is a default behavior that is added to all actors. When the actor leaves the scene, the actor disappears.

Gravity

> This adds a continuous downward motion on the actor that acts much like gravity would.

AllowJumpFromGround

> This will update the `CanJump` property for the actor to 1 when the actor is in contact with solid ground.

RunRight

> Move the actor to the right when the right arrow key is pressed.

RunLeft

> Move the actor to the left when the left arrow key is pressed.

Jump

> This will make the actor jump upward when the spacebar is pressed. This event will fire only when the `CanJump` property is set to 1 from the `AllowJumpFrom Ground` property.

DisallowJumpOtherwise

> This behavior will set the `CanJump` property to 0 every frame. The value will be overridden by the `AllowJumpFromGround` behavior defined earlier. This is designed to make it so that the actor can jump only while on solid ground.

One thing we'll want to do is increase the movement speed of our Main actor when he's moving to the right. To do that, select the RunRight behavior and click the Motion button to edit how the Main actor will move, as shown in Figure 2-34.

Figure 2-34. *The RunRight behavior for the Main actor*

This brings up the motion designer with a number of different settings that allow you to finely tune how you want the actor to behave, as shown in Figure 2-35. Starting from the left, you can see that we are going to be moving east relative to the scene. Because we want to make our car drive faster, simply increase the acceleration value from "200" to "500". The "Continue Moving" section simply states that the car will continue moving while you are pressing the right arrow key, which has been mapped to the RunRight behavior. You can also experiment with the motion to see it in action by clicking the Preview button, which will run the game using your newly defined values.

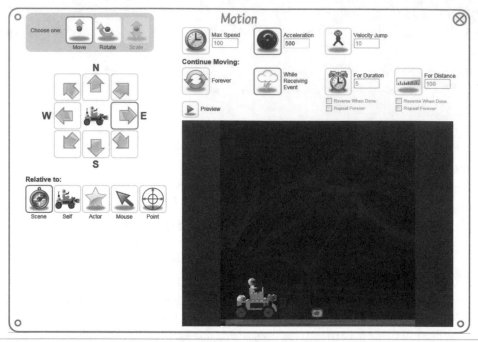

Figure 2-35. *Increasing the acceleration when the Main actor moves to the right*

Building the Catapult Behavior

The final behavior we'll add for the Main actor is a motion behavior that will launch the Main actor into the air when it jumps on top of the Catapult actor. As you can probably imagine, we want the Catapult behavior to launch the Main actor in the air when the Main actor collides with the top of the Catapult. To do this, create a blank motion behavior by clicking on the motion button in the left-hand list of behaviors, as shown in Figure 2-36.

Figure 2-36. *A newly defined motion behavior*

Next, click the event button for "Motion1" to set what event will trigger this event to fire. We want to have this motion behavior activate when our Main actor is on top of the Catapult actor. To do this, set the event as a collision event, as shown in Figure 2-37.

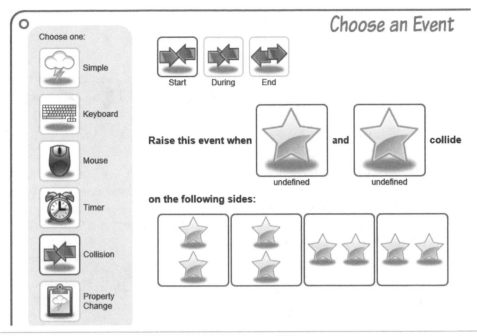

Figure 2-37. *Creating a collision event*

In Figure 2-37, we want to click the two stars in between the "Raise this event when *actor* and *actor* collide". Click on either of the actor icons (order doesn't matter) and select the radio button labeled "Myself (the current instance of Main)" to set the Main actor as the first actor in the collision event, as shown in Figure 2-38.

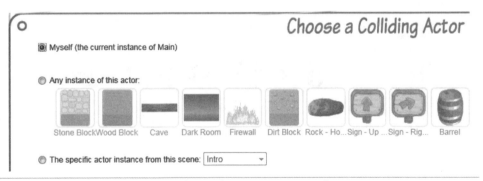

Figure 2-38. *Selecting the current actor in a collision event*

For the other actor, select the radio button labeled "Any instance of this actor" and click on the Catapult actor, as shown in Figure 2-39. This will enable the collision event between the Main actor and any Catapult actors added to our scene.

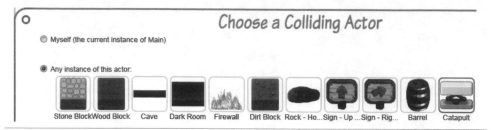

Figure 2-39. *Selecting any instance of the Catapult actor*

The last thing we need to do is set the collision event to fire only when the Main actor is on top of the catapult. You can do this by clicking and unclicking sides to set where you want the event to fire from. We only want the event to fire when the Main actor is on top of the Catapult, and so we will unclick the "bottom", "right", and "left" sides. The finished collision event should look like Figure 2-40.

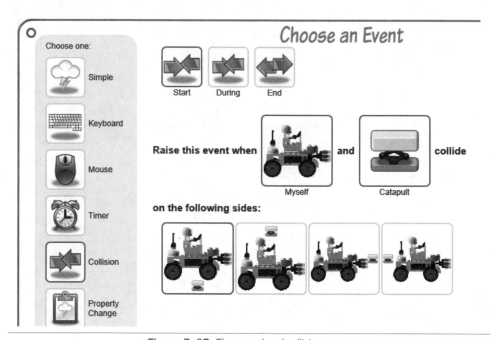

Figure 2-40. *The completed collision event*

Now that we've defined the collision event for when our event will fire, we now need to add what our event will do. To do this, click on the motion button in the "Motion1" behavior (see Figure 2-36). We want to define the motion such that the Main actor will launch upward in the air when he's on top of the Catapult actor. The nice thing is that Popfly includes a built-in motion called "Velocity Jump" that adds a spring-like effect. Let's set the properties of our motion as follows:

- Set the direction of the motion to be upward.
- Click the "Velocity Jump" button and set its value to 40.
- Click the "For Duration" button and set the duration of the jump to 0.5 seconds.

When complete, the motion behavior should look like Figure 2-41.

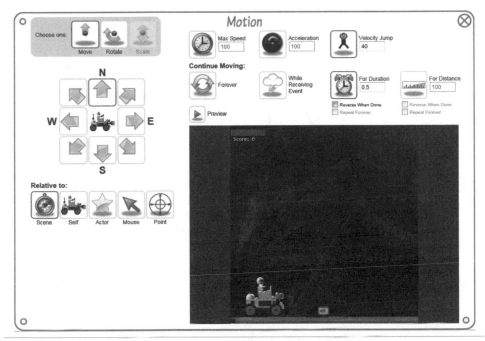

Figure 2-41. *The completed Catapult motion behavior*

Building the LEGO Security Actor Behaviors

For our LEGO Security actor, we want his behavior to be a bit unpredictable so that the actor shoots and jumps at random intervals.

Adding Gravity and Jump Behaviors Using Shortcuts

The first thing we'll do is reuse the built-in "run and jump by pressing keys (side view)" shortcut we showed earlier in "Adding Main Actor Behaviors Using Shortcuts," to create the gravity and jumping behaviors automatically. We're doing this to save time and avoid the errors that might be introduced when manually building these behaviors. Since the Security actor will have random motion and not keyboard-based motion, delete the RunLeft and RunRight behaviors. With those deleted, the LEGO Security actor should only have the behaviors listed in Figure 2-42.

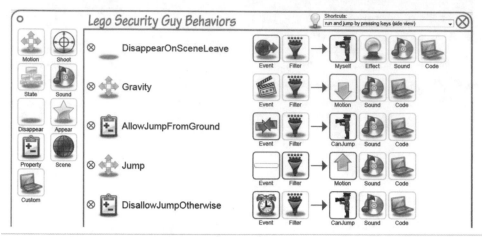

Figure 2-42. *Using shortcuts to speed up the addition of common behaviors*

Setting a Random Jump Behavior

The one change we'll want to make for these prebuilt behaviors is the Jump behavior's event, which is currently mapped to the spacebar. Click on the Jump behavior's event to change it from a keyboard event to a random time interval between 2 and 8 seconds, as shown in Figure 2-43. As you can imagine, this will make our Security actor randomly jump in the air every 2 to 8 seconds.

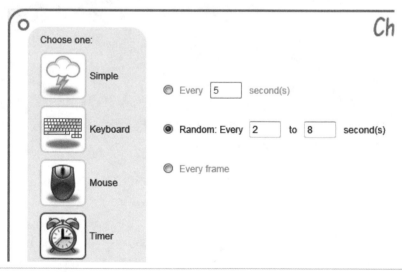

Figure 2-43. *Setting an event's behavior to fire at a random time interval*

Adding a Random Motion Behavior

Next, let's create a new motion behavior so that in addition to jumping randomly, the Security actor will also move left and right at a random time interval. To do this, create a new motion behavior and set the event for the motion behavior to be the same random time interval from Figure 2-43.

Next, set the motion for this behavior to be left (west), but then reverse when done so that it will go east after a couple of seconds, as shown in Figure 2-44.

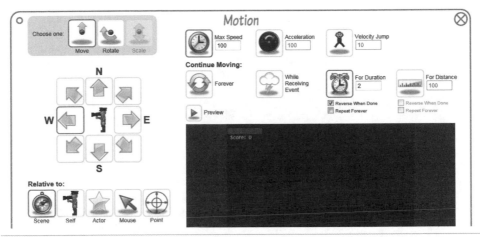

Figure 2-44. *Set the motion behavior to move left for 2 seconds, then reverse when done*

Adding a Shooting Behavior

The next thing we want to do is add a new behavior to shoot a projectile at our Main actor. To do this, add a new shoot behavior to the list of behaviors for the Security actor, as shown in Figure 2-45.

Figure 2-45. *A newly added shoot behavior*

Like we did previously with the motion and jumping behaviors, we will also add a random time interval event for when the shoot behavior should be triggered. To do this, click the "Shoot1" event, select the timer option, and set the timer to be "Random every 2 to 8 seconds" (see Figure 2-43).

Next, we will select the Projectile actor (aka the bullet) to use for our shooting behavior. Click the Projectile button to see a list of Popfly projectile actors and select the "Fire Bullet" actor, as shown in Figure 2-46.

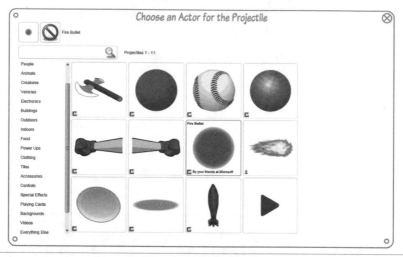

Figure 2-46. Selecting the Fire Bullet projectile

We'll also need to set the motion behavior for this projectile. To do this, click the motion button for the "Shoot1" behavior (see Figure 2-44). We'll set the motion for the projectile to move to the left and increase the "Max Speed" of the projectile to 250, as shown in Figure 2-47.

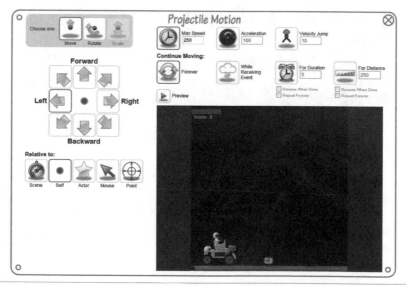

Figure 2-47. Setting the motion for the Projectile actor

Adding a Disappear Behavior

Next, we need to add a behavior for when the Security actor should "die," or disappear. To do that, add a new disappear behavior for the Security actor, as shown in Figure 2-48.

Figure 2-48. *A newly added disappear behavior*

Click the Event button for the "Disappear1" behavior to add a collision event that defines when the Security actor should disappear. Select the collision event, and select "Myself (the current instance of this actor)" and the Main actor for the collision event, as shown in Figure 2-49.

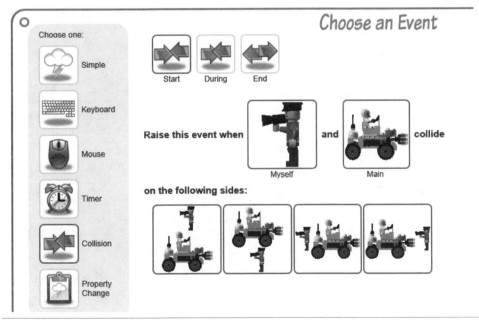

Figure 2-49. *The disappear collision event*

With the disappear collision event defined, the Security actor will now disappear whenever it runs into the Main actor.

Building the Fire Bullet Projectile Behaviors

Since our game uses a health bar, one thing we need to do is add and modify behaviors for the Fire Bullet projectile that was set up in the "Adding a Shooting Behavior" section.

Updating the DisappearOnCollision Behavior

The first change we're going to make is to the existing "DisappearOnCollision" behavior. To do this, select the Fire Bullet from the list of actors and click the Behaviors button to see the list of behaviors for the Fire Bullet, as shown in Figure 2-50.

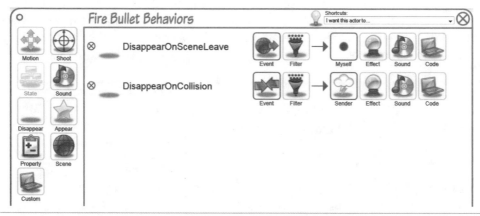

Figure 2-50. *Default behaviors for the Fire Bullet actor*

By default, the "DisappearOnCollision" event is set to make both of the colliding actors disappear on a collision event. This is bad because it would make the Main actor disappear from the scene, which is not what we want. Instead, we want the Fire Bullet to disappear on a collision and we want to subtract the Health property for the Main actor.

To update the "DisappearOnCollision" behavior, click the Sender button (see Figure 2-50) and select the "Myself (the current instance of Fire Bullet)" radio button, as shown in Figure 2-51.

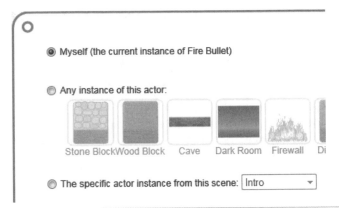

Figure 2-51. *Updating the disappear behavior so that the current instance of the Fire Bullet actor disappears*

Creating a Custom Code Behavior to Lower the Health Property

The next thing we want to add is a custom behavior that will decrease the Health property. To do this, create a new custom behavior, and then click the Event button to set when this behavior should be triggered. In the event designer, select the collision event and set it so that the event will fire when "Myself" (the current instance of the Fire Bullet) and the Main actor collide on any side, as shown in Figure 2-52.

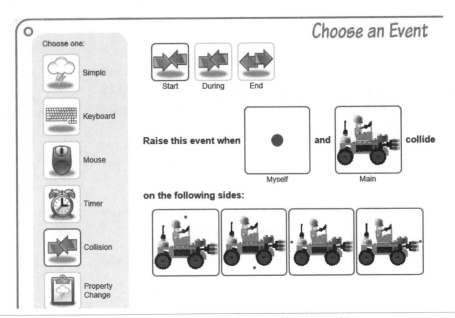

Figure 2-52. *Setting the event for when to update the Health property*

Next, click the code button to bring up the custom code window and add the code in Example 2-4.

Example 2-4. *The Fire Bullet reducing the Health property by 20*

```
Game.SetValue("Health", Game.GetValue("Health") - 20);
```

When complete, the custom code window should look like Figure 2-53. Notice that the custom code window also includes a preview window that enables you to test and run your custom code behavior without having to reload the game in its entirety.

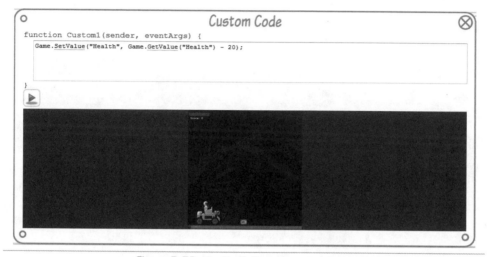

Figure 2-53. *The Fire Bullet custom code event*

Building the LEGO Skeleton Behavior

As the LEGO Skeleton actors should behave like mindless zombies, we're going to have the Skeleton actor mindlessly follow the Main actor when the Skeleton enters the Main viewport.

Adding Gravity and Jump Behaviors Using Shortcuts

Just like we did with the Security actor, let's reuse the built-in "run and jump by pressing keys (side view)" shortcut to create the gravity and jumping behaviors automatically. Remember to delete the RunLeft and RunRight behaviors like we did before.

Updating the Jump Behavior

Like we did previously, we will update the Jump behavior event to fire during a random time interval between 2 and 8 seconds (see Figure 2-43).

Creating a Behavior to Follow the Main Actor

Next we'll create a new motion behavior that will make the Skeleton actors mindlessly follow the Main actor. To do this, create a new motion behavior for the Skeleton actor. Set the event for the motion behavior to be when the Main actor enters the viewport with the Skeleton actor, as shown in Figure 2-54.

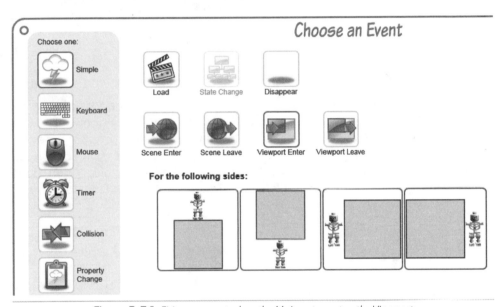

Figure 2-54. *Firing an event when the Main actor enters the Viewport*

Now that the Skeleton's motion will begin when the Main actor enters the scene, next let's configure what the particular motion will be when the event is fired. To do this, click the "Motion1" behavior's Motion button and set the "Relative to" value to the Main actor. When you do this, you'll notice that the directional arrows have changed from "N" and "S" to "Toward" and "Away", as shown in Figure 2-45. Set the motion to be "Toward" the Main actor to complete the motion behavior. With this behavior, when a Skeleton enters the Main actor's viewport (see Figure 2-55), the Skeleton actor will move toward the Main actor forever.

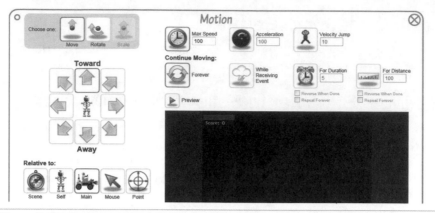

Figure 2-55. *Setting a motion behavior for the Skeleton actor to move toward the Main actor*

Setting the Skeleton Disappear Behavior

The next behavior to add for the Skeleton actor is a disappear behavior, to make the Skeleton disappear when it collides with either the right or the bottom side of our Main actor. To do that, create a new disappear behavior and set its event to be a collision event between the current Skeleton actor (Myself) and the Main actor. Next, unclick the buttons so that the event will fire only when the Main actor lands on top of the Skeleton or runs into the Skeleton on the right side, as shown in Figure 2-56.

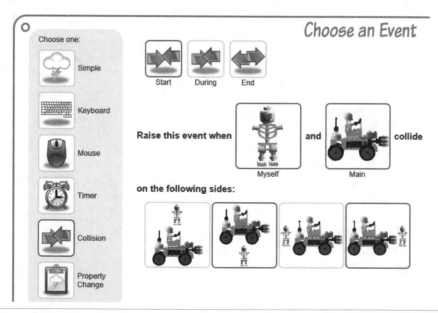

Figure 2-56. *Setting the disappear event to fire when the Main actor is on top or to the right of the Skeleton actor*

In the "Disappear1" behavior, we also want to add a special effect when these two actors collide. To do that, click on the Effect button in the "Disappear1" behavior, as shown in Figure 2-57.

Figure 2-57. *The Disappear1 behavior*

From here, you can choose from a range of special effects or search for one directly in the search box. In the search box, type "Flak" to find the Flak special effect, and click on it to select it, as shown in Figure 2-58. Now, when the Skeleton disappears, you'll see a Flak smoke effect.

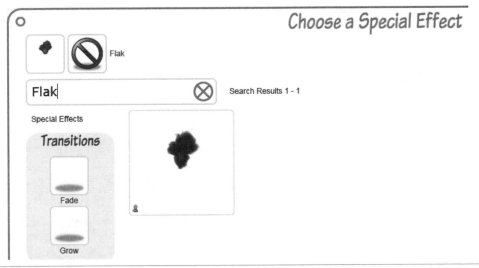

Figure 2-58. *Selecting the Flak special effect*

Creating a Custom Code Behavior to Lower the Health Value

Similar to what we did with the Security actor, we will add a new custom code behavior for the LEGO Skeleton to subtract from the health property. But this time, instead of linking to a projectile, we will make it so that the health will decrease when a Skeleton lands on top of or touches the back of the Main actor.

To do this, create a new custom behavior and set the event for the behavior to be a collision event between Skeleton actor and the Main actor, as shown in Figure 2-59. The key here is to unclick the top and right sides so that this event fires only if the Skeleton actor collides by jumping on top of the Main actor or runs into the rear of the Main actor. You should also make sure to select the "During" event option such that the Main actor will continue losing health while he's in contact with a Skeleton actor that is to the left or on top of him.

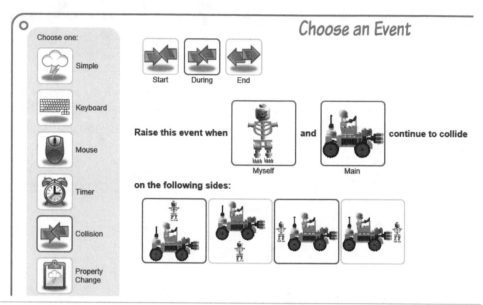

Figure 2-59. *The collision event that defines when the Main actor's health should lower*

Because we set the collision event to fire during any contact (see Figure 2-59), this means that for every frame the Skeleton and the Main actor are in contact, its health will reduce. Because the collision is so frequent (every frame), we will set the code for this behavior to lower the health only by 1 for every frame, as shown in Example 2-5.

Example 2-5. *Lowering the Health bar by 1 every frame*

```
Game.SetValue("Health", Game.GetValue("Health") - 1);
```

As the game is likely to contain around 30 frames per second, that would mean that the Main actor's health bar would reduce by 30 every second.

Adding Behaviors for the Barrel Actor

The Barrel actor should act like a powder keg and explode when it collides with the Skeleton actor. To do this, first we need to add the shortcut to add a gravity motion behavior, just like we did with the Skeleton and Security actors. Next, we want to add a disappear behavior based on a collision event to make any Skeleton actors that fall on the barrel disappear.

Adding the Gravity Shortcut for the Barrel Actor

As we did previously, select the shortcut "run and jump by pressing keys (side view)" and delete all of the newly added behaviors except for Gravity and DisappearOn-SceneLeave, as shown in Figure 2-60. This will make the barrel fall automatically using gravity from the platform upon which they've been placed (as previously shown in Figure 2-22).

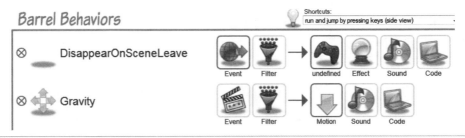

Figure 2-60. *Deleting all but the Gravity and default disappear behaviors for the Barrel actor*

Adding the Disappear Behavior

Like we've done before, add a new disappear behavior and set the behavior's collision event to be between "Myself (the current instance of Barrel)" and the Skeleton actor. Keep the default of all sides for the collision checked so that the default event is as shown in Figure 2-61.

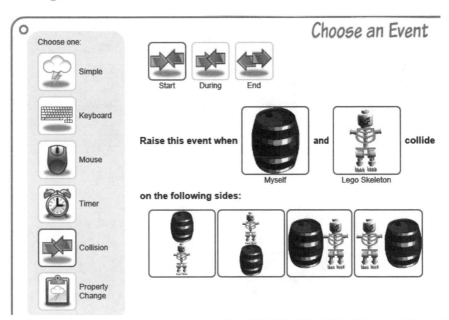

Figure 2-61. *Setting the disappear behavior event for the Barrel*

Next, we need to define which actors should disappear for this event. To do this, click the Myself button for the "Disappear1" behavior, as shown in Figure 2-62.

Figure 2-62. *The Disappear1 event*

From here, we want to select "The event sender" radio button, which will cause both the Barrel actor and the Skeleton actor that collides with it to disappear (see Figure 2-63).

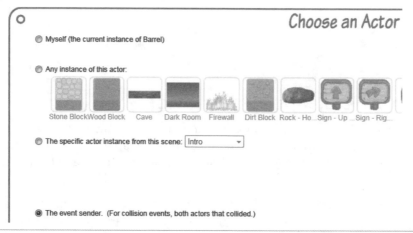

Figure 2-63. *Use the "event sender" option to make both of the colliding actors disappear*

The final touch for the disappear behavior is to add an explosion when the collision occurs. To do that, click the "Disappear1" Effect button and select the "Explosion 2" effect, as shown in Figure 2-64.

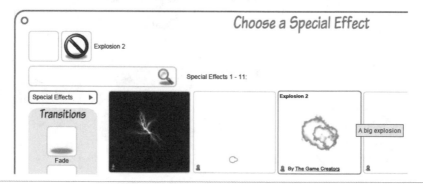

Figure 2-64. *The Barrel explosion effect*

Building the HealthBar Behaviors

As you've noticed, in both the Security Actor and in the Skeleton actor, we've been subtracting the value of the HealthBar property. Now we need to visually show the value of the health decreasing when the Health property changes.

Building a Custom Code Behavior for Updating the HealthBar's HealthValue

Click on the HealthBar actor, switch to its list of behaviors, and click the custom code event to add a new custom code behavior for the HealthBar actor. For the custom code event, select the Property Change event and set it so that whenever the Health property changes, the custom code event will fire (see Figure 2-65).

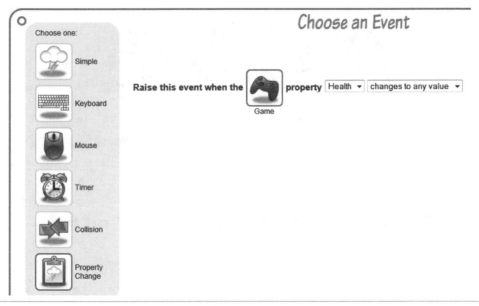

Figure 2-65. *Setting the event to fire whenever the Health property changes*

Next, we'll add the code in Example 2-6 for the custom code event. This code gets a reference to the top-level root of the Silverlight document, finds an XAML object named HealthValue, and then sets the Width of the HealthValue rectangle to the value of the game's Health property.

Example 2-6. *Updating the width of the HealthValue Silverlight rectangle*

```
this.GetVisualRoot().FindName("HealthValue").Width =
    Game.GetValue("Health").toString();
```

This is what happens in the game:

- When the game starts, the Health property is set to 100 (see Figure 2-29).

- When the Main actor collides with the Fire Bullet actor, we reduce the value of the Health property by 20.

- Once this happens, the Health "Property Change" event in Figure 2-65 will fire and the code in Example 2-6 will set the width of the HealthValue rectangle to 80 (100–20).

Figure 2-66 shows the value of the HealthValue rectangle decreasing in width as the Health property decreases.

Figure 2-66. *Visualizing changes to the HealthValue rectangle width when the HealthPropertyChanged event fires*

Creating a Scene Change Behavior to End the Game

The last behavior we want to add for the HealthBar is one that will change to the "Lose" scene if your health is at or below zero. To do that, click the Scene button to add a scene change behavior, as shown in Figure 2-67.

Figure 2-67. *Creating a new scene change behavior*

Next, click the Event button to create the event that will trigger the scene change behavior. We'll define the event to trigger if the Health is less than or equal to 0, as shown in Figure 2-68.

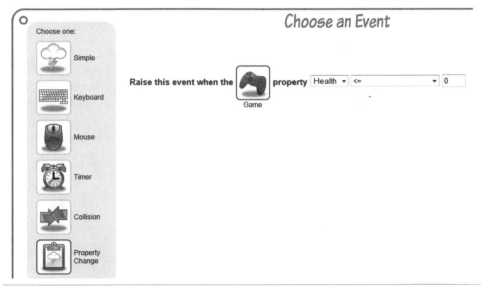

Figure 2-68. *Setting the event to fire when the Health property is at or below zero*

Next, click the Scene button (see Figure 2-67), which will pop up a window from which you can choose the scene to transition to. Since the Health is zero, we have officially lost the game, so we change the scene to the "Lost" scene, as shown in Figure 2-69.

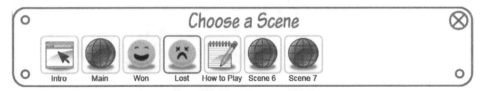

Figure 2-69. *Select the Lost scene for the scene change behavior*

Adding the Blind Scientist Behaviors

Before we define the behaviors for the Blind Scientist, we should spend a little bit of time explaining the XAML that defines the Blind Scientist actor. Inside the Blind Scientist's XAML definition is a Silverlight Storyboard (a time-based animation) that will grow the Blind Scientist in size by 400%. We want to create a behavior that will run the Storyboard animation when our Main actor first collides with the Blind Scientist. Because we don't want the Blind Scientist to grow 400% for every collision with the Main actor, we'll also use a custom property, isHit, as a Boolean field to see whether the growth animation has already executed.

Adding a Custom Code Behavior to Call the Grow Animation Storyboard

To begin, create a new custom code behavior for the Blind Scientist actor and rename the behavior to "RunGrowStoryBoard". Set the event that will run this behavior to be a collision event between the Blind Scientist and the Main actor, as shown in Figure 2-70.

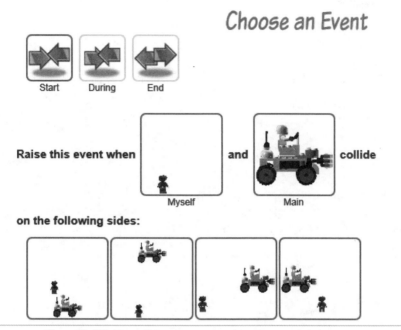

Figure 2-70. *The collision event to run the custom code behavior*

Next, click the Filter button for the "RunGrowStoryBoard" behavior, as shown in Figure 2-71.

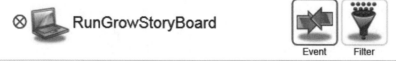

Figure 2-71. *Adding a filter to an event's behavior*

As we explained earlier, a behavior filter lets you filter events so that the behavior will only execute based on some condition. For "RunGrowStoryBoard", we want the animation storyboard to run on the first collision and not subsequent ones, so we will set the filter to run the custom code only when the isHit property is set to "0", as shown in Figure 2-72.

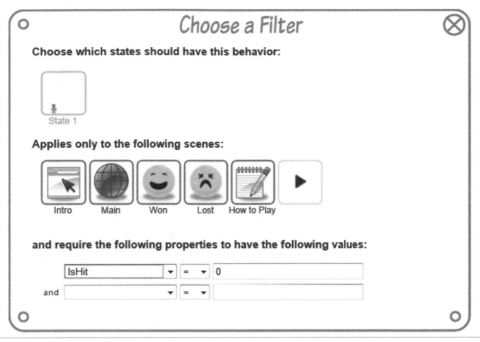

Figure 2-72. *Setting the Filter to run code only when the IsHit property = 0*

Next, we need to write some JavaScript code to call the storyboard and update the IsHit property once we run the animation. To do this, let's first take a look at a snippet of the XAML definition for the Blind Scientist, as shown in Example 2-7.

Example 2-7. *Snippet of XAML for the Blind Scientist actor*

```
<Canvas … Width="500" Height="784" x:Name="canvas">
  <Canvas.Resources>
    <Storyboard x:Name="Grow">
      <!-- Begin Animation XAML -->
…
    </Storyboard>
  </Canvas.Resources>
  <Image Width="125" Height="195" Source="$base$/blindscientist.png" Stretch="Fill"
    Canvas.Top="589" x:Name="image" … >
…
</Canvas>
```

As you can see, the XAML includes a definition for a Storyboard named Grow, which is what we'll need to call programmatically. To do this, we'll add the code in Example 2-8.

```
this.GetVisualRoot().FindName("Grow").begin();
this.SetValue("IsHit", 1);
```

This code finds the Grow Storyboard (see Example 2-7) and calls the Storyboard element's begin() method, which will begin the storyboard animation. Next, it sets the IsHit property of the Blind Scientist actor to "1" to indicate that we have now run the grow animation.

Adding Random Left and Right Motion Behaviors

Given that the Blind Scientist is blind, his motion behaviors should feel a bit random. What we'll do is define two motion behaviors, one to move left and another to move right. Like we did previously, we will set the event for the motion to a random time interval between 2 and 8 seconds (see Figure 2-43, shown previously).

Next, we will have the random motion behaviors start only after the Blind Scientist has grown to 400% his size by using an event filter. Since we know the growth behavior will update the IsHit property to "1", we will run the left and right motion behaviors only if the IsHit property equals "1", as shown in Figure 2-73.

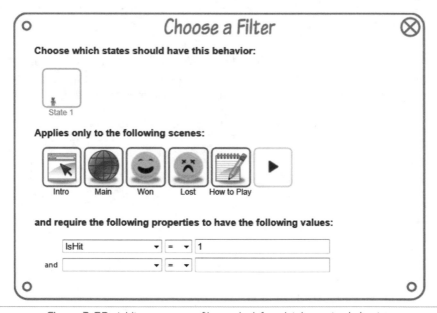

Figure 2-73. *Adding a property filter to the left and right motion behaviors*

For the left motion behavior, we'll set the direction to be left (W), update the Max Speed to "400", and set the motion duration to "1.5" seconds, as shown in Figure 2-74. The right motion behavior will be the same, except that the direction will be to the right (E) instead of to the left.

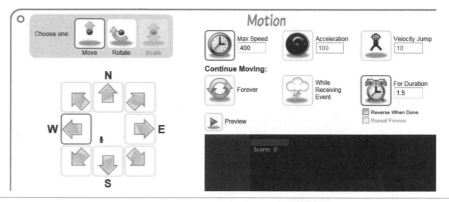

Figure 2-74. *Setting the motion behavior for the Blind Scientist*

Adding a Behavior to Lower the Health Value

Like we did with the Skeleton actor, we will also define a custom code behavior to lower the health of the Main actor's health bar whenever they collide. To do that, add a new custom code behavior and set the event for the behavior to be a collision between the Blind Scientist and the Main actor. In the collision event, set the event to be "during" so that the health will continue to lower for as long as the two are touching. Next, since we will be killing the Blind Scientist by jumping on top of him, make sure to unclick the button where the Main actor is on top of the Blind Scientist. The finished collision event should look like Figure 2-75.

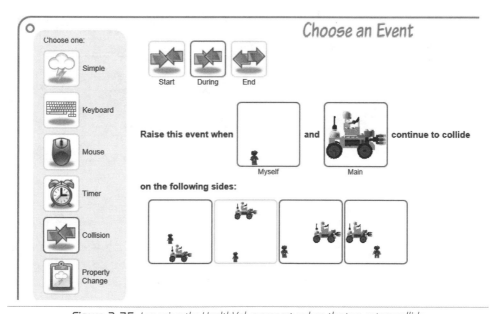

Figure 2-75. *Lowering the HealthValue property when the two actors collide*

Like we did previously, we'll add the code for an event that reduces the health by 1 for every frame in which the Blind Scientist and Main actors are in contact, as shown in Example 2-9.

Example 2-9. *Lowering the Health value by 1*

```
Game.SetValue("Health", Game.GetValue("Health") - 1);
```

Adding the Scene Change Behavior to Win the Game

To win the game, the Main actor will need to jump on top of the Blind Scientist's head. At that point, the user has won the game, and so we should switch the game scene to the Win scene. To do this, we'll create a new scene change behavior for the Blind Scientist actor. Set the event for the scene change behavior to be a collision between the Blind Scientist and the Main actor, as shown in Figure 2-76. Make sure that the only side that will trigger this event is when the Main actor lands on top of the Blind Scientist.

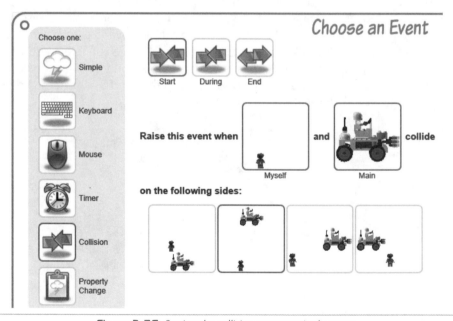

Figure 2-76. *Setting the collision event to win the game*

Next, we will add a filter for this event so that you can win the game only after the IsHit event fires. To do that, click the filter for the event and set it so that the event will fire only when the IsHit property equals "1" (see Figure 2-73).

Next, click the scene button and select the "Won" scene (Figure 2-77), which will officially end the game! The Won and Lost scene are important because Popfly will automatically record users' win/loss records to rank who the best players are.

Figure 2-77. *Switching to the Won scene when the Main actor jumps on top of the Blind Scientist*

Publishing Your Game

Once you have your game built exactly how you like it and are ready to share it with the rest of the world, click the Share button in the top-right corner. This will share your project with the Popfly community and make it so that you can embed your game in a blog, share it on Facebook, or even make it available as a Windows Vista Sidebar Gadget. After your project is shared, a pop-up window (Figure 2-78) will appear that includes a link to your game, the embed code for your game, a link to download the game as a Sidebar Gadget, a link to build the game as a Facebook application, and links to advertise your game on Digg, Reddit, or in email.

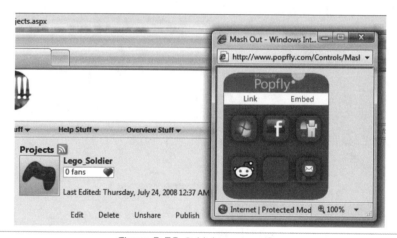

Figure 2-78. *Publishing your game*

Publishing to Facebook

To publish your game on Facebook, click the Facebook icon (the "f") from Figure 2-78. This will then display a set of options for publishing your game, as shown in Figure 2-79.

Figure 2-79. *Publish to Facebook options*

Clicking on the bottom link, "Create Your Own Facebook Application", takes you to a page with step-by-step instructions for how to publish your game, as shown in Figure 2-80.

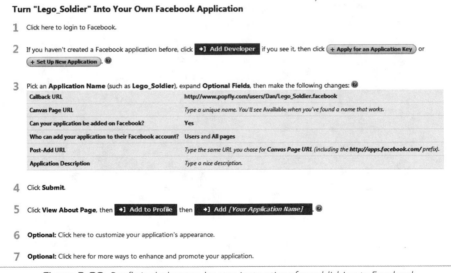

Turn "Lego_Soldier" Into Your Own Facebook Application

1 Click here to login to Facebook.

2 If you haven't created a Facebook application before, click **→] Add Developer** if you see it, then click (**+ Apply for an Application Key**) or (**+ Set Up New Application**).

3 Pick an **Application Name** (such as **Lego_Soldier**), expand **Optional Fields**, then make the following changes:

Callback URL	http://www.popfly.com/users/Dan/Lego_Soldier.facebook
Canvas Page URL	*Type a unique name. You'll see Available when you've found a name that works.*
Can your application be added on Facebook?	Yes
Who can add your application to their Facebook account?	Users and **All pages**
Post-Add URL	*Type the same URL you chose for **Canvas Page URL** (including the **http://apps.facebook.com/** prefix).*
Application Description	*Type a nice description.*

4 Click **Submit**.

5 Click **View About Page**, then **→] Add to Profile** then **→] Add [Your Application Name]** .

6 **Optional:** Click here to customize your application's appearance.

7 **Optional:** Click here for more ways to enhance and promote your application.

Figure 2-80. *Popfly includes step-by-step instructions for publishing to Facebook*

For LegoSoldier, set the application name to "LegoSoldier" and build a unique Facebook URL for your game. The sample in Figure 2-81 sets the Facebook URL to *http://apps.facebook.com/LegoSoldier/*.

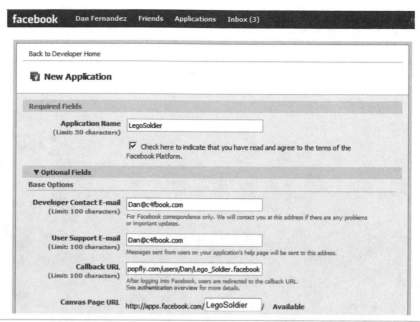

Figure 2-81. *Setting up your game as a new Facebook application*

 If you want to test your application before it's ready to be made public, in the New Application form in Figure 2-81, select the option to only allow developers to see your application. This will publish your application, but make it inaccessible for nondevelopers.

Once you set the properties in step 3 from Figure 2-80 in the new application form (see Figure 2-81), click Submit to submit your new application. You can then navigate directly to your Facebook application page using the Canvas Page URL you set in Figure 2-81. If you've never installed the application before, it will ask whether you want to allow access, as shown in Figure 2-82.

Figure 2-82. *Running the Facebook LegoSoldier application*

Once you allow access to the application, you can then play it directly in Facebook, as shown in Figure 2-83!

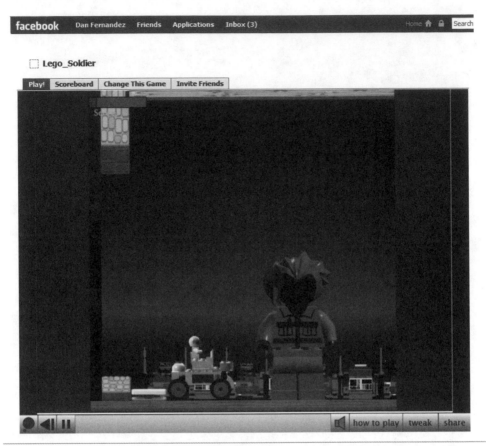

Figure 2-83. *LegoSoldier running inside Facebook*

Final Thoughts

Although LegoSoldier is a relatively short game, it shows off a number of key concepts needed for building more robust games, such as how to build custom actors, how to design scenes, how to build simple enemy AI using random motion behaviors, how to add custom code behaviors for a health bar or for triggering a Silverlight Storyboard, and even how to publish your game on Facebook. Best of all, Popfly's Rip feature makes it easy to copy actors, scenes, sounds, or entire games from anyone else on Popfly, so you can take LegoSoldier and completely customize it to your heart's content.

An In-Game RSS Reader for World of Warcraft

AUTHORS	Gabor Ratky and Dan Fernandez
DIFFICULTY	Intermediate
TIME REQUIRED	2 hours
COST	$19.99 for *World of Warcraft*; $14.99 for monthly fee
SOFTWARE	*World of Warcraft*, AddOn Studio for *World of Warcraft* version 2.0, Visual C# 2008 Express, and Visual Basic 2008 Express or higher, Internet Explorer 7 or higher
HARDWARE	None
DOWNLOAD	*http://www.c4fbook.com/wowfeedreader*

World of Warcraft by Blizzard Entertainment is undoubtedly the most popular massively multiplayer online role-playing game (MMORPG) in the world. Played by an estimated 10 million subscribers, it even holds a Guinness World Record for this feat. While the game that takes place within the fantasy world of Azeroth can easily lock you in front of your computer for hours, what makes *World of Warcraft* really interesting is that its user interface is customizable, allowing all sorts of user modifications, called addons, that can simplify or improve how a player can interact with the world and with other characters, and that can even introduce completely new functionality.

Feed Reader is a *World of Warcraft* addon that adds an in-game RSS Feed Reader so you can read the latest news, forum posts, blogs, sport scores, and more, all while in the comfort of Azeroth!

Overview

Before we delve into how Feed Reader works, let's take a quick tour of its features.

Running Feed Grabber

Since addons cannot access data outside of the game, we'll also build a .NET application named Feed Grabber (Figure 3-1) that sits in your system tray and serializes RSS feeds into Lua, the scripting language that *Warcraft* addons are written in.

Figure 3-1. *Feed Grabber running in the task tray*

Feed Reader

Now that Feed Grabber has converted the RSS feeds into Lua, we can start *World of Warcraft* and see that the Feed Reader addon (Figure 3-2) will display the RSS feeds in-game, so we can read BBC headlines directly in the game!

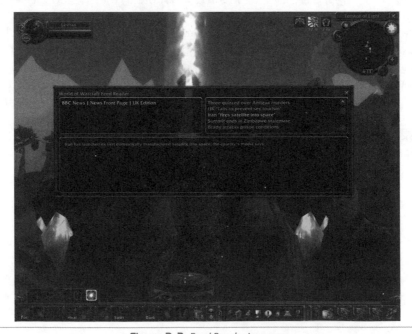

Figure 3-2. *Feed Reader in-game*

Feed Reader Slash Commands

Feed Reader also includes built-in text commands that enable you to show or hide the addon directly from *Warcraft*'s chat window, as in Figure 3-3.

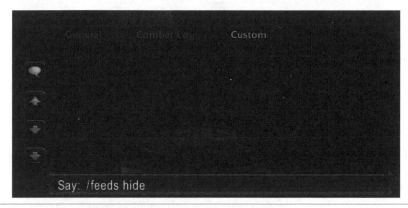

Figure 3-3. *Sending a text command to hide Feed Reader*

Before We Get Started

This chapter assumes that you're a .NET (Visual Basic or C#) developer who plays *World of Warcraft*, and maybe you've used *Warcraft* addons, but you've never written your own. There are many similar concepts that apply to both building *Warcraft* addons and building .NET applications, as you can see in Table 3-1.

Table 3-1. *High-level comparison of* Warcraft *and .NET programming models*

CATEGORY	WARCRAFT ADDONS	.NET
Application files and resources	Table of Contents (*.toc*)	Assembly manifest file
Application metadata (name, author, version)	Table of Contents	AssemblyInfo
UI	FrameXML markup and widgets	XAML markup and controls
Code	Lua	VB/C#
Programming model	Event-based	Event-based
Libraries	WoW Function APIs, third-party libraries	.NET Framework, third-party libraries
Storage	SavedVariables	Isolated storage/ filesystem
Referencing current object	Self	Me (VB); this (C#)
Tools	AddOn Studio for *World of Warcraft*	Visual Studio Express Editions

A Quick Tour of the Lua Programming Language

There are many nuances to the Lua programming language, but the following is a quick glance at its features. For a full reference on the Lua programming language, you can download the language reference from *http://www.lua.org/manual/*.

> **NOTE** *World of Warcraft* uses a slightly modified version of the Lua 5.1 runtime that adds some helper functions and removes operating system and file I/O functions.

Lua types

Lua defines five basic types: a Boolean (true/false), a number, a string, a table (a key/value data type on steroids), and nil (null). Similar to other scripting languages, such as JavaScript, Lua variables are not strongly typed, meaning you do not assign the type when you create a variable. You can also reassign a variable to a different data type without errors.

Variable scopes

Lua has two variable scopes, global and local. Global variables are accessible to anyone, including other addons, whereas local variables are accessible only within the given scope.

For *Warcraft* addon development, global variables should be used sparingly and should be uniquely named to avoid a naming collision with global variables defined in other addons.

Lua functions

Functions are the "meat" of Lua, and the entire *World of Warcraft* API is designed using functions. Functions are mostly equivalent to .NET methods, but there are some important differences you should be aware of:

- Lua functions can be called without the requisite arguments; missing arguments are treated as nil.

- Lua functions can be called with too many arguments; extra arguments are ignored.

- Lua functions can take a variable number of arguments, similar to the `ParamArray` keyword in Visual Basic or the `params` keyword in C#.

- Lua functions can return more than one value.

Table 3-2 contains a basic Lua language reference.

Table 3-2. *Lua language reference*

COMMAND	LUA CODE
Declaring comments	`-- this is a comment`
Declaring a global variable	`message = "hello"`

Declaring a private variable	`-- changing data type is okay`
	`local message = "hello"`
	`message = 5`

Checking for equality	`==`
Checking for inequality	`~=`

If/else	`if (message == "hello") then`
	`    print("hi!")`
	`elseif(message == "goodbye") then`
	`    print("bye!")`
	`else`
	`    print("you still here?")`
	`end`

Concatenating a string	`local message = "hello"`
	`local space = " "`
	`local location = "world"`
	`print(message .. space .. world)`
	`-- prints: hello world`

Declaring a function	`function add(a,b)`
	`    return a+b`
	`end`

Calling a function	`print(add(1,2))  --prints 3`

Declaring a function with multiple results	`function returnThreeVals()`
	`    return "one ", "two ", "three"`
	`end`

Calling a function with multiple results	`val1, val2, val3 = returnThreeVals()`

Table 3-2. *Lua language reference (continued)*

COMMAND	LUA CODE

While loop	```
	i=1
	while i <= 3 do
	    print(i)
	     i = i+1
	end
	--output
	1
	2
	3
	``

For loop	```
	For i=1,3 do
	    print(i)
	end
	--output
	1
	2
	3
	``

Understanding Lua tables

Lua tables are the Swiss-army knife of Lua data structures. Tables can be used to provide behavior similar to enumerations, classes, arrays, collections, and more. Table 3-3 defines a number of common operations you would use for a Lua table.

Table 3-3. *Lua tables quick reference*

COMMAND	LUA CODE
Create an empty table	`feeds  = {}`

Create a table and initialize some data	```
	feeds = {
	    {["Title"] = "Coding4Fun"},
	    {["Title"] = "Channel 9"},
	    {["Title"] = "C4FBook"},
	}
	``

Count the length of items in the table	``` print(#feeds) --prints 3 ```
Print the first item	`print(feeds[1].Title) --prints "Coding4Fun"`

Table 3-3. *Lua tables quick reference (continued)*

COMMAND	LUA CODE
| For loop over a table | ```
-- loop from 1 to length of table
for i=1,#feeds
  print(feeds[i].Title)
end
--prints
Coding4Fun
Channel 9
C4FBook
``` |
| For Each loop over a table using an **ipairs** function | ```
--Note: ipairs() function has multiple
--return values, the index and the value

for index,value in ipairs(feeds) do
    print(index .. ", value=" .. value.Title);
end
-- prints
1, value=Coding4Fun
2, value=Channel 9
3, value=C4FBook
``` |

> **NOTE** Unlike .NET arrays or collection variables, which are zero-based, Lua tables are 1-based, meaning that the index of the first element in a Lua table is 1, not 0.

Feed Reader's Lua table

Using the Feed Grabber tool (see "Feed Grabber," later in this chapter), RSS feeds from the Windows Common Feed List are serialized into a Lua table variable named FEED_READER_FEEDS. The exact format of this data structure is shown in Example 3-1.

Example 3-1. *RSS feeds serialized as a Lua table*

```
FEED_READER_FEEDS = {
  { -- start of first feed
    ["Title"] = "BBC News | News Front Page | UK Edition",
    ["Items"] = {
      {
        ["Title"] = "Politician caught in scandal",
        ["Content"] = "Shock, outrage and dismay",
      }, -- [1]
```

```
      {
        ["Title"] = "Coding4Fun book wins Pulitzer prize",
        ["Content"] = "Authors, media not surprised by latest award.",
      }, -- [2]
    }, -- end of items
  },  -- end of first feed

  { -- start of second feed
    ["Title"] = "NYT > NYTimes.com Home",
    ["Items"] = {
      {
        ["Title"] = "Economy worsening, analysts say",
        ["Content"] = "New data shows economy worsening.",
      }, -- [1]
    }, -- end of items
  },  -- end of second feed
}
```

The Common Feed List is an operating-system-level feature that stores the list of RSS feeds a user has subscribed to. Having a common feed list means that users can share RSS feeds between multiple applications, such as Outlook and Internet Explorer, without needing to manually subscribe to new feeds for every application.

One of the key things to note here is that FEED_READER_FEEDS includes nested tables, meaning there are tables inside of tables. Let's show some ways we can programmatically access this data:

Get the number of feeds
```
    print("Feed count: " .. #FEED_READER_FEEDS)

    Feed count: 2 -- two top-level feeds
```

Get the number of feed items for the second feed
```
    print("Item count: " .. #FEED_READER_FEEDS[2].Items)

    Item count: 1 -- Second feed only has one item
```

Get the content of the second item in the first feed
```
    print(FEED_READER_FEEDS[2].Items[1].Content)
    New data shows economy worsening.
```

Assign the first feed to another table variable
```
    MY_TABLE = FEED_READER_FEEDS[1];
```

Print each feed title
```
    for i=1,#FEED_READER_FEEDS do
      print(FEED_READER_FEEDS[i].Title)
    end

    BBC News | News Front Page | UK Edition
    NYT > NYTimes.com Home
```

FrameXML 101

The user interface of a *World of Warcraft* addon is defined in an XML format called FrameXML. FrameXML is very similar to XAML, the markup language in Windows Presentation Foundation (WPF) and Silverlight. Like XAML, objects are built declaratively in FrameXML, you can set properties in the FrameXML declaration, and later those objects are accessible from code. FrameXML has a number of controls (called a widget element in WoW) that are similar to those in WPF and Windows Forms; see Table 3-4.

Table 3-4. *FrameXML widgets and their .NET counterparts*

FRAMEXML	WPF	WINDOWS FORMS
Frame	Window	Form
FontString	Label	Label
Button	Button	Button
CheckButton	CheckBox	CheckBox
Texture	Image	Image
EditBox	TextBox	TextBox

FrameXML can express complex, dynamic layouts using anchors and templates. Templates are like a combination of WPF templates, styles, and custom controls rolled into one. Before we delve into these, let's take a high-level look at a Hello World example, as shown in Example 3-2.

Example 3-2. *Hello World FrameXML*

```
<Ui … >
  <Script file="Frame.lua" />
  <Frame name="Frame1" parent="UIParent" toplevel="true" enableMouse="true">
    <Size>
      <AbsDimension x="200" y="150" />
    </Size>
    <Anchors>
      <Anchor point="CENTER" />
    </Anchors>
…
    <Layers>
      <Layer level="OVERLAY">
        <FontString name="FontString1" inherits="GameFontNormal" text="Hello world!">
          <Anchors>
            <Anchor point="CENTER">
              <Offset x="0" y="20" />
            </Anchor>
          </Anchors>
```

```
        </FontString>
      </Layer>
    </Layers>
  <Frames />
  <Scripts />
  </Frame>
</Ui>
```

In this example, we first set the associated script file for the FrameXML to be a file named *Frame.lua*. This is similar to .NET's code-behind file, in that event handlers for the frame can be authored in the *Frame.lua* file.

Next, we declare a frame called `Frame1` with some default properties. The frame's size is set to be 200 pixels wide and 150 pixels high. The frame itself is anchored to the center so that it will appear on the center of the screen.

The frame contains a `FontString` widget named `FontString1` that is anchored 20 pixels up from the frame's center point.

The FrameXML from Example 3-2 will render the UI shown in Figure 3-4 in-game.

Figure 3-4. *The Hello world! frame*

Every UI element declared in FrameXML can subsequently be accessed from Lua through a global object with the same name. You can easily try this out by running a small Lua snippet from the chat window by typing:

```
"/script HelloWorldFrameText:SetText("Hello Coding4Fun!");
```

Layout

Every widget in FrameXML can have a combination of a size and one or more anchors. *World of Warcraft* then determines the actual location and size of the widget based on these values before rendering the addon.

A frame's size can be either absolute or relative to its parent.

```
<!-- A button with an absolute size of 100 by 20 pixels -->
<Button>
    <Size>
        <AbsDimension x="100" y="20" />
    </Size>
</Button>

<!-- A frame that has one half of its parent's size -->
<Frame>
    <Size>
        <RelDimension x="0.5" y="0.5" />
    </Size>
</Frame
```

An anchor defines a single point where the widget should be placed. An anchor is always relative to another widget or the screen's point. There are nine points in *World of Warcraft* that can be anchored or anchored to, as shown in Figure 3-5.

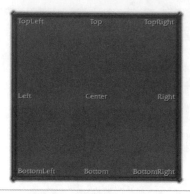

Figure 3-5. *The nine anchor points for a widget*

Table 3-5 lists FrameXML anchor properties.

Table 3-5. *An anchor's properties*

ANCHOR	DESCRIPTION
point	Required. Defines which point of the widget should be anchored.
relativeTo	Optional. The name of the widget whose point the anchor should be relative to. When omitted, the widget's parent is used. If the widget has no parent, the screen is used.
relativePoint	Optional. The point of the widget that the anchor is relative to (see relativeTo). When omitted, the same point as the one anchored is used.
Offset	Optional. An offset in pixels by which the anchored point should be away from the relative point.

In Example 3-3, the anchor positions the CancelButton next to the OKButton by leaving 10 pixels between them. The OKButton is in the bottom-right corner of its parent with a 15-pixel margin.

Example 3-3. *Anchoring two controls relative to each other*

```
<Button name="OKButton" inherits="UIPanelButtonTemplate" text="OK">
<Size>
  <AbsDimension x="80" y="25" />
</Size>
<Anchors>
  <Anchor point="BOTTOMRIGHT">
    <Offset>
      <AbsDimension x="-15" y="15" />
    </Offset>
  </Anchor>
</Anchors>
</Button>
```

```
<Button name="CancelButton" inherits="UIPanelButtonTemplate" text="Cancel">
<Size>
  <AbsDimension x="80" y="25" />
</Size>
<Anchors>
  <Anchor point="RIGHT" relativePoint="LEFT" relativeTo="OKButton">
    <Offset>
      <AbsDimension x="-10" y="0" />
    </Offset>
  </Anchor>
</Anchors>
</Button>
```

AddOn Studio for designing FrameXML

For .NET developers who can't live without Visual Studio, you can use AddOn Studio (AOS) for *World of Warcraft*, a free, open source developer tool that brings a Visual Studio development experience for building *Warcraft* addons. AOS includes a number of features that .NET developers are familiar with, including a visual designer, toolbox for controls, automatic packaging of *Warcraft* deployment files (TOCs), IntelliSense, event and properties window, refactoring, solution control, and more. Figure 3-6 shows how AddOn Studio's designer will render the FrameXML defined in Example 3-3.

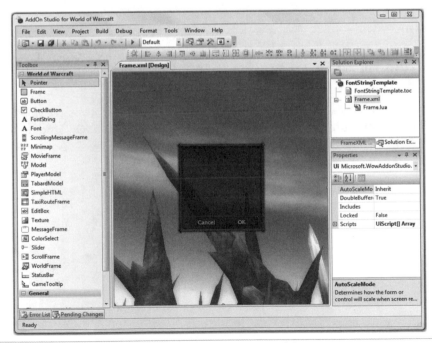

Figure 3-6. *AddOn Studio rendering the FrameXML from Example 3-3*

Rather than manually setting FrameXML anchor properties, you can select the Cancel button and click the Anchors property in the properties window to bring up the Anchor Collection Editor dialog box, as shown in Figure 3-7. The Anchor Collection Editor enables you to visually define all of the FrameXML properties for the Cancel button from Example 3-5.

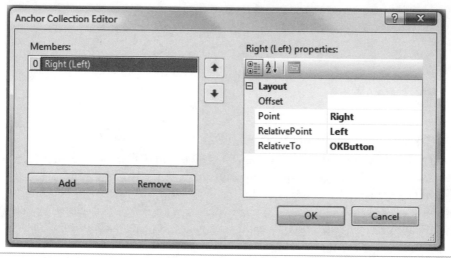

Figure 3-7. *The Anchor Collection Editor*

Templates

Like WPF styles, templates define a common look and feel for FrameXML widgets. *World of Warcraft* defines a number of templates for common UI that you can easily reuse.

To use a template for a widget, such as a `FontString` widget, you simply need to set the `inherits` attribute to a valid `FontString` template. Using AddOn Studio, you can choose from a number of built-in templates by selecting the `inherits` property from the properties window, as shown in Figure 3-8.

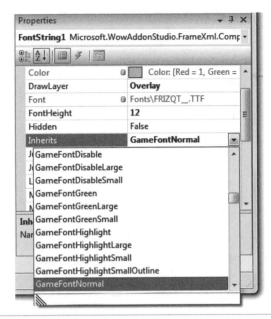

Figure 3-8. *Warcraft predefined templates for a FontString*

Events

Like .NET controls, FrameXML widgets have events that we can assign event handler functions to, much like we would assign a button click event for a button in a .NET application. You can define the Lua function inline in the FrameXML, or you can associate an event with a Lua function that will fire when the event is raised. Example 3-4 shows writing an inline event handler for a button's OnClick event.

Example 3-4. *Button handling the OnClick event*

```
<Button name="ChattyButton" inherits="UIPanelButtonTemplate" text="Click me!">
    <Anchors>
        <!-- ... -->
    </Anchors>
    <Scripts>
        <OnClick>
            message("Hey there!!");
        </OnClick>
    </Scripts>
</Button>
```

One of the most important events is the OnLoad event, which is fired when a frame is loaded. In AddOn Studio, you can easily generate event handlers very similar to the way you would with WPF or Windows Forms projects, by clicking the events tab in the Properties window (Figure 3-9).

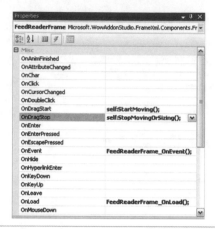

Figure 3-9. *Events of a frame in AddOn Studio for World of Warcraft*

Understanding the Feed Reader Addon

Now that we have a basic understanding of how addons work, let's look at how our Feed Reader addon is built.

Dissecting Feed Reader

The first thing we should do is look at all of the files that make up the Feed Reader addon, as shown in Figure 3-10.

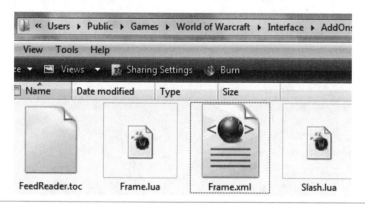

Figure 3-10. *The four files that make up the Feed Reader addon*

The first thing to notice is that Feed Reader is defined in a subdirectory of *Users\Public\Games\World of Warcraft\Interface\AddOns\FeedReader*. All *Warcraft* addons must be in their own custom subdirectory under that path.

Feed Reader includes the following files:

FeedReader.toc

> This is Feed Reader's table of contents (TOC) that defines the addon name, author, version, and, most importantly, the list of all the files in the addon. AddOn Studio will automatically create your TOC file for you, so you won't have to hand-edit these files (click the Project menu to view the addon TOC settings).

Frame.xml

> This defines the look and feel of Feed Reader, including buttons, controls, positioning, colors, and more.

Frame.lua

> This defines a set of Lua functions that map to event handlers for widgets in *Frame. xml*.

Slash.lua

> This is a standalone Lua file that includes slash commands, which are text commands that are registered to *Warcraft*'s chat window (see Figure 3-3).

How Feed Reader and Feed Grabber Work

Next, let's take a 10,000-foot view at the order of execution for Feed Reader and Feed Grabber.

1. Before *Warcraft* starts, Feed Grabber is running in the system executing a background synchronization that takes a set of RSS feeds from the operating system Common Feed List (see Figure 3-1).

2. Feed Grabber takes the in-memory RSS feeds, scrubs them to remove or escape illegal characters, and then serializes the feeds into a Lua table data structure in the file *FeedReader.lua*. *FeedReader.lua* is stored in the directory *Users\Public\Games\ World of Warcraft\WTF\Account\AccountName\SavedVariables*.

3. When *World of Warcraft* starts, the game will scan all subdirectories in the *Users\ Public\Games\World of Warcraft\Interface* directory. It will find the Feed Reader subdirectory, read through the *FeedReader.TOC* file, and read in all of the associated files in "Dissecting Feed Reader."

4. Feed Reader calls into *Warcraft*'s API and registers for the ADDON_LOADED event (see Examples 3-9 and 3-10).

5. *Warcraft* will see that the *FeedReader.TOC* file has declared a saved variable named FEED_READER_FEEDS, and it will load the *FeedReader.lua* file from step #2 and set the FEED_READER_FEEDS variable to the serialized RSS feeds.

6. *Warcraft* finishes loading the addon and fires Feed Reader's OnEvent() function, passing in a number of parameters, including the event name and the addon name that is firing the event (see Example 3-11).

7. Feed Reader calls the SelectFeed function, passing in 1 as a parameter to select the first feed by default (see Example 3-12).

8. The SelectFeed function sets the CURRENT_FEED to be the first feed in FEED_READER_FEEDS (see Example 3-12).

9. The UpdateFeeds function is called to update the UI for the FeedsScrollFrame frame (see Example 3-14).

10. The SelectFeedItem function sets the CURRENT_ITEM to be the first item in the currently selected feed (see Example 3-13).

11. The UpdateFeedItems function is called to update the UI for the FeedItems ScrollFrame frame (see Example 3-15).

12. The UpdateSummary function is called to update the UI to display the content for the currently selected item (see Example 3-18).

13. To get updated news feeds in-game, players must reload their UI. This will force *Warcraft* to save the saved variables to the *FeedReader.lua* file mentioned in step #5.

14. The Feed Grabber .NET application uses a FileSystemWatcher class to monitor when *Warcraft* has updated the saved variables file in step #13, and it will sneak in the updated news feeds to the *FeedReader.lua* file (see Examples 3-30 and 3-31).

The Feed Reader UI

Feed Reader consists of a simple top-level frame using AddOn Studio's default backdrop and styling and a set of three nested frames: the feeds frame, the feed items frame, and the summary frame.

Feed Reader also has a caption FontString in the top-left corner and a close button in the top-right corner.

Example 3-5 shows the top-level definition of the FeedReaderFrame frame.

Example 3-5. *The main Feed Reader frame (children omitted)*

```
<Frame name="FeedReaderFrame" parent="UIParent" toplevel="true" movable="true"
enableMouse="true">
  <Size>
    <AbsDimension x="800" y="300" />
  </Size>
  <Anchors>
    <Anchor point="CENTER" />
  </Anchors>
  <Backdrop bgFile="Interface\DialogFrame\UI-DialogBox-Background"
    edgeFile="Interface\DialogFrame\UI-DialogBox-Border" tile="true">
```

```
<BackgroundInsets>
  <AbsInset left="11" right="12" top="12" bottom="11" />
</BackgroundInsets>
<TileSize>
  <AbsValue val="32" />
</TileSize>
<EdgeSize>
  <AbsValue val="32" />
</EdgeSize>
</Backdrop>
<Layers ... />
<Frames ... />
<Scripts>
  <OnDragStart>self:StartMoving();</OnDragStart>
  <OnDragStop>self:StopMovingOrSizing();</OnDragStop>
  <OnLoad>self:RegisterForDrag("LeftButton"); FeedReaderFrame_OnLoad();
  </OnLoad>
<OnEvent>FeedReaderFrame_OnEvent();</OnEvent>
</Scripts>
</Frame>
```

A button template is also declared for showing the feeds and the feed items. The template specifies the width and height of the items, as well as the fonts to be used (see Example 3-6).

Example 3-6. *ScrollItemTemplate used by FeedReader*

```
<Button name="ScrollItemTemplate" virtual="true">
  <Size>
    <AbsDimension x="150" y="16" />
  </Size>
  <NormalFont style="GameFontNormal" justifyH="LEFT" />
  <HighlightFont style="GameFontHighlight" justifyH="LEFT" />
</Button>
```

Frames

The FeedFrame and the FeedItemsFrame both show a scrollable list of items. They both contain a ScrollFrame and five buttons based on the ScrollItemTemplate template. By inheriting the ScrollFrame from the built-in FauxScrollFrameTemplate, *World of Warcraft* takes care of the scrollbar UI for us (although we will have to manually code scrolling the frame; see the upcoming section "The UpdateFeeds and UpdateFeed-Items function"). Figure 3-11 displays a tree view of all of the controls in the *Frame.xml* file.

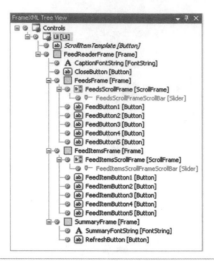

Figure 3-11. *Tree view of Feed Reader's UI*

Each button in `FeedsFrame` and `FeedItemsFrame` contains a short script to handle the `OnClick` event that calls a Lua function to update the UI (see Examples 3-18 and 3-20). The index of the button is passed in as a parameter. The buttons are positioned by anchoring them to the previous button, except for the top buttons, which are anchored to the frame in which they reside. The code for `FeedButton2` is shown in Example 3-7.

Example 3-7. *FeedButton2*

```
<Button name="FeedButton2" inherits="ScrollItemTemplate" text="Feed2">
    <Anchors>
        <Anchor point="TOPLEFT" relativeTo="FeedButton1" relativePoint="BOTTOMLEFT" />
        <Anchor point="TOPRIGHT" relativeTo="FeedButton1" relativePoint="BOTTOMRIGHT" />
    </Anchors>
    <Scripts>
        <OnClick>
            FeedButton_Clicked(2);
        </OnClick>
    </Scripts>
</Button>
```

Adding Code for Frame.xml

Now that we've defined Feed Reader's appearance using FrameXML, we need to show the code that powers the addon's click events and displays the RSS feeds in *Frame. lua*.

Global variables

Feed Reader defines three global variables defined as table types, as shown in the code in Example 3-8.

Example 3-8. *Three global table variables*

```
FEED_READER_FEEDS = {}
CURRENT_FEED = {}
CURRENT_ITEM = {}
```

FEED_READER_FEEDS

This table variable is defined as a *saved variable* in the *FeedReader.TOC* file, meaning that *Warcraft* will populate this variable with the serialized value from *Users\ Public\Games\World of Warcraft\WTF\Account\AccountName\SavedVariables* (see Example 3-1, earlier in this chapter).

CURRENT_FEED

This stores the currently selected feed when we loop through the FEED_READER_ FEEDS table.

CURRENT_ITEM

Stores the currently selected item when we loop through all of the items in CURRENT_FEED.

Defining a variable as a saved variable

To define a variable as a saved variable (one that is saved between gaming sessions), in AddOn Studio, click on the Project menu, select the Project Properties pane, and add in the name(s) of the SavedVariables you want to use (Figure 3-12). For multiple saved variables, simply comma-delimit each variable.

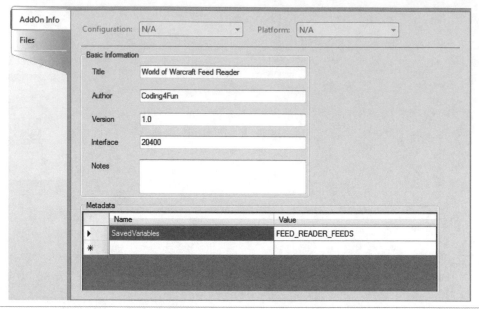

Figure 3-12. *Defining a SavedVariable in AddOn Studio's Project Properties*

Registering for *Warcraft* events

When Feed Reader first starts, WoW will look at what scripts and events have been added to the *Frame.xml* file, as shown in Example 3-9.

Example 3-9. *Feed Reader scripts*

```
<Scripts>
...
  <OnLoad>FeedReaderFrame_OnLoad();</OnLoad>
  <OnEvent>FeedReaderFrame_OnEvent();</OnEvent>
</Scripts>
```

It will first run the OnLoad function, which registers the addon for the ADDON_LOADED event that is shown in Example 3-10.

Example 3-10. *Feed Reader Load events*

```
function FeedReaderFrame_OnLoad()
  this:RegisterEvent("ADDON_LOADED");
end
```

The OnEvent function is a generic function that you will register for any *Warcraft* events to fire. This means that if you register for other FrameXML events or in-game events, such as a combat log event or a chat event, all of those events will be raised to the

OnEvent function. To determine what event is firing the OnEvent function, we can use the global event variable.

Using the event variable, we can determine whether the event is an ADDON_LOADED event, as that's the event we care about, and handle just that event.

The second "gotcha" we'll face is that the ADDON_LOADED event will fire for every add-on that we have installed. However, we can inspect the arg1 variable, a variable that includes the name of the loaded addon, to make sure we fire our event handler only when it's the Feed Reader addon.

If this explanation seems confusing, hopefully the code in Example 3-11 will clarify that we are checking for the correct event and the correct addon for the event before we call the SelectFeed function.

Example 3-11. Capturing events in your addon

```
function FeedReaderFrame_OnEvent()
  if ((event == "ADDON_LOADED") and (arg1 == 'FeedReader')) then
    SelectFeed(1);
  end
end
```

Why Doesn't the OnLoad Function Just Call the SelectFeed Function?

You may be wondering why the **OnLoad** event bothers to register for the **ADDON_LOADED** event, instead of just calling the **SelectFeed** method directly. The reason for this is that when the **OnLoad** function fires, the **FEED_READER_FEEDS** saved variable has not yet been loaded into memory. When the **ADDON_LOADED** event does fire, you can be assured that any saved variables are loaded and available for the addon.

The SelectFeed and SelectFeedItems functions

The SelectFeed and SelectFeedItem functions are used to assign the CURRENT_FEED and CURRENT_ITEM variables, respectively.

When you call the SelectFeed function, you pass in a feedIndex with the index of the FEED_READER_FEEDS table that you want to assign to the CURRENT_FEED table. It looks to see whether we have already selected the feed, and if not, sets the value for the CURRENT_FEED variable. Next, it calls the UpdateFeeds function to update the frame UI and the SelectFeedItems function with a parameter of 1 to select the first feed item (Example 3-12).

Example 3-12. *Updating the currently selected feed with the SelectFeed function*

```
function SelectFeed(feedIndex)
  if (FEED_READER_FEEDS[feedIndex] ~= CURRENT_FEED) then
    --Set CURRENT_FEED as the currently selected feed
    CURRENT_FEED = FEED_READER_FEEDS[feedIndex];
    UpdateFeeds();
    SelectFeedItem(1);
  end
end
```

The SelectFeedItem function

The SelectFeedItem function works almost identically to the SelectedFeed function from Example 3-13, just one level down the hierarchy. So while SelectFeed sets the CURRENT_FEED variable to store the currently selected feed, SelectFeedItem sets the CURRENT_ITEM variable to the currently selected item. When the function is first run, we compare the current item to the index in CURRENT_FEED.Items, and if the index doesn't match, we need to set the value for CURRENT_FEED and then call UpdateFeed Items to update which feed items are visible in the FeedItemsScrollFrame, as shown in Example 3-13.

Example 3-13. *Updating the currently selected item with the SelectFeedItem function*

```
function SelectFeedItem(feedItemIndex)
  if (CURRENT_FEED.Items[feedItemIndex] ~= CURRENT_ITEM) then
    --Set CURRENT_ITEM as the currently selected item
    CURRENT_ITEM = CURRENT_FEED.Items[feedItemIndex];
    UpdateFeedItems();
    UpdateSummary();
  end
end
```

The UpdateFeeds and UpdateFeedItems functions

The UpdateFeeds and UpdateFeedItems functions are used to update the Feeds ScrollFrame and FeedItemsScrollFrame frames, respectively.

As a .NET developer, you've likely become accustomed to using a control such as a ComboBox or ListBox that encapsulates for you all of the behavior around scrolling up and down. Since *Warcraft* doesn't have those control primitives, you will have to manually toggle the visible text of each item in the scroll frame.

Both FeedsScrollFrame and FeedItemsScrollFrame define five buttons that we will need to loop through and set each button's text value based on our current position in the scrolling list.

To better explain how this works, examine Table 3-6, which is an in-memory representation of the FEED_READER_FEEDS variable and the five buttons we defined in the FeedsScrollFrame.

Table 3-6. *Assigning visible values in the FeedsScrollFrame*

INDEX	TITLE	BUTTON
1	Feed Title 1	FeedButton1
2	Feed Title 2	FeedButton2
3	Feed Title 3	FeedButton3
4	Feed Title 4	FeedButton4
5	Feed Title 5	FeedButton5
6	Feed Title 6	Hidden
7	Feed Title 7	Hidden

When UpdateFeeds first runs, it loops through the first five items and assigns the text from the first title to the text of FeedButton1, the text of the second title to the text of FeedButton2, and so on for all five buttons.

When a user clicks on the *scroll down* button for FeedsScrollFrame, the UpdateFeeds function will fire again to assign feed titles to buttons. The difference is that we've now moved down one item, and so all items shift down by one:

- The first item is no longer visible.
- The second item is now the first visible item and assigned to FeedButton1.
- The sixth item, which previously was hidden, is now visible and assigned to Feed Button5.

The newly assigned values are shown in Table 3-7.

Table 3-7. *Scrolling down shifts the visible content down by one*

INDEX	TITLE	BUTTON
1	Feed Title 1	Hidden
2	Feed Title 2	FeedButton1
3	Feed Title 3	FeedButton2
4	Feed Title 4	FeedButton3
5	Feed Title 5	FeedButton4
6	Feed Title 6	FeedButton5
7	Feed Title 7	Hidden

The UpdateFeeds function

Let's now walk through the UpdateFeeds function defined in Example 3-14, which will update the UI of the Feed Reader addon. Since the FeedScrollFrame frame inherits from the FauxScrollFrameTemplate template, we first need to tell the frame how to behave by calling FauxScrollFrame_Update with the following parameters:

- The frame we want to update, FeedsScrollFrame.

- The total number of feeds we have (seven in our example).

- The number of items that we're scrolling through, which is five (five buttons defined in the FeedsScrollFrame).

- The height of each button so that when we scroll down, the scroll moves that number of pixels. The height is 16 pixels by default.

Next, we need to loop through and assign the text for each of the five buttons. In the loop, we need to make sure we get the right index for the starting element, so that if the user has scrolled down the frame, we increment the feedIndex by the number of times he's scrolled down using the GetOffset function for the frame.

Let's assume that we are going through the first loop in the for loop and that the user has scrolled down once. The GetOffset function would return 1 since he scrolled down once, which when added to the i variable counter would set the feedIndex to 2. Since the feedIndex is 2, the first button is now assigned to the second item (feedIndex), and so on.

The getglobal function will return the FeedButton widget, and we set its text to the index. If the index is less than or equal to the number of elements, we'll hide the control, since we don't have any text to show in it.

To provide a visual cue as to which feed is currently selected, we will use the LockHighlight function (Example 3-14) to add a highlight effect to the currently selected feed.

Example 3-14. *Updating the FeedsScrollFrame UI*

```
function UpdateFeeds()
   -- Pass in the frame to update, the total num of feeds,
   -- the number of buttons, and the height of each button
   FauxScrollFrame_Update(FeedsScrollFrame, #FEED_READER_FEEDS, 5, 16);

   local i;
   local feedIndex;

   for i = 1, 5 do
     feedIndex = i + FauxScrollFrame_GetOffset(FeedsScrollFrame);

     if (feedIndex <= #FEED_READER_FEEDS) then
```

```
      getglobal("FeedButton" .. i):SetText(FEED_READER_FEEDS[feedIndex].Title);
      getglobal("FeedButton" .. i):Show();
    else
      getglobal("FeedButton" .. i):Hide();
    end

    if (FEED_READER_FEEDS[feedIndex] == CURRENT_FEED) then
      getglobal("FeedButton" .. i):LockHighlight();
    else
      getglobal("FeedButton" .. i):UnlockHighlight();
    end
  end
end
```

The UpdateFeedItems function

The UpdateFeedItems function works just like the UpdateFeed function, except that it updates the FeedItemsScrollFrame (versus the FeedsScrollFrame) and sets Feed ItemButton (versus FeedButton) controls. See Example 3-15.

Example 3-15. *Updating the FeedItemsScrollFrame UI*

```
function UpdateFeedItems()
  FauxScrollFrame_Update(FeedItemsScrollFrame, #(CURRENT_FEED.Items), 5, 16);
  local i;
  local feedItemIndex;
  for i = 1, 5 do
    feedItemIndex = i + FauxScrollFrame_GetOffset(FeedItemsScrollFrame);
    if (feedItemIndex <= #(CURRENT_FEED.Items)) then
      getglobal("FeedItemButton" .. i):SetText(
        CURRENT_FEED.Items[feedItemIndex].Title);
      getglobal("FeedItemButton" .. i):Show();
    else
      getglobal("FeedItemButton" .. i):Hide();
    end
    if (CURRENT_FEED.Items[feedItemIndex] == CURRENT_ITEM) then
      getglobal("FeedItemButton" .. i):LockHighlight();
    else
      getglobal("FeedItemButton" .. i):UnlockHighlight();
    end
  end
end
```

Updating the summary

After the UpdateFeedItems function is executed, the SelectFeedItem function then calls the UpdateSummary function to update the content of the current item, as shown in Example 3-16.

Example 3-16. *Updating the SummaryFontString*

```
function UpdateSummary()
  SummaryFontString:SetText(CURRENT_ITEM.Content);
end
```

OnClick event for Feed buttons

As we saw earlier when we defined the FrameXML for Feed Reader, all of the buttons in the FeedsScrollFrame have the same OnClick button event handler, with the only difference being that each button passes its index into the function (FeedButton1 passes in 1, FeedButton2 passes in 2, etc). When the clicked function fires (Example 3-17), we receive the button number, and we add the offset to that, since that will determine which line item is actually being read. For example:

1. We click FeedButton1, which is displaying the second item.

2. The FeedButton_Clicked event fires, passing in 1.

3. We call the GetOffset function and receive an offset of 1, meaning the user has scrolled down and that the second item is now the first item.

4. We pass 2 to the SelectFeed function.

Example 3-17. *The OnClick function for all FeedButton controls*

```
function FeedButton_Clicked(i)
  local feedIndex = i + FauxScrollFrame_GetOffset(FeedsScrollFrame);
  SelectFeed(feedIndex);
end
```

OnClick event for FeedItem buttons

Just like with the FeedsScrollFrame, all of the FeedItemButton controls in the Feed ItemsScrollFrame have the same OnClick event handler that passes in the button number. We'll add the button number to the GetOffset function to determine the current feed ItemIndex and call SelectFeedItem, passing in the feedItemIndex (Example 3-18).

Example 3-18. *The OnClick function for all FeedItemButton controls*

```
function FeedItemButton_Clicked(i)
  local feedItemIndex = i + FauxScrollFrame_GetOffset(FeedItemsScrollFrame);
  SelectFeedItem(feedItemIndex);
end
```

Adding a basic slash command

The final part we'll add to Feed Reader is a basic slash command handler. In it, we'll define two commands, one to "show" the FeedReaderFrame frame and another to "hide" it. To register a slash command, you must follow these steps:

1. Create a function that you want to fire when your slash command is received, such as FeedReader_OnCommand.

2. Create an all-uppercase variable name following this pattern: SLASH_ADDON NAME1. For Feed Reader, this means our slash command will be SLASH_FEED READER1. The number at the end of the variable name is required for the slash command to be correctly registered. We'll assign SLASH_FEEDREADER1 to the name of the slash command you are registering, which for Feed Reader will be "/feeds."

3. Register the function from step #1 into *Warcraft*'s internal SlashCmdList table using the addon's name (in uppercase) as the table key.

The code for registering and handling the slash command is shown in Example 3-19. Now, when a user types "/feeds show" into *Warcraft*'s chat window, the text "show" is passed as an argument named arg into the FeedReader_OnCommand function. We then call the FeedReaderFrame:Show() function to show the frame.

Example 3-19. *Feed Reader's slash command*

```
function FeedReader_OnCommand(arg)
  if arg == "show" then
    FeedReaderFrame:Show();
  end

  if arg == "hide" then
    FeedReaderFrame:Hide();
  end
end

SLASH_FEEDREADER1 = "/feeds";
SlashCmdList["FEEDREADER"] = FeedReader_OnCommand;
```

Feed Grabber

We've seen that addons can do powerful things, and it's up to your imagination how you improve *World of Warcraft*'s interface, but they can't really communicate with the outside world. Although Lua comes with standard libraries that provide features such as opening and reading files and accessing operating system services, these libraries are not available inside *World of Warcraft* for security reasons. Thus, Feed Reader cannot download the feeds itself. If only there was a way to provide that information from outside *World of Warcraft*....

Saved variables provides a great way to persist data for an addon between multiple sessions, and is stored as an ordinary Lua file under *World of Warcraft*'s installation directory. Although the file is used to save and load the variables listed as SavedVariables in the addon's TOC file by *World of Warcraft*, nobody said it can't be modified by another application. We just have to make sure we save the information at the right time.

Feed Grabber is a simple application that sits in the task tray and saves the content of the top-level feeds in Windows Common Feed List to the SavedVariables file associated with Feed Reader.

Common Feed List

The Common Feed List is available on Windows XP SP2 with Internet Explorer 7 installed and on Windows Vista. It maintains a list of RSS feeds in a folder hierarchy and can be enabled to periodically download these feeds. Whenever Internet Explorer 7 detects an RSS feed on the current page, the feed icon on the toolbar lights up in orange, which means you can add it to the Feed List. The list of subscribed feeds can be accessed through the menu by clicking View→Explorer Bar→Feeds or by pressing Ctrl+Shift+J, as shown in Figure 3-13.

Figure 3-13. *The Common Feed List in Internet Explorer 7*

The Common Feed List is also accessible using a COM-based API, which means it's a breeze to use from any .NET language, such as C# or VB. We can add a reference to this COM API by using the Add Reference dialog box, selecting the COM tab, and selecting the "Microsoft Feeds" COM object, as shown in Figure 3-14.

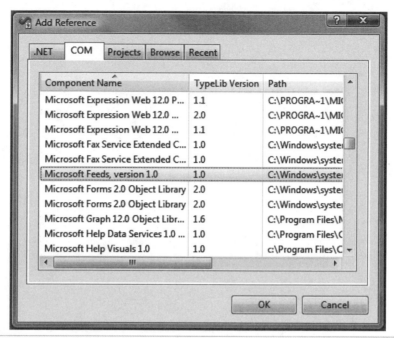

Figure 3-14. *Microsoft Feeds in the Add Reference dialog box*

To use the Feeds library, first you need to create an instance of the FeedsManager Class. The FeedsManagerClass has a number of properties that we will want to use, including:

- The hierarchy of all feeds available in the RootFolder property
- Whether background synchronization of feeds is enabled
- The default time interval between synchronizations

Programmatically getting feeds

First, we'll define two classes, Feed and FeedItem, that we will use to store an RSS Feed, as shown in Examples 3-20 and 3-21. As you can see from the class definitions, these classes are exactly like the structure in the FEED_READER_FEEDS table.

[C#] Example 3-20. *The Feed and FeedItem classes in C#*

```csharp
public class Feed
{
    public string Title { get; set; }
    public FeedItem[] Items { get; set; }
}
```

```
public class FeedItem
{
    public string Title { get; set; }
    public string Content { get; set; }
}
```

Example 3-21. *The Feed and FeedItem classes in VB*

```
Public Class Feed
  Private privateTitle As String
  Public Property Title() As String
    Get
      Return privateTitle
    End Get
    Set(ByVal value As String)
      privateTitle = value
    End Set
  End Property

  Private privateItems As FeedItem()
  Public Property Items() As FeedItem()
    Get
      Return privateItems
    End Get
    Set(ByVal value As FeedItem())
      privateItems = value
    End Set
  End Property
End Class

Public Class FeedItem
  Private privateTitle As String
  Public Property Title() As String
    Get
      Return privateTitle
    End Get
    Set(ByVal value As String)
      privateTitle = value
    End Set
  End Property

  Private privateContent As String
  Public Property Content() As String
    Get
      Return privateContent
```

```
        End Get
        Set(ByVal value As String)
          privateContent = value
        End Set
      End Property
    End Class
```

With our classes defined, we'll next call into the Microsoft Feeds COM objects to re-trieve the RSS feeds from the Common Feed List. To do this, we'll use the GetTopLevel Feeds method in the FeedGrabber class, which gets all of the top-level feeds from the rootFolder, downloads any feeds that haven't been downloaded, and returns the list of feeds, as shown in Examples 3-22 and 3-23.

C# | **Example 3-22.** *Returning a list of Feed objects from the Common Feed List in C#*

```csharp
using System;
using System.Collections.Generic;
using System.Linq;
using System.IO;
using System.Threading;
using System.Lua;
using System.Lua.Serialization;
using Microsoft.Feeds.Interop;
using System.Diagnostics;

public class FeedGrabber
{
  private IFeedsManager feedsManager;
  ...
  private Feed[] GetTopLevelFeeds()
  {
    var rootFolder = (IFeedFolder)feedsManager.RootFolder;
    var topLevelFeeds = (IFeedsEnum)rootFolder.Feeds;

    List<Feed> feeds = new List<Feed>(topLevelFeeds.Count);

    foreach (IFeed feed in topLevelFeeds)
    {
      // If a feed is not yet downloaded, download now
      if (feed.DownloadStatus != FEEDS_DOWNLOAD_STATUS.FDS_DOWNLOADED)
        feed.Download();

      // Skip feed if it could not be downloaded
      if (feed.DownloadStatus != FEEDS_DOWNLOAD_STATUS.FDS_DOWNLOADED)
        continue;
```

```
        feeds.Add(CreateFeed(feed));
      }
      return feeds.ToArray();
    }
```

```vb
Imports Microsoft.VisualBasic
Imports System
Imports System.Collections.Generic
Imports System.Linq
Imports System.IO
Imports System.Threading
Imports System.Lua
Imports System.Lua.Serialization
Imports Microsoft.Feeds.Interop
Imports System.Diagnostics

Public Class FeedGrabber
  Private feedsManager As IFeedsManager
  …
  Private Function GetTopLevelFeeds() As Feed()
    Dim rootFolder = CType(feedsManager.RootFolder, IFeedFolder)
    Dim topLevelFeeds = CType(rootFolder.Feeds, IFeedsEnum)

    Dim feeds As List(Of Feed) = New List(Of Feed)(topLevelFeeds.Count)

    For Each feed As IFeed In topLevelFeeds
      ' If a feed is not yet downloaded, download now
      If feed.DownloadStatus <> FEEDS_DOWNLOAD_STATUS.FDS_DOWNLOADED Then
        feed.Download()
      End If

      ' Skip feed if it could not be downloaded
      If feed.DownloadStatus <> FEEDS_DOWNLOAD_STATUS.FDS_DOWNLOADED Then
        Continue For
      End If

      feeds.Add(CreateFeed(feed))
    Next feed

    Return feeds.ToArray()
  End Function
```

As you may have noticed, the last line of the for each loop in the FeedGrabber method in Examples 3-22 and 3-23 calls the CreateFeed method. The CreateFeed method is used to convert a Microsoft.Feed.IFeed object into a Feed object. The Create Feed method in turn calls the CreateFeedItem method to convert a Microsoft.Feed. IFeedItem into a FeedItem object, as shown in Examples 3-24 and 3-25. When complete, a feed and all the feed items are returned as an array of Feed objects.

C# Example 3-24. *Creating Feed and FeedItem objects in C#*

```csharp
private static Feed CreateFeed(IFeed feed)
{
  var feedItems = (IFeedsEnum)feed.Items;
  return new Feed
    {
      Title = feed.Title,
      Items = feedItems.OfType<IFeedItem>().Select(feedItem =>
        CreateFeedItem(feedItem)).ToArray()
    };
}


private static FeedItem CreateFeedItem(IFeedItem feedItem)
{
  return new FeedItem
  {
    Title = feedItem.Title,
    Content = feedItem.Description
  };
}
```

VB Example 3-25. *Creating Feed and FeedItem objects in VB*

```vb
Private Shared Function CreateFeed(ByVal feed As IFeed) As Feed
  Dim feedItems = CType(feed.Items, IFeedsEnum)
  Return New Feed With {.Title = feed.Title, _
    .Items = feedItems.OfType(Of IFeedItem)().Select(Function(feedItem) _
    CreateFeedItem(feedItem)).ToArray()}
End Function

Private Shared Function CreateFeedItem(ByVal feedItem As IFeedItem) As FeedItem
  Return New FeedItem With {.Title = feedItem.Title, .Content = feedItem.Description}
End Function
```

Serializing to Lua

Now that we have a list of Feed and FeedItem objects, we need to serialize them into a *FeedReader.Lua* file that contains our FEED_READER_FEEDS saved variable.

To do this, we'll use System.Lua, a custom-built library that is designed similarly to the classes in the System.Xml namespace.

System.Lua includes a LuaSerializer class that uses reflection to serialize classes and arrays into Lua tables, and primitive types and strings to their Lua counterparts. The actual writing of the file to disk is done by the LuaWriter class, which provides a fast, non-cached, forward-only way of generating streams of files containing Lua code.

To serialize the feeds into the *FeedReader.Lua* file, we'll call the SaveFeeds method, which gets an array of Feed objects, initializes a LuaWriter object with the path to the *FeedReader.lua* saved variable, and writes the data to the file stream, as shown in Examples 3-26 and 3-27.

C#   Example 3-26. *The SaveFeeds method in C#*

```csharp
public void SaveFeeds()
{
  Feed[] feeds = this.GetTopLevelFeeds();
  if (feeds != null)
  {
    using (var luaWriter = LuaWriter.Create(savedVariablesPath))
    {
      var luaSerializer = new LuaSerializer();

      luaWriter.WriteStartAssignment(feedsVariableName);
      luaSerializer.Serialize(luaWriter, feeds);
      luaWriter.WriteEndAssignment();
    }
  }
}
```

VB   Example 3-27. *The SaveFeeds method in VB*

```vb
Public Sub SaveFeeds()
  Dim feeds() As Feed = Me.GetTopLevelFeeds()
  If feeds IsNot Nothing Then
    Using Writer = LuaWriter.Create(savedVariablesPath)
      Dim luaSerializer = New LuaSerializer()

      Writer.WriteStartAssignment(feedsVariableName)
      luaSerializer.Serialize(Writer, feeds)
```

```
        Writer.WriteEndAssignment()
      End Using
    End If
  End Sub
```

LuaWriter ensures that all strings written to the Saved Variables file are valid Lua strings so that Feed Reader will be able to show them inside *World of Warcraft*.

Sneaking in data updates by monitoring the Saved Variables file

When *World of Warcraft* first loads, it pulls data directly from the Saved Variables file, in our case *FeedReader.lua*, to initialize the FEED_READER_FEEDS variable.

During the course of a game when a player's character switches zones, the UI is reloaded, and rather than reading data from the *FeedReader.lua* Saved Variable files, *Warcraft* overwrites whatever data is stored in that file. This means that after the initial first load, any updates that Feed Grabber (or any application, for that matter) makes to Saved Variables files are lost!

The good news is that it takes *Warcraft* a couple of seconds from the initial writing out of the Saved Variables data before it reads that data back in, and it's during those precious few seconds that we can sneak data into the game!

In order to do this, Feed Grabber will use a FileSystemWatcher object to monitor the Saved Variables file for changes so that it can detect when *World of Warcraft* is saving the variables as part of its process to reload the UI. When we detect this moment, we can sneak our new data in the game.

The first thing we'll do is initialize the FileSystemWatcher object in the Initialize FileSystemWatcher method to listen to changed or deleted events for our Saved Variables file, *FeedReader.lua*, as shown in Examples 3-28 and 3-29.

C# Example 3-28. *InitializeFileSystemWatcher method in C#*

```csharp
private void InitializeFileSystemWatcher()
{
  FileSystemWatcher watcher = new FileSystemWatcher(
    Path.GetDirectoryName(savedVariablesPath), Path.GetFileName(savedVariablesPath));
  watcher.NotifyFilter = NotifyFilters.LastAccess | NotifyFilters.LastWrite |
    NotifyFilters.FileName;
  watcher.Changed += OnFileChangedOrDeleted;
  watcher.Deleted += OnFileChangedOrDeleted;
  watcher.EnableRaisingEvents = true;
}
```

```vb
Private Sub InitializeFileSystemWatcher()
    fileSystemWatcher = New FileSystemWatcher(Path.GetDirectoryName( _
        savedVariablesPath), Path.GetFileName(savedVariablesPath))
    fileSystemWatcher.NotifyFilter = NotifyFilters.LastAccess Or _
        NotifyFilters.LastWrite Or NotifyFilters.FileName
    AddHandler fileSystemWatcher.Changed, AddressOf OnFileChangedOrDeleted
    AddHandler fileSystemWatcher.Deleted, AddressOf OnFileChangedOrDeleted
    fileSystemWatcher.EnableRaisingEvents = True
End Sub
```

Now when the Saved Variables file is changed or deleted, the `OnFileChangedOr Deleted` method will fire. The first thing we do in our method is turn off the `Enable RaisingEvents` property. We need to do this because our method changes the file, and that file change would call the method again and we would be in a recursive loop.

Next, we attempt to save new data to replace the old values in *FeedReader.lua* every five milliseconds in a loop (Examples 3-30 and 3-31). Once the data is written, our loop exits, we turn the `EnableRaisingEvents` property back on, and our addon will now load *Warcraft* with updated RSS feeds!

```csharp
private void OnFileChangedOrDeleted(object sender, FileSystemEventArgs e)
{
    // Suspend change events
    fileSystemWatcher.EnableRaisingEvents = false;

    bool success = false;

    do
    {
        try
        {
            this.SaveFeeds();
            success = true;
        }
        catch (IOException) { Thread.Sleep(5); }
    } while (!success);

    // Resume change events
    fileSystemWatcher.EnableRaisingEvents = true;
}
```

```vb
Private Sub OnFileChangedOrDeleted(ByVal sender As Object, _
  ByVal e As FileSystemEventArgs)

  ' Suspend change events
  fileSystemWatcher.EnableRaisingEvents = False
  Debug.WriteLine("inside FileChanged, time: " & DateTime.Now.TimeOfDay.ToString())
  Dim success As Boolean = False
  Do
    Try
      Me.SaveFeeds()
      success = True
    Catch e1 As IOException
      Thread.Sleep(5)
    End Try
  Loop While Not success
  ' Resume change events
  fileSystemWatcher.EnableRaisingEvents = True
End Sub
```

Final Thoughts

Although this chapter isn't a comprehensive overview of everything you'll need to build your own addons, we hope you have the basics down for how all of the pieces of an addon work together. For more in-depth information on building *Warcraft* addons, we suggest *World of Warcraft Programming* by Wiley Publishing. For free, online reference information on *Warcraft*'s API, *http://www.wowprogramming.com* and *http://www.wowwiki.com* are invaluable resources for getting started. Also, remember that you can open any third-party addon and see for yourself how the code works. Looking at the source code for well-established addons is a great way to learn best practices in addon development.

Although there is certainly a learning curve to understand how to build addons for *World of Warcraft*, the ability to read data in and out of the game can bring about an entirely new class of applications to your gaming experience. Imagine being able to read and write email in game, or synchronizing opponent statistics from Wowarmory.com, or checking your guild's raiding calendar directly in game, or better yet, text messaging your friends when you're online and playing so that they can join you. It's all possible, and it's a lot easier than you might think.

Section 2

Software and Web

AUTHOR	Dan Fernandez
DIFFICULTY	Advanced
TIME REQUIRED	20+ hours
COST	Free
SOFTWARE	Visual C# 2008 Express Edition with Service Pack 1, Visual Basic 2008 Express Edition with Service Pack 1, iTunes version 7.0 or higher
HARDWARE	Optional iPod, iPhone, or Zune device for syncing
DOWNLOAD	*http://www.codeplex.com/InnerTube/* and *http://www.c4fbook.com/InnerTube*

OK, I'll admit it. I love YouTube. It's the only site on the Web where you can be endlessly entertained with everything from classic movie clips from *Pulp Fiction* or *The Big Lebowski* to Internet celebrities like Tron Guy, Kimbo Slice, or Tay Zonday (aka Mr. Chocolate Rain).

In short, YouTube has it all, except for portability, as you can watch YouTube videos only if you have an Internet connection. The goal of InnerTube is to work around that pesky limitation by enabling you to download videos automatically from YouTube, convert them to a more user-friendly file format, and even synchronize your downloaded videos with an iPod or Zune device.

Overview

To see InnerTube in action, let's take a quick tour of some of its key features.

InnerTube's Main UI

As you can see in Figure 4-1, InnerTube's main UI uses a three-pane design similar to Outlook, with the left pane holding the list of video feeds, the center pane listing the videos from the selected feed, and the rightmost pane showing a detailed view of the selected video.

Figure 4-1. *A screenshot of InnerTube*

Running InnerTube for the First Time

When InnerTube first runs, it detects if you have iTunes and/or the Zune client software installed and automatically suggests where your downloaded videos will be stored. If iTunes and Zune are not detected, the option to sync to them will be disabled (see Figure 4-2).

Figure 4-2. *InnerTube configuring itself for your PC*

Adding Videos

Clicking Add Videos from the main menu enables you to easily add different types of YouTube feeds (see Figure 4-3). When you add a feed you can also set properties, such as which user's favorites to download or a time interval for the Top Rated Over Time videos.

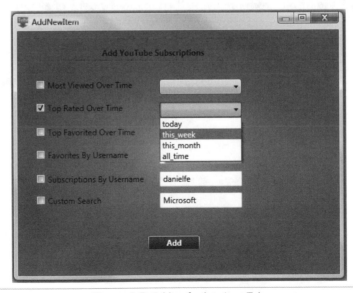

Figure 4-3. *Adding feeds to InnerTube*

How InnerTube Works

Now that we've seen what InnerTube does, we'll go through the key parts of how InnerTube is built, including the following:

- How YouTube's API works

- InnerTube's classes for videos and feeds

- Converting XML from YouTube's API into InnerTube objects

- How to download videos from YouTube

- How to convert the media format for YouTube videos

- A quick overview of how InnerTube's background processing works

- How to sync to iTunes and Zune

- Building the InnerTube application

- Building the InnerTube WPF user interface

How YouTube's API Works

YouTube's API is a REST service that uses Google's Gdata format to enable you to perform operations such as searching for and retrieving information about videos as well as uploading videos to YouTube.

Unlike other services, such as those from Live.com or Amazon.com, you do not need to sign up for a developer account or an API key to read data from YouTube's API. Figure 4-4 shows the results from retrieving the top rated videos of all time on YouTube using Firefox.

 NOTE For full documentation on what services are available from YouTube, go to *http://code.google.com/apis/youtube/developers_guide_protocol.html*.

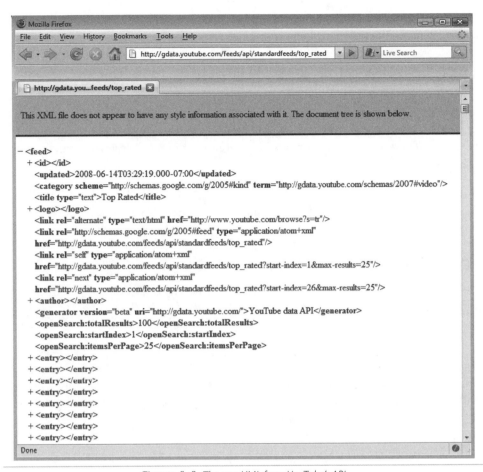

Figure 4-4. *The raw XML from YouTube's API*

Standard YouTube Feeds

If you look closely at the URL in Figure 4-4's image, you'll notice that the Top Rated video feed is a "Standard Feed." YouTube defines a number of standard feeds, including:

- Top Rated: *http://gdata.youtube.com/feeds/api/standardfeeds/top_rated*
- Top Favorited: *http://gdata.youtube.com/feeds/api/standardfeeds/top_favorites*
- Most Viewed: *http://gdata.youtube.com/feeds/api/standardfeeds/most_viewed*

You can further restrict the results from standard feeds by appending a `time` parameter to the query string. For example, this parameter will only retrieve the most viewed videos this week:

```
http://gdata.youtube.com/feeds/api/standardfeeds/most_viewed?time=this_week
```

The `time` parameter can have the following values: today, this_week, this_month, and all_time. The default value is all_time if no parameter is provided.

User-Specific YouTube Feeds

By default, YouTube makes user data (such as your favorite videos or video subscriptions) public and available via its API. To get a user's favorites or subscriptions, just replace the *username* in the following URLs with a valid YouTube username. Unlike the generic YouTube feeds, you cannot add a time parameter to filter user-specific feeds by a time interval.

- Favorites by user: *http://gdata.youtube.com/feeds/api/users/username/favorites*
- Subscriptions by user: *http://gdata.youtube.com/feeds/api/users/username/subscriptions*

YouTube Search

YouTube also provides a search API that can be called by appending vq=*searchterm*. For example, the search URL here will search YouTube for all Microsoft videos:

```
http://gdata.youtube.com/feeds/api/videos?vq=Microsoft
```

Optional Query String Parameters

InnerTube's YouTube wrapper provides a simple implementation for its search, but the YouTube API adds additional search features, such as paging or ordering by appending query string values. The following is a sampling of query string parameters:

orderby
Specify how you want videos sorted—say, by relevance, rating, published date, or number of views. By default, this is set to relevance.

max-results
Specify the maximum number of results. By default, this is set to 25.

start-index
Enable paging through data by setting the start-index to the point from which you want the result set to start. If you set the start-index to 100, the API would retrieve the 100–125th search results. By default, this is set to 0.

 NOTE For a full list of parameters and options, see the YouTube Query Parameter Definitions at *http://code.google.com/apis/youtube/reference.html#Query_parameter_definitions*.

Other Important YouTube URLs

YouTube uses a number of other, well-defined URLs that we'll need to know for the purposes of building our application. Here are quick explanations for each:

Watch

This is the link you commonly see when linking to a video: *http://www.youtube .com/watch?v=VideoID*

Embed

This is the link used for embedding a video on another site, such as MySpace: *http://www.youtube.com/v/VideoID*

Thumbnail

This is the link to the largest image thumbnail available for a video (425×344): *http://img.youtube.com/vi/VideoID/0.jpg*

Download

This is the (hidden) link that we'll use to download a video: *http://www.youtube .com/get_video?video_id=VideoID&t=sessiontoken*

 The Download link to download a video will work only if you append a valid, time-based session token. This is done to try to prevent end users from downloading YouTube videos directly. We'll show how you can work around this restriction in the "Downloading Videos from YouTube" section, later in this chapter.

Building Classes for YouTube Feeds and Videos

Now that you've seen how the YouTube API works, we will show how you can represent the data types from the YouTube API as .NET classes (see Figure 4-5).

InnerTubeTime

This is an enumeration that represents the possible time parameter values we can pass in to YouTube. We'll use this in the InnerTubeService class as an optional parameter to pass into YouTube's API.

InnerTubeFeed

This class represents a specific video feed, such as the Top Rated videos. The Feed Name is a user-friendly name describing the feed, and the URL points to a YouTube API like the ones listed earlier.

InnerTubeVideo

This class represents a single YouTube video and includes most of the fields we get from YouTube (author, comments, categories), as well as a set of download properties that point to the location indicating where that video is stored on disk (once we download it).

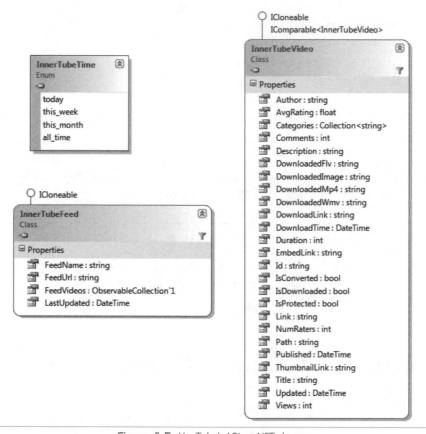

Figure 4-5. *YouTube's API as .NET classes*

Strings or Uri Classes?

You may have noticed that the **InnerTubeVideo** class uses **strings** rather than the **Uri** class to store URLs. In general, using the **Uri** class is the preferred mechanism for storing URLs, but InnerTube needs to serialize (save) its classes to your hard drive using the **Xml Serializer** class. Unfortunately, the **Uri** class is not serializable and will throw an exception if you attempt to serialize a **Uri** class, because **Uri** does not provide a parameter-less constructor class.

Calling the InnerTubeService Class

Now that we have our classes designed, let's show how we can convert the XML from Figure 4-4 into the objects represented in Figure 4-5. To do this, we'll use another class, our `InnerTubeService` class. As you can see in Figure 4-6, the common feeds—Top Rated, Most Viewed, etc.—from YouTube's API are all available as methods. The return type for all of the methods in `InnerTubeService` is an `ObservableCollection<InnerTubeVideo>`.

Figure 4-6. *IntelliSense showing the available methods for retrieving YouTube data*

Why Use ObservableCollection?

One thing to note here is that the collection data type for videos is an **Observable Collection**. The `ObservableCollection` is just like a `Collection` class, but it implements a couple of events, `CollectionChanged` and `PropertyChanged`, respectively, that enable it to easily update data bound data sources in WPF. We'll get into data binding in the "Dissecting MainWindow.xaml" section later in the chapter, but the point here is that we use this particular type because it will automatically update our UI elements when the collection changes, without us needing to rebind the data.

Converting YouTube XML into .NET Objects

The `InnerTubeService` class actually has only one real method that does the work of converting XML into objects, and that's the `ConvertYouTubeXmlIntoObjects` method. The reason for this is that each YouTube XML API call has an identical structure, whether it is for search results or top-rated videos, so we can use the same code to parse the XML but still maintain some "convenience" methods, such as `Search(string query)`, to make it easier to reuse the library.

As you can see in Examples 4-1 and 4-2, the ConvertYouTubeXmlToObjects method takes two parameters, the Uri for a valid YouTube API, and a Setting object, which we must pass in for configuring the directories on your PC that we will save video files (thumbnail, video, etc.). We will cover the Setting class in depth later, in the "Application Settings" section.

C# Example 4-1. *C# code for ConvertYouTubeXmlToObjects method signature*

```csharp
public static ObservableCollection<InnerTubeVideo> ConvertYouTubeXmlToObjects(
  Uri youTubeUrl, Setting setting)
```

VB Example 4-2. *Visual Basic code for ConvertYouTubeXmlToObjects method signature*

```vb
Public Shared Function ConvertYouTubeXmlToObjects(ByVal youtubeUrl As Uri, _
  ByVal setting As Setting) As ObservableCollection(Of InnerTubeVideo)
```

Inside the ConvertYouTubeXmlToObjects method, we declare a number of XNamespace variables, which are required because the XML we receive back from YouTube makes heavy use of XML namespaces (see Examples 4-3 and 4-4).

C# Example 4-3. *C# code to declare XML namespaces*

```csharp
XNamespace nsBase = @"http://www.w3.org/2005/Atom";
XNamespace nsGData = @"http://schemas.google.com/g/2005";
XNamespace nsYouTube = @"http://gdata.youtube.com/schemas/2007";
```

VB Example 4-4. *Visual Basic code to declare XML namespaces*

```vb
Dim nsBase As XNamespace = "http://www.w3.org/2005/Atom"
Dim nsGData As XNamespace = "http://schemas.google.com/g/2005"
Dim nsYouTube As XNamespace = "http://gdata.youtube.com/schemas/2007"
```

To get the actual data "over-the-wire," we'll call the YouTube service using the Web-Client class in the System.Net namespace by passing in the URL for the service and calling the OpenRead() method with YouTube's schema URL. This is equivalent to how we previously opened our browser to peruse the XML from Figure 4-5. We'll then use the XDocument class to load the XML with the XmlTextReader as shown in Examples 4-5 and 4-6.

C# Example 4-5. *C# code to make a web request to YouTube's API*

```csharp
//Use to call service
WebClient wc = new WebClient();

//Get Data
XmlTextReader xr = new XmlTextReader(wc.OpenRead(youTubeUrl));
XDocument rawData = XDocument.Load(xr);
```

```vb
'Use to call service
Dim wc As New WebClient()

'Get Data
Dim xr As New XmlTextReader(wc.OpenRead(youTubeUrl))
Dim rawData As XDocument = XDocument.Load(xr)
```

At this point, we have the raw XML results with a listing of videos in memory, with each <entry> element (a YouTube video) being an XElement object. Next, we want to use LINQ for XML to loop through every entry element and create a new InnerTube Video object, setting properties such as the video author, categories, title, and more, as shown in Examples 4-7 and 4-8.

In the first line of Examples 4-7 and 4-8, you'll notice that we pass in the nsBase + "entry" as a parameter to the Descendents method. This is required because the entry element is in the nsBase namespace, and without this namespace, your LINQ query would throw an exception saying the element attribute does not exist. Also note that we are not concatenating strings, but instead using the overloaded + operator for the XNamespace class. This is why the Visual Basic code uses the + operator instead of the concatenation operator (&).

C# Example 4-7. *C# code to loop through entry elements and assign properties*

```csharp
var query = from entry in rawData.Descendants(nsBase + "entry")
  select new InnerTubeVideo
  {
    Author = entry.Element(nsBase + "author").Element(nsBase + "name").Value,
    Categories = ParseCategories(entry.Elements(nsBase + "category")),
    Id = ParseID(entry.Element(nsBase + "id").Value),
    Published = DateTime.Parse(entry.Element(nsBase + "published").Value),
    Updated = DateTime.Parse(entry.Element(nsBase + "updated").Value),
    Title = entry.Element(nsBase + "title").Value,
    Description = entry.Element(nsBase + "content").Value,
    ...
```

VB Example 4-8. *Visual Basic code to loop through entry elements and assign properties*

```vb
Dim query = From entry In rawData.Descendants(nsBase + "entry") _
  Select New InnerTubeVideo With _
  { _
    .Author = entry.Element(nsBase + "author").Element(nsBase + "name").Value, _
    .Categories = ParseCategories(entry.Elements(nsBase + "category")), _
    .Id = ParseID(entry.Element(nsBase + "id").Value), _
    .Published = DateTime.Parse(entry.Element(nsBase + "published").Value), _
```

```
.Updated = DateTime.Parse(entry.Element(nsBase + "updated").Value), _
.Title = entry.Element(nsBase + "title").Value, _
.Description = entry.Element(nsBase + "content").Value, _
...
```

As mentioned previously, some fields that we want to retrieve are in different namespaces, so we have to, in code, swap out the namespace to read that field. To show exactly what this means, Example 4-9 contains the raw XML received from You-Tube's API for the total number of views for a video.

Example 4-9. *Snippet of XML for the total number of views for a YouTube video*

```
<yt:statistics viewCount="130534" favoriteCount="1210" />
```

Since the viewCount attribute lives in the <yt> (YouTube) XML namespace, we must explicitly add the nsYouTube namespace variable to get the value. In Examples 4-10 and 4-11, we start at the root entry element and get the statistics element, and then pull the viewCount attribute.

 Example 4-10. *C# code to parse the viewCount attribute from XML*

```
Views = int.Parse(entry.Element(nsYouTube +
        "statistics").Attribute("viewCount").Value),
```

 Example 4-11. *Visual Basic code to parse the viewCount attribute from XML*

```
.Views = Integer.Parse(entry.Element(nsYouTube + _
        "statistics").Attribute("viewCount").Value), _
```

To keep the parsing relatively compact, one nice thing you can do with LINQ for XML is pass in a chunk of XML to a function. For example, Johnny Lee's head-tracking video (*http://www.youtube.com/watch?v=cl1AwZN4ZYg*) includes 15 different YouTube video categories, like the listing in Example 4-12.

Example 4-12. *Snippet of XML for a YouTube video's categories*

```
<category scheme="…" term="wiimote" />
<category scheme="…" term="display" />
<category scheme="…" term="3D" />
<category scheme="…" term="reality" />
<category scheme="…" term="nintendo" />
...
```

What we want to do is convert the term attributes in the <category> elements from Example 4-12 into a nice Collection<string> variable, with each term stored as a string. To do this, we'll call ParseCategories, as shown in Examples 4-13 and 4-14.

 Example 4-13. *C# code to send XML to the ParseCategories method*

```
Categories = ParseCategories(entry.Elements(nsBase + "category")),
```

Example 4-14. *Visual Basic code to send XML to the ParseCategories method*

```
.Categories = ParseCategories(entry.Elements(nsBase + "category")), _
```

ParseCategories receives an IEnumerable<Xelement>, which will be formatted exactly like the <category> elements shown in Example 4-12. We can then use LINQ
to pull the value of the <term> attribute from each category and return it all as a
Collection<string> class, as shown in Examples 4-15 and 4-16.

C# Example 4-15. *C# code to parse the value of the term attributes*

```
private static Collection<string> ParseCategories(IEnumerable<XElement> Categories)
{
  var vals = from c in Categories.Attributes("term")
    select c.Value;
  return (Collection<string>)vals;
}
```

VB Example 4-16. *Visual Basic code to parse the value of the term attributes*

```
Private Shared Function ParseCategories(ByVal Categories As IEnumerable(Of XElement))
As Collection(Of String)
  Dim vals = From c In Categories.Attributes("term") _
  Select c.Value
  Return vals.ToCollection()
End Function
```

Examples 4-17 and 4-18 show the ConvertYouTubeXmlToObjects method in its
entirety.

C# Example 4-17. *C# code for the ConvertYouTubeXmlToObjects method*

```
public static ObservableCollection<InnerTubeVideo> ConvertYouTubeXmlToObjects(
  Uri youTubeUrl, Setting setting)
{
  XNamespace nsBase = @"http://www.w3.org/2005/Atom";
  XNamespace nsGData = @"http://schemas.google.com/g/2005";
  XNamespace nsYouTube = @"http://gdata.youtube.com/schemas/2007";

  //Use to call service
  WebClient wc = new WebClient();

  //Get Data
  XmlTextReader xr = new XmlTextReader(wc.OpenRead(youTubeUrl));
  XDocument rawData = XDocument.Load(xr);
  var query = from entry in rawData.Descendants(nsBase + "entry")
  select new InnerTubeVideo
  {
```

```
        Author = entry.Element(nsBase + "author").Element(nsBase + "name").Value,
        Categories = ParseCategories(entry.Elements(nsBase + "category")),
        Id = ParseID(entry.Element(nsBase + "id").Value),
        Published = DateTime.Parse(entry.Element(nsBase + "published").Value),
        Updated = DateTime.Parse(entry.Element(nsBase + "updated").Value),
        Title = entry.Element(nsBase + "title").Value,
        Description = entry.Element(nsBase + "content").Value,
        ThumbnailLink = _BaseThumbnailUrl + ParseID(entry.Element(nsBase + "id").Value) +
          @"/0.jpg",
        Link = _BasewatchUrl + ParseID(entry.Element(nsBase + "id").Value),
        EmbedLink = _baseEmbedUrl + ParseID(entry.Element(nsBase + "id").Value),
        DownloadLink = _BaseDownloadUrl + ParseID(entry.Element(nsBase + "id").Value),
        Views = int.Parse(entry.Element(nsYouTube +
                "statistics").Attribute("viewCount").Value),
        AvgRating = float.Parse(entry.Element(nsGData +
                  "rating").Attribute("average").Value),
        NumRaters = int.Parse(entry.Element(nsGData +
                  "rating").Attribute("numRaters").Value),

        //set download locations
        DownloadedImage = FileHelper.BuildFileName(setting.SubPath,
          ParseID(entry.Element(nsBase + "id").Value), FileType.Image),
        DownloadedFlv = FileHelper.BuildFileName(setting.SubPath,
          entry.Element(nsBase + "title").Value, FileType.Flv),
        DownloadedMp4 = FileHelper.BuildFileName(setting.VideoPath,
          entry.Element(nsBase + "title").Value, FileType.Mp4),
        DownloadedWmv = FileHelper.BuildFileName(setting.VideoPath,
          entry.Element(nsBase + "title").Value, FileType.Wmv)
    };

    return query.ToObservableCollection<InnerTubeVideo>();
}
```

Example 4-18. *Visual Basic code for the ConvertYouTubeXmlToObjects method*

```
Public Shared Function ConvertYouTubeXmlToObjects(ByVal youTubeUrl As Uri, _
  ByVal setting  As Setting) As ObservableCollection(Of InnerTubeVideo)

  Dim nsBase As XNamespace = "http://www.w3.org/2005/Atom"
  Dim nsGData As XNamespace = "http://schemas.google.com/g/2005"
  Dim nsYouTube As XNamespace = "http://gdata.youtube.com/schemas/2007"

  'Use to call service
  Dim wc As New WebClient()
```

```
'Get Data
Dim xr As New XmlTextReader(wc.OpenRead(youTubeUrl))
Dim rawData As XDocument = XDocument.Load(xr)
Dim query = From entry In rawData.Descendants(nsBase + "entry") _

Select New InnerTubeVideo With _
{ _
  .Author = entry.Element(nsBase + "author").Element(nsBase + "name").Value, _
  .Categories = ParseCategories(entry.Elements(nsBase + "category")), _
  .Id = ParseID(entry.Element(nsBase + "id").Value), _
  .Published = DateTime.Parse(entry.Element(nsBase + "published").Value), _
  .Updated = DateTime.Parse(entry.Element(nsBase + "updated").Value), _
  .Title = entry.Element(nsBase + "title").Value, _
  .Description = entry.Element(nsBase + "content").Value, _
  .ThumbnailLink = _BaseThumbnailUrl & ParseID(entry.Element(nsBase + _
    "id").Value)& "/0.jpg", _
  .Link = _BasewatchUrl & ParseID(entry.Element(nsBase + "id").Value), _
  .EmbedLink = _baseEmbedUrl & ParseID(entry.Element(nsBase + "id").Value), _
  .DownloadLink = _BaseDownloadUrl & ParseID(entry.Element(nsBase + "id").Value), _
  .Views = Integer.Parse(entry.Element(nsYouTube + _
    "statistics").Attribute("viewCount").Value), _
  .AvgRating = Single.Parse(entry.Element(nsGData + _
    "rating").Attribute("average").Value), _
  .NumRaters = Integer.Parse(entry.Element(nsGData + _
    "rating").Attribute("numRaters").Value), _
  .DownloadedImage = FileHelper.BuildFileName(setting.SubPath, _
    ParseID(entry.Element(nsBase + "id").Value), FileType.Image), _
  .DownloadedFlv = FileHelper.BuildFileName(setting.SubPath, _
    entry.Element(nsBase + "title").Value, FileType.Flv), _
  .DownloadedMp4 = FileHelper.BuildFileName(setting.VideoPath, _
    entry.Element(nsBase + "title").Value, FileType.Mp4), _
  .DownloadedWmv = FileHelper.BuildFileName(setting.VideoPath, _
    entry.Element(nsBase + "title").Value, FileType.Wmv) _
}

Return query.ToObservableCollection()


End Function
```

Now that we know how to retrieve information about YouTube videos, let's see how we can use this data to programmatically download a YouTube video.

Downloading Videos from YouTube

Now that we've seen how YouTube's API works, we'll now show how to download You-Tube videos, first manually with your browser and then programmatically with code.

Downloading a YouTube Video with Your Browser

YouTube videos are stored in the Flash video (FLV) format, which is what we'll want to download.

Before we show how you can programmatically download a YouTube video, let's look at how you can download a video just by using your browser. To begin with, open any YouTube video page—say, the infamous Tay Zonday "Chocolate Rain" video, which is at *http://www.youtube.com/watch?v=EwTZ2xpQwpA*. From this URL, we can determine that the video ID (v=) is "EwTZ2xpQwpA".

YouTube Blocks You (by Design)

YouTube has a (hidden) URL that you can use to directly download a video, but you need to pass in two things, a `video_id` and a *session token*. A session token is an identifier that YouTube assigns to a browser that lasts for approximately 15 minutes. If you don't have a valid session token, YouTube will block your request to download a Flash video.

To see this in action, open your browser, go to *http://www.youtube.com/get_video?video_id=EwTZ2xpQwpA*, and notice how YouTube pretends the URL is a bad URL by sending back an HTTP 404 Not Found error to Internet Explorer browsers (Firefox 3 users will see a blank page), as shown in Figure 4-7. You get a 404 error because you must append a valid session token to the URL for the request to work.

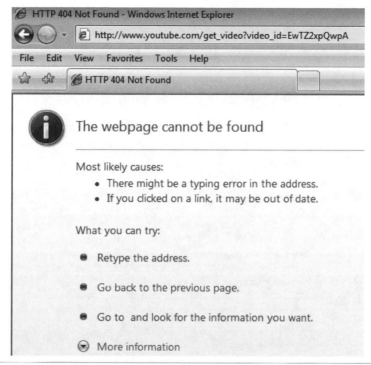

Figure 4-7. *YouTube will return a 404 error in Internet Explorer unless you provide a session token*

Getting a Session Token from JavaScript

To get a valid session token from YouTube, we will have to open a browser to the You-Tube page for "Chocolate Rain" at: *http://www.youtube.com/watch?v=EwTZ2xpQwpA* and click View Source to view the page's HTML contents. In the HTML, you'll find a JavaScript variable named swfArgs that YouTube uses to pass in a number of parameters to the Flash player as shown in Example 4-19.

Example 4-19. *The swfArgs Javascript variable needed to play a YouTube video*

```
var swfArgs = {"usef": 0, "cust_p": "jMWn75PwKgutJQOJ3mrLbA", "iv_storage_
server": "http://www.google.com/reviews/y/", "ad_module": "http://s.ytimg.com/yt/
swf/ad-vfl59966.swf", "ad_channel_code": "invideo_overlay_480x70_cat10,afv_overlay",
"video_id": "EwTZ2xpQwpA", "l": 292, "fmt_map": "34/0/9/0/115", "ad_host":
"ca-host-pub-5311789755034317", "sk": "_N53QD2GOB79IwT2MIi7nNSvpkgWSWWwC",
"invideo": true, "t": "OEgsToPDskJUt8xv3hrKiGOAYlLYcl1L", "hl": "en", "plid":
"AARaIAIC2yUqgjl1AAAA-YT8YQA", "vq": null, "iv_module": "http://s.ytimg.com/yt/swf/
iv_module-vfl57703.swf", "afv": true, "ad_host_tier": "12789", "ad_video_pub_id":
"ca-pub-6219811747049371", "tk": "5Eu9v6C5n2lxivxOtoUqRqTOyNnUmUCs3oR7ZzuDg8_
JZHd6DyO2jw=="};
```

Houston, We Have a Token!

Buried deep inside the swfArgs variable, is the name/value pair "t": "OEgsTo PDskJUt8xv3hrKiGOAYlLYcl1L", which represents a valid session token that can be used to download the video. Now try the *same* download URL for which YouTube previously returned a 404 error, except this time we'll append the "t" session token value as shown below:

http://www.youtube.com/get_video?video_id=EwTZ2xpQwpA&t=OEgsToPDskJUt8 xv3hrKiGOAYlLYcl1L

>
>
> The exact download URL will not work because, by the time you read this, the session token (t= part) would have expired. If you want to try this in your browser, you will first have to navigate to a YouTube video page, click view source in your browser and manually copy/paste the session token into the download URL. If you try to use a session token after the session has expired, you will receive a HTTP 410 Gone Error saying the page does not exist. Session tokens are also unique to a video such that you cannot use the same session token to download a different video.

You should now be prompted to save the 11.3 MB FLV file to your hard drive as shown in Figure 4-8. Let's now see how we can do the same thing using code.

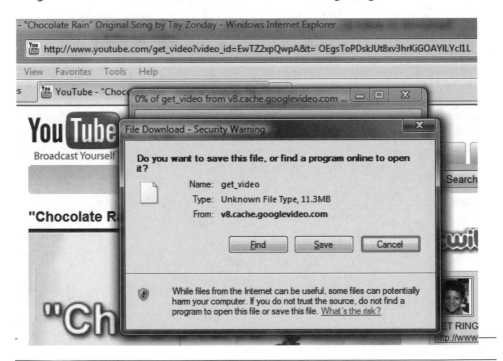

Figure 4-8. *Prompt to save a YouTube video to your PC*

Getting a Token Programmatically

Now that we've shown how you can do it in a browser, we want to replicate the process of getting a token in code by reading the HTML from the video page, pulling the swfArgs Javascript parameter, and then calling the download link with a valid session token.

> **NOTE** HTML parsing like this is brittle and subject to breaking when YouTube changes the way they do session tokens or if they rename their Javascript variables. Given that there is no API to download videos, developers building applications that depend on HTML internals of a website need to continually test and make sure a change to the site doesn't cause an application to break.

To do this in code, we've created a method in the Download class called CreateToken-Request. When given an InnerTubeVideo, it makes a WebClient request to download the video page HTML as a string. It then parses out the swfArgs Javascript variable and retrieves the "t:" argument, just like we did manually with the browser.

The code in Examples 4-20 and 4-21 retrieves the HTML from the web page using the WebClientDownloadStringmethod passing in the Link (the URL for the YouTube video). Next, it gets the index of the swfArgs variable (see Example 4-19) in the HTML string. Once we find the location of swfArgs, we can retrieve the variable's value by finding the index of the bracket characters "{" and "}" which contain the value. Once we get the index of both of those characters, we then use the SubString method to retrieve the value in between the brackets and load that into the variable fullString.

C# Example 4-20. *C# code to programmatically get a session token*

```csharp
private static string CreateTokenRequest(InnerTubeVideo video)
{
  //YouTube variables
  const string jsVariable = "swfArgs";
  const string argName = "t";

  //get raw html from YouTube video page
  string rawHtml;
  using (WebClient wc = new WebClient())
  {
    rawHtml = wc.DownloadString(video.Link);
  }

  //extract the Javascript name/value pairs
```

```
int jsIndex = rawHtml.IndexOf(jsVariable);
int startIndex = rawHtml.IndexOf("{", jsIndex);
int endIndex = rawHtml.IndexOf("}", startIndex);
string fullString = rawHtml.Substring(startIndex + 1, endIndex - startIndex - 1);

//remove all quotes (")
fullString = fullString.Replace("\"", "");

//split all values
string[] allArgs = fullString.Split(',');

//loop through javascript parameters
foreach (string swfArg in allArgs)
{
  if (swfArg.Trim().StartsWith(argName))
  {
    var nameValuePair = swfArg.Split(':');
    return string.Format("{0}={1}", argName, nameValuePair[1].Trim());
  }
}
throw new Exception(string.Format("token not found in swfArgs," +
  " make sure {0} is accessible", video.Link));
}
```

VB Example 4-21. *Visual Basic code to programmatically get a session token*

```
Private Shared Function CreateTokenRequest(ByVal video As InnerTubeVideo) As String
  'YouTube variables
  Const jsVariable As String = "swfArgs"
  Const argName As String = "t"

  'get raw html from YouTube video page
  Dim rawHtml As String
  Using wc As New WebClient()
    rawHtml = wc.DownloadString(video.Link)
  End Using

  'extract the JavaScript name/value pairs
  Dim jsIndex As Integer = rawHtml.IndexOf(jsVariable)
  Dim startIndex As Integer = rawHtml.IndexOf("{", jsIndex)
  Dim endIndex As Integer = rawHtml.IndexOf("}", startIndex)
  Dim fullString As String = rawHtml.Substring(startIndex + 1, _
    endIndex - startIndex - 1)

  'remove all quotes (")
```

```
    fullString = fullString.Replace("""", "")

    'split all values
    Dim allArgs() As String = fullString.Split(","c)

    'loop through javascript parameters
    For Each swfArg As String In allArgs
      If swfArg.Trim().StartsWith(argName) Then
        Dim nameValuePair = swfArg.Split(":"c)
        Return String.Format("{0}={1}", argName, nameValuePair(1).Trim())
      End If
    Next swfArg
    Throw New Exception(String.Format("token not found in swfArgs, " & _
      "make sure {0} is accessible", video.Link))
End Function
```

Once the `fullString` variable holds the value of `swfArgs`, we'll need to do a little bit more work to parse the session token. To do that, we'll remove quotes from the string and split the contents of the variable (each argument is comma delimited). Finally, we'll loop through each argument looking for the `"t"` argument (the session token). Once found, we return a string in the format `"Name=Value"`, which, for this video, would return the following:

```
t=OEgsToPDskJUt8xv3hrKiGOAYlLYcl1L
```

Downloading the Video

Now that we've solved how to get the session token programmatically, we now need to download the file to our hard drive. To do this, we will use the `DownloadVideo` method of the `Download` class which is included in its entirety below in Examples 4-22 and 4-23.

The first thing our code does is make sure we haven't downloaded the Flash video (FLV) before by checking if the file already exists.

Next, we build the download URL which, like in our browser example, is a combination of the download URL, the video ID, and the session token that we get from calling the `CreateTokenRequest` from above.

We open a request to the file stream of the YouTube Flash video file on YouTube's server using the download URL we previously built. At the same time, we also create a FileStream on our hard drive that we'll use to save the video file. The code will read 65K of data from the web stream of the video and write those bytes directly to the hard drive file stream. The code continues looping, reading 65K from the Web and writing it to the hard drive until we reach the end of the file, at which point calling ReadBytes from the web stream will return 0 and we exit the loop.

> **NOTE** Both the WebStream and the FileStream are wrapped in using statements that automatically handle the proper disposal of these resources in an automatically generated try/finally block. We do this to ensure that even if an exception is thrown, we will still clean up system resources properly.

C# Example 4-22. *C# code for the DownloadVideo method*

```csharp
public static void DownloadVideo(InnerTubeVideo source, string destination)
{
  if (!File.Exists(destination))
  {
    UriBuilder final = new UriBuilder(source.DownloadLink);
    final.Query = "video_id=" + source.Id + "&" + CreateTokenRequest(source);

    WebRequest request = WebRequest.Create(final.ToString());
    request.Timeout = 500000;

    try
    {
      WebResponse response = request.GetResponse();

      using (Stream webStream = response.GetResponseStream())
      {
        try
        {
          int _bufferSize = 65536;

          using (FileStream fs = File.Create(destination, _bufferSize))
          {
            int readBytes = -1;
            byte[] inBuffer = new byte[_bufferSize];

            //Loop until we hit the end
            while (readBytes != 0)
```

```
        {
          //read data from web into filebuffer, then write to file
          readBytes = webStream.Read(inBuffer, 0, _bufferSize);
          fs.Write(inBuffer, 0, readBytes);
        }
      }
    }
    catch (Exception ex)
    {
      Debug.WriteLine("Error in Buffer Download");
      Debug.Indent();
      Debug.WriteLine(ex.Message);
    }
  }
}
catch (Exception ex)
{
  Debug.WriteLine("Error in request.GetResponse()");
  Debug.Indent();
  Debug.WriteLine(ex.Message);
}
    }
  }
}
```

VB Example 4-23. *Visual Basic code for the DownloadVideo method*

```vb
Public Shared Sub DownloadVideo(ByVal source As InnerTubeVideo, ByVal destination As
String)
  If (Not File.Exists(destination)) Then
    Dim final As New UriBuilder(source.DownloadLink)
    final.Query = "video_id=" & source.Id & "&" & CreateTokenRequest(source)

    Dim request As WebRequest = WebRequest.Create(final.ToString())
    request.Timeout = 500000

    Try
      Dim response As WebResponse = request.GetResponse()

      Using webStream As Stream = response.GetResponseStream()
        Try
          Dim _bufferSize As Integer = 65536

          Using fs As FileStream = File.Create(destination, _bufferSize)
            Dim readBytes As Integer = -1
            Dim inBuffer(_bufferSize - 1) As Byte
```

```
                    'Loop until we hit the end
                    Do While readBytes <> 0
                      'read data from web into filebuffer, then write to file
                      readBytes = webStream.Read(inBuffer, 0, _bufferSize)
                      fs.Write(inBuffer, 0, readBytes)
                    Loop
                  End Using
                  Catch ex As Exception
                    Debug.WriteLine("Error in Buffer Download")
                    Debug.Indent()
                    Debug.WriteLine(ex.Message)
                End Try
              End Using
          Catch ex As Exception
            Debug.WriteLine("Error in request.GetResponse()")
            Debug.Indent()
            Debug.WriteLine(ex.Message)
          End Try
      End If
  End Sub
```

Downloading a Video's Thumbnail Image

In addition to downloading a YouTube video, InnerTube also downloads the large thumbnail image, sized 425 pixels x 344 pixels, to use as the preview image before a video starts playing. The format of the large image thumbnail URL is *http://img.you tube.com/vi/VideoID/0.jpg.*

The code to download the image (Examples 4-24 and 4-25) simply checks whether the file has already been downloaded, and if it hasn't, calls the DownloadFile method, passing in the location for the source file to download and the destination *filename.*

C# Example 4-24. *C# code to download a video's thumbnail image*

```csharp
public static void DownloadImage(InnerTubeVideo source, string destination)
{
    //if we haven't downloaded the image yet, download it
    if (!File.Exists(destination))
    {
        using (WebClient wc = new WebClient())
        {
            wc.DownloadFile(new Uri(source.ThumbnailLink), destination);
        }
    }
}
```

```
Public Shared Sub DownloadImage(ByVal source As InnerTubeVideo, ByVal destination As
String)
  'if we haven't downloaded the image yet, download it
  If (Not File.Exists(destination)) Then
    Using wc As New WebClient()
      wc.DownloadFile(New Uri(source.ThumbnailLink), destination)
    End Using
  End If
End Sub
```

WebRequest Class Versus WebClient Class

As you may have noticed in the earlier examples, we use the **WebRequest** class to download a video and the **WebClient** class to download an image thumbnail. In comparing the code between the two mechanisms, it should be clear that the **WebClient** class is easier to use than the more complex stream and byte array manipulation we're doing with the **WebRequest** class. The truth is that an earlier version of InnerTube originally did use the **WebClient** class for the **DownloadVideo** method, but the problem was that while downloading videos, the **WebClient** class would intermittently throw **WebExceptions** saying that the underlying request had timed out. As the **WebClient** class does not provide a way to set a request timeout, the solution was to use the **WebRequest** class and set a lengthy **Timeout** property (50K milliseconds or 8.3 minutes) to avoid the intermittent timeout errors.

Converting YouTube Videos Using ffmpeg

We now have the video on our hard drive in the Flash (FLV) format, and although we could build a simple HTML page to embed the Flash videos to watch them locally, what we really want to do is convert the video from FLV format to WMV (Zune) or MP4 (iTunes) format. To do that, we'll use an open source tool called *ffmpeg*, which is a C++ library and command-line tool for converting, resizing, or resampling media from one format to another, with more than 50 formats supported.

In its simplest form, you can call *ffmpeg.exe* by passing in two command-line arguments, the source file that you want to convert and the name of the new file you want it converted to. For example, we can convert a Flash video file named *source.flv* into an MP4 (MPEG-4) format file named *destination.mp4* using the command shown in Example 4-26.

Example 4-26. *Converting a flash video to the MP4 video format*

```
ffmpeg.exe -i "source.flv" "destination.mp4"
```

To convert the *source.flv* file into a *.wmv* (Windows Media Video) file, add the −vcodec wmv2 command-line arguments, as shown in Example 4-27.

Example 4-27. *Converting a flash video to the WMV video format*

```
ffmpeg.exe -i "source.flv" -vcodec wmv2 "destination.wmv"
```

You can even add metadata—such as the author, title, and comment—to the newly converted video by setting additional *ffmpeg.exe* command-line arguments, as shown in Example 4-28.

Example 4-28. *Setting metadata when converting a video*

```
ffmpeg.exe -title "My Video Title" -author "Dan" -comment "best video ever" -i
"source.flv" -vcodec wmv2 "destination.wmv"
```

To call *ffmpeg.exe* programmatically, first we'll build a ConversionType enum to state the possible types of conversion our application allows (see Examples 4-29 and 4-30).

C# **Example 4-29.** *C# code for the ConversionType enum*

```csharp
public enum ConversionType
{
    Mp4,
    Wmv
}
```

VB **Example 4-30.** *Visual Basic code for the ConversionType enum*

```vb
Public Enum ConversionType
    Mp4
    Wmv
End Enum
```

We want to programmatically call the *ffmpeg.exe* console application from code using the System.Diagnostics.Process class. The call to *ffmpeg* is wrapped in the VideoConverter class, which has one method, ConvertFlv, with multiple overloads. The ConvertFlv method overload we'll want to use accepts an InnerTubeVideo and a ConversionType enum (MP4 or WMV). We use this overload because we'll use the video's title, author, and description to set the video's metadata, as described in Example 4-28. Since these fields might contain illegal characters, in which case *ffmpeg.exe* would not work, we will use the ReplaceIllegalCharacters method to clean them up.

As you can see in Exampled 4-31 and 4-32, we are building the command-line arguments to pass into *ffmpeg.exe* based on the type of conversion we are doing (MP4 or WMV).

C# Example 4-3 I. *C# code for setting ffmpeg parameters*

```csharp
public static void ConvertFlv(InnerTubeVideo source, ConversionType conversion)
{
  string title = FileHelper.ReplaceIllegalCharacters(source.Title);
  string author = FileHelper.ReplaceIllegalCharacters(source.Author);
  string description = FileHelper.ReplaceIllegalCharacters(source.Description);

  //set values based on switch
  string cmdLineArgs = String.Empty;
  string destination = String.Empty;

  switch (conversion)
  {
    case ConversionType.Mp4:
    //ffmpeg.exe -title "Chocolate Rain" -author "TayZonday" -comment "Original
    //Song by Tay Zonday" -i "Chocolate Rain.flv" "Chocolate Rain.mp4"
      destination = source.DownloadedMp4;
      cmdLineArgs = String.Format(" -title \"{0}\" -author \"{1}\" -comment \"{2}\"
        -i \"{3}\" \"{4}\"",title, author, description, source.DownloadedFlv,
        destination);
    break;
    case ConversionType.Wmv:
    //ffmpeg.exe -title "Chocolate Rain" -author "TayZonday" -comment "Original
    //Song by Tay Zonday" -i "Chocolate Rain.flv" -vcodec wmv2 "Chocolate Rain.wmv"
      destination = source.DownloadedWmv;
      cmdLineArgs = String.Format(" -title \"{0}\" -author \"{1}\" -comment \"{2}\"
      -i \"{3}\" -vcodec wmv2 \"{4}\"", title, author, description,
      source.DownloadedFlv, destination);
    break;
  }
  ConvertFlv(source.DownloadedFlv, destination, cmdLineArgs);
}
```

VB Example 4-32. *Visual Basic code for setting ffmpeg parameters*

```vb
Public Shared Sub ConvertFlv(ByVal source As InnerTubeVideo, ByVal conversion _
  As ConversionType)
  Dim title As String = FileHelper.ReplaceIllegalCharacters(source.Title)
  Dim author As String = FileHelper.ReplaceIllegalCharacters(source.Author)
  Dim description As String = FileHelper.ReplaceIllegalCharacters(source.Description)

  'set values based on switch
```

```
    Dim cmdLineArgs As String = String.Empty
    Dim destination As String = String.Empty
    Select Case conversion
      Case ConversionType.Mp4
        'ffmpeg.exe -title "Chocolate Rain" -author "TayZonday" -comment "Original Song
        'by Tay Zonday" -i "Chocolate Rain.flv" "Chocolate Rain.mp4"
        destination = source.DownloadedMp4
        cmdLineArgs = String.Format(" -title ""{0}"" -author ""{1}"" " & _
          "-comment ""{2}"" -i ""{3}"" ""{4}""", title, author, _
          description, source.DownloadedFlv, destination)
      Case ConversionType.Wmv
        'ffmpeg.exe -title "Chocolate Rain" -author "TayZonday" -comment "Original Song
        'by Tay Zonday" -i "Chocolate Rain.flv" -vcodec wmv2 "Chocolate Rain.wmv"
        destination = source.DownloadedWmv
        cmdLineArgs = String.Format(" -title ""{0}"" -author ""{1}"" -comment " & _
          " ""{2}"" -i ""{3}"" -vcodec wmv2 ""{4}""", title, author, description, _
          source.DownloadedFlv, destination)
    End Select
    ConvertFlv(source.DownloadedFlv, destination, cmdLineArgs)
  End Sub
```

As you may have noticed in Examples 4-31 and 4-32, the last line of code calls another overload for the ConvertFlv method, which actually calls *ffmpeg* from the command line, which we'll discuss next.

In Examples 4-33 and 4-34, the ConvertFlv method code includes the location of the *ffmpeg.exe* executable. The file itself is distributed in the *SharedUtilities* directory in an *ffmpeg* folder, so we can call Environment.CurrentDirectory to point to the executable and store the path into the exePath variable.

We'll also make sure that we have the source file and don't have the destination file. Assuming we have everything to run, we create a process and set some properties, such as the command-line arguments, the location of the *.exe* file, and other properties that will keep the console window from appearing while we convert a file. To get everything running, you call the Start method of the convert class. Since *ffmpeg. exe* will automatically close when it is finished converting a file, we'll use the Wait ForExit() method, which means that the ConvertFlv method will not return until the conversion is complete.

C#   Example 4-33. *C# code to create a process and call ffmpeg.exe*

```
    private static void ConvertFlv(string sourceFile, string destination,
      string cmdLineArgs)
    {
      //point to ffmpeg conversion tool
      string exePath = Path.Combine(Environment.CurrentDirectory, @"ffmpeg\ffmpeg.exe");
```

```
      //ensure sourceFile files exist and the destination doesn't
      if (File.Exists(sourceFile) && File.Exists(exePath) && !File.Exists(destination))
      {
        //Start a Process externally as we're converting from the command line
        using (Process convert = new Process())
        {
          //Set properties
          convert.StartInfo.WindowStyle = ProcessWindowStyle.Hidden;
          convert.StartInfo.CreateNoWindow = true;
          convert.StartInfo.RedirectStandardOutput = true;
          convert.StartInfo.UseShellExecute = false;
          convert.StartInfo.Arguments = cmdLineArgs;
          convert.StartInfo.FileName = exePath;
          convert.Start();
          convert.WaitForExit();
        }
      }
    }
```

VB Example 4-34. *Visual Basic code to create a process and call ffmpeg.exe*

```
    Private Shared Sub ConvertFlv(ByVal sourceFile As String, ByVal destination As _
      String, ByVal cmdLineArgs As String)
      'point to ffmpeg conversion tool
      Dim exePath As String = Path.Combine(Environment.CurrentDirectory, _
        "ffmpeg\ffmpeg.exe")

      'ensure sourceFile files exist and the destination doesn't
      If File.Exists(sourceFile) AndAlso File.Exists(exePath) AndAlso _
        (Not File.Exists(destination)) Then

        'Start a Process externally as we're converting from the command line
        Using convert As New Process()
          'Set properties
          convert.StartInfo.WindowStyle = ProcessWindowStyle.Hidden
          convert.StartInfo.CreateNoWindow = True
          convert.StartInfo.RedirectStandardOutput = True
          convert.StartInfo.UseShellExecute = False
          convert.StartInfo.Arguments = cmdLineArgs
          convert.StartInfo.FileName = exePath
          convert.Start()
```

```
        convert.WaitForExit()
    End Using
  End If
End Sub
```

Now that we have converted the Flash videos into MP4 and/or WMV files, let's show how you can sync them to iTunes or the Zune client software.

Syncing YouTube Videos to iTunes and Zune

iTunes and Zune provide different mechanisms for syncing videos, but we will build one interface that we can use for both videos, to keep a standard mechanism for syncing files (see Examples 4-35 and 4-36). This interface will sync files for a given device based on the file path.

C#   Example 4-35. *C# interface for syncing to iTunes and Zune*

```
interface IVideoService
{
  void Sync(string filePath);
}
```

VB   Example 4-36. *Visual Basic interface for syncing with iTunes and Zune*

```
Friend Interface IVideoService
  Sub Sync(ByVal filePath As String)
End Interface
```

Syncing Videos to iTunes

To sync YouTube videos to iTunes, we'll use the iTunes COM interop library. This library is automatically included when you install iTunes, and you can add it to your Visual Studio project by clicking in the Solution Explorer and selecting Add Reference…. Then, click the COM tab and select the iTunes 1.11 Type Library, which is a COM wrapper class that simplifies automating iTunes with .NET code.

As you can see in Examples 4-37 and 4-38, we import the iTunesLib namespace and create a private member named iTunes.

C#   Example 4-37. *C# class declaration for iTunes class*

```
using iTunesLib;
public class iTunesSync : IVideoService
{
  iTunesApp iTunes = new iTunesApp();
  …
```

VB Example 4-38. *Visual Basic class declaration for iTunes class*

```
Imports iTunesLib
Public Class iTunesSync
Implements IVideoService
  Private iTunes As New iTunesApp()

...
```

The next step is to implement the IVideoService Sync interface, as shown in Examples 4-39 and 4-40. To do this, we filter the list of files in the filePath variable to only those files with an MP4 file extension. Once we've filtered the list of videos, we then loop through each video and add it to the iTunes Library. When the Sync() method is called, iTunes will open (if it's not already open) and will begin adding videos to your library. As iTunes builds a thumbnail for each video, it may take 1–3 seconds for each video to be added to your library, depending on your machine's performance.

C# Example 4-39. *C# code for implementing the Sync interface*

```csharp
#region IVideoService Members
public void Sync(string filePath)
{
  //only get MP4 files
  string[] fileList = Directory.GetFiles(filePath, "*.mp4",
    SearchOption.TopDirectoryOnly);
  try
  {
    foreach (var f in fileList)
    {
      //Add file
      iTunes.LibraryPlaylist.AddFile(f);
    }
  }
  catch (Exception ex)
  {
    System.Diagnostics.Debug.WriteLine("iTunes error: " + ex.Message);
  }
  finally
  {
    this.iTunes = null;
  }
}
#endregion
```

```vb
#Region "IVideoService Members"
Public Sub Sync(ByVal filePath As String) Implements IVideoService.Sync
  'only get MP4 files
  Dim fileList() As String = Directory.GetFiles(filePath, "*.mp4", _
    SearchOption.TopDirectoryOnly)
  Try
    For Each f In fileList
      'Add file
      iTunes.LibraryPlaylist.AddFile(f)
    Next f
  Catch ex As Exception
    System.Diagnostics.Debug.WriteLine("iTunes error: " & ex.Message)
  Finally
    Me.iTunes = Nothing
  End Try
End Sub
#End Region
```

> **NOTE**
> The reason we filter the list of files instead of looping through all the files in
> the directory is that per the iTunes COM SDK, the **AddFile** method will fail
> if you add a file that is not supported by iTunes (for example, a Windows
> Media Video file). The SDK suggests using the iTunes **ConvertFile** meth-
> od, which will convert the file to a format iTunes understands. Although
> **ConvertFile** is one option for developers, ***ffmpeg.exe*** supports more file
> formats and has easy programmatic access.

We can, with one line of code, tell iTunes to update an iPod (if it's connected), as
shown in Examples 4-41 and 4-42. Finally, as this is COM and since the iTunesApp class
doesn't implement Dispose, make sure to clean up the memory by setting the variable
to null.

```csharp
public void UpdateIPod()
{
  iTunes.UpdateIPod();
}

~iTunesSync()
{
  if (this.iTunes != null)
  {
    //cleanup
```

```
        this.iTunes = null;
    }
}
```

 Example 4-42. *Visual Basic to update an iPod and cleanup memory*

```
Public Sub UpdateIPod()
  iTunes.UpdateIPod()
End Sub

Protected Overrides Sub Finalize()
If Me.iTunes IsNot Nothing Then
  'cleanup
  Me.iTunes = Nothing
End If

End Sub
```

Syncing Videos to Zune

The process for syncing videos to Zune is quite different than syncing videos to iTunes. Although the Zune team doesn't provide an API we can call programmatically, Zune does make it very easy to add files to its library by simply copying the files to directories that Zune monitors.

> **NOTE** Underneath the covers, Zune continuously runs a process called **Zune-Launcher.exe**. Conceptually, **ZuneLauncher** implements the same functionality that a .NET `FileSystemWatcher` class, as it monitors changes to a set of folders for audio and video files.

Zune monitored folders

To pull the list of folders that Zune is monitoring, we will need to go spelunking into the Windows registry. Specifically, we will need to open the *HKEY_CURRENT_USER\ Software\Microsoft\Zune\Groveler* registry key, as shown in Figure 4-9.

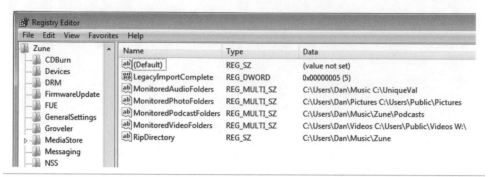

Figure 4-9. *Zune monitored folders are stored in the registry*

To do the same thing programmatically, we'll create an enum named ZuneMonitored
Folders that will represent each monitored folder registry key. We can then call Get
ZuneMonitoredFolders to get a string array of folders by calling the GetValue
method for the Groveler subkey using the Registry class, as shown in Examples 4-43
and 4-44.

C# Example 4-43. *C# code to programmatically extract Zune monitored folders from the registry*

```csharp
public enum ZuneMonitoredFolders
{
  MonitoredAudioFolders,
  MonitoredVideoFolders,
  MonitoredPhotoFolders,
  MonitoredPodcastFolders
}

public class ZuneSync : IVideoService
{
  public static string[] GetZuneMonitoredFolders(ZuneMonitoredFolders folder)
  {
    //Pull registry
    string hive = @"Software\Microsoft\Zune\Groveler\";
    string[] values =
      (string[])Registry.CurrentUser.OpenSubKey(hive).GetValue(folder.ToString());
    return values;
  }
  ...
```

VB Example 4-44. *Visual Basic code to programmatically extract Zune monitored folders from the registry*

```vb
Public Enum ZuneMonitoredFolders
  MonitoredAudioFolders
  MonitoredVideoFolders
```

```
      MonitoredPhotoFolders
      MonitoredPodcastFolders
   End Enum

   Public Class ZuneSync
      Implements IVideoService

      Public Shared Function GetZuneMonitoredFolders(ByVal folder As _
         ZuneMonitoredFolders) As String()
         'Pull registry
         Dim hive As String = "Software\Microsoft\Zune\Groveler\"
         Dim values() As String = _
         CType(My.Computer.Registry.CurrentUser.OpenSubKey(hive). _
            GetValue(folder.ToString()), String())

         Return values
      End Function
      ...
```

Like we did with the iTunes wrapper, we will implement the IVideoService.Sync interface for Zune, as shown in Examples 4-45 and 4-46. In the implementation of the Sync method, we first get the list of video folders that are being monitored. If the passed-in folder is already being monitored, then we are done because new videos being added will automatically show up in Zune. If it's not in the list of monitored folders, we're going to pick the first monitored folder, currentFolders[0], and similar to the iTunes code, we filter just those files with the *.wmv* extension and copy them to the first monitored folder.

C#   Example 4-45. *C# code for implementing the Sync interface*

```csharp
#region VideoService Members
public void Sync(string filePath)
{
  string[] currentFolders = ZuneSync.GetZuneMonitoredFolders(
    ZuneMonitoredFolders.MonitoredVideoFolders);
  bool found = currentFolders.Contains(filePath);
  //check if we are already added the files to the folder
  if (!found)
  {
    //copy the files to the first specified directory
    if (currentFolders.Length >0)
    {
      string destinationPath = currentFolders[0];
      string[] Files = Directory.GetFiles(filePath, "*.wmv",
        SearchOption.TopDirectoryOnly);
      foreach (var f in Files)
```

```
      {
        File.Copy(f, destinationPath, true);
      }
    }
    else
    {
      throw new ArgumentException("Zune is not configured to monitor *any* " +
        "folders, to fix this, open zune.exe, click settings, " +
        "and add a video folder");
    }
  }
}
#endregion
```

```
#Region "VideoService Members"
Public Sub Sync(ByVal filePath As String) Implements IVideoService.Sync
  Dim currentFolders() As String = ZuneSync.GetZuneMonitoredFolders( _
    ZuneMonitoredFolders.MonitoredVideoFolders)
  Dim found As Boolean = currentFolders.Contains(filePath)
  'check if we are already adding the files to the folder
  If (Not found) Then
  'copy the files to the first specified directory
    If currentFolders.Length >0 Then
      Dim destinationPath As String = currentFolders(0)
      Dim Files() As String = Directory.GetFiles(filePath, "*.wmv", _
        SearchOption.TopDirectoryOnly)
      For Each f In Files
        File.Copy(f, destinationPath, True)
      Next f
    Else
      Throw New ArgumentException("Zune is not configured to monitor *any* " & _
        "folders,to fix this, open zune.exe, click settings, and add a video folder")
    End If
  End If
End Sub
#End Region
```

Putting It All Together

At this point, you've seen how we can:

- Convert YouTube's API XML into objects

- Download a YouTube video and a YouTube image thumbnail
- Convert a YouTube video into WMV and MP4 formats
- Sync videos to iTunes and Zune

What we now want to do is combine those four tasks and make them run asynchronously, so that we can still use our application while we're downloading videos. To do all of the tasks just listed asynchronously, we'll use the `InnerTubeFeedWorker` class.

To give you an idea of the size of the asynchronous operations that InnerTube needs to do, let's walk through an example set of feeds that an InnerTube user might have:

Top Rated Videos of All Time
   This represents the top-rated videos that have ever been on YouTube.

Most Viewed Videos This Week
   This represents the most viewed videos for the current week.

That means that, at a high level, `InnerTubeFeedWorker` needs to do the following:

1. Make two HTTP requests to YouTube's API for each feed (two feeds requested once each).

2. Make 50 image download requests for the thumbnails (2 feeds x 25 videos each = 50 images).

3. Make 50 session token requests to get a valid token to download a video (2 feeds x 25 videos = 50 requests), and then make another 50 download video requests for the FLV videos (2 feeds x 25 videos each = 50 video files).

4. Convert all 50 videos from the Flash format to Windows Media Video (WMV) format. If the user has opted to sync with iTunes, this would mean 100 video conversions because each video would need to be converted to both WMV format (InnerTube requires this) and the MP4 format (iTunes requires this).

5. Sync the newly converted videos to iTunes and Zune.

Because of the scale of these tasks, InnerTube is designed to run in the background and uses `SmartThreadPool`, a *www.codeproject.com* library built by Ami Bar that enables you to build and control multiple thread pools.

To put this all together, look at Figure 4-10, which shows the five main tasks involved.

- The Update Feed Pool task updates each of the feeds. Because these requests are relatively small (3–10K), we leave three threads to work on these tasks, as each thread will complete relatively quickly.

- The Download Video Pool task is where we download the thumbnail images and videos. As this task is a long-running task that could potentially download hundreds of megabytes, we will spin up five threads to handle the work. This task tends to be the most network- and disk-intensive, as it is pulling large files and saving them on disk.

- The Convert Video Pool task runs once we've downloaded all the videos. This task is very CPU intensive, and you will see your machine crank up to 100% utilization with this task. Because of this, we use only two threads to convert video files.

- The Update Master List task updates our in-memory collection of videos that we will use for our application UI.

- The Sync to iTunes/Zune Task adds the newly converted videos to your iTunes and/or Zune music collection.

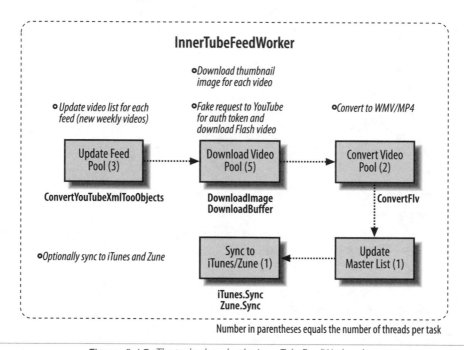

Figure 4-10. *The tasks done by the InnerTubeFeedWorker class*

> **NOTE** Rather than duplicate the documentation in Ami Bar's CodeProject.com article where he walks through how to use the library, here we show how to call the InnerTubeFeedWorker background worker. For detailed documentation on SmartThreadPool, visit *http://www.codeproject.com/KB/threads/smartthreadpool.aspx*.

Calling InnerTubeFeedWorker

As you can see in the upcoming code, instead of using the new keyword to create an instance of InnerTubeFeedWorker, instead we use the static GetInstance method, which will retrieve an instance of the InnerTubeFeedWorker class. This is done so that there is only one instance of InnerTubeFeedWorker at one time and to prevent bad things from happening, such as multiple attempts to download and convert videos on different threads, as each thread would attempt to write to the same file stream, resulting in exceptions or data corruption.

When we call GetInstance, we pass in the list of InnerTubeFeeds and our application settings. We will cover the App class and the Setting class later in the "Global variables" section.

We can also set up event handlers for InnerTubeFeedWorker when it reports progress and when it's finished executing, as shown in Examples 4-47 and 4-48.

C# Example 4-47. *C# code for InnerTubeFeedWorker event handlers*

```
InnerTubeFeedWorker iWork = InnerTubeFeedWorker.GetInstance(App.InnerTubeFeeds,
  App.Settings);

iWork.ProgressChanged += new System.ComponentModel.ProgressChangedEventHandler(
  iWork_ProgressChanged);
iWork.RunWorkerCompleted += new System.ComponentModel.
  RunWorkerCompletedEventHandler(iWork_RunWorkerCompleted);
```

VB Example 4-48. *Visual Basic code for InnerTubeFeedWorker event handlers*

```
Dim iWork As InnerTubeFeedWorker = InnerTubeFeedWorker.GetInstance( _
  App.InnerTubeFeeds, App.Settings)

AddHandler iWork.ProgressChanged, AddressOf iWork_ProgressChanged
AddHandler iWork.RunWorkerCompleted, AddressOf iWork_RunWorkerCompleted
```

InnerTubeFeedWorker has a WorkType enumeration that will tell what specific tasks InnerTubeFeedWorker should execute, as explained in the code comments in Examples 4-49 and 4-50.

C# Example 4-49. *C# code for the types of work the InnerTubeFeedWorker class can do*

```
public enum WorkType
{
  UpdateFeeds, //just Update YouTube API feeds
  Download, //just download FLV files
  DownloadAndConvert, //download and convert FLV files
  Convert, //just convert FLV files
  All //do all of the above
}
```

```
Public Enum WorkType
  UpdateFeeds 'just Update YouTube API feeds
  Download 'just download FLV files
  DownloadAndConvert 'download and convert FLV files
  Convert 'just convert FLV files
  All 'do all of the above
End Enum
```

To actually start the background worker, we need to call the RunWorkerAsync method and pass in the WorkType enum we want it to complete. This method will execute immediately, with all of the processing for InnerTubeFeedWorker taking place on separate, background threads.

To receive progress updates from InnerTubeFeedWorker, you can read e.UserState, which will contain a string with progress updates, such as when a video download is starting, when it's complete, and so forth, as shown in Examples 4-51 and 4-52. Similarly, when InnerTubeFeedWorker finishes executing, it will return an updated list of InnerTubeFeeds with which we can cast and update our InnerTubeFeeds variable.

C# Example 4-51. *C# code to read progress changed events*

```
void iWork_ProgressChanged(object sender,
  System.ComponentModel.ProgressChangedEventArgs e)
{
  string s = (string)(e.UserState);
  …


void iWork_RunWorkerCompleted(object sender,
  System.ComponentModel.RunWorkerCompletedEventArgs e)
{
  App.InnerTubeFeeds = (ObservableCollection<InnerTubeFeed>)e.Result;
  …
```

VB Example 4-52. *Visual Basic code to read progress changed events*

```
Private Sub iWork_ProgressChanged(ByVal sender As Object, _
  ByVal e As System.ComponentModel.ProgressChangedEventArgs)
  Dim s As String = CStr(e.UserState)
  …


Private Sub iWork_RunWorkerCompleted(ByVal sender As Object, _
  ByVal e As System.ComponentModel.RunWorkerCompletedEventArgs)
  App.InnerTubeFeeds = CType(e.Result, ObservableCollection(Of InnerTubeFeed))
```

Setting Up the InnerTube WPF Application

Now that you've seen the core libraries, let's show how you can build a WPF application that can display our list of videos. The first thing we need to do is set up a couple of conventions for our application, namely where we will store global variables, such as the list of feeds and our application setting variables, whether iTunes or Zune is installed, and what location we will save downloaded videos to.

Global Variables

When you create a WPF project, it includes an Application class named `App.xaml`, which includes a code-behind file that, since it's an application-level scope class, would be a perfect place for us to store our global variables. To do that, we declare our list of feeds and our application settings as static properties, as shown in Examples 4-53 and 4-54.

C# Example 4-53. *C# code for InnerTube's global variables*

```csharp
public partial class App : Application
{
  public static ObservableCollection<InnerTubeFeed> InnerTubeFeeds { get; set; }
  public static Setting Settings { get; set; }
```

VB Example 4-54. *Visual Basic code for InnerTube's global variables*

```vb
Partial Public Class App
    Inherits Application
    Private Shared privateInnerTubeFeeds As ObservableCollection(Of InnerTubeFeed)
    Public Shared Property InnerTubeFeeds() As ObservableCollection(Of InnerTubeFeed)
      Get
        Return privateInnerTubeFeeds
      End Get
      Set(ByVal value As ObservableCollection(Of InnerTubeFeed))
        privateInnerTubeFeeds = value
      End Set
    End Property

    Private Shared privateSettings As Setting
    Public Shared Property Settings() As Setting
      Get
        Return privateSettings
      End Get
      Set(ByVal value As Setting)
        privateSettings = value
      End Set
```

```
End Property
...
```

As `InnerTubeFeeds` is a global variable storing all of the feeds and feed videos, we will need to update it during the following conditions:

- When a user adds a feed in the `AddNewFeed.xaml` window
- When a user right-clicks and deletes a feed or feed video from the *MainWindow.xaml* window
- When a user kicks off the `InnerTubeFeedWorker` process, which will add/update the list videos in a feed (say, by downloading a new favorite or top-rated video)

Application Settings

Our application has a number of different settings that we will need to use and store. The following are the fields for the `Setting` class, along with a description of what each property does.

AppName
: The name of the application and, more importantly, the name of the directory we'll use to store our application's files. Its default value is `InnerTube`.

FirstRun
: A Boolean field used to determine whether it's the first time the application has been run. It determines whether we should show the `FirstRunWindow.xaml` file and build an initial set of feeds for the user. Its default value is `true`.

InnerTubeFeedFile
: This is the exact location of the *InnerTubeFeeds.xml* file when it's saved to disk.

SubPath
: This is the directory on your hard drive that we'll use to store files such as the thumbnail images, unconverted FLV files, or serialized classes, such as the `InnerTubeFeed` class and the `Setting` class. It is named using the `AppName` property, and its default value is `C:\Users\`*Username*`\Videos\InnerTube`.

VideoPath
: This is the directory on your hard drive that we'll use to save videos once we convert them. Its default value is `C:\Users\`*Username*`\Videos\`.

iTunesInstalled
: This is a Boolean field that will tell us whether iTunes is installed. Its default value is `false`.

ZuneInstalled
: This is a Boolean field that will tell us whether the Zune software is installed. Its default value is `false`.

UpdateFeedPoolThreads

This is an integer field that sets the number of threads to use for the UpdateFeed Pool process. Its default value is 3 threads.

DownloadPoolThreads

This is an integer field that sets the number of threads to use for the Download Pool process. Its default value is 5 threads.

ConversionPoolThreads

This is an integer field that sets the number of threads to use for the Conversion Pool process. Its default value is 2 threads.

When our application is first run, the *FirstRunWindow.xaml* file will check whether a *Settings* file has already been created. If it hasn't, it will call the SettingService. BuildDefaultSettings method, which will initialize the fields just listed to the machine-specific default values.

Building the InnerTube UI

The InnerTube UI uses a three-pane Microsoft Outlook–like UI, with the left pane representing a list of InnerTubeFeed objects, the middle pane representing a list of InnerTubeVideos for the selected feed, and the rightmost pane showing the detail for the selected video. The next section walks through the skeleton of the UI, and then we'll show a screenshot of the actual UI and describe the required controls.

InnerTube Skeleton

This is the skeleton of the WPF controls contained in the application (see Figure 4-11):

- At the highest level inside MainWindow, we have a DockPanel control that we use to set the Menu and ToolBar controls so they dock to the top of our window.

- For the three-column layout, we use a Grid control with three column definitions and specify the column width with a wildcard (*), which, as with web applications, means the column size can grow when resized.

- The first column (remember columns are zero-based) is a ListBox control that will hold the list of InnerTubeFeed objects for our application.

- The second column is also a ListBox control, and will list the videos for a particular feed.

- The third column contains a canvas control with multiple controls: a user control for the media player, TextBlock controls for fields such as the video title, and so on.

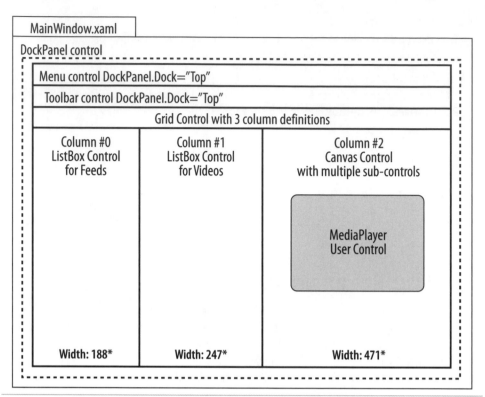

Figure 4-11. *The primary controls in MainWindow.xaml*

NOTE InnerTube uses the *C4fStyle.xaml* file to define the appearance of buttons, ListBox controls, and more. To see what's included in the C4fStyle, see the Appendix.

Dissecting MainWindow.xaml

Since it can be difficult to explain exactly how you take a set of skeleton controls and turn them into a fully functioning UI, we'll dissect *MainWindow.xaml* into the three pieces, labeled 1, 2, and 3 in Figure 4-12. You can refer back to this screenshot to follow along with the expected UI.

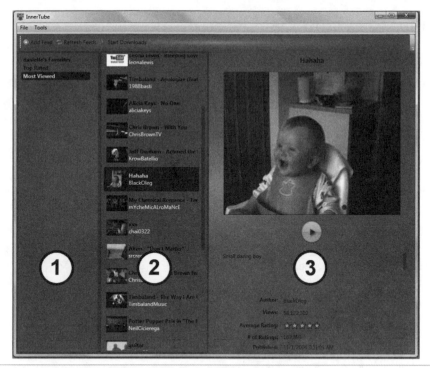

Figure 4-12. *The three Grid columns in MainWindow.xaml*

Setting the MainWindow.xaml data context

Previously we defined a global variable named `InnerTubeFeeds` that holds the list of feeds and the corresponding list of videos. To data bind all of the controls in `Main Window` to `InnerTubeFeeds`, we will set the `DataContext` for the window using the `Window_Loaded` event, as shown in Examples 4-55 and 4-56.

`C#` Example 4-55. *C# code to set the MainWindow.xaml data context*

```
private void Window_Loaded(object sender, RoutedEventArgs e)
{
…
    this.DataContext = App.InnerTubeFeeds;
}
```

`VB` Example 4-56. *Visual Basic code to set the MainWindow.xaml data context*

```
Private Sub Window_Loaded(ByVal sender As Object, ByVal e As RoutedEventArgs)
…
  Me.DataContext = App.InnerTubeFeeds
End Sub
```

Part 1: The Feed List ListBox

For the Feed List UI, we will use a templated `ListBox` control, as shown in Example 4-57. As the main UI is comprised of a `Grid` control, we need to add the control to the first column of the `Grid` control by setting the `Grid.Column` attribute for `ListBox` to zero (the first column). We won't discuss this in detail here, but you'll notice that we have a `ContextMenu` defined to delete a feed (when right-clicked). Next, we'll delve into how we data bind using the `ListBox` `ItemTemplate`.

Example 4-57. XAML code for the first column in MainWindow.xaml

```
<!--First Column-->
<ListBox Grid.Column="0" x:Name="feedList" IsSynchronizedWithCurrentItem="True"
  ItemsSource="{Binding}"  Background="{x:Null}">
  <ListBox.ContextMenu>
    <ContextMenu>
      <MenuItem Click="DeleteFeed" CommandParameter="{Binding Path=/}"
        Header="Delete Feed" >
        <MenuItem.Icon>
          <Image Source="images/cross.png"></Image>
        </MenuItem.Icon>
      </MenuItem>
    </ContextMenu>
  </ListBox.ContextMenu>
  <ListBox.ItemTemplate>
    <DataTemplate>
      <StackPanel Orientation="Horizontal">
        <TextBlock FontWeight="Bold" Text="{Binding Path=FeedName}"/>
      </StackPanel>
    </DataTemplate>
  </ListBox.ItemTemplate>
</ListBox>
```

Data binding the feedList ListBox

To data bind the `feedList` `ListBox` control, we will set a couple of properties:

`ItemSource`

> This is the data source you are binding to. Since we already set up a `DataContext` for all of *MainWindow.xaml*, this is just `"{Binding}"`.

`IsSynchronizedWithCurrentItem`

> This property must be set to true so that all of the controls on the window stay in sync, meaning that if a user clicks on another feed, the `ListBox` control that contains the list of videos and the details pane controls should update to show the videos in that feed.

DataTemplate
   This template controls how each data-bound item will be displayed. In this exam-
   ple, we can data bind the Text property to the FeedName property from App.Inner
   TubeFeeds using Text="{Binding Path=FeedName}" as the binding expression.

Part 2: The VideoList ListBox

In the middle column, we will display a list of videos for the selected feed, including a
thumbnail image, the video title, and the author of each video that belongs to the currently selected feed. Just like we did before, we declare the ListBox control and define
the Grid.Column property, but this time we set it to 1, which is the second column.
We also have a ContextMenu control that is bound to the Delete key by setting the
InputGestureText, and we have a ListBox ItemTemplate that defines the UI for the
ListBox, as shown in Example 4-58.

Example 4-58. *XAML code for the second column in MainWindow.xaml*

```xml
<!--Second Column-->
<ListBox Grid.Column="1"  IsSynchronizedWithCurrentItem="True"
  ItemsSource="{Binding Path=FeedVideos}" Name="VideoList"
  Background="{x:Null}" >
  <ListBox.ItemTemplate>
    <DataTemplate>
      <StackPanel Orientation="Horizontal">
        <StackPanel.ContextMenu>
          <ContextMenu Name="mnuDeleteVideo">
            <MenuItem Click="DeleteVideo" CommandParameter="{Binding}"
              Header="Foo" InputGestureText="Del" >
              <MenuItem.Icon>
                <Image Source="images/cross.png"></Image>
              </MenuItem.Icon>
            </MenuItem>
          </ContextMenu>
        </StackPanel.ContextMenu>
        <Image Margin="2,2,2,2" Source="{Binding Path=DownloadedImage,
          Converter={StaticResource img} }"
          Width="48" Height="48" VerticalAlignment="Center"></Image>
        <StackPanel VerticalAlignment="Center">
          <TextBlock  FontWeight="Bold" Text="{Binding Path=Title}"
            TextTrimming="WordEllipsis"  TextWrapping="Wrap" />
          <TextBlock Foreground="White"  Text="{Binding Path=Author}" />
        </StackPanel>
      </StackPanel>
    </DataTemplate>
  </ListBox.ItemTemplate>
</ListBox>
```

The Data Template UI

Let's take a second to understand how we get XAML to produce a template that looks like Figure 4-13. All of the controls in the data template are defined in a StackPanel with the orientation set to Horizontal, meaning they will stack left to right.

Starting left to right in Example 4-59, we have an image, which itself has a margin of 2 (device-independent) pixels on each side, and a fixed width and height. The next control is another StackPanel control, and because it doesn't explicitly have an Orientation, this means the Orientation is vertical (top to bottom). Inside the StackPanel we have two TextBlock controls, representing the title and author of the video.

Figure 4-13. *The ListBox data template*

Example 4-59. *XAML data template for video list ListBox*

```
<DataTemplate>
...
  <StackPanel Orientation="Horizontal">
    <Image Margin="2,2,2,2" Source="{Binding Path=DownloadedImage,
      Converter={StaticResource img} }"
      Width="48" Height="48" VerticalAlignment="Center">
    </Image>
    <StackPanel VerticalAlignment="Center">
      <TextBlock  FontWeight="Bold" Text="{Binding Path=Title}"
        TextTrimming="WordEllipsis"  TextWrapping="Wrap" />
      <TextBlock Foreground="White"  Text="{Binding Path=Author}" />
    </StackPanel>
  </StackPanel>
</DataTemplate>
```

Data Binding the Video List ListBox

Just like we did with the Feed List ListBox, we'll set a couple of properties to enable data binding for the Video List:

ItemSource

> As the top-level data binding is set to InnerTubeFeeds, we want to bind to just FeedVideos, so we'll set ItemSource to "{Binding Path=FeedVideos}". The FeedVideos property is simply a collection of InnerTubeVideo classes, which means that we can set the Binding Path to any property in the InnerTubeVideo class.

IsSynchronizedWithCurrentItem

> Just like before, we must be set this to true so that all of the controls on the window stay in sync.

Binding to an Image

Take a second to examine the binding syntax for the Image and the two TextBlock controls in Example 4-59. While the TextBlock controls simply bind to the Title and Author properties, the Image binding adds something new, a Converter and a Static Resource. We'll quickly explain what's going on here and how to use converters and static resources.

Building the Image Value Converter

We're using a converter for the image because we want to have some custom code run when we data bind, to make sure that the DownloadedImage value actually exists; if it doesn't, we can swap in a default image. A Converter is a .NET class that implements an interface named IValueConverter. IValueConverter has two methods, Convert and ConvertBack, which both receive a value of type object and have a return type of object, as shown in Examples 4-60 and 4-61.

`C#` Example 4-60. *C# code for the IValueConverter interface*

```csharp
public interface IValueConverter
{
  object Convert(object value, Type targetType,
    object parameter, CultureInfo culture);

  object ConvertBack(object value, Type targetType,
    object parameter, CultureInfo culture);
}
```

`VB` Example 4-61. *Visual Basic code for the IValueConverter interface*

```vb
Public Interface IValueConverter
  Function Convert(ByVal value As Object, ByVal targetType As Type, _
    ByVal parameter As Object, ByVal culture As CultureInfo) As Object
```

```
    Function ConvertBack(ByVal value As Object, ByVal targetType As Type, _
        ByValparameter As Object, ByVal culture As CultureInfo) As Object
    End Interface
```

The next piece of code defines our implementation for IValueConverter. Let's explain
exactly what will happen when we data bind. Since we declared the Converter for the
Image source, WPF will first pass the value of DownloadedImage property to Converter
Image.Convert. The Convert method will check whether the DownloadedImage value
is null, empty, or doesn't exist. If it does exist, it'll just return the image path. If the image doesn't exist, then we'll instead return a default "placeholder" image. The full code
for the ConverterImage class is shown in Examples 4-62 and 4-63.

C#   Example 4-62. C# code for the Image Converter

```
[ValueConversion(typeof(object), typeof(string))]
public class ConverterImage : IValueConverter
{
public object Convert(object value, Type targetType, object parameter,
  System.Globalization.CultureInfo culture)
{
  string path = (string)value;
  return SetImage(path);
}

public static object SetImage(string imagePath)
{
  //if the path doesn't exist
  if (String.IsNullOrEmpty(imagePath) || (!File.Exists(imagePath)))
  {
    //use default image
    return FileHelper.DefaultImage;
  }
  else
  {
    return imagePath;
  }
}

public object ConvertBack(object value, Type targetType,
  object parameter, System.Globalization.CultureInfo culture)
  {
    // we don't intend this to ever be called
    return null;
  }
}
```

```
<ValueConversion(GetType(Object), GetType(String))> _
Public Class ConverterImage
  Implements IValueConverter

  Public Function Convert(ByVal value As Object, ByVal targetType As Type, _
    ByVal parameter As Object, _
    ByVal culture As System.Globalization.CultureInfo) As Object
    Implements IValueConverter.Convert

    Dim path As String = CStr(value)
      Return SetImage(path)
  End Function

  Public Shared Function SetImage(ByVal imagePath As String) As Object
    'if the path doesn't exist
    If String.IsNullOrEmpty(imagePath) OrElse ((Not File.Exists(imagePath))) Then
      'use default image
      Return Path.Combine(App.Settings.SubPath, FileHelper.DefaultImage)
    Else
      Return imagePath
    End If
  End Function

  Public Function ConvertBack(ByVal value As Object, ByVal targetType As Type, _
    ByVal parameter As Object, _
    ByVal culture As System.Globalization.CultureInfo) As Object
    Implements IValueConverter.ConvertBack
    ' we don't intend this to ever be called
    Return Nothing
  End Function
End Class
```

Setting Up a Class As a Static Resource

Now that we've seen how to define a class that implements IValueConverter, let's show how you can call that class declaratively using XAML by setting it as a Static Resource in *MainWindow.xaml*. A static resource is a way to define a class or other resource file in XAML. We can set the ConverterImage class shown earlier to be a Static Resource by doing a couple of things. First, we need to explicitly define the namespace that the ConverterImage class lives in and set up an alias for the namespace, which I chose to be Util, as shown in Example 4-64.

Example 4-64. *Code to declare a .NET Namespace in XAML*

```
<Window
    xmlns:Util="clr-namespace:InnerTube"
```

Second, we define the `ConverterImage` class as a `StaticResource` by declaring it in a `ResourceDictionary` in the format shown in the next code example. Notice that we reference the InnerTube namespace (aka `Util`), followed by the class name, and then define the Key that we can use to reference the `StaticResource` in XAML, as shown in Example 4-65.

Example 4-65. Code to declare a class and assign a key in XAML

```
<Window.Resources>
 <ResourceDictionary>
      <!-- Value Converters for databinding -->
        <Util:ConverterImage x:Key="img" />
    </ResourceDictionary>
</Window.Resources>
```

Part 3: The Details Pane

As is evident by the name, the details pane displays the details of the currently selected `InnerTubeVideo`. The pane itself is made up of a `Canvas` element with a `Grid.Column` property of 2, which indicates the third column since the `Grid` Index starts at zero. The `Canvas` is made up of a set of controls that define their `Canvas.Top` and `Canvas.Left` properties, as shown in Example 4-66.

> **NOTE**
> Experienced WPF developers normally don't like using the **Canvas** control, as it has fixed pixel values and doesn't resize as gracefully as other controls. But it is fine for some scenarios, and there are benefits of using Visual Studio's snap lines to align labels and their corresponding values without having to manually muck with XAML.

Example 4-66. XAML code for the details pane

```
<!-- 3rd Column -->
<Canvas Grid.Column="2" Name="canvas1">
  <!-- Title -->
  <TextBlock Text="{Binding Path=FeedVideos/Title}" Name="VideoTitle"
    TextAlignment="Center" Height="28.453" Canvas.Left="18.859" Canvas.Top="9.228"
    Width="438.133" FontSize="16" FontWeight="Bold"></TextBlock>

  <!-- Video -->
  <Util:MediaPlayer InnerTubeVideoFile="{Binding Path=FeedVideos/}"
    x:Name="VideoPlayer" Canvas.Left="18.571" Canvas.Top="47.678" Height="398.342"
    Width="438.421" />

  <!-- Description -->
  <ScrollViewer Canvas.Left="32.867" Canvas.Top="458.425" Height="86.684"
```

```
       Name="scrollViewer1" Width="424.413">
    <TextBlock Height="180" Text="{Binding Path=FeedVideos/Description}"
       Name="txtDescription" TextDecorations="None" TextWrapping="Wrap" />
  </ScrollViewer>

  <!-- Author -->
    <Label Canvas.Left="46" Canvas.Top="551.777" Height="28.339" Name="lblAuthor"
       Width="120" HorizontalContentAlignment="Right">Author:</Label>
    <TextBlock Text="{Binding Path=FeedVideos/Author}" Canvas.Left="173"
       Canvas.Top="559.209" Height="20.907" Name="txtAuthor" Width="120" />

  <!-- Views -->
    <Label Canvas.Left="46" Canvas.Top="580.116" Height="28.339" Name="lblViews"
       Width="120" HorizontalContentAlignment="Right">Views:</Label>
    <TextBlock Text="{Binding Path=FeedVideos/Views,StringFormat=N0 }"
     Name="txtViews" Canvas.Left="173" Canvas.Top="587.548" Height="20.907"
     Width="120"/>

  <!-- Average Rating -->
  <Label Canvas.Left="46" Canvas.Top="610.122" Height="28.339" Name="lblRaters"
     Width="120" HorizontalContentAlignment="Right">Average Rating: </Label>
  <Util:RatingUserControl StarRating="{Binding Path=FeedVideos/AvgRating}"
     x:Name="Rating" Canvas.Left="173" Canvas.Top="615.123" Height="16.67" />

  <!-- Number of Ratings  >
  <Label Name="lblNumRating" Canvas.Left="46" Canvas.Top="636.794" Height="28.339"
     Width="120" HorizontalContentAlignment="Right"># of Ratings:</Label>
  <TextBlock Text="{Binding Path=FeedVideos/NumRaters, StringFormat=N0}"
    Name="txtNumRating" Canvas.Left="173" Canvas.Top="641.795" Height="21.671"
    Width="120" />

  <!-- Publish Date -->
  <Label Canvas.Left="46" Canvas.Top="660.132" Height="28.339" Name="lblPublished"
     Width="120" HorizontalContentAlignment="Right">Published:</Label>
  <TextBlock Text="{Binding Path=FeedVideos/Published}" Name="txtPublished"
     Canvas.Left="173" Canvas.Top="665.133" Height="21.671" Width="216" />
</Canvas>
```

Formatting Numbers in WPF

For fields such as txtViews and txtNumRating, we can format the values using the
StringFormat property and set its value to a valid .NET Framework formatting string
such as N0 (numbers with commas), as shown in Example 4-67.

Example 4-67. *Data binding the total views for a video using a value converter*

```
<TextBlock Text="{Binding Path=FeedVideos/Views,StringFormat=N0 }" …
```

As the txtViews property is an int data type, if we were to data bind without the StringFormat property, we would get the following example value: 8675309.

After setting the StringFormat property, the txtViews property will appear as 8,675,309.

Data Binding in the Details Pane

Unlike the previous two columns, the details pane is made up of separate, unlinked controls, so we do not define an ItemSource or set the IsSynchronizedProperty.

As a result, the binding syntax for each of the controls is slightly different. Specifically, each Binding Path will start at the root of the InnerTubeFeed class, so to get to the title of a particular video, we need to set the path starting at the FeedVideos property, as in Example 4-68.

Example 4-68. *Data binding the video title*

```
<TextBlock Text="{Binding Path=FeedVideos/Title}" …
```

Data Binding to User Controls

Back in the details pane XAML listing, you'll notice that for actually playing the video, we are data binding to a custom user control named MediaPlayer, which has a custom property named InnerTubeVideoFile. As you can see, the Path value is set to FeedVideos/, which means that we will pass in the entire currently selected Inner TubeVideo class to the InnerTubeVideoFile property when we data bind, as shown in Example 4-69.

Example 4-69. *XAML code to pass an InnerTubeVideo to the MediaPlayer user control*

```
<Util:MediaPlayer InnerTubeVideoFile="{Binding Path=FeedVideos/}"
```

MediaPlayer User Control UI

The UI for the MediaPlayer user control is a Grid that contains four elements. The first two are the Image and MediaElement controls, which are placed directly on top of each other (notice the same Margin values for both), as shown in Example 4-70. We will use the Image control to display a video's preview image when the control first loads, but once a video starts playing, we will hide the image. As both of the elements are stacked right on top of each other, we can use the Grid.ZIndex attribute to state that the Image, which has a higher ZIndex, should appear on top of the MediaElement.

Next is a StackPanel control, which contains one element, a ToggleButton to toggle between playing and pausing a video. Inside of it is a Path, which is an XAML shape for the Play button.

Example 4-70. *XAML for the MediaPlayer user control*

```
<Grid>
  <Image Grid.ZIndex="1" Margin="5,0,5,73" Name="PreviewImage" ></Image>
  <MediaElement Grid.ZIndex="0" Margin="5,0,5,73" Name="VideoPlayer"
    LoadedBehavior="Manual"></MediaElement>
  <StackPanel Orientation="Horizontal" HorizontalAlignment="Center"
    VerticalAlignment="Bottom">
    <ToggleButton Margin="0,0,0,10" Height="50" Width="50"
      Name="PlayButton" Style="{StaticResource PlayButton}"
      Click="Play">
      <Path Data="F1M149.333,406L149.333,598 317.333,502 149.333,406z"
        Fill="#80000000" Height="14" Margin="4,0,0,0" Name="Path" Stretch="Fill"
        Width="14" />
    </ToggleButton>
  </StackPanel>
</Grid>
```

MediaPlayer Data Binding

To enable data binding with the MediaPlayer control, we need to create a special type of WPF property known as a *dependency property*, which enables you to make your controls data-bindable in WPF (among other benefits).

You can see the definition for the InnerTubeVideoFile dependency property in the MediaPlayer code-behind file shown next. The first step is to build a property like you normally would, with the getter returning the DependencyProperty value (C# developers should not use C# 3.0's automatic properties for this), as shown in Examples 4-71 and 4-72.

Next, you declare and register the dependency property, passing in the name, the type you'll receive, the class you are registering for, and finally an event handler that will fire when the value is changed. This event handler replaces the set code in the property because that code will never execute, and therefore change values should be handled via the event handler.

⌐C#⌐ Example 4-71. *C# code for the InnerTubeVideoFile dependency property*

```
public InnerTubeVideo InnerTubeVideoFile
{
  get { return (InnerTubeVideo)GetValue(InnerTubeVideoProperty); }
  set { /* don't write code here it won't execute */ }
}

public static readonly DependencyProperty InnerTubeVideoProperty =
  DependencyProperty.Register("InnerTubeVideoFile",
  typeof(InnerTubeVideo),
```

```
        typeof(MediaPlayer),
        new UIPropertyMetadata(MediaPlayer.InnerTubeVideoFileChanged));
```

 Example 4-72. *Visual Basic code for the InnerTubeVideoFile dependency property*

```
    Public Property InnerTubeVideoFile() As InnerTubeVideo
      Get
        Return CType(GetValue(InnerTubeVideoProperty), InnerTubeVideo)
      End Get
      Set(ByVal value As InnerTubeVideo)
        'Don't write code here it won't execute
      End Set
    End Property

    Public Shared ReadOnly InnerTubeVideoProperty As DependencyProperty = _
      DependencyProperty.Register("InnerTubeVideoFile", _
      GetType(InnerTubeVideo), _
      GetType(MediaPlayer), _
      New UIPropertyMetadata(AddressOf MediaPlayer.InnerTubeVideoFileChanged))
```

Let's now take a look at a snippet of the InnerTubeVideoFile event handler, which will fire any time the property changes (Examples 4-73 and 4-74). There are a couple of things to notice here. First, the event is static and therefore doesn't have access to instance members of the current MediaPlayer control (using this.foo will not work in the event handler). The nice thing is that the current instance class is passed into you as the DependencyObject d, which you can then cast to a MediaPlayer and set instance properties.

The second thing to note is that we can retrieve the passed-in class and cast it to an InnerTubeVideo through the DependencyPropertyChangedEventArgs e variable.

Now that we have the current instance and the new value, we can set the properties for the Image and the MediaElement controls, as shown in the code snippets.

> **NOTE** The **MediaElement** control does not support MP4 video playback, so we must data bind to a Windows Media (WMV) file.

C# Example 4-73. *Snippets from the C# event that fires when the InnerTubeVideFile property changes*

```
    private static void InnerTubeVideoFileChanged(DependencyObject d,
      DependencyPropertyChangedEventArgs e)
    {
      MediaPlayer player = (MediaPlayer)d;
      InnerTubeVideo newVideo = (InnerTubeVideo)e.NewValue;

      ...

      ImageSourceConverter imageConvert = new ImageSourceConverter();
```

```
...
player.PreviewImage.Source =
(ImageSource)imageConvert.ConvertFromString(newVideo.DownloadedImage);

...

//Set Video File
player.VideoPlayer.Source = new Uri(newVideo.DownloadedWmv);

...
```

VB Example 4-74. *Snippets from the Visual Basic event that fires when the InnerTubeVideoFile property changes*

```
Private Shared Sub InnerTubeVideoFileChanged(ByVal d As DependencyObject, _
   ByVal e As DependencyPropertyChangedEventArgs)
Dim player As MediaPlayer = CType(d, MediaPlayer)
Dim newVideo As InnerTubeVideo = CType(e.NewValue, InnerTubeVideo)

...

Dim imageConvert As New ImageSourceConverter()

...

player.PreviewImage.Source = CType(imageConvert.ConvertFromString( _
   newVideo.DownloadedImage), ImageSource)

...

'Set Video File
player.VideoPlayer.Source = New Uri(newVideo.DownloadedWmv)

...
```

Playing and Pausing Video

The final thing we'll look at is the `ToggleButton` `Click` event, which is declared as shown in Example 4-75.

Example 4-75. *Declaring the ToggleButton in XAML*

```
< ToggleButton … Name="PlayButton" Click="Play">
```

In the `Play` event, we can cast the `ToggleButton` to see whether it's currently checked, and do things such as hide the preview image, as shown in Examples 4-76 and 4-77. The `MediaElement` control has static methods to `Play()` and `Pause()` audio and video files, assuming a source has been set.

C# Example 4-76. *C# code for the ToggleButton's Click method*

```
void Play(object sender, RoutedEventArgs args)
{
  ToggleButton tb = (ToggleButton)sender;
  if (isVideo)
  {
    //Hide image if it's a video
    this.PreviewImage.Visibility = Visibility.Hidden;
```

```
      if ((bool)tb.IsChecked)
      {
        VideoPlayer.Play();
      }
      else
      {
        VideoPlayer.Pause();
      }
    }
  }
```

VB Example 4-77. *Visual Basic code for the ToggleButton's Click method*

```
Private Sub Play(ByVal sender As Object, ByVal args As RoutedEventArgs)
  Dim tb As ToggleButton = CType(sender, ToggleButton)
  If isVideo Then
    'Hide image if it's a video
    Me.PreviewImage.Visibility = Visibility.Hidden
    If CBool(tb.IsChecked) Then
      VideoPlayer.Play()
    Else
      VideoPlayer.Pause()
    End If
  End If
End Sub
```

Final Thoughts

In this chapter, you've seen how YouTube's API works, how to circumvent YouTube's restrictions for downloading videos, how to convert video files easily using *ffmpeg*, how to programmatically sync videos to iTunes and Zune, and how to put it all together in one application.

Although InnerTube will never replace YouTube (nor was it designed to), I can't tell you how many times I have ended up stuck somewhere with either my Zune or my laptop with time to kill but no Internet connection. Then I excitedly remember that I have a fresh new set of popular YouTube videos downloaded to my hard drive to watch and entertain myself.

You can of course adapt this code to work with other Flash video websites, such as Break.com or CollegeHumor.com, and build a way to automatically download and convert any Flash video on the Web!

AUTHOR	Dan Fernandez
DIFFICULTY	Advanced
TIME REQUIRED	10+ hours
COST	Free
SOFTWARE	Visual C# Express or Visual Basic Express, Windows Vista
HARDWARE	Two PCs, one running at home and another one working remotely
DOWNLOAD	*http://www.c4fbook.com/PeerCast*

PeerCast is a Windows Presentation Foundation (WPF) application that enables you to stream videos between PCs over an ad-hoc peer-to-peer network.

Overview

I can't help but sound like an obnoxiously loud TV infomercial salesman wearing a cheap polyester suit with too many question marks when I try to describe what Peer Cast does. The truth is PeerCast is pretty basic: it streams video from one PC to another. Here's the kicker, though: if both PCs are on the Internet and can communicate using Peer Name Resolution Protocol (PNRP), you can stream videos from anywhere in the world. No special software, no monthly subscription fee, no custom hardware—just your videos, streamed to you anytime and anywhere. Let me clear my throat while I get my polyester suit on:

> "Bored at work? Wish you could watch recorded episodes of *Law and Order* on your Media Center to pass the time? Now you can with PeerCast! Or maybe you're traveling for work in the middle of nowhere, with just an Internet connection (that works with PNRP). You could be watching any video file on your home PC with PeerCast! How much do you think Peer-Cast costs? Would you believe it if we told you that PeerCast is completely FREE? Would you believe us if we told you that we are just giving away this code?!! We'd have to be c-r-a-z-y to give PeerCast away for free, crazy enough to wear cheesy polyester suits covered in question marks!"

Now that we got that awkwardness out of our system, let's take a tour of PeerCast's features.

A Tour of PeerCast

PeerCast is designed to stream videos from one PC that acts as a server and another PC that acts as a client and requests to stream videos directly from the server.

Client or Server Mode

When PeerCast first runs, you'll be prompted to select whether to run in client or server mode, as shown in Figure 5-1. Although PeerCast is designed to work across the Internet and on multiple PCs, you can run two instances of PeerCast at the same time on the same machine, where one is configured as a client and another as a server.

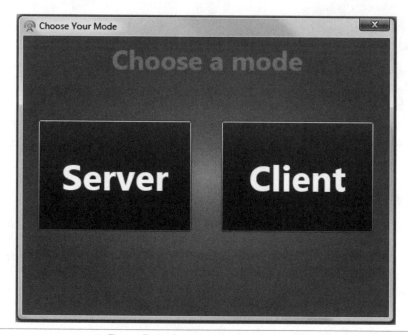

Figure 5-1. *Choosing server or client mode*

Server mode

In server mode, PeerCast will just sit and wait to receive commands from clients that ask to stream a particular video. In server mode, you can set the location on the server for the videos you want to make available for viewing by clicking the Select button, which pops up a folder browser dialog, as shown in Figure 5-2.

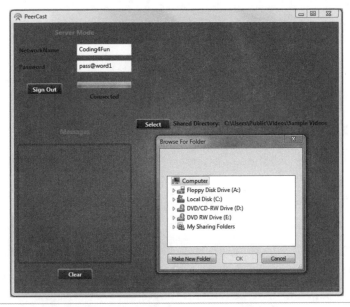

Figure 5-2. *Running PeerCast in server mode*

Client mode

In client mode (Figure 5-3), we make requests to see what videos the server has made available to watch and start streaming them directly over the P2P network.

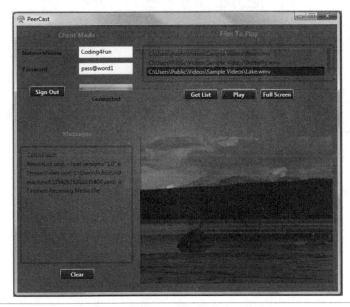

Figure 5-3. *Streaming videos from PeerCast*

Depending on how your network is set up, you may not be able to get the PeerCast application working. As there are a number of reasons why the connection may fail, we have listed some troubleshooting tips on **http://www.c4fbook.com** to help readers diagnose networking issues.

How PeerCast Works

Now that you've seen what PeerCast does, let's explain the technology that makes PeerCast work, including:

- How Peer Channel applications work
- Building the NetworkManager class
- Listening to P2P events using Network Manager
- Understanding how the login process works
- Understanding how chat messages work
- Understanding how video streaming works
- Building the *MainWindow.xaml* UI
- Adding the *MainWindow.xaml* code

How Peer Channel Applications Work

Before we get into any code, we need to explain, at a high level, how Peer Channel applications work.

Key P2P terms

This chapter is written assuming you have no previous experience building P2P applications, and so we'll start off by explaining the key terminology used in P2P applications:

C4FP2P

An abbreviation for the Coding4Fun peer-to-peer library that provides a wrapper of the Peer Channel protocol.

Mesh

An ad-hoc network of nodes with the same mesh name. When you run PeerCast, you'll enter a network name and password, which will create a custom mesh. The term "mesh" in this context has no relation to Microsoft Live Mesh.

NetPeerTcpBinding

A Windows Communication Foundation (WCF) class that implements the Peer Channel protocol.

Node
> A computer, device, or application that uses the Peer Channel protocol. Any PC running PeerCast would be considered a node.

Peer-to-peer (P2P)
> P2P applications use decentralized communication where clients communicate amongst peers instead of communicating to a central server.

Peer Channel
> A protocol for building P2P applications that broadcasts messages over an ad-hoc network of nodes (a mesh). PeerCast uses Peer Channel for all P2P communication.

Peer Name Resolution Protocol (PNRP)
> A protocol to register your node and find other nodes in the cloud.

Peer Channel by example

To help explain how Peer Channel networks work, let's compare and contrast a client/ server website to a Peer Channel network. When you open a browser to a website— say, *www.msn.com*—under the covers, your PC makes a request to a Domain Name Server (DNS) to resolve the IP address for the *www.msn.com* website. Once you have the IP address, your browser then connects directly to that machine, and the site sends a response back to you in HTML. Multiple visitors to the site all connect directly to the server rather than each other.

Peer Channel networks use PNRP, which is conceptually similar to DNS in that they both allow you to register and resolve names into IP addresses over the Internet. PNRP has a number of advantages over DNS for name resolution, such as the ability to register and unregister a new name in the PNRP cloud in real time versus DNS name registration, which can take 24–48 hours to replicate worldwide.

Unlike client-server networks where there is one server machine and multiple clients, a P2P network has decentralized communication with peers communicating with one another each other in a *mesh*, an ad-hoc network of nodes. A mesh network is kind of like a chat room that any PC can create and connect to. The mesh itself is password protected (and optionally encrypted), and the PCs in the mesh can send messages (.NET objects, text, photos, video) between each other anywhere in the world without the need for a central server.

How exactly the machines communicate is not something developers have to worry about, because that is all taken care of for you by the Peer Channel protocol: the connections are optimized, redundant, and fault tolerant (in other words, if one of the machines disconnects, the mesh will reconfigure itself to send messages between other PCs in the mesh). For those interested in the full details of the Peer Channel protocol, please visit the official document specification at *http://msdn.microsoft.com/en-us/ library/cc219453.aspx*.

Building a Peer Channel Application

Now that you have a conceptual understanding of how the Peer Channel protocol works, let's switch gears and discuss how we can use Peer Channel in our application. We'll use the Coding4Fun P2P library, an open source Peer Channel wrapper that includes built-in support for connecting to a custom Peer Channel network, sending text messages, and streaming video. Given the size of the Coding4Fun P2P library, we won't delve too deeply into its code; instead, we'll explain just enough to be able to reuse the library's key features.

Listening to P2P messages asynchronously

One of the key design decisions for PeerCast is that all network communication should happen on a background thread. We do this so that the application UI doesn't appear to freeze or hang while we receive P2P messages or process incoming data, like when we receive a video stream.

We'll use a BackgroundWorker object for processing P2P messages on a background thread and use the BackgroundWorker's ReportProgress event to send data from the background thread to the UI thread. This is important because WPF applications use a Single-Threaded Apartment (STA) thread model, and so all UI changes must happen on the UI thread.

If the background thread receives some data from the P2P network, such as an updated list of videos, it *cannot* directly update controls on a WPF form, and attempting to do so will throw an InvalidOperationException exception stating that only the thread that created the WPF control can update the controls value. To make updates to the UI thread, the UI thread will subscribe to the ProgressChanged event, which will fire any time the ReportProgress method is called on the background thread. Using the ProgressChanged event means we have a thread-safe way to shuttle data from the background thread to the UI thread.

Structuring messages from the background thread to the UI thread

To help clarify what data we're sending from the background thread to the UI thread, we'll explicitly define the types of UI messages that will be sent using the UiMessage enumeration, as shown in Examples 5-1 and 5-2.

 Example 5-1. *Defining the types of messages sent between threads in C#*

```csharp
public enum UiMessage
{
  StreamVideo,
  UpdateStatus,
  ReceivedVideoList,
  ToggleUi,
```

```
        Log
    }
```

Example 5-2. *Defining the types of messages sent between threads in VB*

```
    Public Enum UiMessage
        StreamVideo
        UpdateStatus
        ReceivedVideoList
        ToggleUi
        Log
    End Enum
```

Let's quickly define what each of these message notifications means:

StreamVideo

> The server is going to start streaming a video.

UpdateStatus

> The application has either connected or disconnected to the mesh network.

ReceivedVideoList

> We've received an XML string of videos from the server that needs to be deserialized.

ToggleUi

> We've logged in or out, so the UI should be reset.

Log

> A command has been sent across the P2P network.

We'll use the ThreadMessage class and include the UiMessage enumeration and the string Message to be sent from the background thread to the UI thread, as shown in Examples 5-3 and 5-4. ThreadMessage also includes a helper method named Create to easily create a ThreadMessage object.

C# Example 5-3. *The ThreadMessage class in C#*

```
    public class ThreadMessage
    {
      public UiMessage MessageType { get; set; }
      public string Message { get; set; }

      public static ThreadMessage Create(UiMessage messageType, string message)
      {
        return new ThreadMessage() { MessageType = messageType, Message = message };
      }
    }
```

```
Public Class ThreadMessage
  Private privateMessageType As UiMessage
  Public Property MessageType() As UiMessage
    Get
      Return privateMessageType
    End Get
    Set(ByVal value As UiMessage)
      privateMessageType = value
    End Set
  End Property

  Private privateMessage As String
  Public Property Message() As String
    Get
      Return privateMessage
    End Get
    Set(ByVal value As String)
      privateMessage = value
    End Set
  End Property

  Public Shared Function Create(ByVal messageType As UiMessage, _
    ByVal message As String) As ThreadMessage
    Return New ThreadMessage() With {.MessageType = messageType, .Message = message}
  End Function
End Class
```

The NetworkManager Class

The NetworkManager class handles all of the P2P features in the C4FP2P library, including connecting to the cloud, receiving text messages, streaming a video, and more. The C4FP2P library is a wrapper over the NetPeerTcpBinding Windows Communication Foundation class.

Let's walk through all of the pieces that make up the NetworkManager class.

NetworkManager variables and constructor

When the NetworkManager is created, we initialize a number of member variables that are explained here:

P2pWorker

> This is a BackgroundWorker object that will create a connection to the mesh network and wait for incoming events. Its value is initialized in the NetworkManager constructor.

userName
> An autogenerated value created using the number of DateTime ticks. This value must be different between client and server.

NetworkName
> The name of the mesh network we're connecting to. The networkName must match exactly between client and server.

Password
> The password of the mesh network we're connecting to. This must also match exactly between client and server.

p2p
> This is the C4FP2P library that handles all of the Peer Channel communication, including the connection process, sending and receiving messages across nodes (PCs), and streaming video files.

VideoHttpListener
> The server uses this object to set what methods will be used to break a video file into StreamPacket objects (a chunk of a video file). On the client, when a Stream Packet is received from the server, we'll use the videohttpListener's Stream Changed to write a StreamPacket to a localhost URL on the client machine.

ProgressBarValue
> Used to set the value of the MainWindow progress bar so users have a visual indica tion that the application is processing data. By default this is set to zero.

CurrentState
> This is a SystemState enumeration that tells us whether we are logged in, logged out, or in the process of logging in.

The SystemState enum that we use for the CurrentState property is defined in the C4FP2P library, and the enum defines the three possible states of our NetworkManager class, as shown in Examples 5-5 and 5-6.

C# Example 5-5. *SystemState enum in C#*

```
public enum SystemState
{
  LoggedOut,
  LoggingIn,
  LoggedIn,
}
```

```
Public Enum SystemState
  LoggedOut
  LoggingIn
  LoggedIn
End Enum
```

The NetworkManager variables and the class constructor are defined in Examples 5-7 and 5-8.

C# Example 5-7. *NetworkManager variables and constructor in C#*

```
using System;
using System.ComponentModel;
using System.Windows;
using C4F.VistaP2P.Common;

public class NetworkManager
{
  #region Variables
  public BackgroundWorker P2pWorker;
  private string userName = "machine" + DateTime.Now.Ticks;
  private string networkName;
  private string password;
  private P2PLib p2p;
  private StreamingHttpListener videoHttpListener;
  private int progressBarValue = 0;
  public SystemState CurrentState = SystemState.LoggedOut;
  #endregion

  public NetworkManager()
  {
    P2pWorker = BackgroundWorkerUtility.Create();
  }
  ...
```

VB Example 5-8. *NetworkManager variables and constructor in VB*

```
Imports Microsoft.VisualBasic
Imports System
Imports System.ComponentModel
Imports System.Windows
Imports C4F.VistaP2P.Common

Public Class NetworkManager
  #Region "Variables"
  Public P2pWorker As BackgroundWorker
```

```
Private userName As String = "machine" & DateTime.Now.Ticks
Private networkName As String
Private password As String
Private p2p As P2PLib
Private videoHttpListener As StreamingHttpListener
Private progressBarValue As Integer = 0
Public CurrentState As SystemState = SystemState.LoggedOut
#End Region


Public Sub New()
  P2pWorker = BackgroundWorkerUtility.Create()
End Sub
```

The NetworkManager constructor shown in Examples 5-7 and 5-8 calls the Create() method of the BackgroundWorkerUtility class, which builds a BackgroundWorker object, turns on the ability to report progress back to the main thread, and enables canceling the background worker process, as shown in Examples 5-9 and 5-10.

C# Example 5-9. *The BackgroundWorkerUtility class in C#*

```csharp
public static class BackgroundWorkerUtility
{
  public static BackgroundWorker Create()
  {
    BackgroundWorker worker = new BackgroundWorker()
    {
      WorkerReportsProgress = true,
      WorkerSupportsCancellation = true
    };
    return worker;
  }
}
```

VB Example 5-10. *The BackgroundWorkerUtility class in VB*

```vb
Public NotInheritable Class BackgroundWorkerUtility
  Public Shared Function Create() As BackgroundWorker
    Dim worker As New BackgroundWorker() With {.WorkerReportsProgress = True, _
      .WorkerSupportsCancellation = True}
    Return worker
  End Function
End Class
```

Starting a connection

To connect to a mesh network, you call the PeerChannelWrapperStart method of the P2PLib object, which accepts a nodeName, a networkName, and a password, as shown in the method signature in Examples 5-11 and 5-12.

 Example 5-11. *Starting a P2P connection in C#*

```csharp
public bool PeerChannelWrapperStart(String nodeName, String networkName, _
    String password)
```

 Example 5-12. *Starting a P2P connection in VB*

```vb
public Boolean PeerChannelWrapperStart(String nodeName, String networkName, _
    String password)
```

If we pass in "*MyHomePC*", "*Coding4Fun*", and "*myPassword*" for values, after "*MyHomePC*" is registered in PNRP, a new mesh named "*Coding4Fun*" will be created (assuming it didn't already exist) and assigned the password "*myPassword*".

> **NOTE** When running PeerCast, the network name and the password must match exactly between client and server.

We will wrap the call to this method in NetworkManager's StartConnection method; that way, clients only need to pass in the networkName and password since the userName is dynamically generated (see Examples 5-7 and 5-8). In StartConnection, we'll call the ValidateResetConnection() to ensure that the P2PLib class has been properly closed, and then we update the CurrentState to show we are in the process of logging in. Next, we set the method that will run on the background thread, P2pWorkerAsync, and then start the background thread running by calling the RunWorkerAsync method. This will start executing the P2pWorkerAsync method, but on a background thread instead of the UI thread in which StartConnection is executing. The StartConnection method is included in Examples 5-13 and 5-14 in its entirety.

 Example 5-13. *Starting a P2P connection in C#*

```csharp
public void StartConnection(string networkName, string password)
{
    this.networkName = networkName;
    this.password = password;

    if (ValidateResetConnection())
    {
        //update the network state
        this.CurrentState = SystemState.LoggingIn;
```

```
    P2pWorker.DoWork += new
      System.ComponentModel.DoWorkEventHandler(P2pWorkerAsync);

    //start working
    P2pWorker.RunWorkerAsync();
  }
}
```

VB Example 5-14. *Starting a P2P connection in VB*

```
Public Sub StartConnection(ByVal networkName As String, ByVal password As String)
  Me.networkName = networkName
  Me.password = password

  If ValidateResetConnection() Then
    'update the network state
    Me.CurrentState = SystemState.LoggingIn

    AddHandler P2pWorker.DoWork, AddressOf P2pWorkerAsync

    'start working
    P2pWorker.RunWorkerAsync()
  End If
End Sub
```

The ValidateResetConnection method called from inside the StartConnection method simply checks whether the p2p class is null, as shown in Examples 5-15 and 5-16. Although p2p will be null when the application first starts and we will reset it to null when the connection ends in the EndConnection method (see "Ending a connection"), there is a small chance that the p2p class doesn't get disposed of properly and therefore would not work correctly, hence the check here.

C# Example 5-15. *Ensuring that the P2PLib has been reset in C#*

```
//p2pConnection may not "die" when setting to null so need to check here
private bool ValidateResetConnection()
{
  if (p2p != null)
  {
    MessageBox.Show("An Error occurred when trying to initialize the Network." +
      "Please restart the application");
    return false;
  }
  return true;
}
```

```vb
'p2p may not "die" when setting to null so need to check here
Private Function ValidateResetConnection() As Boolean
  If p2p IsNot Nothing Then
    MessageBox.Show("An Error occurred when trying to initialize the Network." & _
      "Please restart the application")
    Return False
  End If
  Return True
End Function
```

Running on a background thread

Once the StartConnection method calls the RunWorkAsync() method, we'll immediately begin running the P2pWorkerAsync method on a background thread, as shown in Examples 5-17 and 5-18. In P2pWorkerAsync, we call the Report Progress method and send back a ThreadMessage class with a ClientMessage type of "ToggleUi". This tells the UI thread that our SystemState has changed since we are now in the process of logging in.

Next we create a new instance of the P2PLib class and call the Peer ChannelWrapper Start method, passing in the username, network name, and password. This method will return false if there was a problem setting up the connection; otherwise, it returns true. A response of "true" doesn't mean that we are now connected, but rather that a request to start the connection was successful.

Since the entire process of registering a PC and creating an ad-hoc network can take on average 10–30 seconds, we instead need to subscribe to the StatusChanged event in the P2PLib class to find out when we have successfully connected to the network. We'll delve into handling StatusChanged events later in Examples 5-25 and 5-26.

```csharp
private void P2pWorkerAsync(object sender, DoWorkEventArgs doWorkArgs)
{
  //Send back a text that we're logging in
  P2pWorker.ReportProgress(0, ThreadMessage.Create(UiMessage.ToggleUi,
    string.Empty));

  //Create new p2p
  p2p = new P2PLib();

  //Connect to the PeerChannel
  bool start = p2p.PeerChannelWrapperStart(userName, networkName, password);

  //check for connection error
```

```
    if (!start)
    {
      EndConnection();
    }

    SubscribeToPeerChannelEvents();

    //PeerChannel connection may take a while so cycle the ProgressBar
    CycleProgressBarUntilConnected();

    SitAndWait();
  }
```

VB **Example 5-18.** *Connecting to the P2P network in VB*

```
  Private Sub P2pWorkerAsync(ByVal sender As Object, ByVal doWorkArgs As _
    DoWorkEventArgs)
    'Send back a text that we're logging in
    P2pWorker.ReportProgress(0, ThreadMessage.Create(UiMessage.ToggleUi, String.Empty))

    'Create new p2p
    p2p = New P2PLib()

    'Connect to the PeerChannel
    Dim start As Boolean = p2p.PeerChannelWrapperStart(userName, networkName, password)

    'check for connection error
    If (Not start) Then
      EndConnection()
    End If

    SubscribeToPeerChannelEvents()

    'PeerChannel connection may take a while so cycle the ProgressBar
    CycleProgressBarUntilConnected()
    SitAndWait()
  End Sub
```

Subscribing to P2PLib events

The C4FP2P library uses events to send data over the P2P network. For PeerCast, we'll subscribe to the StatusChanged event, the ChatChanged event, and if we're in client mode, we'll subscribe to the StreamChanged event as shown in Examples 5-19 and 5-21. These three events are described here:

StatusChanged
> This fires whenever anyone joins or leaves the mesh network.

ChatChanged
> This fires any time a chat message is sent across the mesh network.

StreamChanged
> This fires any time a StreamedPacket (a slice of a streamed video file) is received.

Although we won't go into detail on what the StreamingHttpListener class does until the "Setting up a video stream" section, the only thing to remember here is that this is the method where we create the videoHttpListener object.

C# **Example 5-19.** *Subscribe to Peer Channel events in C#*

```csharp
private void SubscribeToPeerChannelEvents()
{
  //hook up the events we care about...text and status for the server
  p2p.StatusChanged += new
    EventHandler<StatusChangedEventArgs>(P2PLib_StatusChanged);
  p2p.TextPeerChannelHelper.ChatChanged += new
    EventHandler<ChatChangedEventArgs>(P2PLib_ChatChanged);

  //only setup the listener in client mode
  if (!App.IsServerMode)
  {
    p2p.StreamedVideo.StreamChanged += new
      EventHandler<StreamedChangedEventArgs>(P2PLib_StreamChanged);
  }

  //required by server for start/send stream, used by client for StreamChanged event
  //defined above)
  videoHttpListener = new StreamingHttpListener(userName + "/video/",
    MediaFinished,
    LogMessage,
    p2p.StreamedVideo.StartStream,
    p2p.StreamedVideo.SendStream);
}
```

VB **Example 5-20.** *Subscribe to Peer Channel events in VB*

```vb
Private Sub SubscribeToPeerChannelEvents()
  'hook up the events we care about...text and status for the server
  AddHandler p2p.StatusChanged, AddressOf P2PLib_StatusChanged
  AddHandler p2p.TextPeerChannelHelper.ChatChanged, AddressOf P2PLib_ChatChanged

  'only setup the listener in client mode
  If (Not App.IsServerMode) Then
```

```
    AddHandler p2p.StreamedVideo.StreamChanged, AddressOf P2PLib_StreamChanged
  End If

  'required by server for start/send stream, used by client for StreamChanged event
  'defined above)
  videoHttpListener = New StreamingHttpListener(userName & "/video/", _
    AddressOf MediaFinished, AddressOf LogMessage, _
    AddressOf p2p.StreamedVideo.StartStream, AddressOf p2p.StreamedVideo.SendStream)
End Sub
```

Reporting progress to the UI thread while we wait for a connection

After subscribing to the P2PLib events, we need to wait until we're connected to the network to do anything meaningful. When the StatusChanged event does fire, indicating we've connected to the network, the SystemState for the NetworkManager will change to SystemState.LoggedIn. Until that change happens, though, we do need to send some form of feedback from the background thread to the UI thread.

To do this, we'll use the CycleProgressBarUntilConnected method, which will check the SystemState for the application. If the SystemState shows that the application is still logging in, it will add one to the progressBarValue integer and send the value back to the UI thread using the ReportProgress method, as shown in Examples 5-21 and 5-22. Once the progressBarValue hits 100, we reset the value to zero, which will effectively cycle the progress bar from 0 to 100%. To prevent the CPU from throttling to 100% usage while this is happening, the loop also uses Thread.Sleep to make the background thread hibernate for 100 milliseconds. We'll exit the loop once the SystemState changes to either LoggedOff or LoggedIn.

C# Example 5-21. *Cycling the progressBarValue in C#*

```csharp
private void CycleProgressBarUntilConnected()
{
  //spin while we log in and update the progress bar.
  while (this.CurrentState == SystemState.LoggingIn)
  {
    System.Threading.Thread.Sleep(100);
    if (progressBarValue >= 100)
    {
      progressBarValue = 0;
    }
    else
    {
      progressBarValue++;
    }
```

```
     //Send back to UI thread
     P2pWorker.ReportProgress(progressBarValue);
     if (P2pWorker.CancellationPending)
     {
       P2pWorker.ReportProgress(0);
     }
   }
   //when complete, report 100 as the progress
   P2pWorker.ReportProgress(100);
 }
```

VB Example 5-22. *Cycling the progressBarValue in VB*

```
Private Sub CycleProgressBarUntilConnected()
  'spin while we log in and update the progress bar.
  Do While Me.CurrentState = SystemState.LoggingIn
    System.Threading.Thread.Sleep(100)
    If progressBarValue >= 100 Then
      progressBarValue = 0
    Else
      progressBarValue += 1
    End If

    'Send back to UI thread
    P2pWorker.ReportProgress(progressBarValue)
    If P2pWorker.CancellationPending Then
      P2pWorker.ReportProgress(0)
    End If
  Loop

  'when complete, report 100 as the progress
  P2pWorker.ReportProgress(100)
End Sub
```

Keeping the BackgroundWorker thread alive

Once our status has changed to LoggedIn, the CycleProgressBarUntilConnected loop ends and the last method we call is SitAndWait. The SitAndWait method is an infinite loop that does not end until a CancellationPending message is received, as shown in Examples 5-23 and 5-24. Since we assigned the event handlers for the P2PLib events on the background thread, the events themselves will also fire in the background thread.

Example 5-23. *Keeping the background thread alive in C#*

```csharp
private void SitAndWait()
{
  //continuous loop to sit and wait for PeerChannel or form events
  while (true)
  {
    System.Threading.Thread.Sleep(1000);
    if (P2pWorker != null)
    {
      if (P2pWorker.CancellationPending || CurrentState == SystemState.LoggedOut)
      {
        P2pWorker.ReportProgress(0);
        break;
      }
    }
  }
}
```

Example 5-24. *Keeping the background thread alive in VB*

```vbnet
Private Sub SitAndWait()
  'continuous loop to sit and wait for PeerChannel or form events
  Do
    System.Threading.Thread.Sleep(1000)
    If P2pWorker IsNot Nothing Then
      If P2pWorker.CancellationPending OrElse CurrentState = SystemState.LoggedOut
Then
        P2pWorker.ReportProgress(0)
        Exit Do
      End If
    End If
  Loop
End Sub
```

Listening to P2P Events Using Network Manager

Now that the P2pWorker background thread will be spinning infinitely (at least until we cancel or log out), we will just be waiting for the P2PLib class to fire the events that we've subscribed to. Let's go through how we handle these three events.

Understanding how the login process works

Before we delve into the StatusChanged event handler, let's recap what we've done so far and how the login process works, as illustrated in Figure 5-4.

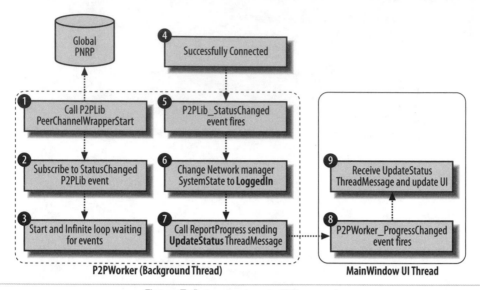

Figure 5-4. *Logging into the P2P network*

1. PeerChannelWrapperStart starts the connection using the C4FP2P library, which itself calls the Global PNRP network to register your node (see Examples 5-17 and 5-18).

2. To receive updates on the connection status, you must subscribe to the Status Changed event (see Examples 5-19 and 5-20).

3. We'll keep the P2PWorker background thread spinning in an infinite loop so that when the P2P events do fire, they will fire on the background thread and not cause our UI to freeze (see Examples 5-23 and 5-24).

4. Assuming you have no issues connecting to the global cloud (like an old router that doesn't support UPnP), your node will be registered in the Global PNRP using an IPv6 address.

5. Once the node is registered, the C4FP2P library will receive a notification and fire the StatusChanged event, indicating that a node has either joined or left (see Examples 5-25 and 5-26).

6. Now that we know we're logged in, we'll change the Network Manager's System-State to LoggedIn (see Examples 5-25 and 5-26).

7. To tell the UI thread that we've logged in, we'll call use the ReportProgress method to send back an UpdateStatus ThreadMessage.

8. On the UI thread, the ProgressChanged event will fire, and it will include the UpdateStatus ThreadMessage from the P2PWorker background thread.

9. The UI thread receives a ThreadMessage object to update the UI in the Receive UpdateStatus method, which checks the NetworkManager's System State set in step 6 to see whether we are logged in or not (see Examples 5-77 and 5-78).

The StatusChanged event

The StatusChanged event will fire when a status change, such as joining or leaving the network, has occurred in any node. The StatusChangedEventArgs object allows you to inspect which user has fired the status changed event (e.Member) and to check whether the updated status indicates that you are now connected (e.NewNodeJoined). In our event handler, we will first check to see whether our username is the member that the StatusChanged event is firing for. If the event is for our user, we'll check whether the event indicates that we have successfully joined or left the P2P network, and then use ReportProgress to tell the UI thread that we have either logged in and set the progressBar value to 100 or logged out and should set the progressBar to 0, as shown in Examples 5-25 and 5-26.

 Example 5-25. *Checking whether we've logged in or out of the network in C#*

```csharp
protected void P2PLib_StatusChanged(object sender, StatusChangedEventArgs e)
{
  if (userName == e.Member)
  {
    if (e.NewNodeJoined)
    {
      this.CurrentState = SystemState.LoggedIn;
      P2pWorker.ReportProgress(100, ThreadMessage.Create(UiMessage.UpdateStatus,
        "Connected"));
    }
    if (e.NodeLeft)
    {
      P2pWorker.ReportProgress(0, ThreadMessage.Create(UiMessage.UpdateStatus,
        "Disconnected..."));
      this.CurrentState = SystemState.LoggedOut;
    }
  }
}
```

VB Example 5-26. *Checking whether we've logged in or out of the network in VB*

```vb
Protected Sub P2PLib_StatusChanged(ByVal sender As Object, _
  ByVal e As StatusChangedEventArgs)
  If userName = e.Member Then
    If e.NewNodeJoined Then
      Me.CurrentState = SystemState.LoggedIn
      P2pWorker.ReportProgress(100, ThreadMessage.Create(UiMessage.UpdateStatus, _
        "Connected"))
    End If
```

```
        If e.NodeLeft Then
          P2pWorker.ReportProgress(0, ThreadMessage.Create(UiMessage.UpdateStatus, _
            "Disconnected..."))
          Me.CurrentState = SystemState.LoggedOut
        End If
      End If
    End Sub
```

Sending commands using chat messages

For PeerCast, we need to send commands between the client and server nodes—for example, to signal to a server that a client would like it to start streaming a video. To send those commands, we're going to use the text messaging features in P2PLib. We'll explicitly define the commands our application uses in the ChatCommand enumeration, shown in Examples 5-27 and 5-28.

C# Example 5-27. *ChatCommand enumeration in C#*

```csharp
public enum ChatCommand
{
  GetList,
  ReturnList,
  StreamVideo
}
```

VB Example 5-28. *ChatCommand enumeration in VB*

```vb
Public Enum ChatCommand
  GetList
  ReturnList
  StreamVideo
End Enum
```

The following are brief descriptions of what each ChatCommand does:

GetList
> A client is requesting the list of video files a server can stream.

ReturnList
> A server is sending back the list of videos to the client.

StreamedVideo
> A client is requesting a particular video that the server should start streaming.

Similar to how we created the ThreadMessage class to send messages from the background thread to the UI thread, we'll create a ChatMessage class to explicitly define what we will communicate from one node on the network to another.

The ChatMessage class includes two properties: the ChatCommand, which we explained earlier, and a Message string, as shown in Examples 5-29 and 5-30. ChatMessage also includes a helper method named Create that simplifies creating a ChatMessage object.

 Example 5-29. *The ChatMessage class in C#*

```csharp
using System;
using System.Collections.Generic;
using System.Linq;
using System.Text;

public class ChatMessage
{
  public ChatCommand CommandType { get; set; }
  public string Message { get; set; }

  public static ChatMessage Create(ChatCommand command, string message)
  {
    return new ChatMessage() { CommandType = command, Message = message };
  }
  ...
```

VB Example 5-30. *The ChatMessage class in VB*

```vb
Public Class ChatMessage
  Private privateCommandType As ChatCommand
  Public Property CommandType() As ChatCommand
    Get
      Return privateCommandType
    End Get
    Set(ByVal value As ChatCommand)
      privateCommandType = value
    End Set
  End Property

  Private privateMessage As String
  Public Property Message() As String
    Get
      Return privateMessage
    End Get
    Set(ByVal value As String)
      privateMessage = value
    End Set
  End Property
```

```
Public Shared Function Create(ByVal command As ChatCommand, _
  ByVal message As String) As ChatMessage
  Return New ChatMessage() With {.CommandType = command, .Message = message}
End Function
```

To actually send a message over the wire, the NetworkManager class has a SendChat-Message method that takes a ChatMessage object and forwards the request to the P2PLib's SendTextMessage method. Since SendTextMessage has two parameters, a sender and a message parameter, we'll set the ChatMessage ChatCommand.To String() value as the sender and ChatMessage.Message as the message parameter, as shown in Examples 5-31 and 5-32.

 Example 5-31. *Sending a ChatMessage in C#*

```csharp
public void SendChatMessage(ChatMessage message)
{
  p2p.TextPeerChannelHelper.SendTextMessage(message.CommandType.ToString(),
    message.Message);
}
```

VB Example 5-32. *Sending a ChatMessage in VB*

```vb
Public Sub SendChatMessage(ByVal message As ChatMessage)
  p2p.TextPeerChannelHelper.SendTextMessage(message.CommandType.ToString(), _
    message.Message)
End Sub
```

One of the gotchas with the design of P2PLib's TextPeerChannelHelper class is that the message contents sent using the SendTextMessage method are actually modified when they are sent over the wire!

For example, imagine you send the StreamVideo string (the result of calling To String() on ChatCommand.StreamVideo) to start streaming a video named *Bear.wmv*, as shown in Examples 5-33 and 5-34.

C# Example 5-33. *Sending a chat message using P2PLib in C#*

```csharp
SendTextMessage("StreamVideo", @"C:\Users\Public\Bear.wmv");
```

VB Example 5-34. *Sending a chat message using P2PLib in VB*

```vb
SendTextMessage("StreamVideo", "C:\Users\Public\Bear.wmv")
```

We'd expect to receive something like this:

```
"StreamVideo C:\Users\Public\Bear.wmv"
```

but the P2PLib class inserts the text " said: " in between the command and the message (including one space to the left and the right), and so the message we actually receive is this:

```
"StreamVideo said: C:\Users\Public\Bear.wmv"
```

To remove the extra text that we don't need for our application, we'll create a helper method named P2PLibParse for the ChatMessage class that parses out the " said: " text and converts the remaining strings into a ChatMessage class, as shown in Examples 5-35 and 5-36. The P2PLibParse method does some basic text parsing that:

1. Splits the text into three parts in the msgParts variable:

    a. Element 0: "StreamVideo"

    b. Element 1: " said: "

    c. Element 2: "C:\Users\Public\Bear.wmv"

2. Combines the first two array elements (0 and 1) and a blank space, and removes the combined string from the original text:

    a. Original message: "StreamVideo said: C:\Users\Public\Bear.wmv"

    b. First two parts: "StreamVideo said: "

    c. Subtract step b from a to get just the path: "C:\Users\Public\Bear.wmv"

3. Creates a new ChatCommand by parsing the msgParts[0] element, "StreamVideo", into an enum and setting the message to the message variable from step 2.

C# Example 5-35. *Parsing out extra text added in a text message in C#*

```
public static ChatMessage P2PLibParse(string text)
{
    //ex:"StreamVideo said: C:\Users\Public\Bear.wmv"

    //split the string based on spaces
    var msgParts = text.Split(' ');

    //combine the first parts of the text
    string firstPart = msgParts[0] + " " + msgParts[1] + " ";

    //now remove from the original text
    string message = text.Remove(0, firstPart.Length);

    //create a text and return it
    ChatMessage msg = new ChatMessage();

    //create a ChatCommand enum
    msg.CommandType = (ChatCommand)Enum.Parse(typeof(ChatCommand), msgParts[0]);
    msg.Message = message;
    return msg;
}
```

```vb
Public Shared Function P2PLibParse(ByVal text As String) As ChatMessage
    'ex:"StreamVideo said: C:\Users\Public\Bear.wmv"

    'split the string based on spaces
    Dim msgParts = text.Split(" "c)

    'combine the first parts of the text
    Dim firstPart As String = msgParts(0) & " " & msgParts(1) & " "

    'now remove from the original text
    Dim message As String = text.Remove(0, firstPart.Length)

    'create a text and return it
    Dim msg As New ChatMessage()

    'create a ChatCommand enum
    msg.CommandType = CType(System.Enum.Parse(GetType(ChatCommand), msgParts(0)), _
        ChatCommand)
    msg.Message = message
    Return msg
End Function
```

Understanding how chat messages work

At this point, we know how to send a chat message over the network and how to convert a received text string into a ChatMessage class. Next, we'll explain what actions a client and server will take when they receive chat commands in the ChatChanged event, as shown in Figure 5-5.

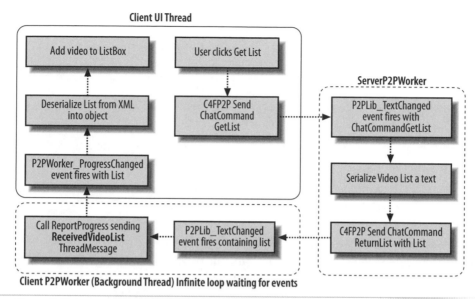

Figure 5-5. *How a request to get a video list is sent and received across the P2P network and across background and UI threads*

1. Assuming we are running PeerCast in client mode and we've already connected to the P2P network, the chat communication starts when a user clicks the Get List button, which calls the Network Manager's SendChatMessage method, passing in a GetList ChatCommand as the parameter (see Examples 5-88 and 5-89).

2. The SendChatMessage message sends the GetList command across the network using the C4FP2P SendTextMessage method (see Examples 5-31 and 5-32).

3. The message is sent across the network, and assuming we are running PeerCast on another PC that is in server mode, the TextChanged event will fire on the server's background thread and we parse the newly received text message into a GetList ChatCommand using the P2PLibParse method (see Examples 5-35 and 5-36).

4. The server checks the message type and begins processing the GetList request by serializing the list of videos into an XML text string (see Examples 5-45 and 5-46). Next, the server sends back the XML list by calling the Network Manager's SendChatMessage method, passing in a ReturnList command as a parameter (see Examples 5-39 and 5-40).

5. The client receives the server response using the TextChanged event and parses it into a ReturnList ChatMessage, with the message contents being the XML list of videos (see Examples 5-37 and 5-38).

6. Since the list of videos needs to be displayed in the PeerCast UI, we need to send data from the background thread to the UI thread using the ReportProgress method. To do this, we'll create a ReceivedVideoList ThreadMessage and include the XML list of videos in the ThreadMessage to the UI thread (see Examples 5-39 and 5-40).

7. The ProgressChanged event fires on the UI thread, and we determine the type of ThreadMessage being passed in (see Examples 5-74 and 5-75).

8. The list of videos is deserialized from an encoded XML string into a List of strings class (see Examples 5-80 and 5-81).

9. We add the items in the video list to the MediaList ListBox control (see Examples 5-78 and 5-79).

Receiving chat messages in the ChatChanged event handler

When a chat message is sent over the wire, our P2PLib_ChatChanged event will fire with the message stored in the ChatChangeEventArgs e.Message property, as shown in Examples 5-37 and 5-38. When this happens, the first thing we'll do is call Report Progress to tell the UI thread to display the chat command we just received.

Next, we check whether the chat message we received starts with the string machine, since we know that this message is an automatic message that the P2PLib object fires when it starts and finishes sending a video. We don't need to take any action when the machine text is received, and so we'll simply exit the ChatChanged method.

If the message doesn't start with machine, we know it's a ChatMessage and we can use the P2PLibParse method explained earlier to convert the chat string into a ChatMessage object. Once it's converted, we can handle client and server events. If PeerCast is running in ServerMode, we'll call the ProcessServerMessage method. Otherwise, we'll check to see if the ChatCommand we received is the ReturnList command; if it is, we'll send the message (the list of videos as an XML string) back to the UI thread to be deserialized.

C# Example 5-37. *Receiving commands using ChatChanged in C#*

```csharp
protected void P2PLib_ChatChanged(object sender, ChatChangedEventArgs e)
{
  //Sends text to chat window
  P2pWorker.ReportProgress(100, ThreadMessage.Create(UiMessage.Log, e.Message));

  if (e.Message.StartsWith("machine"))
  {
    return; //exit
  }

  ChatMessage msg = ChatMessage.P2PLibParse(e.Message);
```

```
  if (App.IsServerMode)
  {
    ProcessServerCommand(msg);
  }
  else
  {
    if (msg.CommandType == ChatCommand.ReturnList)
    {
      ChatMessage.P2PLibParse(e.Message);
      P2pWorker.ReportProgress(100,
        ThreadMessage.Create(UiMessage.ReceivedVideoList, msg.Message));
    }
  }
}
```

VB Example 5-38. *Receiving commands using ChatChanged in VB*

```
Protected Sub P2PLib_ChatChanged(ByVal sender As Object, _
  ByVal e As ChatChangedEventArgs)
  'Sends text to chat window
  P2pWorker.ReportProgress(100, ThreadMessage.Create(UiMessage.Log, e.Message))
  If e.Message.StartsWith("machine") Then
    Return 'exit
  End If

  Dim msg As ChatMessage = ChatMessage.P2PLibParse(e.Message)
  If App.IsServerMode Then
    ProcessServerCommand(msg)
  Else
    If msg.CommandType = ChatCommand.ReturnList Then
      ChatMessage.P2PLibParse(e.Message)
      P2pWorker.ReportProgress(100, ThreadMessage.Create( _
        UiMessage.ReceivedVideoList, msg.Message))
    End If
  End If
End Sub
```

Processing commands on the server

When PeerCast is in server mode, it needs to look for two types of ChatCommands,
the GetList and StreamVideo commands. If the ChatCommand is a GetList command, we'll use the Serializer.SerializeFileList method to serialize a List of
strings containing the video filenames from the server into XML. Once we have the
serialized list as an XML string, the server will send it back to the client by calling the
SendChatMessage with the ReturnList ChatCommand to indicate to the client

that we're returning a list of videos from the server, as shown in Examples 5-39 and 5-40.

The other command we're listening for in server mode is a StreamVideo Chat Command. When the server receives this, it will check to make sure we have a valid videoHttpListener class, and if we're already streaming a video, it will call the CancelSendingStream method to cancel the current stream.

To start streaming a video back to the client, the server will call the SendStreaming Data method, passing in the filename to stream. This will start streaming the video by reading chunks of the stream into StreamPacket objects and sending them back to the client over the network.

C# Example 5-39. *Handling server commands in C#*

```csharp
private void ProcessServerCommand(ChatMessage msg)
{
  switch (msg.CommandType)
  {
    case ChatCommand.GetList:
      string list = Serializer.SerializeFileList();
      this.SendChatMessage(ChatMessage.Create(ChatCommand.ReturnList, list));
      break;
    case ChatCommand.StreamVideo:
      if (videoHttpListener != null)
      {
        //Cancel current stream if streaming
        if (p2p.StreamedVideo.StreamedState == StreamedStateType.Communicating)
        {
          p2p.StreamedVideo.CancelSendingStream();
        }
        //start streaming file back to the client
        videoHttpListener.SendStreamingData(msg.Message);
      }
      break;
  }
}
```

VB Example 5-40. *Handle server commands in VB*

```vb
Private Sub ProcessServerCommand(ByVal msg As ChatMessage)
  Select Case msg.CommandType
    Case ChatCommand.GetList
      Dim list As String = Serializer.SerializeFileList()
      Me.SendChatMessage(ChatMessage.Create(ChatCommand.ReturnList, list))
    Case ChatCommand.StreamVideo
      If videoHttpListener IsNot Nothing Then
```

```
        'Cancel current stream if streaming
        If p2p.StreamedVideo.StreamedState = StreamedStateType.Communicating Then
          p2p.StreamedVideo.CancelSendingStream()
        End If
        'start streaming file back to the client
        videoHttpListener.SendStreamingData(msg.Message)
      End If
  End Select
End Sub
```

The GetList ChatCommand

When PeerCast is run in server mode, it uses the `FileDirectory` user-level variable defined in the Settings tab to define the default directory containing videos that the server is making available to stream, as shown in Figure 5-6.

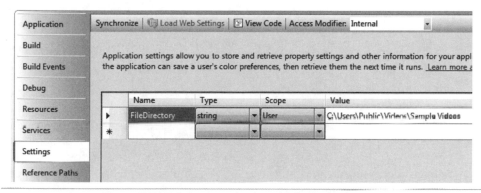

Figure 5-6. *Defining a user-level variable for the file directory*

Now that we know where to locate the video files (the value of the `FileDirectory` variable), we can use the `FileUtility` `GetVideoList` method to search the top directory (subdirectories will not be included) for *.wmv* format files, as shown in Examples 5-41 and 5-42. The `Directory.GetFiles` method returns an array of string objects, and so we convert that array to a generic `List` of type string using the `ToList()` extension method.

C# Example 5-41. *Getting the video list in C#*

```csharp
using System.Collections.Generic;
using System.IO;
using System.Linq;

public static class FileUtility
{
  public static List<string> GetVideoList()
```

```
  {
    List<string> videos =
      Directory.GetFiles(Properties.Settings.Default.FileDirectory,
      "*.wmv", SearchOption.TopDirectoryOnly).ToList();
    return videos;
  }
}
```

```
Imports Microsoft.VisualBasic
Imports System.Collections.Generic
Imports System.IO
Imports System.Linq

Public Class FileUtility

  Public Shared Function GetVideoList() As List(Of String)
    Dim videos As List(Of String) = Directory.GetFiles( _
      My.Settings.Default.FileDirectory,"*.wmv", _
      SearchOption.TopDirectoryOnly).ToList()
    Return videos
  End Function
End Class
```

If we were to call the FileUtility.GetVideoList() method using the default value for FileDirectory, *C:\Users\Public\Videos\Sample Videos*, on Windows Vista, we
would get back a List of strings object with three elements and an internal memory
structure similar to Example 5-43.

Example 5-43. *In-memory representation of videos from GetVideoList*

```
[0]: "C:\Users\Public\Videos\Sample Videos\Bear.wmv"
[1]: "C:\Users\Public\Videos\Sample Videos\Butterfly.wmv"
[2]: "C:\Users\Public\Videos\Sample Videos\Lake.wmv"
```

Since we need to send this list over the network using the SendChatMessage, which
only accepts a string as a message, we'll need to serialize the GetVideoList variable
into one long XML string. To do that, we'll use the SerializeFileList, which calls the
GetVideoList method defined in Example 5-41 and converts the results into the XML
string shown in Example 5-44.

Example 5-44. *The list of videos serialized into an XML string*

```
<?xml version="1.0" encoding="utf-8"?>
  <ArrayOfString xmlns:xsi="http://www.w3.org/2001/XMLSchema-instance"
    xmlns:xsd="http://www.w3.org/2001/XMLSchema">
  <string>C:\Users\Public\Videos\Sample Videos\Bear.wmv</string>
  <string>C:\Users\Public\Videos\Sample Videos\Butterfly.wmv</string>
```

```
<string>C:\Users\Public\Videos\Sample Videos\Lake.wmv</string>
<string>C:\Users\Public\Videos\Sample Videos\Viva Chihuahuas!.wmv</string>
</ArrayOfString>
```

The XML conversion in Examples 5-45 and 5-46 is done by taking the videoList, building a MemoryStream named contents to hold the contents of the file, using an Xml TextWriter and an XmlSerializer to serialize the videoList into XML, and creating a new UTF8Encoding object to convert the contents memory stream into a string of text.

The exact semantics of using these classes isn't as important as understanding that what we're doing is converting an in-memory object into an encoded XML string to send it across the P2P network.

C# Example 5-45. *Serializing a list of videos in C#*

```csharp
using System;
using System.Collections.Generic;
using System.Text;
using System.IO;
using System.Xml.Serialization;
using System.Xml;

public class Serializer
{
  public  static string SerializeFileList()
  {
    List<string> videoList = FileUtility.GetVideoList();

    MemoryStream contents = new MemoryStream();
    XmlTextWriter writer = new XmlTextWriter(contents, Encoding.UTF8);

    XmlSerializer xs = new XmlSerializer(typeof(List<string>));
    xs.Serialize(writer, videoList);

    contents = (MemoryStream)writer.BaseStream;
    UTF8Encoding encoding = new UTF8Encoding();

    return encoding.GetString(contents.ToArray());
  }
  ...
```

VB Example 5-46. *Serializing a list of videos in VB*

```vbnet
Imports Microsoft.VisualBasic
Imports System
Imports System.Collections.Generic
```

```vbnet
Imports System.Text
Imports System.IO
Imports System.Xml.Serialization
Imports System.Xml

Public Class Serializer
  Public Shared Function SerializeFileList() As String
    Dim videoList As List(Of String) = FileUtility.GetVideoList()

    Dim contents As New MemoryStream()
    Dim writer As New XmlTextWriter(contents, Text.Encoding.UTF8)

    Dim xs As New XmlSerializer(GetType(List(Of String)))
    xs.Serialize(writer, videoList)

    contents = CType(writer.BaseStream, MemoryStream)
    Dim encoding As New UTF8Encoding()

    Return encoding.GetString(contents.ToArray())
  End Function
  ...
```

Using C4FP2P to Stream Videos

The most complex part of using the C4FP2P library is trying to understand how to stream a video file. This can be confusing because there are some limitations in Windows Communication Foundation (WCF) and in the MediaElement control:

No native streaming support
> Windows Communication Foundation does not include native support for streaming. This means that the C4FP2P library has to manually break a video file into a set of sequentially numbered StreamPacket classes (a byte array of the contents), send each packet across the network, and reassemble the packets on the client PC.

The streaming source must be a URI
> The P2P library was designed to support streaming to a MediaElement control. This raises a unique challenge in that you can set the video source of a Media Element control only to a Uri, such as a file or a website address, and not to an in-memory stream. The C4FP2P dev team first attempted to stream the packets into a file stream on the disk and set the MediaElement to the file path, but they were unsuccessful; if the MediaElement ever reached the end of the file, it would stop streaming. Instead, the C4FP2P team built a custom localhost address on the receiving machine to write out the StreamPacket byte array directly to that URL. As new packets come in, they are written to the URL, and a MediaElement control using that localhost address simply streams the contents. Since it's an open HTTP

connection, the MediaElement also doesn't close the connection when it reaches the end, meaning we can start and stop writing data to the URL.

Understanding how video streaming works

Like we've done previously with the status change and chat messaging events, next we'll explain what happens conceptually when we stream a video, as illustrated in Figure 5-7.

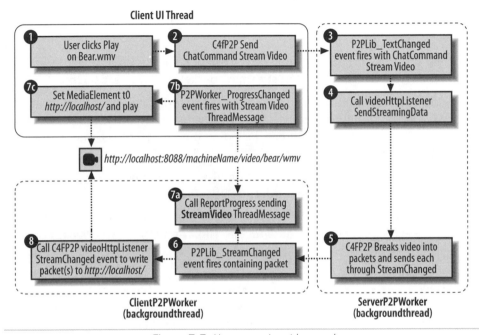

Figure 5-7. *How streaming videos work*

1. The user running PeerCast in client mode selects the video he wants to start streaming from the MediaList Listbox. The play button event handler creates a ChatMessage with a StreamVideo ChatCommand and the name of the video we want to stream as the message. The newly created ChatMessage is then sent using the Network Manager's SendChatMessage method (see Examples 5-84 and 5-85).

2. The SendChatMessage sends the StreamVideo command and the video to be streamed across the network using the C4FP2P SendTextMessage method (see Examples 5-31 and 5-32).

3. The message is sent across the P2P network and, assuming we are running Peer-Cast on another PC that is in server mode, the TextChanged event will fire on the server's background thread. We parse the newly received text message into a StreamVideo ChatCommand using the P2PLibParse method (see Examples 5-35 and 5-36).

4. To start streaming the video file, we call the videoHttpListener SendStreaming Data method, passing in the file path we want to stream (see Examples 5-39 and 5-40).

5. When the videoHttpListener object is first created (see Examples 5-19 and 5-20), we registered several methods as parameters in the constructor, such as Start Stream and SendStream, that are part of the C4FP2P library. These methods break a video file into hundreds of small StreamPacket objects. Each of these packets is then sent back to the client node through the StreamChanged event.

6. The StreamChanged event on the client will fire once for every StreamPacket it receives from the server.

7. When the very first StreamPacket is received in the StreamChanged event, we need to get the UI ready to start streaming packets to the user's screen.

   a. To tell the UI thread that we're starting to receive packets of the video file, we'll use the ReportProgress method and send a StreamVideo Thread Message back to the UI thread, including the URL on the client's PC that will contain the video stream (see Examples 5-51 and 5-52).

   b. The ProgressChanged event fires and we determine the type of Thread Message being passed in (see Examples 5-74 and 5-75).

   c. The UI thread receives the StreamVideo ThreadMessage and it sets the Media Element control to the *http://localhost* URL where the StreamPacket objects will be written to on the background thread (see Examples 5-82 and 5-83).

8. In parallel to step 7 but on the background thread, we forward the Stream Packet we received from step 6 to the videoHttpListener's StreamChanged event. This listener's StreamChanged event, which is different from the P2PLib's StreamChanged event (see "Two different StreamChanged events"), takes a StreamPacket and writes the contents of the StreamPacket (a byte array containing a sliver of the video) to the *http://localhost* path on the client machine (see Examples 5-51 and 5-52).

9. The user will now start seeing the contents of the video as it is streamed to his PC.

Setting up a video stream

The C4FP2P library includes two classes used for streaming a video file. The first class is the StreamingHelper class. The P2PLib object exposes an instance of the Streaming Helper class as a property named StreamedVideo. The two important methods we'll reuse from the StreamingHelper class are:

StartStream
    This method is called when you first want to start streaming a video. It initializes the video stream and opens the video file.

SendStream

This method does the actual work of opening up a file stream and looping through the entire video file, sending 12K of bytes at a time across the network in StreamPacket objects.

Again, you do not need to know the inner workings of these methods, but you do need to know they exist, as they must be set as parameters when we create a Streaming HttpListener object. Let's look at the method signature for the Streaming HttpListener class, as shown in Examples 5-47 and 5-48.

C# Example 5-47. *StreamingHttpListener class constructor in C#*

```csharp
public StreamingHttpListener(String uniqueStreamName, _
    WorkerThreadFinished threadFinishedDelegate,LogMessage msg, _
    StartStream startStream, SendStream sendStream)
```

VB Example 5-48. *StreamingHttpListener class constructor in VB*

```vb
Public Sub New(ByVal uniqueStreamName As String, _
    ByVal threadFinishedDelegate As WorkerThreadFinished, ByVal msg As LogMessage, _
    ByVal startStream As StreamingHttpListener.StartStream, _
    ByVal sendStream As StreamingHttpListener.SendStream)
```

When you create an instance of the StreamingListener class, you must pass in the five required parameters, as they are part of the class constructor. Let's take a minute to explain what each of these parameters does:

UniqueStreamName

This string is used to assign a unique localhost address on the client PC to write the contents of a StreamPacket we receive. The stream name for a video stream has the following format:

http://localhost:8088/machineName/video/FileName

An actual example for PeerCast would be:

http://localhost:8088/machine633540078269940000/video/bear.wmv

threadFinishedDelegate

This method fires once the streaming of a file is completed. This is useful for detecting whether an error occurred while streaming a video or when you need to execute code after the streaming has completed.

LogMessage

This method fires to send status messages to describe the current status of the StreamingHttpListener class. The following is a list of messages that will be sent to the LogMessage method when you start streaming a file:

- When the server starts streaming a video, it will send *"Sending Media File: filename"*.

- When the server has finished streaming a video, it will send *"Finished Sending Media"*.

- When the client has finished receiving the file, it will send *"Finished Receiving Media File"*.

- If there was a connection issue and there was a timeout, it will send *"Stream Timed out"*.

StartStream

This method fires when you first start streaming a file. This must be assigned to the P2PLib's StreamedVideo.StartStream method that we explained earlier.

SendStream

This method actually does the work of streaming the file. This must be assigned to the P2PLib's StreamedVideo.SendStream method explained earlier.

Now that you have an understanding of what the parameters are used for, let's review in Examples 5-49 and 5-50 how we constructed the videoHttpListener object from Example 5-19.

`C#` Example 5-49. *Constructing the videoHttpListener object in C#*

```
videoHttpListener = new StreamingHttpListener(userName + "/video/",
    MediaFinished,
    LogMessage,
    p2p.StreamedVideo.StartStream,
    p2p.StreamedVideo.SendStream);
```

`VB` Example 5-50. *Constructing the videoHttpListener object in VB*

```
videoHttpListener = New StreamingHttpListener(userName & "/video/", _
    AddressOf MediaFinished, AddressOf LogMessage, _
    AddressOf p2p.StreamedVideo.StartStream, AddressOf p2p.StreamedVideo.SendStream)
```

When the server fires the SendStreamingData method to start streaming a video, the C4FP2P library will fire the methods assigned in the videoHttpListener constructor, including LogMessage when we start and end sending a file and StartStream and SendStream to break the video file on the server into multiple StreamPacket objects and send them to the client.

When it's finished streaming the video, the MediaFinished method indicates we're done streaming. To send data over the network, the SendStream method will send the StreamPacket object from the server to the client using the StreamChanged event.

Two different StreamChanged events

One of the confusing aspects of the C4FP2P library is that two different classes include StreamChanged event handlers, and although they share the same name, the functionality is completely different!

P2PLib StreamChanged

This StreamChanged event is used to send back a StreamPacket from the server to the client PC.

`StreamingHttpListener StreamChanged`
This `StreamChanged` event takes a `StreamPacket` and writes it out to the localhost URL on the client PC.

To add to the confusion, we actually use both of these events one after another. First we use the `P2PLib StreamChanged` event to send a video packet from the server to the client. When the client receives that packet, we fire the other `StreamingHttpListener StreamChanged` event to write out the `StreamPacket` we just received to the localhost URL.

The P2PLib StreamChanged event

The `P2PLib StreamChanged` event is fired every time a `StreamPacket` is received over the network. What this means is that this event will fire hundreds or thousands of times depending on the size of the video file you are streaming. The `StreamPacket` objects are passed in through the `StreamChangedEventArgs e.StreamedPacket` variable.

We will forward the newly received `StreamPacket` to the `videoHttpListener Stream Changed` event. This event in turn writes out the `StreamPacket` to *http://localhost*, as shown in Examples 5-51 and 5-52.

We also need to do a little bit of setup when the event fires for the first time (meaning we received a `StreamPacket` with a `packetNumber` of 0). What we'll do is set up a URL variable with the same format as the `P2PLib` class uses and send the URL back to the UI thread so that we can set the `MediaElement` control's `Source` property to be the URL that the `P2PLib` object will begin writing to.

| C# | **Example 5-51.** *P2PLib StreamChanged event handler in C#*

```csharp
void P2PLib_StreamChanged(object sender, StreamedChangedEventArgs e)
{
    //take packet from server & use videoHttpListener to write to localhost
    videoHttpListener.StreamedChanged(e);

    //set client to listen to stream
    if (e.StreamedPacket.packetNumber == 0)
    {
        string file = StreamingHttpListener.SafeHttpString(e.StreamedPacket.fileName);
        string url = String.Format(@"http://localhost:8088/{0}/video/{1}", userName,
        file);
        P2pWorker.ReportProgress(100, ThreadMessage.Create(UiMessage.StreamVideo, url));
    }
}
```

Example 5-52. *P2PLib StreamChanged event handler in VB*

```vb
Private Sub P2PLib_StreamChanged(ByVal sender As Object, _
  ByVal e As StreamedChangedEventArgs)

  'take packet from server & use videoHttpListener to write to localhost
  videoHttpListener.StreamedChanged(e)

  'set client to listen to stream
  If e.StreamedPacket.packetNumber = 0 Then
    Dim file As String = StreamingHttpListener.SafeHttpString(_
      e.StreamedPacket.fileName)

    Dim url As String = String.Format("http://localhost:8088/{0}/video/{1}", _
      userName, file)

    P2pWorker.ReportProgress(100, ThreadMessage.Create(UiMessage.StreamVideo, url))
  End If
End Sub
```

Woohoo! At this point, we are officially streaming a video to the uniqueStreamName *http://localhost* address!

Logging messages when streaming a video

When we created the videoHttpListener object (see Examples 5-49 and 5-50), one of the parameters we had to pass into the videoHttpListener constructor was a LogMessage method. The LogMessage method will fire two events for a streaming video, one to indicate that the server is starting to stream a file, and a second when the streaming of the video is complete. For example, we'll see the following two messages fire when we stream a video:

- Sending Media File: *C:\Users\Public\Videos\Sample Videos\Bear.wmv*

- Finished Sending Media

The messages themselves come from deep within the P2PLib class, and we won't do anything other than forward them on to the UI thread so that users can see the application progress, as shown in Examples 5-53 and 5-54.

Example 5-53. *Logging streaming messages in C#*

```csharp
public void LogMessage(string msg)
{
  P2pWorker.ReportProgress(100, ThreadMessage.Create(ClientMessage.Log, msg));
}
```

Example 5-54. *Logging streaming messages in VB*

```vb
Public Sub LogMessage(ByVal msg As String)
  P2pWorker.ReportProgress(100, ThreadMessage.Create(UiMessage.Log, msg))
End Sub
```

Finished streaming a video

Once a video finishes streaming, the MediaFinished event will fire. In this event handler, we'll check whether there was a streaming error, and if there was, we'll display a MessageBox with the error message and end the connection, as shown in Examples 5-55 and 5-56.

`C#` Example 5-55. *Checking for exceptions in the MediaFinished event in C#*

```csharp
protected void MediaFinished(object sender, RunWorkerCompletedEventArgs e)
{
    //End connection on error
    if (e.Error != null)
    {
        MessageBox.Show(String.Format("Error streaming this video:{0}", _
            e.Error.Message));
        EndConnection();
    }
}
```

`VB` Example 5-56. *Checking for exceptions in the MediaFinished event in VB*

```vb
Protected Sub MediaFinished(ByVal sender As Object, ByVal e As RunWorkerCompleted
Protected Sub MediaFinished(ByVal sender As Object, _
    ByVal e As RunWorkerCompletedEventArgs)
    'End connection on error
    If e.Error IsNot Nothing Then
        MessageBox.Show(String.Format("Error streaming this video:{0}", e.Error.Message))
        EndConnection()
    End If
End Sub
```

Ending a connection

The last bit of work we'll do in the NetworkManager class is clean up when we're done. Specifically, we want to tell the UI thread to reset itself back to the state before we started to connect to the network. We also need to close and set to null (or set to nothing in VB) the P2PLib wrapper and the videoHttpListener objects and cancel the background worker thread, as shown in Examples 5-57 and 5-58.

`C#` Example 5-57. *Ending a connection in C#*

```csharp
public void EndConnection()
{
    //make sure we're not calling this multiple times
    if (this.CurrentState != SystemState.LoggedOut)
    {
        this.CurrentState = SystemState.LoggedOut;
```

```
    //reset UI after changing SystemState
    P2pWorker.ReportProgress(0, ThreadMessage.Create(UiMessage.ToggleUi,
      string.Empty));

    //close and set classes to null
    if (p2p != null)
    {
      p2p.Close();
      p2p = null;
    }
    if (videoHttpListener != null)
    {
      videoHttpListener.Stop();
      videoHttpListener.Quit();
      videoHttpListener = null;
    }
    if (P2pWorker != null)
    {
      P2pWorker.CancelAsync();
    }
  }
}
```

VB **Example 5-58.** *Ending a connection in VB*

```
Public Sub EndConnection()
  'make sure we're not calling this multiple times
  If Me.CurrentState <> SystemState.LoggedOut Then
    Me.CurrentState = SystemState.LoggedOut
    'reset UI after changing SystemState
    P2pWorker.ReportProgress(0, ThreadMessage.Create(UiMessage.ToggleUi, _
      String.Empty))

    'close and set classes to null
    If p2p IsNot Nothing Then
      p2p.Close()
      p2p = Nothing
    End If

    If videoHttpListener IsNot Nothing Then
      videoHttpListener.Stop()
      videoHttpListener.Quit()
      videoHttpListener = Nothing
    End If
```

```
    If P2pWorker IsNot Nothing Then
      P2pWorker.CancelAsync()
    End If
  End If
End Sub
```

Building the Application UI

At this point, we've covered all of the network communication in the `NetworkManager` class, but we haven't built the actual application UI, which is the next step in building PeerCast.

Choosing the Application Mode

When PeerCast first runs, the *ChooseMode.xaml* window will load, as shown in Figure 5-8, with two buttons, one named Client and another named Server, representing the two application modes.

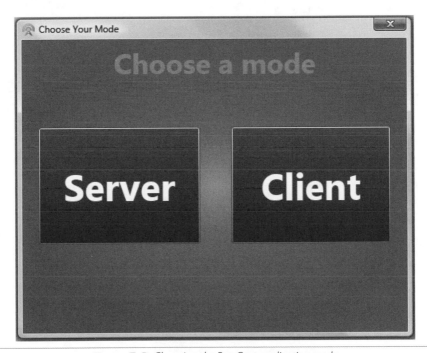

Figure 5-8. *Choosing the PeerCast application mode*

Both buttons have the same click event, `SetMode`, which sets the application-level `IsServerMode` variable defined in Examples 5-61 and 5-62. The code also opens the *MainWindow.xaml* window and closes the *ChooseMode.xaml* window, as shown in Examples 5-59 and 5-60.

```csharp
private void SetMode(object sender, RoutedEventArgs e)
{
    var button = (Button)sender;
    if (button.Name == "Server")
    {
        App.IsServerMode = true;
    }
    else
    {
        App.IsServerMode = false;
    }

    //open Main Window
    MainWindow w = new MainWindow();
    w.Show();

    //close current Window
    this.Close();
}
```

VB Example 5-60. *The ChooseMode Button event handler in VB*

```vbnet
Private Sub SetMode(ByVal sender As Object, ByVal e As RoutedEventArgs)
    Dim button = CType(sender, Button)
    If button.Name = "Server" Then
        App.IsServerMode = True
    Else
        App.IsServerMode = False
    End If

    'open Main Window
    Dim w As New MainWindow()
    w.Show()

    'close current Window
    Me.Close()
End Sub
```

Storing the PeerCast mode

To store the mode in which PeerCast is running, we'll define an application-level variable in the *App.xaml* (*Application.xaml* in VB), as shown in Examples 5-61 and 5-62. The application mode will be stored in a Boolean property named IsServerMode that will be true if we're running as a server or false if we're running as a client.

```csharp
using System.Windows;

public partial class App : Application
{
  public static bool IsServerMode;
}
```

```vb
Imports Microsoft.VisualBasic
Imports System.Windows
Partial Public Class App
  Inherits Application

  Public Shared IsServerMode As Boolean

End Class
```

Building the MainWindow.xaml UI

The user interface for PeerCast's main window is designed as a four-cell grid (see Figure 5-9):

Login cell
> The top-left cell contains the login control for connecting to the P2P network.

Message cell
> The bottom-left cell contains controls for messages that are received over the peer network.

Client controls cell
> The top-right cell holds controls that are visible only when the application is in client mode.

Server controls and media player cell
> The bottom-right cell holds a set of controls for selecting which videos a server will make available for clients to stream and the MediaElement control used in client mode to stream videos.

> **NOTE** PeerCast uses the *C4fStyle.xaml* file to define the appearance of buttons, ListBox controls, and more. To see what's included in the C4fStyle, see the Appendix.

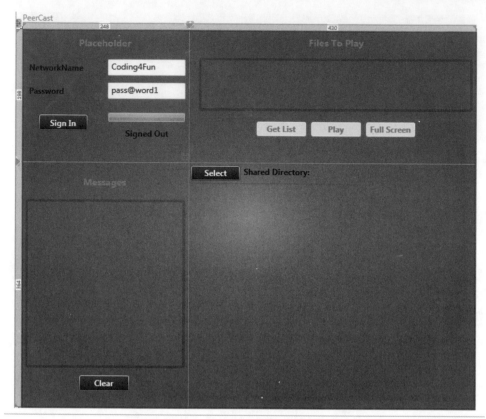

Figure 5-9. *The MainWindow four-cell grid*

Defining the four-cell grid

To begin with, we'll define the *MainWindow.xaml* file with some basic sizing properties, as well as a custom application icon and the *C4fStyle.xaml* SilverGradient. Next,
we define a two-column, two-row grid that will hold our application controls with
defined height and width values, as shown in Example 5-63.

Example 5-63. *MainWindow XAML*

```
<Window x:Class="P2PVideoClient.MainWindow"
  xmlns="http://schemas.microsoft.com/winfx/2006/xaml/presentation"
  xmlns:x="http://schemas.microsoft.com/winfx/2006/xaml"
  Title="P2P Video" Height="600" Width="700" MinWidth="500" MinHeight="400"
  Background="{DynamicResource SilverGradient}" Icon="/P2PVideoClient;component/icon.
png">
  <Grid>
    <Grid.ColumnDefinitions>
      <ColumnDefinition Width="260*"/>
```

```
      <ColumnDefinition Width="450*" />
    </Grid.ColumnDefinitions>
    <Grid.RowDefinitions>
      <RowDefinition Height="198*"></RowDefinition>
      <RowDefinition Height="364*"></RowDefinition>
    </Grid.RowDefinitions>
  </Grid>
</Window>
```

The login cell

The login cell pictured in Figure 5-10 encompasses the top-left corner of the window and includes nested Grid controls with a two-column by four-row layout. To tell
the WPF rendering engine that we want our nested Login grid to be in the first row
and first column (the top-left corner), we must explicitly set the Grid.Row and Grid.
Column properties to zero (the first row/column).

The first row in the login grid is a label that spans both columns to display the application mode. The next two rows are a series of labels and textboxes for the network
name and the password. The fourth and final row has the SignInButton button in the
first column, and a StackPanel control with a progressBar and a label stacked vertically (one on top of the other), as shown in Example 5-64.

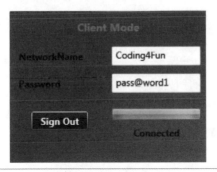

Figure 5-10. *The login cell*

Example 5-64. *XAML for the login cell*

```
<!-- Login Grid 2 columns x 4 rows -->
<Grid Grid.Row="0" Grid.Column="0" Name="Login">
  <Grid.ColumnDefinitions>
    <ColumnDefinition Width="150*"/>
    <ColumnDefinition Width="150*"/>
  </Grid.ColumnDefinitions>

  <Grid.RowDefinitions>
    <RowDefinition Height="Auto"></RowDefinition>
```

```xml
        <RowDefinition Height="Auto"></RowDefinition>
        <RowDefinition Height="Auto"></RowDefinition>
        <RowDefinition Height="Auto"></RowDefinition>
    </Grid.RowDefinitions>

    <!-- First Row -->
    <Label Grid.ColumnSpan="2" Grid.Row="0" Margin="5" HorizontalAlignment="Center"
      Name="AppModeLabel" Style="{DynamicResource HeaderStyle}">Placeholder</Label>

    <!-- Second Row-->
    <Label Margin="5" Grid.Row="1" Grid.Column="0" Name="NetworkNameLabel" Height="25"
      VerticalAlignment="Top" >NetworkName</Label>
    <TextBox Grid.Column="1" Grid.Row="1" Margin="5" Name="NetworkName" Height="25"
      VerticalAlignment="Top"></TextBox>

    <!-- Third Row-->
    <Label Grid.Column="0" Grid.Row="2" HorizontalAlignment="Left" Margin="5"
      Name="PasswordLabel" Height="25"  Width="112">Password</Label>
    <TextBox Grid.Column="1" Grid.Row="2" Margin="5" Height="25" Name="Password">
      </TextBox>

    <!-- Fourth Row-->
    <Button Grid.Column="0" Margin="5" Width="75" Height="25" Grid.Row="3"
      Name="SignInButton" Click="SignInButton_Click" >Sign In</Button>
    <StackPanel Grid.Column="1"  Grid.Row="3">
      <ProgressBar Grid.Column="0" Grid.Row="2"  x:Name="progressBar1"
        VerticalAlignment="Top" Margin="5,15,5,0" Height="15" />
      <Label Grid.Column="1" Grid.Row="2" Margin="3" Name="StatusValue"
        HorizontalContentAlignment="Center">Signed Out</Label>
    </StackPanel>
  </Grid>
```

The Message cell

The Message cell pictured in Figure 5-11 is used to write out chat messages we receive over the P2P network.

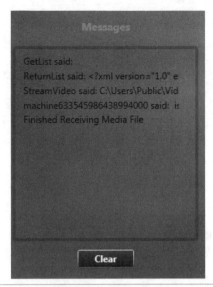

Figure 5-11. *The Message cell*

In the second row of the first column (the bottom left-hand corner) is the MessageCell StackPanel control. To define the location of the MessageCell StackPanel, we set its Grid.Column to zero (the first column) and the Grid.Row to one (the second row). Inside the StackPanel, we define a Label, setting its Style property to the C4fStyle HeaderStyle. Any messages we receive will be written to the Messages ListBox control. Finally, we also include the ClearMessages button that will simply remove any items from the Messages Listbox. The XAML is shown in Example 5-65.

Example 5-65. *XAML for the message cell*

```
<StackPanel Grid.Column="0" Grid.Row="1" Margin="0,10,0,0" Name="MessageCell">
  <Label Margin="5" Height="30" Width="120" HorizontalContentAlignment="Center"
    Style="{DynamicResource HeaderStyle}">Messages</Label>
  <ListBox Margin="5" Name="Messages" MinHeight="250" MaxHeight="300" />
  <Button Height="25" Margin="5" Name="ClearMessages" VerticalAlignment="Bottom"
    HorizontalAlignment="Center" Width="75" Click="ClearMessages_Click">Clear</But-
ton>
</StackPanel>
```

The Client controls cell

In the first row of the second column (the top-right corner) of PeerCast, we define a set of controls to list and play videos, as illustrated in Figure 5-12.

Figure 5-12. *The Client controls cell*

Like we did with the login cell, we add a nested `Grid` control named `ClientControls` with one column and two rows. In the first row, we define a header `Label` and a `List Box` control that will contain the list of video files the server has returned to us. In the second row, we define a `StackPanel` with a horizontal orientation and three buttons:

GetList
  Makes a request to the server to get the list of available videos.

Play
  Makes a request to the server to play the selected video from the `MediaList` `ListBox`.

FullScreen
  Like `Play`, this makes a request to play the selected video from the `MediaList` `ListBox`, but it opens up a new window, *FullScreen.xaml*, to play it in.

The buttons are disabled by default, and are enabled once we receive a `StatusChanged` message indicating that we are logged in. Since the client controls are relevant only when PeerCast is running in client mode, we will actually hide the entire `Client Controls` grid when we're in server mode by setting its visibility property to hidden. The XAML is shown in Example 5-66.

Example 5-66. *The ClientControls XAML*

```
<!-- Second Column -->
<Grid Grid.Column="1" Grid.Row="0" Margin="9.89,0,0,0" Name="ClientControls">
  <Grid.ColumnDefinitions>
    <ColumnDefinition ></ColumnDefinition>
  </Grid.ColumnDefinitions>
  <Grid.RowDefinitions>
    <RowDefinition Height="200*"></RowDefinition>
    <RowDefinition Height="100*"></RowDefinition>
  </Grid.RowDefinitions>
```

```xaml
<!-- First ClientControls Row -->
<StackPanel Grid.Row="0" >
  <Label Height="30" HorizontalAlignment="Center" VerticalAlignment="Top"
    Margin="3" Name="FilesToPlay" Style="{DynamicResource HeaderStyle}">
    Files To Play</Label>
  <ListBox Margin="5" Name="MediaList" MinWidth="300" MinHeight="75"
    MaxHeight="300" IsEnabled="False" RenderTransformOrigin="0.5,0.5"
    Height="80" >
    <ListBox.RenderTransform>
      <TransformGroup>
        <ScaleTransform ScaleX="1" ScaleY="1"/>
        <SkewTransform AngleX="0" AngleY="0"/>
        <RotateTransform Angle="0"/>
        <TranslateTransform X="0" Y="0"/>
      </TransformGroup>
    </ListBox.RenderTransform>
  </ListBox>
</StackPanel>

<!-- Second ClientControls Row -->
<StackPanel Grid.Row="1" Height="30" Orientation="Horizontal"
  VerticalAlignment="Top" HorizontalAlignment="Center">
  <Button Height="23" Margin="3" Name="GetList" Width="75" Click="GetList_Click"
    IsEnabled="False" >Get List</Button>
  <Button Height="23" Margin="3" Name="Play" Width="75" Click="Play_Click"
    IsEnabled="False">Play</Button>
  <Button Height="23" Margin="3" Name="FullScreen" Width="75"
    Click="FullScreen_Click" IsEnabled="False">Full Screen</Button>
</StackPanel>
</Grid>
```

Server controls and the media player cell

The final cell in *MainWindow.xaml* is in the second row, second column of our top-level grid (the bottom right-hand corner). This cell defines the server directory controls and the media player, as illustrated in Figure 5-13.

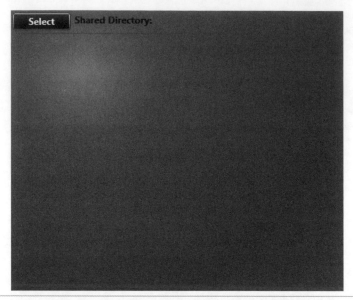

Figure 5-13. *The server controls and media player cell*

In this section, we include a StackPanel control with a horizontal orientation. The ServerControls StackPanel includes a button control to pop up a FolderBrowser Dialog control that enables users to select the directory on the server that will be made available for clients to stream. We will also display the currently selected directory using the FilePath label. Since we will pick the directory to stream files only when we are in server mode, we will set the visibility of the ServerControls StackPanel to be hidden when PeerCast is run in client mode. Underneath the StackPanel is the MediaPlayer MediaElement control. This control is what we will use to stream videos when we hit the Play button on the client. The XAML is shown in Example 5-67.

Example 5-67. *XAML for server controls and media player*

```
<!-- Server Controls -->
<StackPanel Grid.Row="1" Grid.Column="1" Name="ServerControls" Margin="3,0,0,0"
Height="30" VerticalAlignment="Top" Orientation="Horizontal">
  <Button Name="OpenDialog" Click="OpenDialog_Click" Width="75" Height="23">Select
  </Button>
  <Label Name="ChooseDirectory">Shared Directory:</Label>
  <Label Name="FilePath" />
</StackPanel>
<!-- Media Player -->
<MediaElement Grid.Row="1" Grid.Column="1" Name="MediaPlayer" LoadedBehavior="Manual"
  Margin="10,31,10,10" MinHeight="300"  />
```

Adding the MainWindow.xaml Code

Now that we've defined the appearance of our application, next we need to define the properties and events for *MainWindow.xaml*.

MainWindow properties

MainWindow defines two properties, as shown in Examples 5-68 and 5-69: one for the NetworkManager class that we will use to send and receive data from P2PLib, and another for the FullScreen window that we'll create when a user clicks on the FullScreen button.

Example 5-68. *MainWindow properties in C#*

```csharp
using System;
using System.Collections.Generic;
using System.ComponentModel;
using System.Linq;
using System.Windows;
using C4F.VistaP2P.Common;

public partial class MainWindow : Window
{
  #region Properties
  //net is the wrapper for all async/P2P work
  private NetworkManager net = new NetworkManager();
  FullScreen fullWindow;
  #endregion
  ...
```

VB Example 5-69. *MainWindow properties in VB*

```vbnet
Imports Microsoft.VisualBasic
Imports System
Imports System.Collections.Generic
Imports System.ComponentModel
Imports System.Linq
Imports System.Windows
Imports C4F.VistaP2P.Common

Partial Public Class MainWindow
  Inherits Window

  #Region "Properties"
  'net is the wrapper for all async/P2P work
```

```
Private net As New NetworkManager()
Private fullWindow As FullScreen
#End Region
```

MainWindow constructor

The MainWindow constructor calls the default InitializeComponent() method as well as the FirstLoad method, which initializes the MainWindow form. When First Load runs, we check whether we are running in client or server mode, set the AppMode Label, and hide the opposite mode's controls (if we're in client mode, we hide the server controls). If we're in server mode, we also set the FilePath label to the File Directory user setting we created in Figure 5-6. The other thing we do is subscribe to the P2pWorker's background worker, ProgressChanged, and RunWorkerCompleted events. This is important because we will make heavy use of the P2pWorker's Progress Changed event to send updates from the background thread to the UI thread. The constructor and the FirstLoad method are shown in Examples 5-70 and 5-71.

 Example 5-70. *The MainWindow constructor in C#*

```csharp
public MainWindow()
{
  InitializeComponent();
  FirstLoad();
}
...
private void FirstLoad()
{
  //Set Text
  if (App.IsServerMode)
  {
    AppModeLabel.Content = "Server Mode";
    FilePath.Content = Properties.Settings.Default.FileDirectory;
    ClientControls.Visibility = Visibility.Hidden;
  }
  else
  {
    AppModeLabel.Content = "Client Mode";
    ServerControls.Visibility = Visibility.Hidden;
  }
  //Setup Event handlers as all messages from NetworkManager comes through here
  net.P2pWorker.ProgressChanged += new
    ProgressChangedEventHandler(P2PWorker_ProgressChanged);
  net.P2pWorker.RunWorkerCompleted += new System.ComponentModel.
    RunWorkerCompletedEventHandler(P2PBackgroundWorkerCompleted);
}
```

Example 5-71. *The MainWindow constructor in VB*

```vb
Public Sub New()
  InitializeComponent()
  FirstLoad()
End Sub

Private Sub FirstLoad()
  'Set Text
  If App.IsServerMode Then
    AppModeLabel.Content = "Server Mode"
    FilePath.Content = My.Settings.Default.FileDirectory
    ClientControls.Visibility = Visibility.Hidden
  Else
    AppModeLabel.Content = "Client Mode"
    ServerControls.Visibility = Visibility.Hidden
  End If
  'Setup Event handlers as all messages from NetworkManager comes through here
  AddHandler net.P2pWorker.ProgressChanged, AddressOf P2PWorker_ProgressChanged
  AddHandler net.P2pWorker.RunWorkerCompleted, AddressOf P2PBackgroundWorkerCompleted
End Sub
```

Signing in

To connect to the P2P network, we'll click the SignIn button. The SignIn button acts as a toggle button in that its effect depends on whether you are already signed in. If you are not signed in, it will validate the NetworkName and then start a connection by passing in the name of the network and its password, as shown in Examples 5-72 and 5-73. However, if you are already signed in and connected, the SignIn button will actually end the network connection.

C# **Example 5-72.** *Starting a P2P connection in C#*

```csharp
//Sign In Button starts Connection
private void SignInButton_Click(object sender, RoutedEventArgs e)
{
  if (net.CurrentState == SystemState.LoggedOut)
  {
    if (ValidateFields())
    {
      net.StartConnection(NetworkName.Text, Password.Text);
    }
  }
  else
  {
    net.EndConnection();
  }
```

```
    }

    private bool ValidateFields()
    {
      if (string.IsNullOrEmpty(NetworkName.Text) &&
        NetworkName.Text.Trim().Contains(' '))
      {
        MessageBox.Show("Please Enter a non-null NetworkName that contains " +
          "only alphanumeric characters");
        return false;
      }
      return true;
    }
```

VB Example 5-73. *Starting a P2P connection in VB*

```
'Sign In Button starts Connection
Private Sub SignInButton_Click(ByVal sender As Object, ByVal e As RoutedEventArgs)
  If net.CurrentState = SystemState.LoggedOut Then
    If ValidateFields() Then
      net.StartConnection(NetworkName.Text, Password.Text)
    End If
    Else
      net.EndConnection()
    End If
End Sub

Private Function ValidateFields() As Boolean
  If String.IsNullOrEmpty(NetworkName.Text) AndAlso _
    NetworkName.Text.Trim().Contains(" "c) Then
    MessageBox.Show("Please Enter a non-null NetworkName that contains only " & _
      "alphanumeric characters")
    Return False
  End If
  Return True
End Function
```

Receiving UI updates from ProgressChanged

As we explained earlier, PeerCast handles processing in the NetworkManager class
in the background thread. Since the background thread cannot directly update the
UI thread, we'll use the ProgressChanged event as a thread-safe way to send updates from the background thread to the UI thread, as shown in Examples 5-74 and
5-75. To do this, the NetworkManager class will send back a ThreadMessage object
(see Examples 5-3 and 5-4) and the current progress bar value. Once we receive the

ThreadMessage object, we check the MessageType and either update the UI inline or forward the message onto other event handlers to process.

Example 5-74. *Receiving messages from the background thread in C#*

```csharp
void P2PWorker_ProgressChanged(object sender, ProgressChangedEventArgs e)
{
  //update progress bar
  progressBar1.Value = e.ProgressPercentage;

  //Read messages from the Network Manager
  if (e.UserState != null)
  {
    ThreadMessage message = (ThreadMessage)(e.UserState);
    switch (message.MessageType)
    {
      case UiMessage.UpdateStatus:
        StatusValue.Content = message.Message;
        break;
      case UiMessage.Log:
        Messages.Items.Add(message.Message);
        break;
      case UiMessage.StreamVideo:
        PlayVideo(message.Message);
        break;
      case UiMessage.ReceivedVideoList:
        UpdateVideoList(message.Message);
        break;
      case UiMessage.ToggleUi:
        ToggleUi();
        break;
    }
  }
}
```

Example 5-75. *Receiving messages from the background thread in VB*

```vb
Private Sub P2PWorker_ProgressChanged(ByVal sender As Object, ByVal e As Progress-
ChangedEventArgs)
  'update progress bar
  progressBar1.Value = e.ProgressPercentage

  'Read messages from the Network Manager
  If e.UserState IsNot Nothing Then
    Dim message As ThreadMessage = CType(e.UserState, ThreadMessage)
    Select Case message.MessageType
```

```
      Case UiMessage.UpdateStatus
        StatusValue.Content = message.Message
      Case UiMessage.Log
        Messages.Items.Add(message.Message)
      Case UiMessage.StreamVideo
        PlayVideo(message.Message)
      Case UiMessage.ReceivedVideoList
        UpdateVideoList(message.Message)
      Case UiMessage.ToggleUi
        ToggleUi()
    End Select
  End If
End Sub
```

Toggling the UI

The ToggleUi method is called when we receive a ToggleUi ThreadMessage in the
ReportProgress event handler. This method simply resets, enables, or disables con-
trols in the MainWindow form based on whether we are logged in or out, as shown in
Examples 5-76 and 5-77.

C# **Example 5-76**. *Toggling the UI based on our SystemState in C#*

```
private void ToggleUi()
private void ToggleUi()
{
  if (net.CurrentState == SystemState.LoggedIn ||
    net.CurrentState == SystemState.LoggingIn)
  {
    SignInButton.Content = "Sign Out";
    StatusValue.Content = "Signing In...";
    OpenDialog.IsEnabled = false;
    GetList.IsEnabled = true;
    Play.IsEnabled = true;
    FullScreen.IsEnabled = true;
    MediaList.IsEnabled = true;
  }
  else
  {
    SignInButton.Content = "Sign In";
    StatusValue.Content = "Disconnected";
    GetList.IsEnabled = false;
    Play.IsEnabled = false;
    FullScreen.IsEnabled = false;
    MediaList.IsEnabled = false;
  }
}
```

```vb
Private Sub ToggleUi()
  If net.CurrentState = SystemState.LoggedIn OrElse _
    net.CurrentState = SystemState.LoggingIn Then
    SignInButton.Content = "Sign Out"
    StatusValue.Content = "Signing In..."
    GetList.IsEnabled = True
    Play.IsEnabled = True
    FullScreen.IsEnabled = True
    MediaList.IsEnabled = True
  Else
    SignInButton.Content = "Sign In"
    StatusValue.Content = "Disconnected"
    GetList.IsEnabled = False
    Play.IsEnabled = False
    FullScreen.IsEnabled = False
    MediaList.IsEnabled = False
  End If
End Sub
```

Receiving a video list

The UpdateVideoList method shown in Examples 5-78 and 5-79 is called when we receive a ReceivedVideoList ThreadMessage in the ReportProgress event handler. This method deserializes the video list that has been sent as XML (see Examples 5-45 and 5-46) into a generic List of string objects, and then just loops through them to add them to the MediaList ListBox control.

C# Example 5-78. *Updating the MediaList ListBox in C#*

```csharp
private void UpdateVideoList(string serializedList)
{
  List<string> videos = Serializer.DeserializeFileList(serializedList);
  //clear list
  MediaList.Items.Clear();

  //add each item
  foreach (string s in videos)
  {
    MediaList.Items.Add(s);
  }
}
```

```
Private Sub UpdateVideoList(ByVal serializedList As String)
  Dim videos As List(Of String) = Serializer.DeserializeFileList(serializedList)
  'clear list
  MediaList.Items.Clear()

  'add each item
  For Each s As String In videos
    MediaList.Items.Add(s)
  Next s
End Sub
```

Deserializing the file list

The Serializer class also defines a DeserializeFileList method that does the opposite of the SerializeFileList (see Example 5-45), in that it converts an XML string
into an object, as shown in Examples 5-80 and 5-81. The code converts the XML into
a byte array and reads it into the contents MemoryStream. From there, we can use
the XmlTextWriter and XmlSerializer to deserialize the XML into a List of strings.
Again, the exact semantics don't matter here; the key is that we're taking an XML string
and building it into a List object.

C# Example 5-80. *Converting an XML string into a List of string object in C#*

```
public static List<string> DeserializeFileList(string serializedList)
{
  //deserialize the list of files
  UTF8Encoding encoding = new UTF8Encoding();
  Byte[] byteArray = encoding.GetBytes(serializedList);
  MemoryStream contents = new MemoryStream(byteArray);
  XmlTextWriter writer = new XmlTextWriter(contents, Encoding.UTF8);
  XmlSerializer xs = new XmlSerializer(typeof(List<string>));

  return (List<string>) xs.Deserialize(contents);
}
```

VB Example 5-81. *Converting an XML string into a List of string object in VB*

```
Public Shared Function DeserializeFileList(ByVal serializedList As String) As _
  List(Of String)
  'deserialize the list of files
  Dim encoding As New UTF8Encoding()
  Dim byteArray() As Byte = encoding.GetBytes(serializedList)
  Dim contents As New MemoryStream(byteArray)
  Dim writer As New XmlTextWriter(contents, Text.Encoding.UTF8)
  Dim xs As New XmlSerializer(GetType(List(Of String)))
```

```
    Return CType(xs.Deserialize(contents), List(Of String))
End Function
```

Playing a video

The PlayVideo method is called when we receive a StreamVideo ThreadMessage in the ReportProgress event handler. This method checks whether we should be playing the video in the fullWindow window or in the MainWindow's media player, and then just sets the video URL to start playing from the stream, as shown in Examples 5-82 and 5-83.

 Example 5-82. *Setting the MediaPlayer controls in C#*

```csharp
public void PlayVideo(string url)
{
  if (fullWindow == null)
  {
    MediaPlayer.Source = new Uri(url);
    MediaPlayer.Play();
  }
  else
  {
    fullWindow.SetMediaPlayer(new Uri(url));
    fullWindow.Show();
  }
}
```

VB **Example 5-83.** *Setting the MediaPlayer controls in VB*

```vb
Public Sub PlayVideo(ByVal url As String)
  If fullWindow Is Nothing Then
    MediaPlayer.Source = New Uri(url)
    MediaPlayer.Play()
  Else
    fullWindow.SetMediaPlayer(New Uri(url))
    fullWindow.Show()
  End If
End Sub
```

Sending a Play message

When a user clicks the Play button, we use the NetworkManager's SendChatMessage method to tell it to start streaming the selected video from the MediaList ListBox, as shown in Examples 5-84 and 5-85.

```csharp
private void Play_Click(object sender, RoutedEventArgs e)
{
  //make a request to play a video
  net.SendChatMessage(ChatMessage.Create(ChatCommand.StreamVideo,
  (string)MediaList.SelectedItem));
}
```

VB Example 5-85. *Sending a chat message to play the selected video in VB*

```vb
Private Sub Play_Click(ByVal sender As Object, ByVal e As RoutedEventArgs)
  'make a request to play a video
  net.SendChatMessage(ChatMessage.Create(ChatCommand.StreamVideo, CStr( _
    MediaList.SelectedItem)))
End Sub
```

Sending a full-screen play message

When a user clicks on the FullScreen button, we'll check to see if a fullWindow object has already been created. If it hasn't, we'll create one and add a Closing event handler that will reset the fullWindow variable back to null, as shown in Examples 5-86 and 5-87. We need the Closing event in order to avoid a null reference exception that can occur if a user closes the fullWindow and then presses the Full Screen button again. Just like we did with the Play button previously, we will forward the currently selected video to the server to start a streaming request.

C# Example 5-86. *Playing a video in a separate full-screen window*

```csharp
private void FullScreen_Click(object sender, RoutedEventArgs e)
{
  //open a new window full screen
  if (fullWindow == null)
  {
    fullWindow = new FullScreen();
    fullWindow.Closing += new CancelEventHandler(fullWindow_Closing);
  }
  net.SendChatMessage(ChatMessage.Create(ChatCommand.StreamVideo,
    (string)MediaList.SelectedItem));
}

void fullWindow_Closing(object sender, CancelEventArgs e)
{
  //assign to null so that we won't try to play a video with a Closed window
  //which throws an exception
  fullWindow = null;
}
```

```vb
Private Sub FullScreen_Click(ByVal sender As Object, ByVal e As RoutedEventArgs)
  'open a new window full screen
  If fullWindow Is Nothing Then
    fullWindow = New FullScreen()
    AddHandler fullWindow.Closing, AddressOf fullWindow_Closing
  End If
  net.SendChatMessage(ChatMessage.Create(ChatCommand.StreamVideo, _
    CStr(MediaList.SelectedItem)))
End Sub

Private Sub fullWindow_Closing(ByVal sender As Object, ByVal e As CancelEventArgs)
  'assign to null so that we won't try to play a video with a Closed window
  'which throws an exception
  fullWindow = Nothing
End Sub
```

Getting a list of videos from the server

When a user clicks on the GetList button, we will simply forward a ChatCommand to the server to get the list of videos, as shown in Examples 5-88 and 5-89. The server in turn will send us back the list of videos as XML through the ProgressChanged event. Since we're not passing any other data as a message, we'll simply set it to an empty string.

C# Example 5-88. *Sending a chat request to get the server's video list in C#*

```csharp
private void GetList_Click(object sender, RoutedEventArgs e)
{
  //make a request to get the server's video list
  net.SendChatMessage(ChatMessage.Create(ChatCommand.GetList, string.Empty));
}
```

 Example 5-89. *Sending a chat request to get the server's video list in VB*

```vb
Private Sub GetList_Click(ByVal sender As Object, ByVal e As RoutedEventArgs)
  'make a request to get the server's video list
  net.SendChatMessage(ChatMessage.Create(ChatCommand.GetList, String.Empty))
End Sub
```

Selecting the video streaming directory

If you're running PeerCast in server mode, you can change the default streaming directory with the System.Windows.Forms FolderBrowserDialog class, as shown in Examples 5-90 and 5-91. Assuming a user selects a new directory and clicks OK, the selected directory will be set to the FileDirectory user variable we defined in Figure 5-6. Since FileDirectory is declared as a user setting variable, Visual Studio will handle persisting the newly updated value without us having to manually serialize and deserialize the value.

C# Example 5-90. *Opening the FolderBrowser dialog in C#*

```csharp
private void OpenDialog_Click(object sender, RoutedEventArgs e)
{
    var folder = new System.Windows.Forms.FolderBrowserDialog();
    folder.RootFolder = Environment.SpecialFolder.MyComputer;

    System.Windows.Forms.DialogResult r = folder.ShowDialog();
    if (r == System.Windows.Forms.DialogResult.OK)
    {
        Properties.Settings.Default.FileDirectory = folder.SelectedPath;
        Properties.Settings.Default.Save();
        FilePath.Content = folder.SelectedPath;
    }
}
```

VB Example 5-91. *Opening the FolderBrowser dialog in VB*

```vb
Private Sub OpenDialog_Click(ByVal sender As Object, ByVal e As RoutedEventArgs)
    Dim folder = New System.Windows.Forms.FolderBrowserDialog()
    folder.RootFolder = Environment.SpecialFolder.MyComputer

    Dim r As System.Windows.Forms.DialogResult = folder.ShowDialog()
    If r = System.Windows.Forms.DialogResult.OK Then
        My.Settings.Default.FileDirectory = folder.SelectedPath
        My.Settings.Default.Save()
        FilePath.Content = folder.SelectedPath
    End If
End Sub
```

When P2pWorker completes

Back in the FirstLoad method (see Example 5-70), when we first set up the event handlers for P2pWorker, we also set up a backgroundWorkerCompleted event handler that will fire when the NetworkManager's background worker thread completes its processing, as shown in Examples 5-92 and 5-93. As you might remember from Examples 5-23 and 5-24, the background worker is in an infinite loop, and so this event should fire only if the user closes the connection, or as shown in the examples, an error occurs in the background thread.

```csharp
protected void P2pBackgroundWorkerCompleted(object sender, RunWorkerCompletedEven-
tArgs e)
{
  //error occured
  if (e.Error != null)
  {
    MessageBox.Show(String.Format("An error occurred in the background thread: {0}",
      e.Error.Message));
  }
  else
  {
    net.EndConnection();
  }
}
```

```vb
Protected Sub P2pBackgroundWorkerCompleted(ByVal sender As Object, ByVal e As _
  RunWorkerCompletedEventArgs)
  'error occured
  If e.Error IsNot Nothing Then
    MessageBox.Show(String.Format("An error occurred in the background thread: {0}",
      e.Error.Message))
  Else
    net.EndConnection()
  End If
End Sub
```

Final Thoughts

Building P2P applications can be complex given how many things are going on, ranging from multiple threads to new network protocols, but the real takeaway here is the potential power of peer-enabled networks. The ability to share objects, files, videos, and more across the Internet in a decentralized, secure, and scalable way is huge, and developers can start building some amazing applications with a few event handlers, an understanding of how events work, and a little bit of creativity.

AUTHOR	Clint Rutkas (*http://betterthaneveryone.com/*), Dan Fernandez, and Brian Peek
DIFFICULTY	Intermediate
TIME REQUIRED	3–6 hours
COST	Free
SOFTWARE	Visual Web Developer 2008 Express Edition
HARDWARE	None
DOWNLOAD	*http://www.c4fbook.com/TwitterVote*

Twitter (*http://www.twitter.com*) is a web application that allows friends, family, co-workers, and anyone else to instantly communicate with each other (and to the world at large) by sending quick, short messages via a web browser, cell phone text message, or a variety of other client applications. Many refer to Twitter as a microblogging platform, but it is also a form of mass, public communication via a format similar to instant messaging. A message sent to Twitter is referred to as a "tweet." We'll primarily refer to status updates as tweets for the rest of this chapter.

Twitter is a great tool and has some amazing strengths. For example, it is free, it fosters an astounding community, and it exposes a fairly strong API (application programming interface) model.

In this chapter, we will develop an application called TwitterVote. TwitterVote is a web application that enables you to build custom online polls that allows other users to cast their vote via Twitter. For example, you can create a poll asking your friends what their favorite video game console is, with the choices of "Wii, PS3, Xbox360". They can then reply with their vote, and you can calculate and view the results.

Overview

To use Twitter, you will need to create a free account. This can be done by going to the Twitter site at *http://www.twitter.com/* and joining the service. Select a username and a password you will remember, as you will need both later on to use TwitterVote.

After creating an account, log in and check out the service. You will see a screen similar to the one shown in Figure 6-1 after logging in.

Figure 6-1. *Twitter user interface*

You can update your status by typing a message in the text region at the top of the page and clicking the "update" button.

In Twitter, you can reply to a specific user by using the format *@targetUsername This is a reply*. These replies will show up on the target user's Replies tab.

As you use Twitter, its value increases as you search for other people and follow their tweets, and as your friends join your network. You can even follow the Coding4Fun site by adding @coding4fun (*http://twitter.com/coding4fun*). But for now, we can move on to creating the TwitterVote application.

Twitter Rules and Limitations

Twitter does have a few rules and limitations. One rule is that you can send only 140 characters per message. This limit can greatly affect what you can do with Twitter, but you can also see it as a challenge to keep your tweets short and sweet. Additionally, specific methods in Twitter's API limit you to a certain number of requests per hour per user. This value is currently 100 per hour, but that number may change. Keep these items in mind when querying the Twitter service for this or any other application.

Building TwitterVote

So now that we know a little bit about Twitter, let's discuss the application we are going to build. This web-based application will poll your own user account looking for a keyword that determines a poll has started and find the valid parameters for that poll (either a numeric value or a choice of text values).

The application will then poll the list of replies to your Twitter account and determine which of those are valid poll responses. These responses will be tabulated and displayed on a web page.

Twitter: Under the Hood

Twitter exposes its API via Representational State Transfer (REST). Simply, this means the API is exposed via the Web and will return a chunk of data in a defined format. The following are some examples from Twitter's API. Note that the format can be XML, JSON, RSS, or ATOM, depending on the API. To switch formats, just change the *.xml* extension to *.json*, *.rss*, or *.atom* to retrieve data in the specified format. User tweets: *http://twitter.com/statuses/user_timeline/coding4fun.xml*

- User friends: *http://twitter.com/statuses/friends_timeline.xml*
- User replies: *http://twitter.com/statuses/replies.xml*
- API call counter: *http://twitter.com/account/rate_limit_status.xml*

The Twitter API

Twitter's API model can be found at *http://apiwiki.twitter.com/*. The supported calls you can currently make against the API are listed in Table 6-1.

Table 6-1. *Twitter API methods*

METHOD TYPE	METHODS
Status methods	public_timeline, friends_timeline, user_timeline, show, update, replies, destroy
User methods	friends, followers, featured, show
Direct message methods	direct_messages, sent, new, destroy
Friendship methods	create, destroy, exists
Account methods	verify_credentials, end_session, archive, update_location, update_delivery_device
Favorite methods	favorites, create, destroy
Notification methods	follow, leave
Block methods	create, destroy
Help methods	test, downtime_schedule

TwitterVote will use the methods from the *User* and *Status* groups. Any of these methods can be called by sending a request to the Twitter website, passing the method name as the first word after the forward slash in the URL. For example, to call the user_timeline method for the C4FBook user, you would request *http://twitter.com/statuses/user_timeline/c4fbook.xml*. If you visit this URL in your web browser, you will get back a chunk of XML that looks like that in Example 6-1.

Example 6-1. *XML results for C4FBook user*

```
<?xml version="1.0" encoding="UTF-8"?>
<statuses type="array">
<status>
  <created_at>Sun Aug 10 07:14:47 +0000 2008</created_at>
  <id>883094245</id>
  <text>I am trying out Twitter!</text>
  <source>web</source>
  <truncated>false</truncated>
  <in_reply_to_status_id></in_reply_to_status_id>
  <in_reply_to_user_id></in_reply_to_user_id>
  <favorited></favorited>
  <user>
    <id>15796176</id>
    <name>C4FBook</name>
    <screen_name>C4FBook</screen_name>
    <location></location>
    <description></description>
    <profile_image_url>http://static.twitter.com/images/default_profile_normal.png
    </profile_image_url>
```

```
<url></url>
    <protected>false</protected>
    <followers_count>0</followers_count>
  </user>
  </status>
</statuses>
```

From the XML, you can see C4FBook's most up-to-date tweet, which is stored in the text element:

```
<text>I am trying out Twitter!</text>
```

Twitter Implementation

First, open Visual Web Developer Express 2008 and create a new *ASP.NET Web Application* named *TwitterVote* in C# or Visual Basic, as shown in Figure 6-2.

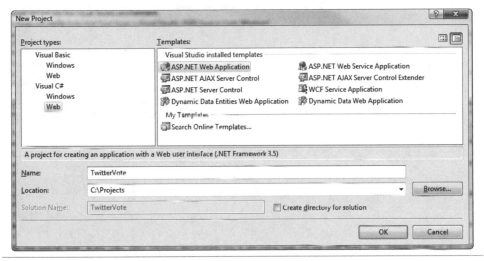

Figure 6-2. *Creating a new ASP.NET Web Application*

When the project is loaded, right-click on the TwitterVote project, select New Folder, and create a new folder named *App_Code*, as shown in Figure 6-3. This will be where all of your code files will be placed for the project.

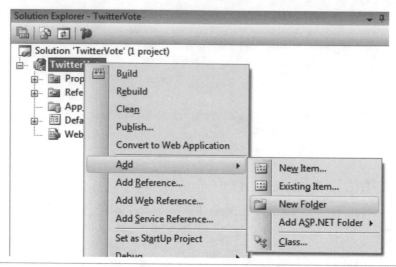

Figure 6-3. *Adding the App_Code folder*

Now let's write the code required for our application to talk to Twitter and parse the results. Add a new class to the *App_Code* folder named Tweet. This will be a pretty simple object with a handful of properties that will be used to store the values of a tweet from a user on Twitter. The code is shown in Examples 6-2 and 6-3.

C#   Example 6-2. *C# code for the Tweet class*

```csharp
using System;

public class Tweet
{
    public string Text { get; set; }
    public DateTime? DateCreated { get; set; }
    public string UserName { get; set; }
}
```

VB   Example 6-3. *Visual Basic code for the Tweet class*

```vb
Imports Microsoft.VisualBasic
Imports System

Public Class Tweet
    Private privateText As String
    Public Property Text() As String
        Get
            Return privateText
        End Get
        Set(ByVal value As String)
```

```
                privateText = value
        End Set
    End Property
    Private privateDateCreated As Nullable(Of DateTime)
    Public Property DateCreated() As Nullable(Of DateTime)
        Get
            Return privateDateCreated
        End Get
        Set(ByVal value As Nullable(Of DateTime))
            privateDateCreated = value
        End Set
    End Property
    Private privateUserName As String
    Public Property UserName() As String
        Get
            Return privateUserName
        End Get
        Set(ByVal value As String)
            privateUserName = value
        End Set
    End Property
End Class
```

We can now write an object to get the data from Twitter and parse it into Tweet objects. Create a new class in the *App_Code* directory named TwitterService.

The constructor will take a Twitter username and password combination that will be used to log into the Twitter service. As discussed earlier, we only require the use of two methods, user_timeline and replies, so let's write and expose two methods that can be called to return the data from these Twitter methods, as shown in Examples 6-4 and 6-5.

C#   Example 6-4. *C# code for the base TwitterService class*

```csharp
using System;
using System.Collections.Generic;
using System.IO;
using System.Xml;
using System.Linq;
using System.Net;
using System.Xml.Linq;
using System.Security;
using System.Globalization;

public class TwitterService
{
    private string username, password;
```

```csharp
        public TwitterService(string user, string pass)
        {
            // store away twitter user/pass
            username = user;
            password = pass;
        }


        public List<Tweet> GetUserTimeline()
        {
          string url =
              string.Format("http://twitter.com/statuses/user_timeline/{0}.xml",
                          username);
              return ConvertTwitterXmlToList(new Uri(url));
        }


        public List<Tweet> GetReplies()
        {
          // HACK: Bug in Twitter is forcing me to do this at the moment...
          int random = (int)(new Random().NextDouble() * 100000);
          return ConvertTwitterXmlToList(new Uri(
              string.Format("http://twitter.com/statuses/replies.xml?since_id={0}",
                          random)));
        }
    }
```

VB **Example 6-5.** *Visual Basic code for the base TwitterService class*

```vbnet
Imports Microsoft.VisualBasic
Imports System
Imports System.Collections.Generic
Imports System.IO
Imports System.Xml
Imports System.Linq
Imports System.Net
Imports System.Xml.Linq
Imports System.Security
Imports System.Globalization

Public Class TwitterService
    Private username, password As String

    Public Sub New(ByVal user As String, ByVal pass As String)
        ' store away twitter user/pass
        username = user
        password = pass
    End Sub
```

```
Public Function GetUserTimeline() As List(Of Tweet)
    Dim url As String = _
        String.Format("http://twitter.com/statuses/user_timeline/{0}.xml", _
                    username)
    Return ConvertTwitterXmlToList(New Uri(url))
End Function

Public Function GetReplies() As List(Of Tweet)
    ' HACK: Bug in Twitter is forcing me to do this at the moment...
    Dim random As Integer = CInt(Fix(New Random().NextDouble() * 100000))
    Return ConvertTwitterXmlToList(New Uri( _
        String.Format("http://twitter.com/statuses/replies.xml?since_id={0}", _
                    random)))
End Function
End Class
```

These two methods simply call a method we're about to write named Convert TwitterXmlToList, passing in a Uri object (Universal Resource Identifier), which is a path to the Twitter API method as described before.

You will notice a bit of a hack on the GetReplies method. There is a bug in the Twitter API that causes responses to be incorrectly cached, which will break our application. To get around this, we change the since_id parameter to a random value, forcing Twitter to request the real, uncached results each time. If and when this bug is fixed, this hack may be removed.

The final ConvertTwitterXmlToList method will call that Uri, return the XML result, parse it into Tweet objects, and return them as a .NET generic list object. This is shown in Examples 6-6 and 6-7.

C# Example 6-6. C# code for ConvertTwitterXmlToList method

```csharp
public List<Tweet> ConvertTwitterXmlToList(Uri TwitterUrl)
{
    Stream s = null;

    //call service
    WebClient wc = new WebClient();
    wc.Credentials = new NetworkCredential(username, password);

    //Get Data
    try
    {
        s = wc.OpenRead(TwitterUrl);
    }
    catch (WebException we)
    {
        // if we get an error
        if(we.Status == WebExceptionStatus.ProtocolError)
```

```
    {
        // get the HTTP status code
        switch((int)((HttpWebResponse)we.Response).StatusCode)
        {
            // HTTP error 400 == twitter rate limit exceeded
            case 400:
                throw new ApplicationException(
                    "Twitter rate limit reached...please try again later.");
            // HTTP error 401 == unauthorized
            case 401:
                throw new SecurityException("User not authorized");
            default:
                throw;
        }
    }
}


XmlTextReader xr = new XmlTextReader(s);
XDocument rawData = XDocument.Load(xr);


// pull the required elements from each status chunk into a new Tweet object
var query = from entry in rawData.Descendants("statuses").Descendants("status")
            select new Tweet
            {
                UserName = entry.Element("user").Element("screen_name").Value,
                Text = entry.Element("text").Value,
                // HTTP-formatted date
                DateCreated = DateTime.ParseExact(entry.Element("created_at").Value,
                            "ddd MMM dd HH:mm:ss zzzz yyyy",
                            CultureInfo.GetCultureInfoByIetfLanguageTag("en-us"),
                            DateTimeStyles.AllowWhiteSpaces)
            };


return query.ToList();
}
```

VB **Example 6-7.** *Visual Basic code for ConvertTwitterXmlToList method*

```vb
Public Function ConvertTwitterXmlToList(ByVal TwitterUrl As Uri) As List(Of Tweet)
    Dim s As Stream = Nothing

    'call service
    Dim wc As New WebClient()
    wc.Credentials = New NetworkCredential(username, password)
```

```
        'Get Data
        Try
            s = wc.OpenRead(TwitterUrl)
        Catch we As WebException
            ' if we get an error
            If we.Status = WebExceptionStatus.ProtocolError Then
                ' get the HTTP status code
                Select Case CInt(Fix((CType(we.Response, HttpWebResponse)).StatusCode))
                    ' HTTP error 400 == twitter rate limit exceeded
                    Case 400
                        Throw New ApplicationException(_
                            "Twitter rate limit reached...please try again later.")
                    ' HTTP error 401 == unauthorized
                    Case 401
                        Throw New SecurityException("User not authorized")
                    Case Else
                        Throw
                End Select
            End If
        End Try

        Dim xr As New XmlTextReader(s)
        Dim rawData As XDocument = XDocument.Load(xr)

        ' pull the required elements from each status chunk into a new Tweet object
        Dim query = From entry In rawData.Descendants("statuses").Descendants("status") _
                Select New Tweet With { _
                    .UserName = entry.Element("user").Element("screen_name").Value, _
                    .Text = entry.Element("text").Value, _
                    .DateCreated = DateTime.ParseExact( _
                            entry.Element("created_at").Value, _
                            "ddd MMM dd HH:mm:ss zzzz yyyy", _
                            CultureInfo.GetCultureInfoByIetfLanguageTag("en-us"), _
                            DateTimeStyles.AllowWhiteSpaces)}
    End Function
```

The first chunk of this code creates a WebClient object, sets its credentials to those passed in via the constructor, and then opens the Uri specified. If an exception is thrown, it determines what the error is and propagates it back to the client. Twitter will return an error 400 code if you have exceeded its rate limit.

The second chunk takes the stream returned from the WebClient request and turns it into an XDocument object, which is a representation of an XML document. We then use *LINQ to XML* to query this XML data to create a List of Tweet objects, filling in the UserName, Text, and DateCreated properties based on the data provided.

Voting Implementation

Now that we can query the Twitter service and receive the data, we need to write some code to create our actual poll and collect the results. Add a new class to the *App_Code* folder named `Poll`.

First, let's set up the using statements, member variables, and base class. The member variables will keep an instance of our `TwitterService` object, the valid responses for a poll, the votes cast by other users, and some timestamps to determine when we last polled Twitter, to see if the newly queried responses are new or old. The constructor will also take the username and password specified in the *web.config* file (which will be seen later) and instantiate a new `TwitterService` object. All of this can be seen in Examples 6-8 and 6-9.

`C#` Example 6-8. *C# code for base Poll class*

```csharp
using System;
using System.Collections.Generic;
using System.Linq;
using System.Configuration;

public class Poll
{
    // Our Twitter API wrapper
    private TwitterService twitter;

    // votes entered by others
    private List<string> votes { get; set; }

    // valid poll responses
    private HashSet<string> validResponses { get; set; }

    // last time we updated the poll information
    private DateTime lastUpdatedVotes;
    private DateTime lastUpdatedPolls;

    // map result to percentage
    Dictionary<string, double> responses;

    public Poll()
    {
        validResponses = new HashSet<string>();
        votes = new List<string>();

        twitter = new TwitterService(
                    ConfigurationManager.AppSettings["TwitterUserName"],
                    ConfigurationManager.AppSettings["TwitterPassword"]);
```

```
        }
    }
```

```vb
Imports Microsoft.VisualBasic
Imports System
Imports System.Collections.Generic
Imports System.Linq
Imports System.Configuration

Public Class Poll
    ' Our Twitter API wrapper
    Private twitter As TwitterService

    ' votes entered by others
    Private privatevotes As List(Of String)
    Private Property votes() As List(Of String)
        Get
            Return privatevotes
        End Get
        Set(ByVal value As List(Of String))
            privatevotes = value
        End Set
    End Property

    ' valid poll responses
    Private privatevalidResponses As HashSet(Of String)
    Private Property validResponses() As HashSet(Of String)
        Get
            Return privatevalidResponses
        End Get
        Set(ByVal value As HashSet(Of String))
            privatevalidResponses = value
        End Set
    End Property

    ' last time we updated the poll information
    Private lastUpdatedVotes As DateTime
    Private lastUpdatedPolls As DateTime

    ' map result to percentage
    Private responses As Dictionary(Of String, Double)
```

```
    Public Sub New()
        validResponses = New HashSet(Of String)()
        votes = New List(Of String)()

        twitter = New TwitterService( _
                ConfigurationManager.AppSettings("TwitterUserName"), _
                ConfigurationManager.AppSettings("TwitterPassword"))
    End Sub
End Class
```

Next, we need a method to search our own tweet list to look for "poll" commands. To
create a poll, the user will send out a tweet of the format poll *pollparameters*, where
pollparameters is either two numbers separated by a hyphen (such as "1-10") or a
comma delimited list of valid responses (such as "A,B,C,D"). If two numbers are specified, it is assumed that the responses will be in the range inclusive of those two values.
For example, 1-10 would create a poll with valid responses of all the numbers between
1 and 10, inclusive.

The UpdatePolls method retrieves the user's timeline. This is simply all the tweets
the user has sent. It runs through this list of Tweet objects looking for those in the format previously described. When one is found, it processes the list of valid responses
using the ProcessParameterList method and stores them away for later use. After
the list is processed, the time of the last message is stored, so when we look at the list
later we can skip all entries we have already seen. All of this is shown in Examples 6-10
and 6-11.

C#　Example 6-10. *C# code for the UpdatePolls and ProcessParameterList methods*

```
private void UpdatePolls()
{
    // get all user's tweets
    List<Tweet> tweets = twitter.GetUserTimeline();

    if (tweets == null || tweets.Count <= 0)
        return;

    foreach (Tweet tweet in tweets)
    {
        // if the tweet is new
        if (tweet.DateCreated.HasValue && tweet.DateCreated > lastUpdatedPolls)
        {
            // looking for "poll params"
            string[] breakdown = tweet.Text.ToLower().Split(' ');

            // if it's a poll command, create a new poll
            if (breakdown.Length == 2 && breakdown[0].ToLower() == "poll")
            {
                ProcessParameterList(breakdown[1]);
```

```
                    break;
                }
            }
        }

        if (tweets.Count > 0)
            lastUpdatedPolls = tweets[0].DateCreated.Value;
    }

    private void ProcessParameterList(string parameterList)
    {
        // currently supported
        // 1-10 \d-\d
        // a,b,c,d comma delimited.

        // numbers X to Y
        if(parameterList.Contains('-'))
        {
            string[] items = parameterList.Split('-');
            if (items.Length == 2)
            {
                // if it's a hyphenated list, we assume it's two numbers, low - high
                int start = int.Parse(items[0]);
                int end = int.Parse(items[1]);

                for (int i = start; i <= end; i++)
                    validResponses.Add(i.ToString());
            }

        }
        // comma delimited list of options
        else if(parameterList.Contains(','))
        {
            string[] items = parameterList.Split(',');
            foreach (string item in items)
                validResponses.Add(item.Trim());
        }
    }
```

VB Example 6-11. *Visual Basic code for the UpdatePolls and ProcessParameterList methods*

```
Private Sub UpdatePolls()
    ' get all user's tweets
    Dim tweets As List(Of Tweet) = twitter.GetUserTimeline()

    If tweets Is Nothing OrElse tweets.Count <= 0 Then
```

```vbnet
            Return
        End If

    For Each tweet As Tweet In tweets
        ' if the tweet is new
        If tweet.DateCreated.HasValue AndAlso _
                tweet.DateCreated > lastUpdatedPolls Then
            ' looking for "poll params"
            Dim breakdown() As String = tweet.Text.ToLower().Split(" "c)

            ' if it's a poll command, create a new poll
            If breakdown.Length = 2 AndAlso breakdown(0).ToLower() = "poll" Then
                ProcessParameterList(breakdown(1))
                Exit For
            End If
        End If
    Next tweet

    If tweets.Count > 0 Then
        lastUpdatedPolls = tweets(0).DateCreated.Value
    End If
End Sub

Private Sub ProcessParameterList(ByVal parameterList As String)
    ' currently supported
    ' 1-10 \d-\d
    ' a,b,c,d comma delimited.

    ' numbers X to Y
    If parameterList.Contains("-"c) Then
        Dim items() As String = parameterList.Split("-"c)
        If items.Length = 2 Then
            ' if it's a hyphened list, we assume it's two numbers, low - high
            Dim start As Integer = Integer.Parse(items(0))
            Dim [end] As Integer = Integer.Parse(items(1))

            For i As Integer = start To [end]
                validResponses.Add(i.ToString())
            Next i
        End If

    ' comma delimited list of options
    ElseIf parameterList.Contains(","c) Then
        Dim items() As String = parameterList.Split(","c)
        For Each item As String In items
```

```
            validResponses.Add(item.Trim())
        Next item
    End If
End Sub
```

Now that the poll is created, we need to find other users' replies to the poll. The UpdateVotes method retrieves the replies sent to the current user and enumerates through the list, looking for those that contain the text of a valid reply (determined earlier). If a valid reply is found, it is added to the votes list for later tabulation. As with the UpdatePolls method, the time of the last reply is stored so we only look at new replies the next time. Additionally, we will add one utility method named UpdateAll, which will use these two methods to find the most recent poll and update the votes, as shown in Examples 6-12 and 6-13.

C# Example 6-12. *C# code for the UpdateVotes and UpdateAll method*

```csharp
private void UpdateVotes()
{
    // get all replies for current user
    List<Tweet> tweets = twitter.GetReplies();

    // a reply will come in the form of @username Vote
    foreach (Tweet tweet in tweets)
    {
        // if we've seen it before, move on
        if (tweet.DateCreated.HasValue && tweet.DateCreated > lastUpdatedVotes)
        {
            // split up the values
            string[] tweetSplit = tweet.Text.ToLower().Split(' ');

            // if it's the right length, and the reply contains a valid vote choice,
            // add it
            if (tweetSplit.Length == 2 && validResponses.Contains(tweetSplit[1]))
                votes.Add(tweetSplit[1]);
        }
    }

    // if we updated, update our date for next time
    if(tweets.Count > 0)
        lastUpdatedVotes = tweets[0].DateCreated.Value;
}

public void UpdateAll()
{
    UpdatePolls();
    UpdateVotes();
}
```

Example 6-13. *Visual Basic code for the UpdateVotes and UpdateAll method*

```vb
Private Sub UpdateVotes()
    ' get all replies for current user
    Dim tweets As List(Of Tweet) = twitter.GetReplies()

    ' a reply will come in the form of @username Vote
    For Each tweet As Tweet In tweets
        ' if we've seen it before, move on
        If tweet.DateCreated.HasValue AndAlso _
                tweet.DateCreated > lastUpdatedVotes Then
            ' split up the values
            Dim tweetSplit() As String = tweet.Text.ToLower().Split(" "c)

            ' if it's the right length, and the reply contains a valid
            ' vote choice, add it
            If tweetSplit.Length = 2 AndAlso _
                    validResponses.Contains(tweetSplit(1)) Then
                votes.Add(tweetSplit(1))
            End If
        End If
    Next tweet

    ' if we updated, update our date for next time
    If tweets.Count > 0 Then
        lastUpdatedVotes = tweets(0).DateCreated.Value
    End If
End Sub

Public Sub UpdateAll()
    UpdatePolls()
    UpdateVotes()
End Sub
```

We now have our poll and our results. Finally, we need to tabulate those results. The GetPollResults method creates a Dictionary table that maps a valid response to the percentage of voters who replied with that option. The votes are enumerated, tallied, and returned to the caller for later display. Additionally, we will add one property that will return the total number of votes named TotalVotes, as shown in Examples 6-14 and 6-15.

Example 6-14. *C# code for the GetPollResults method and TotalVotes property*

```csharp
public Dictionary<string, double> GetPollResults()
{
```

```csharp
    // map result to percentage
    Dictionary<string, double> returnResults =
        new Dictionary<string, double>(validResponses.Count);

    // create an array of valid choices
    foreach (string param in validResponses)
        returnResults[param] = 0;

    // tally results of each vote
    foreach (string vote in votes)
    {
        if (returnResults.Keys.Contains(vote))
            returnResults[vote] += 1;
    }

    if (votes.Count > 0)
    {
        // get percentages
        string[] keys = returnResults.Keys.ToArray();
        foreach (string key in keys)
            returnResults[key] = (returnResults[key] / votes.Count) * 100;
    }

    return returnResults;
}


public int TotalVotes
{
    get { return votes.Count; }
}
```

VB **Example 6-15.** *Visual Basic code for the GetPollResults method and TotalVotes property*

```vbnet
Public Function GetPollResults() As Dictionary(Of String, Double)
    ' map result to percentage
    Dim returnResults As Dictionary(Of String, Double) = _
        New Dictionary(Of String, Double)(validResponses.Count)

    ' create an array of valid choices
    For Each param As String In validResponses
        returnResults(param) = 0
    Next param

    ' tally results of each vote
    For Each vote As String In votes
        If returnResults.Keys.Contains(vote) Then
```

```
            returnResults(vote) += 1
        End If
    Next vote

    If votes.Count > 0 Then
        ' get percentages
        Dim keys() As String = returnResults.Keys.ToArray()
        For Each key As String In keys
            returnResults(key) = (returnResults(key) / votes.Count) * 100
        Next key
    End If

    Return returnResults
End Function

Public ReadOnly Property TotalVotes() As Integer
    Get
        Return votes.Count
    End Get
End Property
```

Displaying Results with Popfly

We can now create a poll, get the responses to the poll, and tabulate the totals, so
we need a way to display them on the screen. To do this we will use a custom Popfly
component that will be embedded into a web page.

Popfly (*http://www.popfly.com/*) allows users with little to no programming experience
to create web mashups. A *mashup* is a web application that can take data from multiple sources and combine it in some fashion to make a single application.

Popfly's main interface consists of dragging large blocks to a surface, configuring
those blocks for a specific task, and then connecting the outputs and inputs of those
blocks so data will flow and be transformed into a final goal.

The component we are going to build is currently publicly shared at *http://www
.popfly.com/users/c4fbook/TwitterVoteGraph*, so we can use that directly. To build your
own Popfly component for displaying the results, just follow the directions in this
section.

Our final Popfly mashup will look like that shown in Figure 6-4.

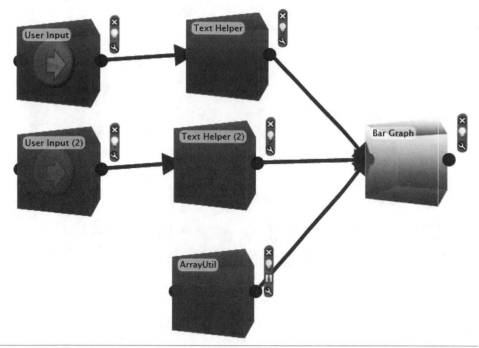

Figure 6-4. *Complete Popfly mashup for TwitterVoteGraph*

To create this, start by making a new mashup in Popfly. Search in the left "Blocks" pane for the *User Input* block, and drag two instances of the block to the mashup area. Do the same for the *Text Helper*, *ArrayUtil*, and *Bar Graph* blocks, and connect them as shown in Figure 6-4.

Next, we need to configure the two *User Input* blocks to pull the labels and values query string items from the URL for parsing. Click on the little wrench icon on the *User Input* blocks, and configure them as shown in Figures 6-5 and 6-6.

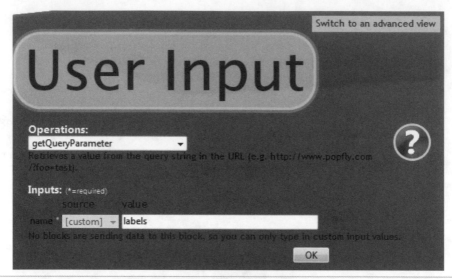

Figure 6-5. *User Input block for labels*

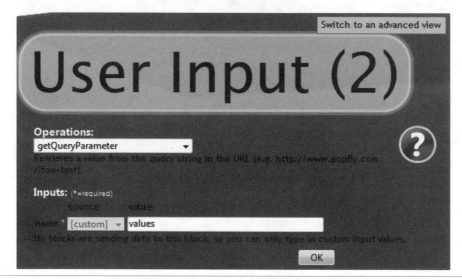

Figure 6-6. *User Input block for values*

Next, we will configure our *Text Helper* blocks to split the labels and values parameters using the | (pipe) character. Configure the two *Text Helper* blocks as shown in Figures 6-7 and 6-8.

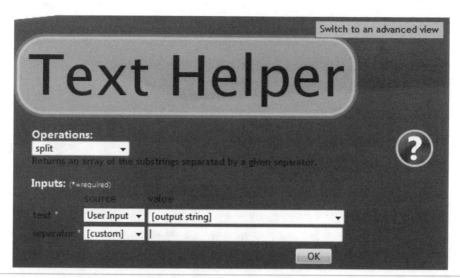

Figure 6-7. *Text Helper block for labels*

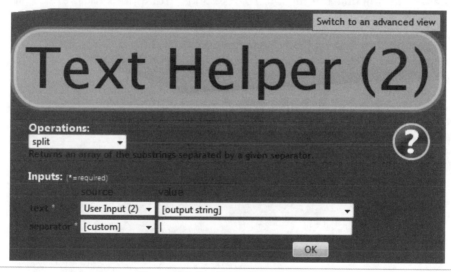

Figure 6-8. *Text Helper block for values*

The *ArrayUtil* block will be used to hold an array of color values that will be passed into the *BarGraph* block to determine the colors of the bars. Configure this block as shown in Figure 6-9.

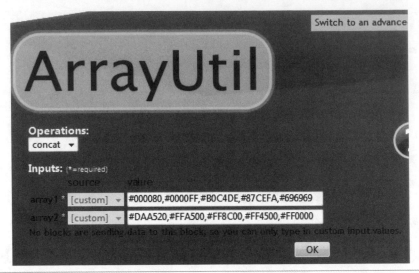

Figure 6-9. *ArrayUtil block configurations*

Finally, we can configure the *Bar Graph* block using the outputs of the previous blocks, as shown in Figure 6-10.

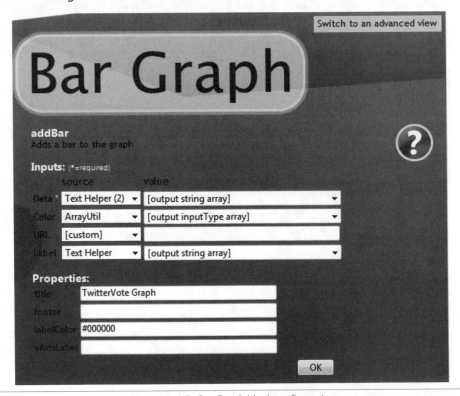

Figure 6-10. *Bar Graph block configuration*

Embedding the Popfly Results Graph

Now that we have our Popfly mashup (either the shared mashup or one you created yourself), we can embed it in our web page and display the results. The HTML side of the *default.aspx* page will be quite simple. We just need a place to insert an <IFRAME> tag, which will contain the Popfly content, a few labels to display the total number of votes, and a button to refresh the graph. The HTML can be found in Examples 6-16 and 6-17.

`C#` Example 6-16. *HTML for the Default.aspx page (C#)*

```
<%@ Page Language="C#" AutoEventWireup="true" CodeFile="Default.aspx.cs"
Inherits="Default" %>
<html>
<head runat="server">
  <title>TwitterVote</title>
</head>
<body style="font-family:Arial">
    <form id="form1" runat="server">
    <div ID="ResultsData" runat="server" />
    <p/>
    <asp:Label ID="TotalVotes" runat="server" Text="Total Votes: "/>
    <asp:Label ID="Total" runat="server" Text="Label" />
    <p/>
    <asp:Button ID="UpdateResults" runat="server" onclick="UpdateResults_Click"
     Text="Update Results" />
    </form>
</body>
</html>
```

`VB` Example 6-17. *HTML for the Default.aspx page (Visual Basic)*

```
<%@ Page Language="vb" AutoEventWireup="true" CodeBehind="Default.aspx.vb"
Inherits="Default" %>
<html>
<head runat="server">
  <title>TwitterVote</title>
</head>
<body style="font-family:Arial">
    <form id="form1" runat="server">
    <div ID="ResultsData" runat="server" />
    <p/>
    <asp:Label ID="TotalVotes" runat="server" Text="Total Votes: "/>
    <asp:Label ID="Total" runat="server" Text="Label" />
    <p/>
    <asp:Button ID="UpdateResults" runat="server" onclick="UpdateResults_Click"
     Text="Update Results" />
```

```
</form>
</body>
</html>
```

The code-behind for this ASP.NET page is also relatively simple. When the page is loaded, we will get the `Poll` object created earlier. If it already exists in the cache, we will use the existing one to save some processing work; otherwise, we create one from scratch. The base code for this code-behind is found in Examples 6-18 and 6-19.

C# Example 6-18. *C# code for the base default.aspx code-behind*

```csharp
using System;
using System.Collections.Generic;
using System.Text;
using System.Web;

public partial class Default : System.Web.UI.Page
{
    private Poll poll;

    protected void Page_Load(object sender, EventArgs e)
    {
        // get the poll object
        poll = GetPoll();

        // update on first load
        if(!Page.IsPostBack)
        {
            poll.UpdateAll();
            DrawPopflyResults();
        }
    }

    private Poll GetPoll()
    {
        // if the Poll object is in the cache, return it
        // otherwise, create a new one
        Poll poll = (Poll)HttpRuntime.Cache["poll"];
        if (poll == null)
        {
            poll = new Poll();
            HttpRuntime.Cache["poll"] = poll;
        }
        return poll;
    }
}
```

```vb
Imports System
Imports System.Collections.Generic
Imports System.Text
Imports System.Web

Partial Public Class [Default]
    Inherits System.Web.UI.Page
    Private poll As Poll

    Protected Sub Page_Load(ByVal sender As Object, ByVal e As EventArgs)

        ' get the poll object
        poll = GetPoll()

        ' update on first load
        If (Not Page.IsPostBack) Then
            poll.UpdateAll()
            DrawPopflyResults()
        End If
    End Sub

    Private Function GetPoll() As Poll
        ' if the Poll object is in the cache, return it
        ' otherwise, create a new one
        Dim poll As Poll = CType(HttpRuntime.Cache("poll"), Poll)
        If poll Is Nothing Then
            poll = New Poll()
            HttpRuntime.Cache("poll") = poll
        End If
        Return poll
    End Function
End Class
```

Next we need to create a method to get the results, format it in the way the Popfly component expects, and then insert the final URL into an <IFRAME> tag to be drawn on the page. The Popfly component will expect two values passed on the query string: labels and values. Both of these must be formatted in a |-delimited list. The code for the DrawPopflyResults method is found in Examples 6-20 and 6-21.

```csharp
private void DrawPopflyResults()
{
    // get the tabulated results
    Dictionary<string, double> results = poll.GetPollResults();
```

```
StringBuilder labels = new StringBuilder();
StringBuilder values = new StringBuilder();

// create a |-delimited list of labels and values for the results graph
foreach(KeyValuePair<string, double> result in results)
{
    labels.AppendFormat("{0}|", result.Key);
    values.AppendFormat("{0}|", result.Value);
}

// create
string graphUrl = string.Format(@"http://www.popfly.com/users/c4fbook/↵
TwitterVoteGraph.content?labels={0}&values={1}", labels, values);
    ResultsData.InnerHtml = string.Format(@"<iframe allowtransparency='true' ↵
frameborder='no' src='{0}' style='width: 800px; height: 600px'></iframe>", graphUrl);

    Total.Text = poll.TotalVotes.ToString();
}
```

VB Example 6-21. *Visual Basic code for the DrawPopflyResults method*

```
Private Sub DrawPopflyResults()
    ' get the tabulated results
    Dim results As Dictionary(Of String, Double) = poll.GetPollResults()

    Dim labels As New StringBuilder()
    Dim values As New StringBuilder()

    ' create a |-delimited list of labels and values for the results graph
    For Each result As KeyValuePair(Of String, Double) In results
        labels.AppendFormat("{0}|", result.Key)
        values.AppendFormat("{0}|", result.Value)
    Next result

    ' create
    Dim graphUrl As String = String.Format("http://www.popfly.com/users/c4fbook/↵
TwitterVoteGraph.content?labels={0}&values={1}", labels, values)
    ResultsData.InnerHtml = String.Format("<iframe allowtransparency='true' ↵
frameborder='no' src='{0}' style='width: 800px; height: 600px'></iframe>", graphUrl)

    Total.Text = poll.TotalVotes.ToString()
End Sub
```

Finally, we will create a button-click event handler to update the poll and draw the
results, as shown in Examples 6-22 and 6-23.

Example 6-22. *C# code for the UpdateResults_Click method*

```csharp
protected void UpdateResults_Click(object sender, EventArgs e)
{
    poll.UpdateAll();
    DrawPopflyResults();
}
```

Example 6-23. *Visual Basic code for the UpdateResults_Click method*

```vb
Protected Sub UpdateResults_Click(ByVal sender As Object, ByVal e As EventArgs)
    poll.UpdateAll()
    DrawPopflyResults()
End Sub
```

Running the Application

The final step in this process is setting up the *web.config* file for our Twitter username and password. If you open the existing *web.config* file, you should see a single line near the top reading <appSettings/>. Simply replace that single line with the application settings as shown in Example 6-24, replacing the username and password with your own Twitter username and password.

Example 6-24. *appSettings section in web.config file*

```xml
<appSettings>
    <add key="TwitterUserName" value="username"/>
    <add key="TwitterPassword" value="password"/>
</appSettings>
```

With that complete, simply press F5 or click Debug→Start Debugging to start the application in debug mode. A local ASP.NET server will be created and the application will start up looking for the newest poll command and results. Create your poll, have people respond, and click the Update Results button to get the latest tabulation. However, do remember what was mentioned previously: Twitter has a rate limit, so don't press that button too many times too quickly, or you may be locked out for a period of time.

Sample Poll and Results

Let's take a look at a sample poll and its results. Figure 6-11 shows a Twitter user named C4FBook asking the question, "What is your favorite video game console?" The user then creates the poll by sending the poll wii,ps3,xbox360 command, which starts the poll and sets up the valid responses of "Wii, PS3, and Xbox 360". Following that, four users reply with their favorite console choices.

Figure 6-11. *Poll question, creation, and responses*

With the poll created and votes in place, we can start the TwitterVote application and view a bar graph of the results using Popfly, as shown in Figure 6-12.

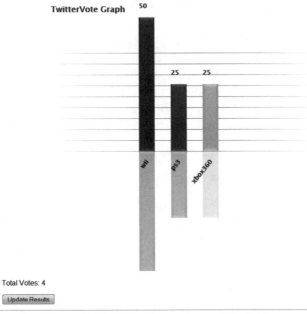

Figure 6-12. *TwitterVote results graph via Popfly*

Final Thoughts

Twitter is a very popular web-based service that exposes a simple API that can be used with minimal effort. TwitterVote is just one simple use of this API and can be expanded to add many features that use other methods exposed by the Twitter service, such as building a simple trivia game. Give it a try and poll your friends to see what features they might like added, and then create them yourself!

WHSMail: 7

An Outlook Webmail Add-in for Windows Home Server

AUTHOR	Brian Peek
DIFFICULTY	Intermediate
TIME REQUIRED	3–6 hours
COST	Free
SOFTWARE	Windows Home Server, Microsoft Outlook 2007 (not Outlook Express/Windows Mail), Visual Basic 2008 Express or Visual C# 2008 Express, Visual Web Developer 2008 Express .NET Framework 3.5 runtime, and Outlook/Office Primary Interop Assemblies (more on this later)
HARDWARE	None
DOWNLOAD	*http://www.c4fbook.com/WHSMail*

This chapter will show you how to build a new website using ASP.NET that can be added to your Windows Home Server (WHS) installation and will allow you to view the Outlook message store running on whatever computer contains your current Outlook installation.

Overview

Windows Home Server is a product from Microsoft that allows home users to manage and share data, including photos, documents, videos, and music. It also provides a very easy way to back up all computers on your home network to a central storage server. Windows Home Server can also be extended via add-ins to enhance the experience and provide new and interesting functionality in addition to what comes in the box.

One feature not present in WHS that I wanted was the ability to view my entire Outlook mail store from the Web at any time. I have six or seven email accounts that are all set up to retrieve via POP3 to Outlook. Most of these accounts do not support IMAP or have a web-based interface. Therefore, Outlook is generally open all day and checking messages, and all of my old mail is also stored there locally. When I'm away from home, it's often inconvenient to have to establish a remote desktop connection into the machine with Outlook running to read my email. Therefore, it would be nice to have a web-based version of my current Outlook folders, so I can view all email (old and new) at any time simply by browsing to a web server at home. Windows Home Server comes with Internet Information Services 6 (IIS6), and one can easily add a new web application to IIS on the server.

Understanding the Setup

Setup can be a bit tricky. Outlook 2007 will need to be installed on your development machine. It does not need to be on the same machine that contains your store at this point, but that would help. Once Outlook 2007 is installed, the *Primary Interop Assemblies* for Office need to be installed. This can be done by choosing *.NET Programming Support* from the list of sub-items in the Microsoft Office Outlook section of the setup program, as shown in Figure 7-1.

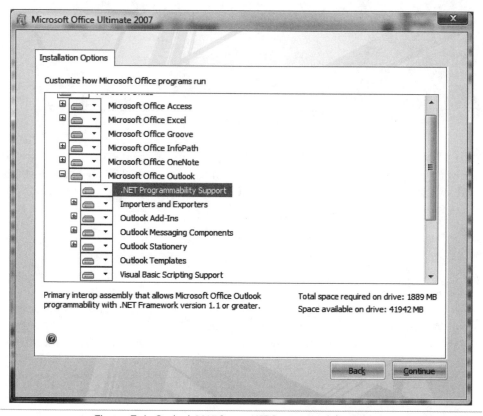

Figure 7-1. *Outlook 2007 Setup, .NET Programmability Support*

Architecture

The architecture we will be using is very similar that of an N-tier application, where there is a client application connecting to a server to get data or perform some operation. The machine running Outlook 2007 with the message store to be viewed is, in essence, the server machine. That machine will run a host process that we will develop that will expose several methods via Windows Communication Foundation (WCF). These methods will be consumed by an ASP.NET application running on the Windows Home Server.

Building the Host Application

Let's start by building the host application. This will run on the computer where Outlook is installed and the messages are stored. The application will be written to run in the notification area next to the Windows system clock.

To start, open Visual C# 2008 Express and create a new Windows Application project named WHSMailHost. Rename the default *Form1.cs* (or *.vb*) file to *frmMain.cs* (or *.vb*). Double-click on the file in the Solution Explorer to bring up the design surface.

In order to get the application to run in the notification area, drag and drop a Notify Icon control from the Toolbox to the design surface. Name it niIcon and then drag over a ContextMenuStrip to the design surface and name it cmsMenu, as shown in Figure 7-2.

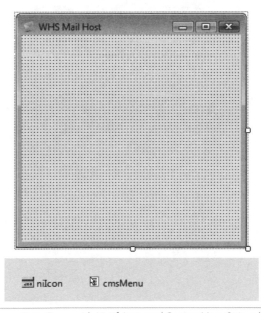

Figure 7-2. *Form with NotifyIcon and ContextMenuStrip added*

Finally, set the properties on the `niIcon` control as shown in Table 7-1 and Figure 7-3.

Table 7-1. *nilcon properties*

PROPERTY	VALUE
Text	WHS Mail Host
ContextMenuStrip	cmsMenu
Visible	True

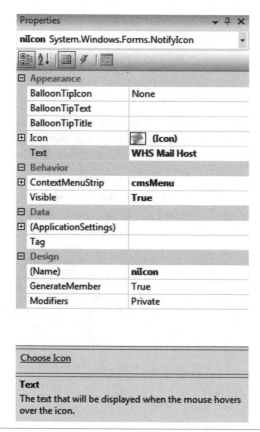

Figure 7-3. *nilcon Properties*

Right-click on the `cmsMenu` control, and select Edit Items... to bring up the Items Collection Editor for the context menu, as shown in Figure 7-4.

▤	View _C_ode
	Edit Items...
✂	Cu_t_
▣	Cop_y_
▣	_P_aste
✕	_D_elete
▤	P_r_operties

Figure 7-4. *Edit Items… menu item*

Here, add a single menu item named mnuExit with its Text property set to &Exit, as shown in Figure 7-5.

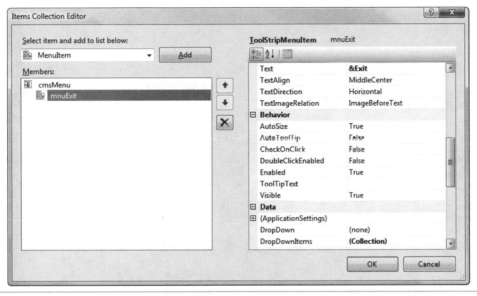

Figure 7-5. *Items Collection Editor*

Click OK to exit the dialog. Back on the form design surface, you should see a menu appear at the top of the form. Double-click the Exit entry you just created from this menu to add a default Click event. In the code for the Click event, simply close the form, as shown in Examples 7-1 and 7-2.

C# Example 7-1. *C# Code for mnuExit_Click event*

```csharp
private void mnuExit_Click(object sender, EventArgs e)
{
    // exit the application
    this.Close();
}
```

```
Private Sub mnuExit_Click(ByVal sender As Object, ByVal e As EventArgs) _
    Handles mnuExit.Click
    ' exit the application
    Me.Close()
End Sub
```

Finally, add the Resize, Load, and FormClosing events to frmMain by selecting them from the Event Property window (see Figure 7-6) and implementing them with the code shown in Examples 7-3 and 7-4.

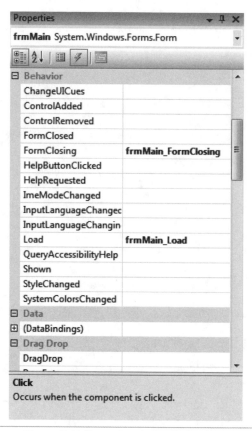

Figure 7-6. *Properties window for frmMain*

C# Example 7-3. *C# code for Resize, Load, and FormClosing events*

```
private void frmMain_Resize(object sender, EventArgs e)
{
    // hide the form
```

```
        this.Hide();
    }

    private void frmMain_Load(object sender, EventArgs e)
    {
        // start the WCF service
        MyServiceHost.StartService();
    }

    private void frmMain_FormClosing(object sender, FormClosingEventArgs e)
    {
        // stop the WCF service
        MyServiceHost.StopService();
    }
```

VB Example 7-4. *Visual Basic code for Resize, Load, and FormClosing events*

```
    Private Sub frmMain_Resize(ByVal sender As Object, ByVal e As EventArgs) _
        Handles MyBase.Resize
        ' hide the form
        Me.Hide()
    End Sub

    Private Sub frmMain_Load(ByVal sender As Object, ByVal e As EventArgs) _
        Handles MyBase.Load
        ' start the WCF service
        MyServiceHost.StartService()
    End Sub

    Private Sub frmMain_FormClosing(ByVal sender As Object, _
                                    ByVal e As FormClosingEventArgs) _
        Handles MyBase.FormClosing
        ' stop the WCF service
        MyServiceHost.StopService()
    End Sub
```

The code above references a class named MyServiceHost. This is what starts the WCF host and will be discussed next.

Windows Communication Foundation (WCF)

Windows Communication Foundation is a feature of the .NET Framework that allows you to build applications that communicate with each other across the network. Essentially, WCF will allow us to call methods on an object that is exposed on another computer as though they were both on the local machine. With this project, there will be one application running on one machine (the client; in this case, the ASP.NET application) that will execute a method on another machine, the host, which will be running Outlook and the application we are writing.

In the WHSMailHost project, add a reference to the *System.ServiceModel* assembly. Then, add a class to the project named WHSMailService. Open the class and add the code shown in Examples 7-5 or 7-6 beneath the generated WHSMailService class implementation.

C# Example 7-5. *C# code for MyServiceHost class*

```csharp
internal class MyServiceHost
{
    internal static ServiceHost myServiceHost = null;

    internal static void StartService()
    {
        // Instantiate new ServiceHost
        myServiceHost = new ServiceHost(typeof(WHSMailService));
        myServiceHost.Open();
    }

    internal static void StopService()
    {
        // Call StopService from your shutdown logic (i.e. dispose method)
        if (myServiceHost.State != CommunicationState.Closed)
            myServiceHost.Close();
    }
}
```

VB Example 7-6. *Visual Basic code for MyServiceHost class*

```vb
Friend Class MyServiceHost
    Friend Shared myServiceHost As ServiceHost = Nothing

    Friend Shared Sub StartService()
        ' Instantiate new ServiceHost
        myServiceHost = New ServiceHost(GetType(WHSMailService))
        myServiceHost.Open()
    End Sub

    Friend Shared Sub StopService()
        ' Call StopService from your shutdown logic (i.e. dispose method)
        If myServiceHost.State <> CommunicationState.Closed Then
            myServiceHost.Close()
        End If
    End Sub
End Class
```

This code simply creates a new WCF ServiceHost that exposes the type WHSMail Service (which we will implement next) and then opens that host so that it may receive incoming connections. We will look at how these connections are configured later in this chapter.

Remember that the code in frmMain called the StartService and StopService methods is located here when the main form loads and closes. This very easily allows us to immediately start the service host when the application starts and close the service host when the application exits.

Contracts and Entities

In WCF, a contract is an interface that defines which methods are exposed by the service and can be consumed by the client application. Both the client application and the server application will need to know what is in this interface, so we will need to create a second project that will contain the interface definition.

Additionally, we will need a way to pass folder and email information to and from each application, so we will define some custom classes to encapsulate those objects.

To begin, add a new *Class Library* project in the current solution named WHSMail Common. In this new project, create a directory named *Contracts* and a directory named *Entities*.

Inside the *Entities* directory, create a new class named Folder. This will represent an Outlook message folder. The class is implemented as shown in Examples 7-7 and 7-8.

C# | Example 7-7. *C# code for the Folder class*

```csharp
using System;
using System.Collections.Generic;

namespace WHSMailCommon.Entities
{
    // entity object representing an Folder
    [Serializable]
    public class Folder : IComparable
    {
        public Folder(string entryID, string name, int unreadMessages,
                    int totalMessages)
        {
            EntryID = entryID;
            Name = name;
            UnreadMessages = unreadMessages;
            TotalMessages = totalMessages;
        }
```

```csharp
            // MAPI unique identifier
            public string EntryID { get; set; }

            // subfolders of this folder
            public List<Folder> Folders { get; set; }
            public string Name { get; set; }
            public int UnreadMessages { get; set; }
            public int TotalMessages { get; set; }

            // used so we can sort the folders alphabetically later on
            public int CompareTo(object obj)
            {
                return string.Compare(this.Name, ((Folder)obj).Name);
            }
        }
    }
```

VB Example 7-8. *Visual Basic code for the Folder class*

```vb
Imports Microsoft.VisualBasic
Imports System
Imports System.Collections.Generic

Namespace WHSMailCommon.Entities
    ' entity object representing an Folder
    <Serializable> _
    Public Class Folder
        Implements IComparable
        Private _entryID As String
        Private _name As String
        Private _folders As List(Of Folder)
        Private _unreadMessages As Integer
        Private _totalMessages As Integer

        Public Sub New(ByVal entryID As String, ByVal name As String, _
                       ByVal unreadMessages As Integer, _
                       ByVal totalMessages As Integer)
            _entryID = entryID
            _name = name
            _unreadMessages = unreadMessages
            _totalMessages = totalMessages
        End Sub

        ' MAPI unique identifier
        Public Property EntryID() As String
            Get
```

```vb
            Return _entryID
        End Get
        Set(ByVal value As String)
            _entryID = value
        End Set
    End Property


    ' subfolders of this folder
    Public Property Folders() As List(Of Folder)
        Get
            Return _folders
        End Get
        Set(ByVal value As List(Of Folder))
            _folders = value
        End Set
    End Property

    Public Property Name() As String
        Get
            Return _name
        End Get
        Set(ByVal value As String)
            _name = value
        End Set
    End Property

    Public Property UnreadMessages() As Integer
        Get
            Return Me._unreadMessages
        End Get
        Set(ByVal value As Integer)
            Me._unreadMessages = value
        End Set
    End Property

    Public Property TotalMessages() As Integer
        Get
            Return Me._totalMessages
        End Get
        Set(ByVal value As Integer)
            Me._totalMessages = value
        End Set
    End Property

    ' used so we can sort the folders alphabetically later on
    Public Function CompareTo(ByVal obj As Object) As Integer _
```

```
        Implements IComparable.CompareTo
            Return String.Compare(Me.Name, (CType(obj, Folder)).Name)
        End Function
    End Class
End Namespace
```

This class defines several properties to describe the folder (EntryID, Name, etc.) and additionally implements the IComparable interface's CompareTo method so that we can easily sort the folders alphabetically later on.

Next, create a class named Email. The code for this class is found in Examples 7-9 and 7-10.

C#   Example 7-9. C# code for the Email class

```
using System;

namespace WHSMailCommon.Entities
{
    // entity object representing an Email
    [Serializable]
    public class Email
    {
        public Email(string entryID, string from, string fromName, string subject,
                    DateTime received, int size)
        {
            EntryID = entryID;
            From = from;
            FromName = fromName;
            Subject = string.IsNullOrEmpty(subject) ? "(no subject)" : subject;
            Received = received;
            Size = size;
        }

        public Email(string entryID, string from, string fromName, string subject,
                    DateTime received, int size, string body) :
                        this(entryID, from, fromName, subject, received, size)
        {
            Body = body;
        }

        // MAPI unique ID
        public string EntryID { get; set; }

        // email address of sender
        public string From { get; set; }
```

```
            // name of sender
            public string FromName { get; set; }

            public string Subject { get; set; }
            public string Body { get; set; }
            public DateTime Received { get; set; }
            public int Size { get; set; }
        }
    }
```

```
Imports Microsoft.VisualBasic
Imports System

Namespace WHSMailCommon.Entities
    ' entity object representing an Email
    <Serializable> _
    Public Class Email
        Private _entryID As String
        Private _from As String
        Private _fromName As String
        Private _subject As String
        Private _received As DateTime
        Private _size As Integer
        Private _body As String

        Public Sub New(ByVal entryID As String, ByVal From As String, _
                    ByVal fromName As String, ByVal subject As String, _
                    ByVal received As DateTime, ByVal size As Integer)
            _entryID = entryID
            _from = From
            _fromName = fromName
            If String.IsNullOrEmpty(subject) Then
                _subject = "(no subject)"
            Else
                _subject = subject
            End If
            _received = received
            _size = size
        End Sub

        Public Sub New(ByVal entryID As String, ByVal From As String, _
                    ByVal fromName As String, ByVal subject As String, _
                    ByVal received As DateTime, ByVal size As Integer, _
                    ByVal body As String)
```

```vbnet
        Me.New(entryID, From, fromName, subject, received, size)
        _body = body
    End Sub

    ' MAPI unique ID
    Public Property EntryID() As String
        Get
            Return _entryID
        End Get
        Set(ByVal value As String)
            _entryID = value
        End Set
    End Property

    ' email address of sender
    Public Property From() As String
        Get
            Return _from
        End Get
        Set(ByVal value As String)
            _from = value
        End Set
    End Property

    ' name of sender
    Public Property FromName() As String
        Get
            Return _fromName
        End Get
        Set(ByVal value As String)
            _fromName = value
        End Set
    End Property

    Public Property Subject() As String
        Get
            Return _subject
        End Get
        Set(ByVal value As String)
            _subject = value
        End Set
    End Property

    Public Property Body() As String
        Get
```

```
                    Return _body
                End Get
                Set(ByVal value As String)
                    _body = value
                End Set
            End Property

            Public Property Received() As DateTime
                Get
                    Return _received
                End Get
                Set(ByVal value As DateTime)
                    _received = value
                End Set
            End Property

            Public Property Size() As Integer
                Get
                    Return _size
                End Get
                Set(ByVal value As Integer)
                    _size = value
                End Set
            End Property
        End Class
    End Namespace
```

This class simply contains properties to describe an email message, such as `Subject`, `Body`, etc.

You will note that both of these classes have the `Serializable` attribute attached to them. When objects are passed through WCF, they are serialized at the source and deserialized at the destination. By marking the objects with the `Serializable` attribute, the .NET CLR can do this for us automatically, since we are not using any complex data types in our entities.

With our entities out of the way, we can now define our contract. Inside the *Contracts* directory, create a new *Interface* file named *IWHSMailService.cs* (or *.vb*).

This interface/contract will define three methods: one to return a tree of `Folder` objects that represent the folder tree in Outlook (`GetFolders`), one method to return a list of `Email` objects inside that folder (`GetMessages`), and one method to return the contents of a single `Email` message (`GetMessage`). The interface code is shown in Examples 7-11 and 7-12.

```csharp
using System.Collections.Generic;
using System.ServiceModel;
using WHSMailCommon.Entities;

namespace WHSMailCommon.Contracts
{
    // list of methods of the WHSMailService service
    [ServiceContract()]
    public interface IWHSMailService
    {
        [OperationContract]
        List<Folder> GetFolders();

        [OperationContract]
        List<Email> GetMessages(string entryID, int numPerPage, int pageNum);

        [OperationContract]
        Email GetMessage(string entryID);
    }
}
```

VB Example 7-12. *Visual Basic code for the IWHSMailService interface*

```vb
Imports Microsoft.VisualBasic
Imports System.Collections.Generic
Imports System.ServiceModel
Imports WHSMailCommon.Entities

Namespace WHSMailCommon.Contracts
    ' list of methods of the WHSMailService service
    <ServiceContract()> _
    Public Interface IWHSMailService
        <OperationContract> _
        Function GetFolders() As List(Of Folder)

        <OperationContract> _
        Function GetMessages(ByVal entryID As String, ByVal numPerPage As Integer, _
                        ByVal pageNum As Integer) As List(Of Email)

        <OperationContract> _
        Function GetMessage(ByVal entryID As String) As Email
    End Interface
End Namespace
```

As with the entities, this interface is also decorated with several attributes. First, any WCF contract interface must be tagged with the ServiceContract attribute to define it as a service contract to WCF. Additionally, all methods that will be exposed for consumption by a client must be marked with the OperationContract attribute; otherwise, you will not be able to call them remotely via WCF.

The implementation and description of these methods will come later when we write the contract implementation.

Configuration

The final thing to set up for the WCF server is the configuration. The service can very easily be configured using an application configuration file. Add an *Application Configuration* file to the WHSMailHost project named *App.config*. Set the contents of the file to that shown in Example 7-13.

Example 7-13. *XML contents of app.config*

```xml
<?xml version="1.0" encoding="utf-8" ?>
<configuration>
    <system.serviceModel>
        <bindings>
            <netTcpBinding>
                <binding name="NewBinding0">
                    <security mode="None" />
                </binding>
            </netTcpBinding>
        </bindings>
        <services>
            <service name="WHSMailHost.WHSMailService">
                <endpoint address="net.tcp://localhost:12345/IWHSMailService"
                    binding="netTcpBinding" bindingConfiguration="NewBinding0"
                    contract="WHSMailCommon.Contracts.IWHSMailService" />
            </service>
        </services>
    </system.serviceModel>
</configuration>
```

The <services> section defines the services that the WCF host will expose. We create a single <service> named WHSMailHost.WHSMailService, which is the full name of the service class that we will implement soon. Inside the <service> tag an endpoint is defined. An endpoint is essentially the address and configuration to which the client connects. The endpoint defined here uses the *net.tcp* protocol and is set to listen on the localhost on port 12345 at the name IWHSMailService. The next thing defined is a binding. This sets the protocol by which the service will communicate, its configuration, and the contract it implements. The binding configuration named NewBinding0 (a default name) can be found in the example inside the <bindings> tag. The only configuration item specified is that security will be turned off for communication between the client and server. Given that these two machines will be connecting to each other on your own local network, security is not a great concern. If you were to use this over a real Internet connection, where the client and server were open to the outside world, you would definitely want to add security.

The final item in the service configuration is the contract. This is set to the fully qualified name of the IWHSMailService interface we just created.

There are around several billion other options, protocols, bindings, etc., etc., etc. that can be configured here. At the end of this chapter, you will find several links to WCF documentation that you can explore to learn more about the WCF internals. Also note that you can configure WCF using a graphical UI with the *Service Configuration Editor* application installed with the Windows SDK or with the full version of Visual Studio 2008.

Using Outlook and MAPI

Messaging Application Programming Interface (MAPI) is a set of COM libraries in Windows that allows one to develop applications and plug-ins for Microsoft Outlook and other messaging applications that support it (Exchange, Windows Messaging, etc.). We will be using MAPI to get the data we require from Outlook for our application.

Earlier, we created a contract named IWHSMailService. This contract will be implemented by the WHSMailService class, also created earlier. To do this, back in the WHSMailHost project, set a reference to the solution's WHSMailCommon assembly. Then, set a reference to the *Microsoft Outlook 12.0 Object Library*, which you will find under the COM tab (assuming Outlook is installed as per the instructions earlier), as shown in Figure 7-7.

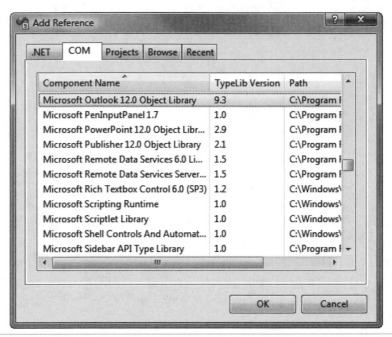

Figure 7-7. *Microsoft Outlook 12.0 Object Library reference*

Then, bring the Contracts and Entities namespaces into the WHSMailService class and set up the interface implementation with the code in either Examples 7-14 or 7-15.

[C#] Example 7-14. *C# code for the base WHSMailService class*

```
using WHSMailCommon.Contracts;
using WHSMailCommon.Entities;
using Outlook = Microsoft.Office.Interop.Outlook;

namespace WHSMailHost
{
    public class WHSMailService : IWHSMailService
    {
    }
}
```

```
Imports WHSMailCommon.Contracts
Imports WHSMailCommon.Entities
Imports Outlook = Microsoft.Office.Interop.Outlook

Public Class WHSMailService
    Implements IWHSMailService
End Class
```

Visual Studio should automatically create the three methods that must be implemented according to the interface: GetFolders, GetMessages, and GetMessage. We will fill those in shortly. But first, we must implement our constructor. When WCF calls the service, a new instance of the object will be created on each call. Therefore, it is easy to set up any initialization code for the service in the default constructor method. In this case, we will initialize the MAPI layer and log onto the default instance.

We need to get an instance of the Outlook ApplicationClass. From there we can get an instance of the MAPI namespace. All methods that we will be using hang off that namespace object. The code for the constructor is shown in Examples 7-16 and 7-17.

C# Example 7-16. *C# code for the WHSMailService constructor*

```
private readonly Outlook.NameSpace _nameSpace;

public WHSMailService()
{
    // get an instance of the MAPI namespace and login
    Outlook.Application app = new Outlook.ApplicationClass();
    _nameSpace = app.GetNamespace("MAPI");
    _nameSpace.Logon(null, null, false, false);
}
```

VB Example 7-17. *Visual Basic code for the WHSMailService constructor*

```
Private ReadOnly _nameSpace As Outlook.NameSpace

Public Sub New()
    ' get an instance of the MAPI namespace and login
    Dim app As Outlook.Application = New Outlook.ApplicationClass()
    _nameSpace = app.GetNamespace("MAPI")
    _nameSpace.Logon(Nothing, Nothing, False, False)
End Sub
```

With a handle to the namespace, we can write our GetFolders method. This method will get the default *Inbox* folder in the default Outlook message store, look at the parent node, recursively enumerate from there, pulling out only those folders that contain mail items, and finally sort them alphabetically (recall the CompareTo method of the IComparable interface we implemented earlier). The implementation of the GetFolders method is shown in Examples 7-18 and 7-19.

Example 7-18. *C# code for the GetFolders method*

```csharp
public List<Folder> GetFolders()
{
    List<Folder> list = new List<Folder>();

    // get the inbox and then go up one level...
    // that *should* be the root of the default store
    Outlook.MAPIFolder root = (Outlook.MAPIFolder)_nameSpace.GetDefaultFolder(
                                Outlook.OlDefaultFolders.olFolderInbox).Parent;

    // add root folder
    Folder folder = new Folder(root.EntryID, root.Name, root.UnReadItemCount,
                                root.Items.Count);
    list.Add(folder);

    // Enumerate the sub-folders
    EnumerateFolders(root.Folders, folder);

    return list;
}

private void EnumerateFolders(Outlook.Folders folders, Folder rootFolder)
{
    foreach(Outlook.MAPIFolder f in folders)
    {
        // ensure it's a folder that contains mail messages
        // (i.e. no contacts, appointments, etc.)
        if(f.DefaultItemType == Outlook.OlItemType.olMailItem)
        {
            if(rootFolder.Folders == null)
                rootFolder.Folders = new List<Folder>();

            // add the current folder and enumerate all sub-folders
            Folder subFolder = new Folder(f.EntryID, f.Name, f.UnReadItemCount,
                                f.Items.Count);
            rootFolder.Folders.Add(subFolder);
            if(f.Folders.Count > 0)
                this.EnumerateFolders(f.Folders, subFolder);
        }
    }
}
```

```
        // alphabetize the list (Folder implements IComparable)
        rootFolder.Folders.Sort();
    }
```

```vb
Public Function GetFolders() As List(Of Folder) Implements IWHSMailService.GetFolders
    Dim list As List(Of Folder) = New List(Of Folder)()

    ' get the inbox and then go up one level...
    ' that *should* be the root of the default store
    Dim root As Outlook.MAPIFolder = _
        CType(_nameSpace.GetDefaultFolder( _
                Outlook.OlDefaultFolders.olFolderInbox).Parent, Outlook.MAPIFolder)

    ' add root folder
    Dim folder As Folder = New Folder(root.EntryID, root.Name, _
                                    root.UnReadItemCount, root.Items.Count)
    list.Add(folder)

    ' Enumerate the sub-folders
    EnumerateFolders(root.Folders, folder)

    Return list
End Function

Private Sub EnumerateFolders(ByVal folders As Outlook.Folders, _
                        ByVal rootFolder As Folder)
    For Each f As Outlook.MAPIFolder In folders
        ' ensure it's a folder that contains mail messages
        ' (i.e. no contacts, appointments, etc.)
        If f.DefaultItemType = Outlook.OlItemType.olMailItem Then
            If rootFolder.Folders Is Nothing Then
                rootFolder.Folders = New List(Of Folder)()
            End If

            ' add the current folder and enumerate all sub-folders
            Dim subFolder As Folder = New Folder(f.EntryID, f.Name, _
                                        f.UnReadItemCount, f.Items.Count)
            rootFolder.Folders.Add(subFolder)
            If f.Folders.Count > 0 Then
                Me.EnumerateFolders(f.Folders, subFolder)
            End If
        End If
    Next f

    ' alphabetize the list (Folder implements IComparable)
```

```
        rootFolder.Folders.Sort()
    End Sub
```

This code will return a generic, hierarchal List of our Folder entity objects that will be displayed in the web application. Note that one of the items assigned to the Folder entity is the EntryID property from the MAPIFolder object. All MAPI items—be they email messages, folders, appointments, etc.—have a unique identifier stored in the EntryID field. We will need this unique value later on to retrieve messages from that folder.

Next, let's implement the GetMessages method. This method will return a list of messages (minus the bodies) from the folder specified using the GetFolderFromID method, sorted by the received date, with the most current first. It will also handle paging so that the entire folder is not returned at once. The implementation for this method is shown in Examples 7-20 and 7-21.

C# | **Example 7-20.** *C# code for the GetMessages method*

```csharp
public List<Email> GetMessages(string entryID, int numPerPage, int pageNum)
{
    List<Email> list = new List<Email>();

    Outlook.MAPIFolder f;

    // if no ID specified, open the inbox
    if(string.IsNullOrEmpty(entryID))
        f = _nameSpace.GetDefaultFolder(Outlook.OlDefaultFolders.olFolderInbox);
    else
        f = _nameSpace.GetFolderFromID(entryID, "");

    // to handle the sorting, one needs to cache their own instance
    // of the items object
    Outlook.Items items = f.Items;

    // sort descending by received time
    items.Sort("[ReceivedTime]", true);

    // pull in the correct number of items based on number of items per page
    // and current page number
    for(int i = (numPerPage*pageNum)+1; i <= (numPerPage*pageNum)+numPerPage &&
                                        i <= items.Count; i++)
    {
        // ensure it's a mail message
        Outlook.MailItem mi = (items[i] as Outlook.MailItem);
        if(mi != null)
            list.Add(new Email(mi.EntryID, mi.SenderEmailAddress, mi.SenderName,
                        mi.Subject, mi.ReceivedTime, mi.Size));
    }
```

```
    return list;

}
```

```
Public Function GetMessages(ByVal entryID As String, ByVal numPerPage As Integer, _
                            ByVal pageNum As Integer) As List(Of Email) _
                   Implements IWHSMailService.GetMessages
    Dim list As List(Of Email) = New List(Of Email)()


    Dim f As Outlook.MAPIFolder


    ' if no ID specified, open the inbox
    If String.IsNullOrEmpty(entryID) Then
        f = _nameSpace.GetDefaultFolder(Outlook.OlDefaultFolders.olFolderInbox)
    Else
        f = _nameSpace.GetFolderFromID(entryID, "")
    End If


    ' to handle the sorting, one needs to cache their own instance
    ' of the items object
    Dim items As Outlook.Items = f.Items


    ' sort descending by received time
    items.Sort("[ReceivedTime]", True)


    ' pull in the correct number of items based on number of items per page
    ' and current page number
    Dim i As Integer = (numPerPage*pageNum)+1
    Do While i <= (numPerPage*pageNum)+numPerPage AndAlso i <= items.Count
        ' ensure it's a mail message
        Dim mi As Outlook.MailItem = (TryCast(items(i), Outlook.MailItem))
        If Not mi Is Nothing Then
            list.Add(New Email(mi.EntryID, mi.SenderEmailAddress, mi.SenderName, _
                        mi.Subject, mi.ReceivedTime, mi.Size))
        End If
        i += 1
    Loop


    Return list
End Function
```

The method takes a string parameter named entryID, which is the unique identifier of the folder from which to return the messages. If no ID is specified, messages are returned from the *Inbox*. This code also handles paging by indexing into the array of Items of the MAPIFolder object at the specified position and counting out numPerPage records to be returned. A list of Email entity objects to be displayed on the web interface is returned from this method.

Finally, let's implement the GetMessage method. This will return a specific message based on the MAPI EntryID using the GetItemFromID method and format the body for plain text or HTML display, as shown in Examples 7-22 and 7-23.

C# Example 7-22. *C# code for the GetMessageMethod*

```csharp
public Email GetMessage(string entryID)
{
    // pull the message
    Outlook.MailItem mi =
        (_nameSpace.GetItemFromID(entryID, "") as Outlook.MailItem);

    if (mi != null)
    {
        string body;

        // if it's a plain format message, wrap it in <pre> tags for nice output
        if(mi.BodyFormat == Outlook.OlBodyFormat.olFormatPlain)
            body = "<pre>" + mi.Body + "</pre>";
        else
            body = mi.HTMLBody;

        return new Email(mi.EntryID, mi.SenderEmailAddress, mi.SenderName,
                        mi.Subject, mi.ReceivedTime, mi.Size, body);
    }
    else
        return null;
}
```

VB Example 7-23. *Visual Basic code for the GetMessage method*

```vb
Public Function GetMessage(ByVal entryID As String) As Email _
        Implements IWHSMailService.GetMessage
    ' pull the message
    Dim mi As Outlook.MailItem = _
        (TryCast(_nameSpace.GetItemFromID(entryID, ""), Outlook.MailItem))

    If Not mi Is Nothing Then
        Dim body As String

        ' if it's a plain format message, wrap it in <pre> tags for nice output
        If mi.BodyFormat = Outlook.OlBodyFormat.olFormatPlain Then
            body = "<pre>" & mi.Body & "</pre>"
        Else
```

```
            body = mi.HTMLBody
        End If

        Return New Email(mi.EntryID, mi.SenderEmailAddress, mi.SenderName, _
                         mi.Subject, mi.ReceivedTime, mi.Size, body)
    Else
        Return Nothing
    End If
End Function
```

With these three methods in place, we can get our folders, get messages in those folders, and get a specific message from a folder.

We are now finished with the "host" application. We've created a Windows Forms application that will sit in the notification area next to the clock, and that will get folders and messages from Outlook via MAPI, serialize them, and send them down to the client application for display.

Now we can switch our attention to the web-based "client" application that will plug into WHS.

ASP.NET "Client"

The client we are going to produce is a very simple three-paned screen, much like Outlook, with folders on the left, messages on the top right, and message text on the bottom right, as shown in Figure 7-8.

Figure 7-8. *Web mail interface*

Open Visual Web Developer Express and create a new *ASP.NET Web Application* named `WHSMailWeb`, as shown in Figure 7-9.

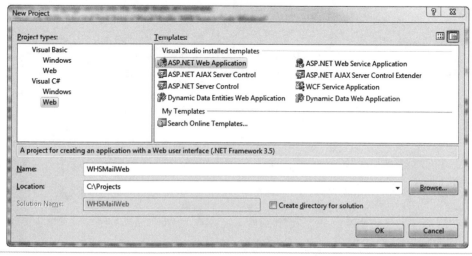

Figure 7-9. *Creating the ASP.NET web application*

When the project loads, we can add our existing WHSMailCommon and WHSMailHost projects to the solution and have everything contained in one place. Make sure these two projects are closed in any other IDEs, and then right-click on the WHSMailWeb solution. From the context menu, select Add→Existing Project... and navigate to the location of your WHSMailCommon and WHSMailHost projects, as shown in Figure 7-10. You can also find this command in the standard File menu in Visual Studio.

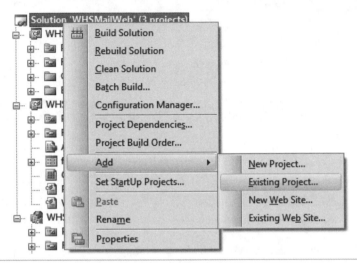

Figure 7-10. *Adding existing projects*

Select the *.csproj* or *.vbproj* for each project. They will now appear in the Solution Explorer and can be edited and compiled from here.

Back in the WHSMailWeb project, set a reference to the WHSMailCommon project, along with the System.ServiceModel assembly.

Now let's configure the ASP.NET application so it can properly call our WCF service running on the host machine. Open the *web.config* file and replace the contents with that shown in Example 7-24.

Example 7-24. *XML contents for the web.config file*

```
<?xml version="1.0"?>
<configuration>
    <system.web>
        <compilation debug="true" />
        <customErrors mode="Off" />
        <!-- INSERT CODE FROM /REMOTE/WEB.CONFIG HERE!!-->
        <!-- DON'T FORGET TO UPDATE THE FORMS AND CUSTOMERRORS KEYS! -->

        <!-- END COPIED CODE-->
    </system.web>
```

```
<system.serviceModel>
    <bindings>
        <netTcpBinding>
            <binding name="NewBinding0" maxReceivedMessageSize="1048576">
                <readerQuotas maxStringContentLength="1048576" />
                <security mode="None" />
            </binding>
        </netTcpBinding>
    </bindings>
    <client>
        <endpoint address="net.tcp://SERVERNAME:12345/IWHSMailService"
            binding="netTcpBinding" bindingConfiguration="NewBinding0"
            contract="WHSMailCommon.Contracts.IWHSMailService"
            name="WHSMailService" />
    </client>
</system.serviceModel>
</configuration>
```

This looks very similar to the configuration information from our host service. You will notice that an endpoint is defined that points to the host server.

 You will need to change the **SERVERNAME** text in the configuration host to the name or IP address of the machine that will run Outlook and the WHSMailHost application.

You will see the same setup for the binding and contract. The name parameter will be used by the code a bit later so WCF knows how to contact the host to instantiate the remote object.

The one thing that is different here is the netTcpBinding configuration. The security mode is set to none as it was before, but we have the addition of maxReceived MessageSize and maxStringContentLength. Both of these are set at 1 megabyte to allow that much data to be transferred from the host to the client. The default is only 64K, which is not enough to return most of the data we need to serialize and transmit between the two machines.

Next, add a class to the project named BasePage. This page will be inherited by all pages in the project, to easily start up and shut down the WCF channel required to retrieve the message data. Implement the BasePage class as shown in Examples 7-25 or 7-26.

C# Example 7-25. *C# code for the BasePage page*

```
using System;
using System.ServiceModel;
using WHSMailCommon.Contracts;
```

```csharp
namespace WHSMailWeb
{
    public partial class BasePage : System.Web.UI.Page
    {
        ChannelFactory<IWHSMailService> _factory = null;
        private IWHSMailService _channel = null;

        protected void Page_Init(object sender, EventArgs e)
        {
            // create a channel factory and then instantiate a proxy channel
            _factory = new ChannelFactory<IWHSMailService>("WHSMailService");
            _channel = _factory.CreateChannel();
        }

        protected void Page_Unload(object sender, EventArgs e)
        {
            try
            {
                _factory.Close();
            }
            catch
            {
                // for the moment, we don't really care what happens here...if it
                // fails, so be it
            }
        }

        public IWHSMailService WHSMailService
        {
            get { return _channel; }
        }

    }
}
```

VB **Example 7-26.** *Visual Basic code for the BasePage page*

```vbnet
Imports Microsoft.VisualBasic
Imports System
Imports System.ServiceModel
Imports WHSMailCommon.Contracts

Namespace WHSMailWeb
    Public Partial Class BasePage
        Inherits System.Web.UI.Page
```

```
        Private _factory As ChannelFactory(Of IWHSMailService) = Nothing
        Private _channel As IWHSMailService = Nothing

        Protected Sub Page_Init(ByVal sender As Object, ByVal e As EventArgs)
            ' create a channel factory and then instantiate a proxy channel
            _factory = New ChannelFactory(Of IWHSMailService)("WHSMailService")
            _channel = _factory.CreateChannel()
        End Sub

        Protected Sub Page_Unload(ByVal sender As Object, ByVal e As EventArgs)
            Try
                _factory.Close()
            Catch
                ' for the moment, we don't really care what happens here...if it
                ' fails, so be it
            End Try
        End Sub

        Public ReadOnly Property WHSMailService() As IWHSMailService
            Get
                Return _channel
            End Get
        End Property

    End Class
End Namespace
```

This code overrides the page's Init and Unload methods. Page_Init is called at the beginning of a page request, and Page_Unload is called just before the request completes.

The Page_Init method here uses WCF to create a ChannelFactory object factory that will return proxy objects of type IWHSMailService. Recall that this is the interface that defines the contract of our service. The name passed as a parameter to the ChannelFactory constructor must match the name of the service in the configuration file, as discussed earlier.

Next, a channel object is created by calling CreateChannel from the ChannelFactory. This is what returns the fake proxy object defined by our contract. A property named WHSMailService at the bottom of the class exposes this so that the inherited pages can easily use the object to call the host service. We'll see this a bit later.

The Page_Unload method simply closes the factory object and very poorly handles any exceptions that may occur when doing so. An error on close isn't critical to this application, but that is certainly not the case for all applications.

Now we will implement the *Default.aspx* page. The HTML of the page is shown in Example 7-27.

Example 7-27. *HTML for the Default.aspx page*

```
<%@ Page Language="C#" AutoEventWireup="true" CodeBehind="Default.aspx.cs"
Inherits="WHSMailWeb._Default" %>
<%@ Import namespace="System.ComponentModel"%>

<!DOCTYPE html PUBLIC "-//W3C//DTD XHTML 1.0 Transitional//EN" "http://www.w3.org/TR/
xhtml1/DTD/xhtml1-transitional.dtd">

<html xmlns="http://www.w3.org/1999/xhtml" >
<head runat="server">
    <title>WHS Email</title>
    <style>
body
{
    margin:0;
    padding:0;
    height:100%;
}
#top
{
    position: absolute;
    left: 16%;
    top: 0px;
    margin: 0px;
    padding: 0px;
    overflow: auto;
    height:54%;
    width:84%;
}

#pager
{
    position: absolute;
    left: 16%;
    top: 54%;
    margin: 0px;
    padding: 0px;
    overflow: auto;
    height: 24px;
    width: 84%;
    text-align: center;
    font-family: Tahoma;
```

```css
        font-size: Smaller;
    }

    #bottom
    {
        position: absolute;
        left: 16%;
        margin: 0px;
        padding: 0px;
        vertical-align: top;
        top: 56%;
        height: 44%;
        width: 84%;
        overflow: auto;
        border-top: thin solid #EFF3FB;
        word-wrap:break-word;
    }

    #folders
    {
        position: absolute;
        left: 0px;
        margin: 0px;
        padding: 0px;
        vertical-align: top;
        height: 100%;
        width: 15%;
        overflow: auto;
        border-right: thin solid #EFF3FB;
    }

    #tblHeader
    {
        color:#FFFFFF;
        font-family: Tahoma;
        font-size: smaller;
    }
    </style>
</head>
<body scroll="no">
    <form id="form1" runat="server">
    <div id="folders">
        <asp:TreeView ID="tvFolders" runat="server"
            OnSelectedNodeChanged="tvFolders_SelectedNodeChanged" ExpandDepth="0"
            ImageSet="Inbox" NodeIndent="10">
```

```
                <ParentNodeStyle Font-Bold="False" />
                <HoverNodeStyle Font-Underline="True" />
                <SelectedNodeStyle Font-Underline="True" HorizontalPadding="0px"
                    VerticalPadding="0px" />
                <NodeStyle Font-Names="Verdana" Font-Size="8pt" ForeColor="Black"
                    HorizontalPadding="5px"
                NodeSpacing="0px" VerticalPadding="0px" />
            </asp:TreeView>
        </div>
        <div id="top">
            <asp:GridView ID="GridView1" runat="server" CellPadding="4"
                ForeColor="#333333" GridLines="Horizontal" AutoGenerateColumns="False"
                CaptionAlign="Top" HorizontalAlign="Center" Width="100%" PageSize="20"
                Font-Names="Tahoma" Font-Size="Small">
                <FooterStyle BackColor="#507CD1" Font-Bold="True" ForeColor="White" />
                <RowStyle BackColor="#EFF3FB" />
                <EditRowStyle BackColor="#2461BF" />
                <SelectedRowStyle BackColor="#D1DDF1" Font-Bold="True"
                    ForeColor="#333333" />
                <PagerStyle BackColor="#2461BF" ForeColor="White"
                    HorizontalAlign="Center" />
                <HeaderStyle BackColor="#507CD1" Font-Bold="True" ForeColor="White" />
                <AlternatingRowStyle BackColor="White" />
                <Columns>
                    <asp:BoundField DataField="From" HeaderText="From" />
                    <asp:TemplateField HeaderText="Subject">
                        <ItemTemplate>
                            <asp:LinkButton ID="btnLink" OnCommand="btnLink_Command"
                                CommandArgument='<%#Eval("EntryID")%>'
                                runat="server"><%#Eval("Subject")%></asp:LinkButton>
                        </ItemTemplate>
                    </asp:TemplateField>
                    <asp:BoundField DataField="Received" HeaderText="Received" />
                    <asp:BoundField DataField="Size" HeaderText="Size" />
                </Columns>
            </asp:GridView>
        </div>
        <div id="pager">
            <asp:LinkButton ID="btnPrev" runat="server"
                OnClick="btnPrev_Click">&lt; Prev</asp:LinkButton> 
            <asp:LinkButton ID="btnNext" runat="server"
                OnClick="btnNext_Click">Next &gt;</asp:LinkButton>
        </div>
        <div id="bottom" runat="server">
            <table cellpadding="0" cellspacing="0" id="tblHeader" bgcolor="#507CD1"
                width="100%" runat="server">
```

```
<tr><td><strong>From:</strong></td><td><asp:Label ID="lblFrom"
    runat="server"/></td></tr>
<tr><td><strong>Subject:</strong></td><td><asp:Label ID="lblSubject"
    runat="server"/></td></tr>
<tr><td><strong>Received:</strong></td><td><asp:Label ID="lblReceived"
    runat="server"/></td></tr>
    </table>
    <div id="msgContent" runat="server"></div>
    </div>
    </form>
</body>
</html>
```

This page contains four <DIV> tags: one contains an ASP.NET TreeView object (the left-most pane), one contains an ASP.NET GridView object (the top-right pane), one contains two ASP.NET LinkButtons that implement a Next/Back paging scheme (the middle-right pane), and the last contains a table to display some header information and a <DIV> to display the message contents (the lower-right pane).

The GridView sets up a variety of styles and then its column information inside the <Columns> tag. The grid contains four columns: the "from" address, the subject, the date the email was received, and the size of the message. The from, received, and size columns are created using the BoundField project. This project will automatically be assigned using data binding, which we will look at later. The subject column is created using a TemplateField, which allows us to insert a LinkButton control on each line so that the subject becomes a clickable link that will display the message text in the lower pane.

As seen previously, this will produce a web page that looks like that shown in Figure 7-11.

Figure 7-11. *Web mail interface*

Now let's implement the actual logic for the page. Open the *Default.aspx* page's code-behind file, and implement the base code as shown in Examples 7-28 and 7-29.

C# Example 7-28. *C# code for the base _Default code-behind*

```
using System;
using System.Collections.Generic;
using System.Web.UI.WebControls;
using WHSMailCommon.Entities;

namespace WHSMailWeb
{
    public partial class _Default : BasePage
    {
    }
}
```

VB Example 7-29. *Visual Basic code for the base _Default code-behind*

```
Imports Microsoft.VisualBasic
Imports System
```

```
Imports System.Collections.Generic
Imports System.Web.UI.WebControls
Imports WHSMailCommon.Entities

Namespace WHSMailWeb
    Public Partial Class _Default
        Inherits BasePage
    End Class
End Namespace
```

Next, let's implement the Page_Load method. This method will be called after the Page_Init method, which is implemented in our parent object and will be called automatically. This can be seen in Examples 7-30 and 7-31.

C# Example 7-30. *C# code for the Page_Load and helper methods*

```csharp
private string _folderEntryID = string.Empty;
private int _pageNum = 0;

protected void Page_Load(object sender, EventArgs e)
{
    // first time in (tvFolders has viewstate enabled
    if(tvFolders.Nodes.Count == 0)
    {
        // get the folder tree
        List<Folder> folderList = this.WHSMailService.GetFolders();

        // add the root node and expand it
        TreeNode node = new TreeNode(folderList[0].Name, folderList[0].EntryID);
        node.Expanded = true;
        tvFolders.Nodes.Add(node);

        // load up the sub-folders
        LoadNode(folderList[0].Folders, node);

        // get the inbox list and bind it to the grid
        List<Email> list = GetMessages();
        BindMessages(list);

        // save off the default page number and folder ID
        ViewState["PageNum"] = _pageNum;
        ViewState["FolderID"] = _folderEntryID;
    }

    _pageNum = int.Parse(ViewState["PageNum"].ToString());
```

```
        _folderEntryID = ViewState["FolderID"].ToString();
    }

    private void LoadNode(List<Folder> folders, TreeNode node)
    {
        foreach(Folder f in folders)
        {
                // add the node with the format of Folder (Unread/Total)
                TreeNode subNode = new TreeNode(f.Name + " (" + f.UnreadMessages + "/" +
                                            f.TotalMessages + ")", f.EntryID);

                // expand and select the inbox
                subNode.Expanded = subNode.Selected = (f.Name == "Inbox");
                node.ChildNodes.Add(subNode);

                // load the subfolders
                if(f.Folders != null)
                        LoadNode(f.Folders, subNode);
        }
    }

    private List<Email> GetMessages()
    {
        // get a group of messages based on the current page number and size
        return this.WHSMailService.GetMessages(_folderEntryID, GridView1.PageSize,
                                        _pageNum);
    }

    private void BindMessages(List<Email> list)
    {
        // load the grid
        GridView1.DataSource = list;
        GridView1.DataBind();

        // save off the new page number
        ViewState["PageNum"] = _pageNum;
    }
```

VB **Example 7-31**. *Visual Basic code for the Page_Load and helper methods*

```
    Private _folderEntryID As String = String.Empty
    Private _pageNum As Integer = 0

    Protected Sub Page_Load(ByVal sender As Object, ByVal e As EventArgs)
    ' first time in (tvFolders has viewstate enabled
    If tvFolders.Nodes.Count = 0 Then
```

```vbnet
        ' get the folder tree
        Dim folderList As List(Of Folder) = Me.WHSMailService.GetFolders()

        ' add the root node and expand it
        Dim node As TreeNode = New TreeNode(folderList(0).Name, _
                                            folderList(0).EntryID)
        node.Expanded = True
        tvFolders.Nodes.Add(node)

        ' load up the sub-folders
        LoadNode(folderList(0).Folders, node)

        ' get the inbox list and bind it to the grid
        Dim list As List(Of Email) = GetMessages()
        BindMessages(list)

        ' save off the default page number and folder ID
        ViewState("PageNum") = _pageNum
        ViewState("FolderID") = _folderEntryID
    End If

    _pageNum = Integer.Parse(ViewState("PageNum").ToString())
    _folderEntryID = ViewState("FolderID").ToString()
End Sub

Private Sub LoadNode(ByVal folders As List(Of Folder), ByVal node As TreeNode)
    For Each f As Folder In folders
        ' add the node with the format of Folder (Unread/Total)
        Dim subNode As TreeNode = New TreeNode(f.Name & " (" & f.UnreadMessages & _
                                                "/" & f.TotalMessages & ")", _
                                                f.EntryID)

        ' expand and select the inbox
        subNode.Selected = (f.Name = "Inbox")
        subNode.Expanded = subNode.Selected
        node.ChildNodes.Add(subNode)

        ' load the subfolders
        If Not f.Folders Is Nothing Then
                LoadNode(f.Folders, subNode)
        End If
    Next f
End Sub

Private Function GetMessages() As List(Of Email)
    ' get a group of messages based on the current page number and size
```

```
            Return Me.WHSMailService.GetMessages(_folderEntryID, GridView1.PageSize, _
                                            _pageNum)
    End Function

    Private Sub BindMessages(ByVal list As List(Of Email))
            ' load the grid
            GridView1.DataSource = list
            GridView1.DataBind()

            ' save off the new page number
            ViewState("PageNum") = _pageNum
    End Sub
```

If the tvFolders tree view has not been filled in, we call our host service's GetFolders method from the WHSMailService property, as defined in the examples. The method then enumerates through the hierarchical list of folders returned, building the same tree structure that exists in Outlook. The Text property of each TreeNode is set to the folder name with a count of messages unread and total count of messages. The Value property of the node is set to the unique MAPI-defined EntryID so that we can later grab that value to return the list of messages from that specific folder.

Next, we call our service's GetMessages method to return messages from the Inbox. We pass in the value from the grid view's PageSize property and a member variable named _pageNum. This will handle our paging scheme, as discussed earlier. Once that list of messages is returned, it is bound to the data grid for display. By setting up the BoundField columns as we did earlier, the columns will be filled in automatically, with no additional effort on our part.

Finally, the default page number and folder entry ID (0 and "", respectively) are stored in the ViewState so they can be assigned back to our member variables on each page request.

Next, we will implement what occurs when a user clicks on a folder in the tree view. We simply pull out the MAPI-unique EntryID (which is stored in the Value field of the selected node), assign it to the local member variable and view state, and then call the GetMessages method from our service to return a list of messages from that folder, just as we did with the inbox earlier. The code for this process is shown in Examples 7-32 and 7-33.

C#   **Example 7-32.** *C# code for the tvFolders_SelectedNodeChanged event handler*

```
    protected void tvFolders_SelectedNodeChanged(object sender, EventArgs e)
    {
        // new folder, so reset the view
        _pageNum = 0;
        _folderEntryID = this.tvFolders.SelectedNode.Value;
        ViewState["FolderID"] = _folderEntryID;
```

```
        List<Email> list = GetMessages();
        BindMessages(list);
    }
```

VB Example 7-33. *Visual Basic code for the tvFolders_SelectedNodeChanged event handler*

```
    Protected Sub tvFolders_SelectedNodeChanged(ByVal sender As Object, _
                                                ByVal e As EventArgs)
        ' new folder, so reset the view
        _pageNum = 0
        _folderEntryID = Me.tvFolders.SelectedNode.Value
        ViewState("FolderID") = _folderEntryID

        Dim list As List(Of Email) = GetMessages()
        BindMessages(list)
    End Sub
```

Next, we can implement the Next/Back link buttons (Examples 7-34 and 7-35). These methods simply increment or decrement the current page number, assign it to the view state for use on the next request, and then, just as before, get the list of messages specific to the currently selected folder, using the unique ID stored in the view state.

C# Example 7-34. *C# code for the btnPrev_Click and btnNext_Click event handlers*

```
    protected void btnPrev_Click(object sender, EventArgs e)
    {
        // first page
        if(_pageNum > 0)
            _pageNum--;

        List<Email> list = GetMessages();
        BindMessages(list);
    }

    protected void btnNext_Click(object sender, EventArgs e)
    {
        // next page
        _pageNum++;
        List<Email> list = GetMessages();

        // if we're out of messages, go back to the previous page
        if(list == null || list.Count == 0)
        {
            _pageNum--;
            list = GetMessages();
```

```
        }
        BindMessages(list);
    }
```

```
    Protected Sub btnPrev_Click(ByVal sender As Object, ByVal e As EventArgs)
        ' first page
        If _pageNum > 0 Then
            _pageNum -= 1
        End If

        Dim list As List(Of Email) = GetMessages()
        BindMessages(list)
    End Sub

    Protected Sub btnNext_Click(ByVal sender As Object, ByVal e As EventArgs)
        ' next page
        _pageNum += 1
        Dim list As List(Of Email) = GetMessages()

        ' if we're out of messages, go back to the previous page
        If list Is Nothing OrElse list.Count = 0 Then
            _pageNum -= 1
            list = GetMessages()
        End If
        BindMessages(list)
    End Sub
```

Finally, we need to implement displaying the actual email body when the user selects a message from the top pane. As discussed previously, if you look at the HTML for the *Default.aspx* page, you will see that the Subject field is bound to a LinkButton control in the grid view via a TemplateField (the rest of the fields are standard Bound Fields). The LinkButton sets the CommandArgument property to the unique EntryID of that message as defined by MAPI. So, all we need to do is listen on the server for the LinkButton's Command event, grab the unique ID, and call our service's Get Message method with that ID to return the message itself, as shown in Examples 7-36 and 7-37.

```
    protected void btnLink_Command(object sender, CommandEventArgs e)
    {
        Email email = this.WHSMailService.GetMessage(e.CommandArgument.ToString());

        // fill out the header with some basic info
        lblFrom.Text = email.FromName + " (" + email.From + ")";
```

```
lblSubject.Text = email.Subject;
lblReceived.Text = email.Received.ToString();

// when a message is selected, write out the content
msgContent.InnerHtml = email.Body;
}
```

 Example 7-37. *Visual Basic code for the btnLink_Command event handler*

```
Protected Sub btnLink_Command(ByVal sender As Object, ByVal e As CommandEventArgs)
    Dim email As Email = Me.WHSMailService.GetMessage(e.CommandArgument.ToString())

    ' fill out the header with some basic info
    lblFrom.Text = email.FromName & " (" & email.From & ")"
    lblSubject.Text = email.Subject
    lblReceived.Text = email.Received.ToString()

    ' when a message is selected, write out the content
    msgContent.InnerHtml = email.Body
End Sub
```

The Email entity is retrieved, its properties are set to the labels in the header, and the message content is assigned to the InnerHtml property of the content-holding <DIV>.

Voilà! A very simple mail reader.

That's it for code. Now we need to deploy the applications and configure Windows Home Server.

> **WARNING**
> There is one caveat here that needs to be mentioned. The web-based client will display the contents of any message without the strict security checking that Outlook would do on its own. Therefore, be careful when viewing unknown messages and clicking unknown links, as Outlook isn't here to protect you.

Deployment

First, install .NET Framework 3.5 on the machine you will use to run the WHSMailHost application, if it isn't already. Then, copy the *WHSMailHost.exe*, *WHSMailHost.exe.config*, and *WHSMailCommon.dll* files to a directory on this machine. You might want to create a shortcut in the Startup group so it will launch automatically when you log into Windows.

Next, open Outlook and select Tools→Trust Center. Choose Programmatic Access, and set the option to "Never warn me about suspicious activity", as shown in Figure

7-12. Unfortunately this security measure must be disabled; otherwise, Outlook will prompt you every time the host process attempts to retrieve any data. There is no way to bypass this on an application-by-application basis, so we have to turn it off for all applications.

> **NOTE** If you are running Windows Vista, you must run Outlook as an Administrator in order to change this setting. Once changed, you may go back to running Outlook as a standard user.

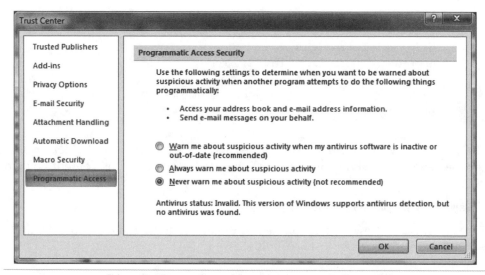

Figure 7-12. *Programmatic Access Security in Outlook 2007*

If you are running firewall software on the PC, ensure that port 12345 will allow traffic to pass through. You may also change port 12345 to a different port, but you must change it in the configuration files for both applications.

Finally, note that Outlook does not need to remain open to use this application. You do, however, need to be logged into the machine with the host running.

WHSMailWeb

For the next few steps, you will need to remote desktop into your Windows Home Server using the true Remote Desktop application, not the Windows Home Server Connector.

On your Windows Home Server machine, install the .NET Framework 3.5 Runtime, which you need in order to use WCF. Next, create a new directory named *mail* inside the existing *c:\inetpub* directory. Copy all *.aspx* pages, *web.config*, *icon.png*, and the *bin* directory to the *mail* directory you just created. Then, open the Internet Information Services (IIS) Manager application from the Administrative Tools group on the Start menu. Open the Web Sites note, right-click on Default Web Site, and select New→Virtual Directory… from the context menu, as shown in Figure 7-13.

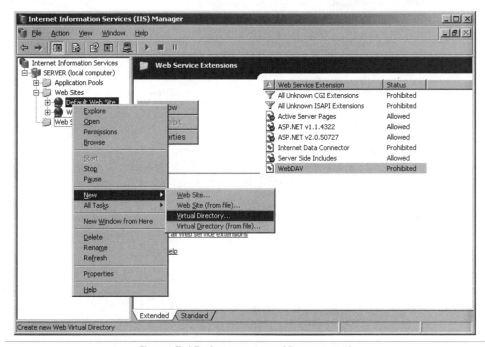

Figure 7-13. *Creating a Virtual Directory in IIS*

When prompted, use the values in Table 7-2.

Table 7-2. *Virtual directory properties*

PROPERTY	VALUE
Alias	Mail
Path	C:\inetpub\mail
Permissions	Read, Run Scripts

The next part is a bit tricky. We want to integrate with the security already provided by Windows Home Server. The WHS *remote* website uses Forms security from ASP.NET. Ideally, you should be able to log into the main page of the WHS remote website and then open the webmail link without having to log in again. Additionally, if the *mail* URL is used directly, you should be prompted for your login credentials.

To achieve this, open the *web.config* file from *c:\inetpub\remote* in Notepad. In the XML between the start and end <system.web> tags, you will find the configuration for the Forms-based authentication used by WHS. In order to use the cookie that is created by this authentication method, we need to have the same key values in our *web.config* file. The easiest way to achieve this is to copy all of the text between the open and closing `<system.web>` tags of the *web.config* file in the remote directory. Next, open the *web.config* file from the *mail* directory that you just copied over, and paste the text between the two lines informing you to do so. The code in Example 7-38 is an example of what this text looks like, but *do not use this exact code*, as it will not work for you. The values are different on each and every machine.

Example 7-38. XML to copy/paste between web.config files

```
<machineKey validationKey="24032958BBC3088B5B117035A7399814727BA88188A044271034A21968
FFCA1621D8F923102D345F9166A42E4F6B6A70F4B838F8127F844D2AB0C492F43AE2F6"
  decryptionKey="3D8D5A023C289F4E19085134E1CACA0842BC363122B058EFD8E6CF796E4406E3"
  validation="SHA1" decryption="AES" />
<authentication mode="Forms">
        <forms name="RemotePortalAuth" loginUrl="logon.aspx" protection="All"
          path="/" timeout="12000" requireSSL="false"/>
    </authentication>
    <authorization>
        <deny users="?"/>
        <allow users="*"/>
    </authorization>
    <httpRuntime executionTimeout="86400" maxRequestLength="2097151" />
    <customErrors mode="On" defaultRedirect="error.aspx"/>
    <trace enabled="false" localOnly="false" pageOutput="false"
     requestLimit="100" traceMode="SortByTime" />
    <sessionState mode="InProc" cookieless="false" timeout="20"/>
    <globalization requestEncoding="utf-8" responseEncoding="utf-8"/>
```

Finally, we need to update the `loginUrl` and `defaultRedirect` paths in the `forms` and `customErrors` keys of our *web.config* file. Add /remote/ to the beginning of each to make them /remote/login.aspx and /remote/error.aspx, respectively, as shown in Example 7-39.

Example 7-39. Updated <forms> and <customErrors> nodes

```
<forms name="RemotePortalAuth" loginUrl="/remote/logon.aspx" protection="All"
  path="/" timeout="12000" requireSSL="false"/>
<customErrors mode="On" defaultRedirect="/remote/error.aspx"/>
```

Finally, be sure that the SERVERNAME item in the endpoint configuration is updated to the name/IP address of the machine running the host process.

With the files copied and edited, ensure that permissions on the file are propagated from the root *mail* directory to the files inside.

Finally, open the *websites.xml* file in the */remote* directory and add the XML shown in Example 7-40 before the end </WebSites> tag.

Example 7-40. *XML addition for websites.xml file*

```
<WebSite name="Outlook Webmail" uri="/mail" imageUrl="/mail/icon.png"
absolute="false"></WebSite>
```

With the configuration done, we need to enable website connectivity in Windows Home Server. Double-click the Windows Home Server Console icon on the desktop. When it loads, click the Settings button in the top-right corner. When the Settings dialog appears, select Remote Access in the left pane, and then click the Turn On button in the right pane, assuming website connectivity is off, as shown in Figure 7-14. If it is already enabled, skip this step.

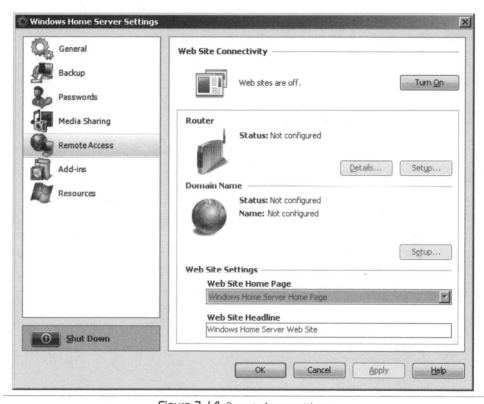

Figure 7-14. *Remote Access settings*

Running the Application

Ensure the *WHSMailHost* application is running on the PC with Outlook installed. Then, browse to your Windows Home Server's default website. After logging in, you should see a link on the right side of the screen named Outlook Webmail, as shown in Figure 7-15.

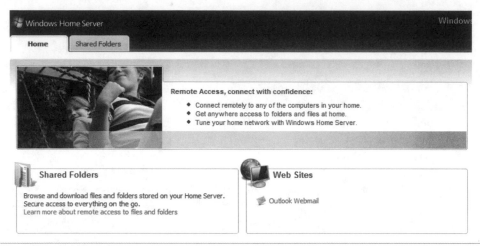

Figure 7-15. *Outlook Webmail icon*

Click that link to start our application, and if everything is working, you should see the web page as shown in the figure.

Final Thoughts

Phew! Two applications and one shared assembly later, we have a web-based add-in for Windows Home Server that allows you to remotely access your Outlook message store. Currently the application is read-only and provides only minimal functionality, but it's a great starting point to create a full-featured webmail client interface that would include support for attachments, and message flags. It could even be expanded to include Outlook calendars, contacts, and tasks.

Section 3

Hardware

Wiimote-Controlled Car

AUTHOR	Brian Peek
DIFFICULTY	Medium
TIME REQUIRED	5 Hours
COST	$40 for Wii Remote (or free if you own a Nintendo Wii console), $80 for a Phidget Interface Kit, $25 for a R/C car
SOFTWARE	Visual C# 2008 Express, Visual Basic 2008 Express, or any full edition of Visual Studio 2008
HARDWARE	Nintendo Wii Remote, Phidget Interface Kit, R/C car with "digital" inputs, soldering iron, solder, wire
DOWNLOAD	*http://www.c4fbook.com/WiimoteCar*

Since its North American launch in November 2006, the Nintendo Wii game console's innovative user interface has taken gaming to a new level. With few exceptions, previous gaming consoles only allowed users to control a game via a standard control pad and buttons. The Nintendo Wii lets users control the games with the motion-sensitive Wii Remote, affectionately known as the *Wiimote* (see Figure 8-1).

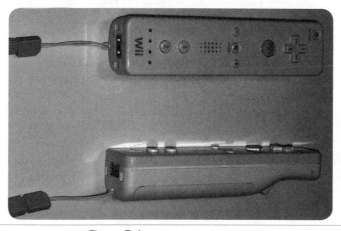

Figure 8-1. *A Wii remote (Wiimote)*

This project will use the motion-sensitive capabilities of the Wiimote to control a standard remote-controlled car, allowing the driver to steer the car left and right by tilting the Wiimote.

Overview

For those unfamiliar with the Wii remote, it is a hand-held, rectangular device similar in shape to a television remote control. It is included with the Nintendo Wii console, or can be purchased separately for about $40.

This controller contains a ton of hardware packed within its shell:

- Three-axis accelerometer
- IR-sensitive camera capable of sensing four points
- Seven push buttons
- Four-way directional control pad
- Four LEDs
- Speaker
- Vibration motor
- Expansion port
- Bluetooth connectivity

That final item in the list, Bluetooth connectivity, is the key to what makes this little device so intriguing. Being Bluetooth compatible, it is possible to pair the Wiimote to almost any computer with a Bluetooth interface and communicate with the device.

Wiimote Definitions

Accelerometer: an electronic component that can measure the force exerted on an axis. The Wiimote's accelerometer can measure force on three axes.

Bluetooth: a short-range wireless transmission protocol. The Wiimote uses this protocol to connect to the Wii console or a PC.

IR; infra-red: a wavelength of light that is invisible to the naked eye. The Wii sensor bar that sits on top of the television emits two IR points, which the Wiimote is able to "see" in order to determine its position in space.

LED: Light Emitting Diode. The Wiimote contains four LEDs at its very bottom, and these can be used to express simple status information.

The second piece of hardware required for this project is a *Phidget Interface Kit*. Phidgets (*http://www.phidgets.com/*) are USB-based devices that allow one to easily perform simple I/O operations with an extremely easy-to-use programming interface. An Interface Kit can be used to open and close switches, read digital inputs, and read the values of analog sensors, such as temperature or force sensors. For this project we will be focusing on the digital output portion of the Interface Kit, which will allow us to open and close the switches of the remote control car's handheld unit, thus simulating the user manipulating the controls directly. Phidget Interface Kits are available in a variety of models, and this project will work with either the 0/16/16 or 0/0/4.

This project requires three things: an interface for the user (the Wiimote), an interface to the car (the car's original handset control unit), and a bridge between the two (the Phidget Interface Kit). The software built in this chapter will read input via the Wiimote, determine which way it is tilted, and then toggle an output on the Phidget Interface Kit either on or off. The Interface Kit will be wired directly to the car's original handheld control unit, so toggling that output on or off will be identical to a person holding the handheld control unit and moving the joysticks (see Figure 8-2).

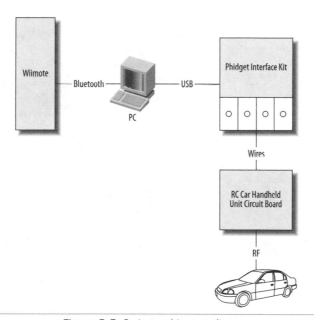

Figure 8-2. *Project architecture diagram*

Building the Hardware

The first step in this project is to get the remote-control car connected to the computer in some manner. The easiest way to do this is to directly wire the handheld control unit to the Phidget Interface Kit, which plugs into the computer's USB port. The key to this step is finding a remote-controlled car that has a "digital" controller. That is, the joysticks, when moved, simply close a switch. A remote-controlled car with "analog" inputs will allow the user to vary the speed and turn the wheels, which certainly adds increased control, but also adds a fair amount of complexity to the project as well as expense for hardware to properly control it. In my experience, the cheaper the car, the more likely it is to have digital inputs. Additionally, cars with remote controllers that contain buttons instead of joysticks are almost always digital input devices.

The car used in this chapter is from the Dub City collection by Jada Toys, and costs about $20 (see Figure 8-3). If that particular car is not available to you, be sure to check out the book's website at *http://www.c4fbook.com/* to see what other models people have successfully used with this project.

If you plan on using more than one remote-controlled car at a time for racing, ensure that you purchase cars that run on different radio frequencies. The box will usually be marked with either the frequency or a letter denoting a frequency, such as A/B/C. If you buy multiple cars with different frequencies (or letters), you should be fine.

Figure 8-3. *Remote-controlled car and handheld control unit*

Start by unscrewing all of the screws on the back of the handheld unit and removing the back cover. Inside you should find a circuit board. If this is screwed into the unit, remove the screws from this as well so it can be removed and flipped over. On the front side of the circuit board, where the joysticks make contact with the board, you should find some simple switches that open and close when the joysticks are moved (see Figure 8-4).

Figure 8-4. *Disassembled handheld unit*

A wire will need to be soldered to each contact of each switch. To do this, cut eight lengths of wire, each about 6 inches long. Almost any wire will do. If you have some spare phone or network cable lying around, feel free to use that. Strip off a bit of insulation from each end. Next, solder one end of each wire to each contact on the circuit board. Each direction will be comprised of two contact points. When those points are closed via the joystick, the circuit is closed, the command is sent to the remote-controlled car, and the car will move (see Figure 8-5).

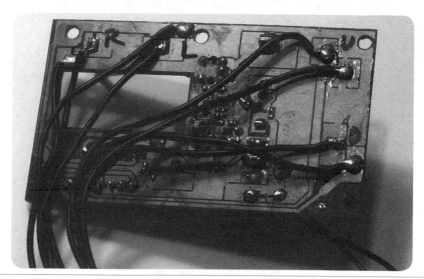

Figure 8-5. *Wired unit*

By soldering these wires onto the contact points, we can toggle that switch open and closed electronically, thereby simulating the joystick doing the work.

Phidgets

With all wires soldered to the board, the opposite ends need to be inserted into the screw terminals of the Phidget Interface Kit. This will be slightly different depending on the Interface Kit used.

For all kits, assume the mappings in Table 8-1 from output port to direction.

Table 8-1. *Output port mappings*

OUTPUT PORT	DIRECTION
0	Forward
1	Backward
2	Left
3	Right

Phidget 0/0/4 Interface Kit

This board contains four relays that can be opened and closed by software. In front of the relays is a strip of screw terminals that expose the relay contacts. Each set of terminals is labeled NO (Normally Open), NC (Normally Closed), and XC (Relay X Common), where *X* is a number from 0 to 3. "Normally Open" means that the switch will be open in its unpowered position, but will close when power is applied. "Normally Closed" is just the opposite; with no power applied, the switch will be closed and applying power will open it. The "Common" terminal can be considered the "ground" for each relay.

We want our circuits on the handheld unit to be open until we close them, so one wire from each contact pair will be connected to the NO terminal of each section, and the other will be connected to the Common terminal (see Figure 8-6).

Figure 8-6. *Phidget 0/0/4 Interface Kit with wires attached*

Phidget 0/16/16 Interface Kit

This board is divided into two sections, labeled Inputs and Outputs. The output section contains 16 digital outputs numbered 0 through 15. There are also eight common ground terminals labeled "G". Connect one wire from each contact pair of the handheld unit to a numbered output as described in Table 8-1, and the other to a common ground terminal (see Figure 8-7).

Figure 8-7. *Phidget 0/16/16 Interface Kit with wires attached*

If you are using a Phidget Interface Kit 0/16/16, there is one additional step that must be performed. Once the wires are connected to the handheld unit and Interface Kit, plug a battery into the handheld unit and turn it on. Next, put batteries in the car, flip it over so the wheels are off the ground, and turn it on as well. Because these boards share a common ground, you may notice that certain functions of the car will be stuck in the "on" position. That is, the car may drive forward, or the wheels may be stuck in one direction. If this occurs, simply swap the wires for that direction on the screw terminals of the Phidget Interface Kit and that direction should "unlock."

Building the Software

Writing the software for the base of this project is relatively easy due to the very simple APIs of both the Wiimote library and the Phidget library.

Software Requirements

Several libraries need to be downloaded and installed for use by this project. First, the Phidget API must be installed so the application can communicate with the attached Phidget Interface Kit. This library is updated frequently, and occasionally changes are made that break existing code. Therefore, the specific version used with this project can be found at the book's website: *http://www.c4fbook.com/WiimoteCar*.

Next, the Managed Wiimote library must be available to the application. This chapter was written using version 1.5.2 of the Wiimote library, which is available at the book's website or at *http://www.codeplex.com/WiimoteLib*.

Software Implementation

Start by creating a new Windows Application in your preferred language, either C# or Visual Basic. Once Visual Studio has set up the application, several references will need to be set. First, the application will be communicating with the Wiimote, so the managed Wiimote library, *WiimoteLib.dll*, needs to be referenced. Copy the *WiimoteLib.dll* file from the distribution to the local project directory so you can easily find it when adding the reference. The application will also use a Phidget Interface Kit, so a reference to the Phidget library, *Phidget21.NET.dll*, also needs to be set (see Figure 8-8).

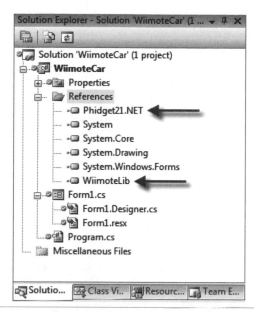

Figure 8-8. *Project references set*

> **NOTE** Note that if you are running a 64-bit version of Windows, the Phidget's assemblies may not show up in the global list of available references. If this is the case, browse to **C:\Program Files (x86)\Phidgets** and select the **Phidget21.NET.dll** assembly manually.

Next, open the design view of *Form1.cs*, and then double-click in any blank area to create the default Load event handler. Before filling in this event handler, the references need to be imported into the form, and member variables need to be created to maintain instances of the Phidget Interface Kit and the Wiimote. To import the appropriate libraries, add the code in Examples 8-1 or 8-2 to the existing import statements.

 Example 8-1. *C# code to import the appropriate libraries*

```
using Phidgets;
using WiimoteLib;
```

VB Example 8-2. *Visual Basic code to import the appropriate libraries*

```
Imports Phidgets
Imports WiimoteLib
```

Next, add one of the two snippets in Examples 8-3 and 8-4 (based on the programming language chosen) to define the required member variables. This code should be added at the form level.

Example 8-3. *C# code to define member variables*

```csharp
// instance of the connected Wiimote
private Wiimote _wiimote;

// instance of the connected Phidget Interface Kit
private InterfaceKit _interfaceKit;
```

Example 8-4. *Visual Basic code to define member variables*

```vb
' instance of the connected Wiimote
Private _wiimote As Wiimote

' instance of the connected Phidget Interface Kit
Private _interfaceKit As InterfaceKit
```

With the member variable definition in place, move back to the generated Load event handler and instantiate, open, and wait for the Phidget Interface Kit to be attached (see Examples 8-5 and 8-6).

Example 8-5. *C# code to instantiate and open the Phidget Interface Kit*

```csharp
// create the InterfaceKit object and open access to the board
_interfaceKit = new InterfaceKit();
_interfaceKit.open();
_interfaceKit.waitForAttachment(5000);
```

Example 8-6. *Visual Basic code to instantiate and open the Phidget Interface Kit*

```vb
' create the InterfaceKit object and open access to the board
_interfaceKit = New InterfaceKit()
_interfaceKit.open()
_interfaceKit.waitForAttachment(5000)
```

The final task to handle in the form load method is to instantiate and configure the Wiimote object. The Wiimote library provides a very simple event-based model to connect to the Wiimote controller. Simply instantiate a new Wiimote object, set up the event handler to receive data from the controller, and then connect to the controller. This process is shown in the next code sample, which should be added to the same Load method as the Phidget code in Examples 8-7 and 8-8.

```
// create the Wiimote object
_wiimote = new Wiimote();

// set up an event handler to be notified when the Wiimote sends a packet of data
_wiimote.WiimoteChanged += Wiimote_WiimoteChanged;

// connect the Wiimote
_wiimote.Connect();

// set the report type to Buttons and Accelerometer data only
_wiimote.SetReportType(InputReport.ButtonsAccel, true);
```

VB Example 8-8. *Visual Basic code to instantiate Wiimote object*

```
' create the Wiimote object
_wiimote = New Wiimote()

' set up an event handler to be notified when the Wiimote sends a packet of data
AddHandler _wiimote.WiimoteChanged, AddressOf Wiimote_WiimoteChanged

' connect the Wiimote
_wiimote.Connect()

' set the report type to Buttons and Accelerometer data only
_wiimote.SetReportType(InputReport.ButtonsAccel, True)
```

With that in place, all that's left is to create the event handler just listed, which will take data from the Wiimote and toggle the appropriate outputs on the Phidget Interface Kit to drive the car.

Create the event handler as shown in Examples 8-9 and 8-10.

C# Example 8-9. *C# code implementing the Wiimote_WiimoteChanged event handler*

```
void Wiimote_WiimoteChanged(object sender, WiimoteChangedEventArgs e)
{
    // get the current Wiimote state
    WiimoteState ws = e.WiimoteState;

    // if button 1 is pressed, toggle the Forward output
    _interfaceKit.outputs[0] = ws.ButtonState.One;

    // if button 2 is pressed, toggle the Backward output
    _interfaceKit.outputs[1] = ws.ButtonState.Two;

    // if the Wiimote is tilted far enough to the left, toggle the Left output
```

```
        _interfaceKit.outputs[2] = (ws.AccelState.Values.Y < -0.07f);

        // if the Wiimote is tilted far enough to the right, toggle the Reft output
        _interfaceKit.outputs[3] = (ws.AccelState.Values.Y >  0.07f);
    }
```

VB Example 8-10. *Visual Basic code implementing the Wiimote_WiimoteChanged event handler*

```
    Private Sub Wiimote_WiimoteChanged(ByVal sender As Object, ByVal e As Wii-
    moteChangedEventArgs)
        ' get the current Wiimote state
        Dim ws As WiimoteState = e.WiimoteState

        ' if button 1 is pressed, toggle the Forward output
        _interfaceKit.outputs(0) = ws.ButtonState.One

        ' if button 2 is pressed, toggle the Backward output
        _interfaceKit.outputs(1) = ws.ButtonState.Two

        ' if the Wiimote is tilted far enough to the left, toggle the Left output
        _interfaceKit.outputs(2) = (ws.AccelState.Values.Y < -0.07f)

        ' if the Wiimote is tilted far enough to the right, toggle the Reft output
        _interfaceKit.outputs(3) = (ws.AccelState.Values.Y > 0.07f)
    End Sub
```

The event handler simply uses the WiimoteState object, which is passed in as an argument to the event handler method to set up the Phidget Interface Kit outputs. If the 1 button is pressed, the output labeled 0 is set. If the 2 button is pressed, the first (1) output is set. If the Wiimote is tilted past the threshold defined to the left or right, the second or third output is set, respectively.

With the relay closed, the switch to the remote-control device is closed. With that switch closed, the signal is sent to the car and the car moves appropriately.

You may find that the threshold values in this example are too sensitive (or not sensitive enough). By changing the values compared against the AccelState.Values.Y property (in our example, 0.07f), you can raise or lower the threshold to something you find more comfortable.

Special steps for 64-bit Windows users

For those of you running a 64-bit version of Windows, there is one additional step that must be taken. The Phidget libraries are not totally compatible with 64-bit editions of Windows, but this can be worked around by creating an x86 (32-bit) target platform configuration, forcing the application to run as a 32-bit application.

To do this, select Build→Configuration Manager… (see Figure 8-9).

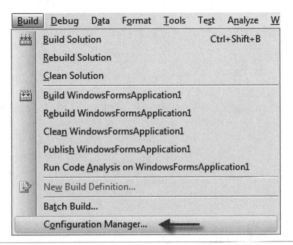

Figure 8-9. *Configuration Manager… menu entry*

From the Configuration Manager dialog box, select <New…> from the "Active solution platform" drop-down at the top-right corner (see Figure 8-10).

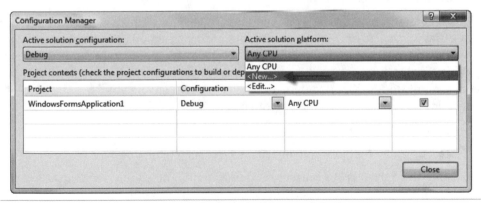

Figure 8-10. *Configuration Manager dialog box*

From the New Solution Platform dialog box, select x86 in the top drop-down box, and Any CPU in the bottom dialog box (see Figure 8-11).

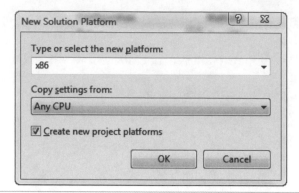

Figure 8-11. *New Solution Platform dialog box*

Close all of the windows and ensure that x86 is selected as the target platform on the standard toolbar (see Figure 8-12).

Figure 8-12. *x86 platform selected on the standard toolbar*

Using the Application

Now comes the fun part: driving the remote-controlled car with the Wiimote. Before this can happen, however, a few items need to be set up.

Pairing the Wiimote

Unfortunately, this step is largely dependent on the Bluetooth adapter and Bluetooth stack that is installed on your computer, so explicit instructions cannot be given. Also note that the Wiimote, although it is a Bluetooth device, is not a standard, 100% compatible Bluetooth device, so it is possible this will just not work using the Bluetooth adapter and stack on your computer. When in doubt, ensure you have the absolute latest drivers installed for your Bluetooth device.

To pair the Wiimote, perform the following steps:

1. Start up your Bluetooth software and have it search for a device.

2. Hold down the 1 and 2 buttons on the Wiimote. You should see the LEDs at the bottom start flashing. Do not let go of these buttons until this entire procedure is complete.

3. The device should show up in the list of devices found as Nintendo RVL-CNT-01. If it is not there, start over and try again.

4. Click Next to move your way through the wizard. If at any point you are asked to enter a security code or PIN, leave the number blank or click Skip. Do not enter a number.

5. You may be asked which service to use from the Wiimote. Select the keyboard/mouse/HID service if prompted (you should see only one service available).

6. Finish the wizard.

The LEDs at the bottom should continue to flash, and you should see the device name in your list of connected Bluetooth devices.

Installing the Phidget Interface Kit

Simply plug the Phidget Interface Kit into any USB port on your PC, and it should be recognized as a USB Human Interface Device (HID) device and not require any special drivers to work.

Driving the Car

Finally, ensure you have batteries in both the handheld controller and the car, and turn everything on. Run the application you just wrote, or run the executable directly if you downloaded the sample code package. The application will connect to the Wiimote and Phidget boards on startup. The window will be fairly boring since there isn't any output; however, the real action is the Wiimote and car, not the Windows form.

Hold the Wiimote with the buttons facing up and the back parallel to the ground, the D-pad to the left and the 1 and 2 buttons to the right, with the narrow sides in your left and right hands, as shown in Figure 8-13.

Figure 8-13. *Holding the Wiimote for driving*

To drive the car, simply press the 1 button to drive forward, or the 2 button to drive backward. To steer, tilt (don't twist!) the Wiimote left and right.

Final Thoughts

There we have it: a Wiimote-controlled car. With the use of a Wiimote, a remote-controlled car, a Phidget Interface Kit, and some soldering, we have a remote-controlled car that can be controlled by a Nintendo Wii Remote.

But don't stop here. With a little effort, there are countless ways to improve upon what is in this chapter and make the project even more interesting. For instance, you could change the control scheme to detect motion forward or backward instead of using the 1 or 2 buttons. You could also add a wireless webcam to create a stealthy spy car.

In the next chapter, we will use the Wiimote to create an entirely different kind of control scheme.

Wiimote Whiteboard

AUTHORS	Johnny Lee (*http://procrastineering.blogspot.com/*), Boon Jin Goh (*http://www.boonjin.com/*), Mike Korcynski, and Brian Peek
DIFFICULTY	Medium
TIME REQUIRED	3 hours
COST	$40 for Wii Remote (or free if you own a Nintendo Wii console), plus a couple of bucks for an IR LED, resistors, and white-erase marker
SOFTWARE	Visual C# 2008 Express, Visual Basic 2008 Express, or any full edition of Visual Studio 2008
HARDWARE	Nintendo Wii Remote, Infrared (IR) LED, normally open momentary switch button, 1.5V battery, white-erase marker, soldering iron, solder, wire
DOWNLOAD	*http://www.c4fbook.com/WiimoteWhiteboard*

Overview

As you saw in the previous chapter using the Wii remote, the controller is quite a versatile tool that contains a number of interesting sensing capabilities and is relatively easy to connect to a PC. This chapter describes how to create a multi-point interactive whiteboard surface using the camera built into the front of each controller.

This chapter will cover only the implementation details specific to creating an interactive whiteboard. It assumes that you have already successfully connected a Wii remote to a Bluetooth-compatible computer. If you are uncertain about how to do this, refer to Chapter 8 for instructions.

Defining an Interactive Whiteboard

When introduced to schools in 1801, the chalkboard was lauded as one of the most powerful and important educational tools ever created. It provides a lecturer with the ability to quickly and easily present visual material to a large audience simply by drawing it on an erasable, reusable wall. Two centuries later, the chalkboard is an icon representing teaching throughout the world. As technology and manufacturing capabilities improved, the chalkboard has evolved through various forms. However, the fundamental purpose remains the same. The modern whiteboard provides a hypo-allergenic, dust-free, clean-erasing, and high-clarity writing surface. Whiteboards are a staple of any modern office environment and many classrooms. However, like paper, the whiteboard is a passive surface. The written material is static. It cannot be easily moved, copied, saved, or recalled at a later date. Once drawn, the information stays on the surface. Once erased, everything is lost.

An interactive whiteboard, sometimes called a digital whiteboard, is an attempt to combine the benefits of digital information such as cut, copy, paste, save, open, and send with all of the physical affordances and benefits of a real whiteboard for presenting, sharing, and drawing visual information. Instead of using markers to leave ink on the surface, touch-sensing technology detects the location of the stylus and a computer displays virtual ink simulating the experience of drawing. Because the information is digital, it can be saved, printed, emailed, and erased at a push of a button. The stylus can draw any color, be any size, simulate a paintbrush, a pencil, or an air brush, and make selections and drag objects just like a mouse cursor. In many cases, commercial interactive whiteboard systems simulate the mouse cursor, allowing you to interact with any software application, such as paint programs, web browsers, simulations, or games.

This allows teachers to control the computer while standing in front of the class by touching the whiteboard surface; integrate materials such as pictures, diagrams, and video into their presentations; make on-screen notes and drawings using a stylus; digitally save classroom materials; or demonstrate interactive software. Businesses use interactive whiteboard systems as collaborative tools when members of a team are not co-located or to perform workflow documentation. The digital markings can be transmitted over the Internet, providing a shared experience for remote participants. Designers can bring up relevant digital materials, perform document manipulations, or create annotations that can be easily archived.

Unfortunately, interactive whiteboard systems can be very expensive, frequently costing several thousands of dollars, not including the projector or the computer. As a result, only institutions that have a very large equipment budget can afford such a luxury. Certainly, this places interactive whiteboard systems outside the realm of personal use for most individuals. Fortunately, in this chapter, you will learn how to create an effective interactive whiteboard system using the Nintendo Wii remote and about

$10 of electronics. This project also works with most computer and television displays, so a projector is optional.

Using the Wii Remote Infrared Camera

One of the ways we can track the location of a stylus to create an interactive display surface is to use a camera. A camera can see where the stylus is in an image, and we can extract those pixel coordinates to tell the computer where the cursor should be on the screen. Several interactive touch systems today use camera-based tracking for touch input, including the Microsoft Surface, the Perceptive Pixel display, and products from Smart Technologies. Often these systems use near infrared (IR) light illumination to highlight the location of touches. Near IR refers to wavelengths of light that are just outside the range of human visibility at the red end of the spectrum. IR light is commonly used in household remote controls to interact with televisions and stereos. Since this light is invisible to us, camera tracking systems can use specialized IR illumination to highlight the visibility of target objects.

Behind the black plastic in the tip of each Wii remote is an IR-sensitive camera. The camera provides pointing capability on the Wii game console by looking for the sensor bar placed near your television. The name "sensor bar" is actually a misnomer since it does not actually contain any sensors but rather two groups of IR emitters. The two groups of emitters appear as two bright dots in the camera image. Using the location of these two dots, the console can determine where you are pointing on the screen.

The camera chip is manufactured by a company named PixArt Imaging, Inc. The interesting feature of the camera is that it does not provide an image, but only the coordinate information of up to four bright dots. The chip has what PixArt calls an integrated "Multi-Object Tracking System (MOTS)." This is an integrated hardware computer vision processor that tracks the location of bright dots. If you were to write your own computer vision software for use with a regular webcam, you would simply step through the array of pixels of each image frame, tag those that were above a particular brightness value, group them into blobs, and then average their coordinates to find a center. This is called blob tracking. Fortunately, the camera chip does all this hard work for us. However, this also means that the raw camera image is not available to the host PC over Bluetooth.

The tracking data returned by the camera has a resolution of 1,024 horizontal pixels by 768 vertical pixels, with a refresh rate of 100 samples per second. The camera will track the locations of up to four IR dots simultaneously. If more than four points are visible, it takes the four brightest points. It could be used to track more than four dots if the lights twinkle or blink, but the software would have to be smarter to handle this.

Using IR Pens

Since the Wii remote camera is sensitive to sources of IR light, if we want to track the location of a stylus on a display, we need to create a stylus with a tip that emits IR light. To do this, we need a couple of components:

- An IR light emitting diode (LED)
- A normally open momentary switch button
- One AAA battery
- Some thin wire (26 AWG or higher)
- A casing to hold everything, such as a dry-erase marker

Building the pen for this project is as much an art as it is a science. If you think the whiteboard is something you'll want to come back to, enhance, and use repeatedly, by all means take the time to fit the assembled circuit in the casing of a whiteboard marker, as shown in Figure 9-1.

Figure 9-1. *Completed IR pen in dry-erase marker*

However, if you struggle with getting the circuit into the marker's cavity, look for alternative casings that may give a little more space to work with. For example, sometimes your circuit can be too bulky in your first attempt to fit in the tight space of a whiteboard marker. A slightly roomier option is to use a spare parts tube from a computer toolkit as the body, and insert a whiteboard marker tip in place of a cap to give it the feeling of a stylus, as seen in Figure 9-2.

Figure 9-2. *Completed IR pen in spare parts tube*

Spare parts tubes are available on Amazon and at other retailers. These tubes are often found in PC toolkits as well, so you may already have one available. Since seating the circuit in a spare parts tube is so easy, we will use that as a fallback and focus here on building the pen with the whiteboard marker.

Building the Circuit

The circuit itself is very simple to build. With a bit of soldering, you can get this together pretty quickly. If you've never soldered before, check the Web for some tutorials before you begin.

Take a second, and think about where you want your button to be in relation to the IR LED. Ideally, you'll want your button to be close to the tip of the pen as this will feel the most natural for a presenter. You also may want to consider leaving your wires long enough that you can set up your circuit in the pen casing before inserting the battery, because being able to see what you're doing is a lot easier than guessing.

Let's take a look at the parts that make up our circuit. LEDs are available in a wide range of colors and are commonly found in modern consumer electronics stores. There is a good chance you have a few LEDs near you right now. LEDs that emit IR light are fairly easy to obtain, either online or at a local store that sells electronics parts, such as RadioShack. You might also be able to salvage one from an old remote control. Though many LEDs will work, the recommended LED is a Vishay TSAL6400, which is a high-powered IR LED rated for a continuous operating current of 100mA. It is available from many online suppliers; one such location is Mouser Electronics (*http://www.mouser.com/*). Search for part number TSAL6400 on their site, and you'll see that the LED can be purchased for about 30 cents. Since you're using a 1.5V AAA battery, you will want to use an LED that has a forward voltage of about 1.7V Max. Doing this allows you to skip using a resistor, which is one less part to fit in the casing and one less part to solder. You'll also need a normally open momentary pushbutton switch. Keep in mind the size of your case when picking out a switch. You will want something similar to the Mountain Switch 10PA019, which can also be found on Mouser's website. Finally, you can simply tape your leads to your battery with some electrical tape, or you can opt for a battery holder. You can fit a AAA battery holder in the body of a whiteboard pen similar to Keystone Electronics 137, Mouser Part 534-137.

Now that we've examined the parts that make up our pen, we need to create a simple circuit that turns on the LED when we push the button. This will allow us to click and drag objects on the screen. A schematic of the circuit is shown in Figure 9-3.

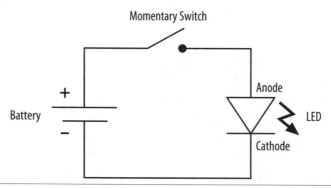

Figure 9-3. *Circuit diagram for the IR pen*

In this configuration, when the switch is closed, the circuit completes a loop, allowing electricity to flow and illuminating the LED. When the switch is released, the circuit loop is disconnected and the LED turns off. It is important to note that LEDs have a positive and a negative end and will work only if the wires are connected in the correct polarity. The anode must lead to the positive terminal of the battery and cathode must lead to the negative terminal of the battery. The documentation that came with your LED should indicate which end is the anode and which is the cathode; however, the longer lead wire on an LED, or the rounded side of the LED (not the flat), is almost always the anode. Test your circuit before putting it into the body of the pen to save time and sanity by making sure it works now.

NOTE For testing if your LED is wired correctly or if your pen is working, many camera phones are able to see IR light. Point your camera phone at the LED and press the marker button to activate it. If everything is working, it should glow in the preview image on your phone.

Preparing the Dry-Erase Marker

Before you begin the final assembly, let's prepare the dry-erase marker. If you haven't already, use a pair of needle nose pliers to remove the back cap from the marker and clean out the inside. Save the cap for later. By the time you're done, you should have an empty marker casing, dry and free of ink. Now drill or cut a hole in the side of the marker for your switch, making the hole just large enough that the switch won't pull through completely. You can use a Dremel for this step, but a regular drill or even an Xacto knife (be careful!) will work. While you are doing this, you could also thin out the walls of the pen tip by inserting the Dremel cutting tool down the pen's tip. Doing this makes getting the LED out through the tip much easier. Also, be sure to remove the washer and nut from the switch at this point.

You're now ready to begin putting together your IR pen. Doing this will most likely be a frustrating test of patience, and not all that different from a game of Operation. You'll want to bend your circuit into a sensible shape to push down the shaft of the pen. Push the circuit into the pen slowly, as it is very easy to accidentally break a lead off the switch or off the LED if you're not careful. It may take some trial and error and reworking the shape of your circuit so that the LED and the tip of the pen line up properly. Try not to force anything. As the LED begins to push through the narrow part of the shaft, start to work on pulling the pushbutton switch through the hole you made. You can do this by using a small loop of wrapping wire to hook the switch and fishing it through the hole. Tweezers and pliers can be too big. Once you have the switch well positioned, put the washer and nut on to hold it in place. Use the method described previously to test your circuit. It's easier to find out a soldered joint has broken now than after you've stuffed all the wires in the pen and put the cap back on. With your circuit properly functioning, get your remaining wires and battery (with or without holder) into the body of the pen.

Now that we have working IR pens, it is time to write the software that will control the mouse cursor.

Setting Up Your Project

Begin by creating a new Windows Application and name it "WiimoteWhiteboard". This will create a project with an empty *Form1.cs* or *Form1.vb* for you. Our program will have three components: a main form that display a graphical user interface and coordinates all the parts of the program, a form for doing touch calibration, and a class for doing some math. This chapter will begin by describing the two smaller components and then go into the form later. It is important to understand what the pieces are before putting it all together.

Warping the Camera Coordinates

From the previous chapter, you learned how to set up a demo program that reads the data from the Wii remote accelerometers. To get the coordinate values of the Wii remote's IR sensor, you can use the `WiimoteState.IRState.IRSensors` array inside of your `WiimoteChangedEventHandler`. You can read the coordinates of each visible dot, but this will only give you the location in the coordinate space of the camera. Unless we have the Wii remote positioned directly in front of our display such that every pixel is accurately aligned, we must transform the raw camera coordinates into sensible display coordinates. Or, more precisely, we must find the correspondence between the camera pixels and the display pixels. To do this, we can use something called a planar homography.

When you look at the world through the lens of a camera, the world is captured as a flat image and everything becomes distorted according to the rules of perspective geometry. Objects that are farther away look smaller and squares transform into trapezoids. When looking at a flat surface, this distortion can be encapsulated by a warping matrix called a planar homography. This is what we need to map our camera coordinates on the display.

Explaining exactly how or why this works is outside the scope of this chapter. It is all part of the magic of linear algebra. But for the sake of using the following code, all you need to know are eight numbers: the corners of a known rectangle on your display, or "destination quad", [(x1,y1), (x2,y2), (x3,y3), (x4,y4)]; and the location of those corners in the camera image, or "source quad", [(x1',y1'), (x2',y2'), (x3',y3'), (x4',y4')]. These eight numbers are sufficient to compute the homography matrix. So when we activate our pen, the camera sees where the dot is and can compute where that corresponds to on the display.

The following code is a fairly common implementation of computing a planar homography as a 4x4 matrix. A 3x3 matrix is sufficient for storing all the parameters of a planar homography, but the 4x4 matrix form can be readily used in 3D rendering pipelines, such as OpenGL and DirectX, for hardware acceleration of warping more complex content. This is not really necessary for this project, but it increases the utility of the code. For more details on the algorithmic underpinnings of homographies, refer to your favorite computer vision textbook.

To begin, create a class named `Warper` in the project. In this class, we set up variables for our source points, destination points, two working matrices, and then the solution warping matrix, as shown in Examples 9-1 and 9-2. A dirty flag helps signal that the data points have been changed and the matrices need to be recomputed.

```csharp
public class Warper
{
    private float[] _srcX = new float[4];
    private float[] _srcY = new float[4];
    private float[] _dstX = new float[4];
    private float[] _dstY = new float[4];
    private float[] _srcMat = new float[16];
    private float[] _dstMat = new float[16];
    private float[] _warpMat = new float[16];
    private bool _dirty;
}
```

VB | Example 9-2. *Visual Basic class-level member variables for the Warper class*

```vb
Public Class Warper
    Private _srcX(3) As Single
    Private _srcY(3) As Single
    Private _dstX(3) As Single
    Private _dstY(3) As Single
    Private _srcMat(15) As Single
    Private _dstMat(15) As Single
    Private _warpMat(15) As Single
    Private _dirty As Boolean
End Class
```

To initialize the Warper object with the identity matrix, a matrix where the values on the main diagonal (top-left to lower-right) are set to 1, we set the source points and destination points to be identical (the corners of a unit square) and run the calculation. The result sets the working matrices and solution matrix to the identity matrix (see Examples 9-3 and 9-4).

C# | Example 9-3. *C# code to initialize the Warper class*

```csharp
public Warper()
{
    SetIdentity();
}

public void SetIdentity()
{
    SetSource(0.0f, 0.0f,
              1.0f, 0.0f,
              1.0f, 1.0f,
              0.0f, 1.0f);

    SetDestination(0.0f, 0.0f,
```

```
                    1.0f, 0.0f,
                    1.0f, 1.0f,
                    0.0f, 1.0f);
    ComputeWarp();
}

public void SetSource(float x0, float y0, float x1, float y1, float x2, float y2,
                    float x3, float y3)
{
    _srcX[0] = x0;
    _srcY[0] = y0;
    _srcX[1] = x1;
    _srcY[1] = y1;
    _srcX[2] = x2;
    _srcY[2] = y2;
    _srcX[3] = x3;
    _srcY[3] = y3;
    _dirty = true;
}

public void SetDestination(float x0, float y0, float x1, float y1, float x2,
                    float y2, float x3, float y3)
{
    _dstX[0] = x0;
    _dstY[0] = y0;
    _dstX[1] = x1;
    _dstY[1] = y1;
    _dstX[2] = x2;
    _dstY[2] = y2;
    _dstX[3] = x3;
    _dstY[3] = y3;
    _dirty = true;
}
```

VB Example 9-4. *Visual Basic code to initialize the Warper class*

```
Public Sub New()
    SetIdentity()
End Sub

Public Sub SetIdentity()
    SetSource(0.0f, 0.0f, 1.0f, 0.0f, 1.0f, 1.0f, 0.0f, 1.0f)
    SetDestination(0.0f, 0.0f, 1.0f, 0.0f, 1.0f, 1.0f, 0.0f, 1.0f)
    ComputeWarp()
End Sub
```

```
Public Sub SetSource(ByVal x0 As Single, ByVal y0 As Single, _
                     ByVal x1 As Single, ByVal y1 As Single, _
                     ByVal x2 As Single, ByVal y2 As Single, _
                     ByVal x3 As Single, ByVal y3 As Single)
    _srcX(0) = x0
    _srcY(0) = y0
    _srcX(1) = x1
    _srcY(1) = y1
    _srcX(2) = x2
    _srcY(2) = y2
    _srcX(3) = x3
    _srcY(3) = y3
    _dirty = True
End Sub

Public Sub SetDestination(ByVal x0 As Single, ByVal y0 As Single, _
                          ByVal x1 As Single, ByVal y1 As Single, _
                          ByVal x2 As Single, ByVal y2 As Single, _
                          ByVal x3 As Single, ByVal y3 As Single)
    _dstX(0) = x0
    _dstY(0) = y0
    _dstX(1) = x1
    _dstY(1) = y1
    _dstX(2) = x2
    _dstY(2) = y2
    _dstX(3) = x3
    _dstY(3) = y3
    _dirty = True
End Sub
```

The workhorse of this class is the ComputeWarp method, which calculates the homography matrix given the source points and destination points. It first computes the matrix necessary to transform a unit square into the destination quadrilateral using ComputeSquareToQuad. This is merely a system of linear equations. It then calculates the matrix necessary to transform the source quadrilateral into a unit square using ComputeQuadToSquare, which is actually just the inverse of the solution to Compute SquareToQuad. Once these two working matrices have been calculated, they can be multiplied together to get the homography matrix that will directly warp the source points into the destination points (see Examples 9-5 and 9-6).

C# **Example 9-5.** *C# code for ComputeWarp and supporting methods*

```
public void ComputeWarp()
{
    ComputeSquareToQuad(_dstX[0], _dstY[0],
                        _dstX[1], _dstY[1],
                        _dstX[2], _dstY[2],
```

```
                          _dstX[3], _dstY[3],
                          _dstMat);
        ComputeQuadToSquare(_srcX[0], _srcY[0],
                            _srcX[1], _srcY[1],
                            _srcX[2], _srcY[2],
                            _srcX[3], _srcY[3],
                            _srcMat);
        MultiplyMatrices(_srcMat, _dstMat, _warpMat);
        _dirty = false;
    }

    public void MultiplyMatrices(float[] srcMat, float[] dstMat, float[] resMat)
    {
        // [ a b ] [w x] [(aw + by) (ax + bz)]
        // [ c d ] * [y z] = [(cw + dy) (cz + dz)]
        for (int row = 0; row < 4; row++)
        {
            int rowIndex = row * 4;
            for (int col = 0; col < 4; col++)
            {
                resMat[rowIndex + col] = (srcMat[rowIndex ] * dstMat[col ] +
                                          srcMat[rowIndex + 1] * dstMat[col + 4] +
                                          srcMat[rowIndex + 2] * dstMat[col + 8] +
                                          srcMat[rowIndex + 3] * dstMat[col + 12]);
            }
        }
    }

    public void ComputeSquareToQuad(float x0,
                                    float y0,
                                    float x1,
                                    float y1,
                                    float x2,
                                    float y2,
                                    float x3,
                                    float y3,
                                    float[] mat)
    {

        float dx1 = x1 - x2,        dy1 = y1 - y2;
        float dx2 = x3 - x2,        dy2 = y3 - y2;
        float sx = x0 - x1 + x2 - x3;
        float sy = y0 - y1 + y2 - y3;
        float g = (sx  * dy2 - dx2 * sy)  / (dx1 * dy2 - dx2 * dy1);
        float h = (dx1 * sy  - sx  * dy1) / (dx1 * dy2 - dx2 * dy1);
        float a = x1 - x0 + g * x1;
        float b = x3 - x0 + h * x3;
        float c = x0;
```

```
        float d = y1 - y0 + g * y1;
        float e = y3 - y0 + h * y3;
        float f = y0;

        mat[ 0] = a;      mat[ 1] = d;      mat[ 2] = 0;      mat[ 3] = g;
        mat[ 4] = b;      mat[ 5] = e;      mat[ 6] = 0;      mat[ 7] = h;
        mat[ 8] = 0;      mat[ 9] = 0;      mat[10] = 1;      mat[11] = 0;
        mat[12] = c;      mat[13] = f;      mat[14] = 0;      mat[15] = 1;
}


public void ComputeQuadToSquare(float x0,
                                float y0,
                                float x1,
                                float y1,
                                float x2,
                                float y2,
                                float x3,
                                float y3,
                                float[] mat)
{
    ComputeSquareToQuad(x0, y0, x1, y1, x2, y2, x3, y3, mat);

    // invert through adjoint
    float a = mat[ 0],  d = mat[ 1], /* ignore */ g = mat[ 3];
    float b = mat[ 4],  e = mat[ 5], /* 3rd col*/ h = mat[ 7];
    /* ignore 3rd row */
    float c = mat[12],  f = mat[13];

    float a1 =      e - f * h;
    float b1 = c * h - b;
    float c1 = b * f - c * e;
    float d1 = f * g - d;
    float e1 =      a - c * g;
    float f1 = c * d - a * f;
    float g1 = d * h - e * g;
    float h1 = b * g - a * h;
    float i1 = a * e - b * d;

    float idet = 1.0f / (a * a1          + b * d1           + c * g1);

    mat[ 0] = a1 * idet;  mat[ 1] = d1 * idet;  mat[ 2] = 0;  mat[ 3] = g1 * idet;
    mat[ 4] = b1 * idet;  mat[ 5] = e1 * idet;  mat[ 6] = 0;  mat[ 7] = h1 * idet;
    mat[ 8] = 0         ;  mat[ 9] = 0          ;  mat[10] = 1;  mat[11] = 0         ;
    mat[12] = c1 * idet;  mat[13] = f1 * idet;  mat[14] = 0;  mat[15] = i1 * idet;
}
```

```
    public float[] GetWarpMatrix()
    {
        return _warpMat;
    }
```

Example 9-6. *Visual Basic code for ComputeWarp and supporting methods*

```
    Public Sub ComputeWarp()
        ComputeSquareToQuad(dstX(0), _dstY(0), _dstX(1), _dstY(1), _dstX(2), _dstY(2), _
                            _dstX(3), _dstY(3), _dstMat)
        ComputeQuadToSquare(srcX(0), _srcY(0), _srcX(1), _srcY(1), _srcX(2), _srcY(2), _
                            _srcX(3), _srcY(3), _srcMat)
        MultiplyMatrices(_srcMat, _dstMat, _warpMat)
        _dirty = False
    End Sub


    Public Sub MultiplyMatrices(ByVal srcMat() As Single, ByVal dstMat() As Single, _
                            ByVal resMat() As Single)
        ' [ a b ]    [w x]   [(aw + by) (ax + bz)]
        ' [ c d ] * [y z] = [(cw + dy) (cz + dz)]
        For row As Integer = 0 To 3
            Dim rowIndex As Integer = row * 4
            For col As Integer = 0 To 3
                    resMat(rowIndex + col) = (srcMat(rowIndex) * dstMat(col) + _
                                             srcMat(rowIndex + 1) * dstMat(col + 4)+ _
                                             srcMat(rowIndex + 2) * dstMat(col + 8) + _
                                             srcMat(rowIndex + 3) * dstMat(col + 12))
             Next col
          Next row
    End Sub


    Public Sub ComputeSquareToQuad(ByVal x0 As Single, ByVal y0 As Single, _
                                   ByVal x1 As Single, ByVal y1 As Single, _
                                   ByVal x2 As Single, ByVal y2 As Single, _
                                   ByVal x3 As Single, ByVal y3 As Single, _
                                   ByVal mat() As Single)

            Dim dx1 As Single = x1 - x2, dy1 As Single = y1 - y2
            Dim dx2 As Single = x3 - x2, dy2 As Single = y3 - y2
            Dim sx As Single = x0 - x1 + x2 - x3
            Dim sy As Single = y0 - y1 + y2 - y3
            Dim g As Single = (sx * dy2 - dx2 * sy) / (dx1 * dy2 - dx2 * dy1)
            Dim h As Single = (dx1 * sy - sx * dy1) / (dx1 * dy2 - dx2 * dy1)
            Dim a As Single = x1 - x0 + g * x1
            Dim b As Single = x3 - x0 + h * x3
            Dim c As Single = x0
            Dim d As Single = y1 - y0 + g * y1
```

```vb
        Dim e As Single = y3 - y0 + h * y3
        Dim f As Single = y0

        mat(0) = a
        mat(1) = d
        mat(2) = 0
        mat(3) = g
        mat(4) = b
        mat(5) = e
        mat(6) = 0
        mat(7) = h
        mat(8) = 0
        mat(9) = 0
        mat(10) = 1
        mat(11) = 0
        mat(12) = c
        mat(13) = f
        mat(14) = 0
        mat(15) = 1
End Sub

Public Sub ComputeQuadToSquare(ByVal x0 As Single, ByVal y0 As Single, _
                        ByVal x1 As Single, ByVal y1 As Single, _
                        ByVal x2 As Single, ByVal y2 As Single, _
                        ByVal x3 As Single, ByVal y3 As Single, _
                        ByVal mat() As Single)
        ComputeSquareToQuad(x0, y0, x1, y1, x2, y2, x3, y3, mat)

        ' invert through adjoint
        ' ignore 3rd column
        Dim a As Single = mat(0), d As Single = mat(1), g As Single = mat(3)
        Dim b As Single = mat(4), e As Single = mat(5), h As Single = mat(7)
        ' ignore 3rd row
        Dim c As Single = mat(12), f As Single = mat(13)

        Dim a1 As Single = e - f * h
        Dim b1 As Single = c * h - b
        Dim c1 As Single = b * f - c * e
        Dim d1 As Single = f * g - d
        Dim e1 As Single = a - c * g
        Dim f1 As Single = c * d - a * f
        Dim g1 As Single = d * h - e * g
        Dim h1 As Single = b * g - a * h
        Dim i1 As Single = a * e - b * d
```

```
        Dim idet As Single = 1.0f / (a * a1 + b * d1 + c * g1)

        mat(0) = a1 * idet
        mat(1) = d1 * idet
        mat(2) = 0
        mat(3) = g1 * idet
        mat(4) = b1 * idet
        mat(5) = e1 * idet
        mat(6) = 0
        mat(7) = h1 * idet
        mat(8) = 0
        mat(9) = 0
        mat(10) = 1
        mat(11) = 0
        mat(12) = c1 * idet
        mat(13) = f1 * idet
        mat(14) = 0
        mat(15) = i1 * idet
    End Sub


    Public Function GetWarpMatrix() As Single()
            Return _warpMat
    End Function
```

Now that we have computed the homography matrix we can use it to warp new points that may be inside or outside the boundaries of the quadrilateral defined by the source points. To do this, we use the following Warp method, which will multiply a new source point (srcX, srcY) by the homography matrix, filling in the corresponding destination point (dstX, dstY) coordinates as shown in Examples 9-7 and 9-8. The static method simply allows the developer to use an alternative warping matrix if desired.

C# | Example 9-7. *C# code for Warp methods*
```csharp
public void Warp(float srcX, float srcY, ref float dstX, ref float dstY)
{
    if (_dirty)
        ComputeWarp();

    Warp(_warpMat, srcX, srcY, ref dstX, ref dstY);
}

public static void Warp(float[] mat, float srcX, float srcY, ref float dstX,
                        ref float dstY)
{
```

```
    float[] result = new float[4];
    float z = 0;
    result[0] = srcX * mat[0] + srcY*mat[4] + z*mat[ 8] + mat[12];
    result[1] = srcX * mat[1] + srcY*mat[5] + z*mat[ 9] + mat[13];
    result[2] = srcX * mat[2] + srcY*mat[6] + z*mat[10] + mat[14];
    result[3] = srcX * mat[3] + srcY*mat[7] + z*mat[11] + mat[15];
    dstX = result[0]/result[3];
    dstY = result[1]/result[3];
}
```

VB Example 9-8. *Visual Basic code for Warp methods*

```
Public Sub Warp(ByVal srcX As Single, ByVal srcY As Single, ByRef dstX As Single, _
            ByRef dstY As Single)
    If _dirty Then
        ComputeWarp()
    End If

    Warp(_warpMat, srcX, srcY, dstX, dstY)
End Sub

Public Shared Sub Warp(ByVal mat() As Single, ByVal srcX As Single, ByVal srcY As
Single, ByRef dstX As Single, ByRef dstY As Single)
    Dim result(3) As Single
    Dim z As Single = 0
    result(0) = srcX * mat(0) + srcY*mat(4) + z*mat(8) + mat(12)
    result(1) = srcX * mat(1) + srcY*mat(5) + z*mat(9) + mat(13)
    result(2) = srcX * mat(2) + srcY*mat(6) + z*mat(10) + mat(14)
    result(3) = srcX * mat(3) + srcY*mat(7) + z*mat(11) + mat(15)
    dstX = result(0)/result(3)
    dstY = result(1)/result(3)
End Sub
```

By entering these four pairs of source and destination points, the computer gains the ability to map each pixel in the camera image to pixels in a flat display. Now we have to create a calibration utility that allows us to quickly and easily enter these four pairs of points.

Touch Calibration

The WiimoteWhiteboard software has two graphical user interfaces: the main control panel and a four-point calibration form. The purpose of the calibration form is to obtain the four pairs of points needed to compute the homography matrix described earlier. It is a full-screen window that displays four crosshairs sequentially at known locations near each corner of the display. The user places the IR pen at each crosshair location, activates the LED, the camera sees the dot, the software pairs the dot location with the known display coordinates of the crosshair, and then proceeds to the next crosshair. Once all four points have been registered, we have enough information to compute the homography matrix and can begin simulating the mouse.

Let's begin by creating our *Calibration Form*. First we need add a new *Windows Form* to our project. In the Solution Explorer, right-click on your project name, which should bring up a menu. Navigate to Add→New Item, select *Windows Form* from the choice of templates, and name it *CalibrationForm.cs* or *CalibrationForm.vb*, depending on your language of choice.

We must set up the form's properties so it will show up as a full-screen window. To do this, set the FormBorderStyle property to None, and StartPosition to Manual. Later, in code, we will manually assign the window position and size to cover the screen.

We want to be able to draw into this form, and one way to do that is to draw into a PictureBox object. From the Toolbox panel, select the *PictureBox* item and draw a region in the form preview. Name this *PictureBox* "pbCalibrate". The size and location of the *PictureBox* is not important, as we will fit it into place programmatically later.

Now, set up an event handler for the KeyDown event on the form. To do this, click the lightning-bolt icon in the Properties window, and then double-click the KeyDown entry, as shown in Figure 9-4.

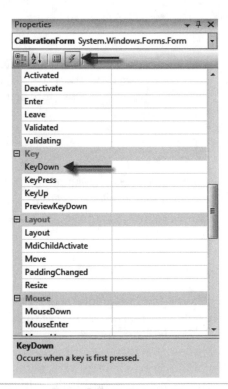

Figure 9-4. *KeyDown event*

This will create a stub method that can be filled in with our own code, as shown in Examples 9-9 and 9-10. The purpose of adding a key event handler is so that we can close the frame before the calibration is finished if the Escape key is pressed.

C# Example 9-9. *C# code for the KeyDown event*

```csharp
private void CalibrationForm_KeyDown(object sender, KeyEventArgs e)
{
    if (e.KeyCode == Keys.Escape)
        this.Close();
}
```

VB Example 9-10. *Visual Basic code for the KeyDown event*

```vb
Private Sub CalibrationForm_KeyDown(ByVal sender As Object, _
                                    ByVal e As KeyEventArgs) Handles MyBase.KeyDown
    If e.KeyCode = Keys.Escape Then
        Me.Close()
    End If
End Sub
```

Next, we add some member variables that provide a bitmap to draw onto and a graphics handle to perform the drawing. Then, we create the constructor for our form. This does several things. First, it grabs the screen size, and then it sets the form to full screen. Next, we initialize the bitmap to match the size of the screen, initialize the graphics handle, and set the picture box we created earlier to also be full screen. Finally, it clears the bitmap to white and invokes an update on the picture box, which will draw our bitmap on the screen (see Examples 9-11 and 9-12).

C# Example 9-11. *C# code for the CalibrationForm member variables and constructor*

```csharp
using System.Drawing;
using System.Drawing.Imaging;
using System.Windows.Forms;

public partial class CalibrationForm : Form
{
    private Bitmap _bmpCalibration;
    private Graphics _gfxCalibration;

    public CalibrationForm()
    {
        InitializeComponent();

        Rectangle rect = Screen.GetWorkingArea(this);

        this.Size = new Size(rect.Width, rect.Height);
```

```
        this.Text = "Calibration - Working area:" +
                    Screen.GetWorkingArea(this).ToString() + " || Real area: " +
                    Screen.GetBounds(this).ToString();

        _bmpCalibration = new Bitmap(rect.Width, rect.Height,
                                     PixelFormat.Format24bppRgb);
        _gfxCalibration = Graphics.FromImage(_bmpCalibration);
        pbCalibrate.Left = 0;
        pbCalibrate.Top = 0;
        pbCalibrate.Size = new Size(rect.Width, rect.Height);
        pbCalibrate.Image = _bmpCalibration;

        _gfxCalibration.Clear(Color.White);
    }
```

VB Example 9-12. *Visual Basic code for the CalibrationForm member variables and constructor*

```
Imports System.Drawing
Imports System.Drawing.Imaging
Imports System.Windows.Forms

Namespace WiimoteWhiteboard
    Partial Public Class CalibrationForm
        Inherits Form
        Private _bmpCalibration As Bitmap
        Private _gfxCalibration As Graphics

        Public Sub New()
            InitializeComponent()

            Dim rect As Rectangle = Screen.GetWorkingArea(Me)

            Me.Size = New Size(rect.Width, rect.Height)
            Me.Text = "Calibration - Working area:" & _
                    Screen.GetWorkingArea(Me).ToString() & _
                    " || Real area: " & Screen.GetBounds(Me).ToString()

            _bmpCalibration = New Bitmap(rect.Width, rect.Height, _
                                         PixelFormat.Format24bppRgb)
            _gfxCalibration = Graphics.FromImage(_bmpCalibration)
            pbCalibrate.Left = 0
            pbCalibrate.Top = 0
            pbCalibrate.Size = New Size(rect.Width, rect.Height)
            pbCalibrate.Image = _bmpCalibration

            _gfxCalibration.Clear(Color.White)
        End Sub
```

The CalibrationForm class, which consists of a routine that clears the screen, draws a single crosshair, and presents it to the screen, is shown in Examples 9-13 and 9-14. This is the method that will be used by our main program for stepping through the calibration process.

Example 9-13. *C# code for the remainder of the CalibrationForm class*

```csharp
public void ShowCalibration(int x, int y, int size, Pen p)
{
    _gfxCalibration.Clear(Color.White);

    // draw crosshair
    _gfxCalibration.DrawEllipse(p, x - size / 2, y - size / 2, size, size);
    _gfxCalibration.DrawLine(p, x-size, y, x+size, y);
    _gfxCalibration.DrawLine(p, x, y-size, x, y+size);

    BeginInvoke((MethodInvoker)delegate() { pbCalibrate.Image = _bmpCalibration; });
}
```

Example 9-14. *Visual Basic code for the remainder of the CalibrationForm class*

```vb
Public Sub ShowCalibration(ByVal x As Integer, ByVal y As Integer, ByVal size As _
                    Integer, ByVal p As Pen)
    _gfxCalibration.Clear(Color.White)

    ' draw crosshair
    _gfxCalibration.DrawEllipse(p, x - size \ 2, y - size \ 2, size, size)
    _gfxCalibration.DrawLine(p, x-size, y, x+size, y)
    _gfxCalibration.DrawLine(p, x, y-size, x, y+size)

    BeginInvoke(CType(AddressOf SetImage, MethodInvoker))
End Sub

Private Sub SetImage()
    pbCalibrate.Image = _bmpCalibration
End Sub
```

Putting It All Together

Now that we have our two small components, *Warper* and *Calibration Form*, we need to create our main form, which will manage these pieces, present a graphical control panel, step through the calibration process, initiate the warping calculation, and simulate the mouse. This may sound like a lot, but it is fairly straightforward administrative work.

To begin, we will add the visual components for the graphical user interface. Open up the form designer for *Form1.cs/vb* by double-clicking it in the Solution Explorer. For our battery monitor, we'll create a *GroupBox* with the label "Wiimote Battery". Inside of the *GroupBox*, add a *ProgressBar* named "pbBattery" and a *Label* named "lblBattery". These will provide a visual and textual representation of the battery level.

Below the *GroupBox*, add another *Label* named "lblIRVisible". This is a diagnostic tool to tell us whether the camera can see the IR pen, which will help us troubleshoot the visibility of the display.

Next, add another *Label* named "lblTrackingUtil". This is another diagnostic that provides feedback on the quality of the Wii remote placement. It calculates what percentage of the camera image is being utilized for tracking on the display, which roughly corresponds to the tracking quality.

Below this label, add a *CheckBox* to enable or disable control of the mouse cursor named "cbCursorControl". This helps prevent erratic cursor behavior when positioning the Wii remote and testing camera visibility.

Finally, add a big *Button* to initiate the calibration process named "btnCalibrate". When you are done, your interface should look something like Figure 9-5.

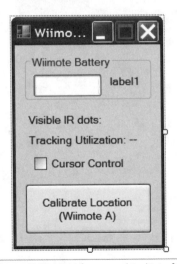

Figure 9-5. Main form graphical interface

Now let's add the code. Again, right-click on *Form1.cs/vb* and select View Code. First, we need a few member variables in our main form, as shown in Examples 9-15 and 9-16. We need a handle to our Wii remote, some helper variables, a handle to a calibration form, and then a *Warper* object.

First, set a reference to the *WiimoteLib* library. Copy the *WiimoteLib.dll* file from the distribution to the local project directory so you can easily find it when adding the reference, and then add a reference to it.

```csharp
using System;
using System.Drawing;
using System.Windows.Forms;
using System.Runtime.InteropServices;
using System.IO;
using WiimoteLib;

namespace WiimoteWhiteboard
{
    public partial class Form1 : Form
    {
        private const string CalibrationFilename = "calibration.dat";

        //instance of the wii remote
        private Wiimote _wm = new Wiimote();

        //helps with event firing
        private WiimoteState _lastWiiState = new WiimoteState();

        private bool _cursorControl;
        private Size _screenSize;

        private int _calibrationState;
        //specifies how far in to draw the crosshairs
        private float _calibrationMargin = .1f;

        //track the number of points stored
        int _smoothingCount = 0;

        //store the number of points to average out (1-10)
        int _smoothingPoints = 5;

        //store the past coordinates for smoothing
        float[] _smoothingX = new float[10];
        float[] _smoothingY = new float[10];

        private CalibrationForm cf;

        private Warper _warper = new Warper();
        private float[] _srcX = new float[4];
        private float[] _srcY = new float[4];
        private float[] _dstX = new float[4];
        private float[] _dstY = new float[4];
```

```
            public Form1()
            {
                InitializeComponent();
            }
        }
    }
```

Example 9-16. *Visual Basic code for member variables for the Form1 class*

```vb
Imports Microsoft.VisualBasic
Imports System
Imports System.Drawing
Imports System.Windows.Forms
Imports System.Runtime.InteropServices
Imports System.IO
Imports WiimoteLib

Namespace WiimoteWhiteboard
    Partial Public Class Form1
        Inherits Form
        Private Const CalibrationFilename As String = "calibration.dat"

        'instance of the wii remote
        Private _wm As New Wiimote()
        Private _lastWiiState As New WiimoteState() 'helps with event firing

        Private _cursorControl As Boolean
        Private _screenSize As Size

        Private _calibrationState As Integer
        'specifies how far in to draw the crosshairs
        Private _calibrationMargin As Single =.1f

        'track the number of points stored
        Private _smoothingCount As Integer = 0
        'store the number of points to average out (1-10)
        Private _smoothingPoints As Integer = 5
        Private _smoothingX(9) As Single 'store the past coordinates for smoothing
        Private _smoothingY(9) As Single

        Private cf As CalibrationForm

        Private _warper As New Warper()
        Private _srcX(3) As Single
```

```
            Private _srcY(3) As Single
            Private _dstX(3) As Single
            Private _dstY(3) As Single

            Public Sub New()
                InitializeComponent()
            End Sub
        End Class
    End Namespace
```

Since we want our software to mimic the behavior of the mouse and keyboard, the easiest way to do this is to programmatically simulate the input events that would normally occur if a user were moving the mouse or typing on the keyboard. To do this, we must artificially construct mouse and keyboard event data and then send it to the event processor of the operating system. Unfortunately, .NET does not fully support what is required, so we have to access the Win32 API with the help of runtime interop services and P/Invoke. So, at the top of our code, we must insert using System. Runtime.InteropServices, which will give us access to unmanaged Win32 libraries for simulating input events. The main routine of interest is the SendInput command, which will send the events to the operating system. But, to use this routine, we have to pass it correctly formatted INPUT data structures, which in turn are composed of MOUSEINPUT data structures. We also need to define a variety of constants that will be used to specify fields in the event information. We also import keybd_event, which is easy to use for generating keyboard events (see Examples 9-17 and 9-18).

C# | Example 9-17. *C# code for constants, structures, and Win32 API imports*

```
//declare consts for mouse messages
public const int INPUT_MOUSE             = 0;
public const int MOUSEEVENTF_MOVE        = 0x01;
public const int MOUSEEVENTF_LEFTDOWN    = 0x02;
public const int MOUSEEVENTF_LEFTUP      = 0x04;
public const int MOUSEEVENTF_RIGHTDOWN   = 0x08;
public const int MOUSEEVENTF_RIGHTUP     = 0x10;
public const int MOUSEEVENTF_ABSOLUTE    = 0x8000;

//declare consts for key scan codes
public const byte VK_LEFT   = 0x25;
public const byte VK_UP     = 0x26;
public const byte VK_RIGHT  = 0x27;
public const byte VK_DOWN   = 0x28;

public const int KEYEVENTF_KEYUP = 0x02;

public struct MOUSEINPUT     //24 bytes
{
```

```
    public int dx;          //4
    public int dy;          //4
    public uint mouseData;  //4
    public uint dwFlags;    //4
    public uint time;       //4
    public IntPtr dwExtraInfo;//4
}

public struct INPUT        //28 bytes
{
    public int type;       // 4 bytes
    public MOUSEINPUT mi;  //24 bytes
}

private const int INPUT_SIZE = 28;

private INPUT[] _buffer = new INPUT[2];

//for firing mouse events
[DllImport("user32.dll", SetLastError = true)]
static extern uint SendInput(uint nInputs, INPUT[] pInputs, int cbSize);

//imports keybd_event function from user32.dll
[DllImport("user32.dll", SetLastError = true)]
public static extern void keybd_event(byte bVk, byte bScan, long dwFlags,
                                  long dwExtraInfo);
```

VB　Example 9-18. *Visual Basic code for constants, structures, and Win32 API imports*

```
'declare consts for mouse messages
Public Const INPUT_MOUSE As Integer = 0
Public Const MOUSEEVENTF_MOVE As Integer = &H01
Public Const MOUSEEVENTF_LEFTDOWN As Integer = &H02
Public Const MOUSEEVENTF_LEFTUP As Integer = &H04
Public Const MOUSEEVENTF_RIGHTDOWN As Integer = &H08
Public Const MOUSEEVENTF_RIGHTUP As Integer = &H10
Public Const MOUSEEVENTF_ABSOLUTE As Integer = &H8000

'declare consts for key scan codes
Public Const VK_LEFT As Byte = &H25
Public Const VK_UP As Byte = &H26
Public Const VK_RIGHT As Byte = &H27
Public Const VK_DOWN As Byte = &H28

Public Const KEYEVENTF_KEYUP As Integer = &H02
```

```
Public Structure MOUSEINPUT '24 bytes
    Public dx As Integer '4
    Public dy As Integer '4
    Public mouseData As UInteger '4
    Public dwFlags As UInteger '4
    Public time As UInteger '4
    Public dwExtraInfo As IntPtr '4
End Structure

Public Structure INPUT '28 bytes
    Public type As Integer ' 4 bytes
    Public mi As MOUSEINPUT '24 bytes
End Structure

Private Const INPUT_SIZE As Integer = 28

'for firing mouse events
<DllImport("user32.dll", SetLastError := True)> _
Shared Function SendInput(ByVal nInputs As UInteger, ByVal pInputs() As INPUT, _
                    ByVal cbSize As Integer) As UInteger
End Function

'imports keybd_event function from user32.dll
<DllImport("user32.dll", SetLastError := True)> _
Public Shared Sub keybd_event(ByVal bVk As Byte, ByVal bScan As Byte,
                    ByVal dwFlags As Long, ByVal dwExtraInfo As Long)
End Sub

Private _buffer(1) As INPUT

' delegate for updating the UI on the original thread
Private Delegate Sub UpdateUIDelegate(ByVal args As WiimoteState)

' delegate for updating tracking info
Private Delegate Sub UpdateTrackingUtilizationDelegate(ByVal utilStatus As String)
```

Once we have our variables declared and have imported the routines we need, it is time to start building our main program. After our form has been loaded, we can initialize a few things, such as the screen size and connection to our Wii remote. If the connection fails, we display an alert and close the form. If the connection is successful, we add an event handler that will get called every time new data is available from the Wii remote, and then load the existing calibration file if there is one. It is good to keep in mind that updates from the Wii remote arrive approximately 100 times per second.

Next, we add functionality to the elements in the user interface. When we close the form, make sure to properly disconnect from the Wii remote. When the calibrate button is pressed, display the calibration form (if it is not already open) and initialize the calibration process. Finally, we bind our enable flag for mouse cursor control to the state of the checkbox.

To start, using the Event Properties window in Visual Studio, add default event handlers for the following controls and events:

- Form1_Load
- Form1_Closed
- btnCalibrate_Click
- cbCursorControl_CheckChanged

For each event, click the control in the designer, and then double-click the event entry in the table. A default, empty event handler will be created. The full implementation of these event handlers with the functionality described previously can be found in Examples 9-19 and 9-20.

C# Example 9-19. C# code for Form1 event handlers

```csharp
private void Form1_Load(object sender, EventArgs e)
{
    _screenSize.Width = Screen.GetBounds(this).Width;
    _screenSize.Height= Screen.GetBounds(this).Height;

    try
    {
        //connect to wii remote
        _wm.Connect();

        //set what features you want to enable for the remote, look at
        //Wiimote.InputReport for options
        _wm.SetReportType(InputReport.IRAccel, true);

        //set wiiremote LEDs with this enumerated ID
        _wm.SetLEDs(true, false, false, false);
    }
    catch (Exception x)
    {
        MessageBox.Show("Exception: " + x.Message);
        this.Close();
    }

    //add event listeners to changes in the wiiremote
    //fired for every input report - usually 100 times per second if accelerometer is
```

```
        //enabled
        _wm.WiimoteChanged += wm_WiimoteChanged;

        LoadCalibrationData();
    }

    private void Form1_FormClosed(object sender, FormClosedEventArgs e)
    {
        //disconnect the wiimote
        _wm.Disconnect();
    }

    private void btnCalibrate_Click(object sender, EventArgs e)
    {
        if(cf == null || cf.IsDisposed)
                cf = new CalibrationForm();

        cf.Show();
        _cursorControl = false;
        _calibrationState = 1;
        DoCalibration();
    }

    private void cbCursorControl_CheckedChanged(object sender, EventArgs e)
    {
        _cursorControl = cbCursorControl.Checked;
    }
```

VB Example 9-20. *Visual Basic code for Form1 event handlers*

```
    Private Sub Form1_Load(ByVal sender As Object, ByVal e As EventArgs) _
        Handles MyBase.Load
        _screenSize.Width = Screen.GetBounds(Me).Width
        _screenSize.Height= Screen.GetBounds(Me).Height

        Try
                'connect to wii remote
                _wm.Connect()

                'set what features you want to enable for the remote,
                ' look at Wiimote.InputReport for options
                _wm.SetReportType(InputReport.IRAccel, True)

                'set wiiremote LEDs with this enumerated ID
                _wm.SetLEDs(True, False, False, False)
        Catch x As Exception
```

```
                    MessageBox.Show("Exception: " & x.Message)
                    Me.Close()
            End Try


            'add event listeners to changes in the wiiremote
            'fired for every input report - usually 100 times per second
            ' if accelerometer is enabled
            AddHandler _wm.WiimoteChanged, AddressOf wm_WiimoteChanged


            LoadCalibrationData()
        End Sub


    Private Sub Form1_FormClosed(ByVal sender As Object, _
                                 ByVal e As FormClosedEventArgs) _
                                 Handles MyBase.FormClosed
            'disconnect the wiimote
            _wm.Disconnect()
        End Sub


    Private Sub btnCalibrate_Click(ByVal sender As Object, ByVal e As EventArgs) _
            Handles btnCalibrate.Click
            If cf Is Nothing OrElse cf.IsDisposed Then
                    cf = New CalibrationForm()
            End If


            cf.Show()
            _cursorControl = False
            _calibrationState = 1
            DoCalibration()
        End Sub


    Private Sub cbCursorControl_CheckedChanged(ByVal sender As Object, _
                                              ByVal e As EventArgs) _
                                                  Handles cbCursorControl.CheckedChanged
            _cursorControl = cbCursorControl.Checked
        End Sub
```

The calibration process is a simple state machine that steps through each of the four points we need and then finishes by computing the warp. Thus, inside of Do Calibration there is a switch statement with five cases. The first four cases specify where to draw the crosshairs on the calibration screen. The _calibrationMargin variable, defined earlier, determines how far from the edge of the screen they should be. The crosshair locations will be our destination points for the warper. The last state computes the warp, closes the calibration form, updates the user interface, and saves the calibration data to a file (see Examples 9-21and 9-22).

```csharp
public void DoCalibration()
{
    if (cf == null)
        return;

    int x;
    int y;
    int size = 25;
    Pen p = new Pen(Color.Red);

    switch (_calibrationState)
    {
        case 1:
            x = (int)(_screenSize.Width * _calibrationMargin);
            y = (int)(_screenSize.Height * _calibrationMargin);
            cf.ShowCalibration(x, y, size, p);
            _dstX[_calibrationState - 1] = x;
            _dstY[_calibrationState - 1] = y;
            break;
        case 2:
            x = _screenSize.Width - (int)(_screenSize.Width * _calibrationMargin);
            y = (int)(_screenSize.Height * _calibrationMargin);
            cf.ShowCalibration(x, y, size, p);
            _dstX[_calibrationState - 1] = x;
            _dstY[_calibrationState - 1] = y;
            break;
        case 3:
            x = (int)(_screenSize.Width * _calibrationMargin);
            y = _screenSize.Height -(int)(_screenSize.Height * _calibrationMargin);
            cf.ShowCalibration(x, y, size, p);
            _dstX[_calibrationState - 1] = x;
            _dstY[_calibrationState - 1] = y;
            break;
        case 4:
            x = _screenSize.Width - (int)(_screenSize.Width * _calibrationMargin);
            y = _screenSize.Height -(int)(_screenSize.Height * _calibrationMargin);
            cf.ShowCalibration(x, y, size, p);
            _dstX[_calibrationState - 1] = x;
            _dstY[_calibrationState - 1] = y;
            break;
        case 5:
            //compute warp
            _warper.SetDestination(_dstX[0], _dstY[0], _dstX[1], _dstY[1], _dstX[2],
                            _dstY[2], _dstX[3], _dstY[3]);
```

```
        _warper.SetSource(_srcX[0], _srcY[0], _srcX[1], _srcY[1], _srcX[2],
                          _srcY[2], _srcX[3], _srcY[3]);
        _warper.ComputeWarp();
        _calibrationState = 0;
        _cursorControl = true;
        BeginInvoke((MethodInvoker)delegate() {
                cf.Close();
                cbCursorControl.Checked = _cursorControl;
        });
        SaveCalibrationData();
        UpdateTrackingUtilization();
        break;
    default:
        break;
    }
}
```

VB Example 9-22. *Visual Basic code for the DoCalibration method*

```
Public Sub DoCalibration()
    If cf Is Nothing Then
        Return
    End If

    Dim x As Integer
    Dim y As Integer
    Dim size As Integer = 25
    Dim p As New Pen(Color.Red)

    Select Case _calibrationState
        Case 1
            x = CInt(Fix(_screenSize.Width * _calibrationMargin))
            y = CInt(Fix(_screenSize.Height * _calibrationMargin))
            cf.ShowCalibration(x, y, size, p)
            _dstX(_calibrationState - 1) = x
            _dstY(_calibrationState - 1) = y
        Case 2
            x = _screenSize.Width - CInt(Fix(_screenSize.Width * _calibrationMargin))
            y = CInt(Fix(_screenSize.Height * _calibrationMargin))
            cf.ShowCalibration(x, y, size, p)
            _dstX(_calibrationState - 1) = x
            _dstY(_calibrationState - 1) = y
        Case 3
            x = CInt(Fix(_screenSize.Width * _calibrationMargin))
            y = _screenSize.Height -CInt(Fix(_screenSize.Height * _
                                        _calibrationMargin))
```

```
                cf.ShowCalibration(x, y, size, p)
                _dstX(_calibrationState - 1) = x
                _dstY(_calibrationState - 1) = y
            Case 4
                x = _screenSize.Width - CInt(Fix(_screenSize.Width * _calibrationMargin))
                y = _screenSize.Height -CInt(Fix(_screenSize.Height * _
                                                _calibrationMargin))
                cf.ShowCalibration(x, y, size, p)
                _dstX(_calibrationState - 1) = x
                _dstY(_calibrationState - 1) = y
            Case 5
                'compute warp
                _warper.SetDestination(_dstX(0), _dstY(0), _dstX(1), _dstY(1), _
                                        _dstX(2), _dstY(2), _dstX(3), _dstY(3))
                _warper.SetSource(_srcX(0), _srcY(0), _srcX(1), _srcY(1), _srcX(2), _
                                    _srcY(2), _srcX(3), _srcY(3))
                _warper.ComputeWarp()
                _calibrationState = 0
                _cursorControl = True
                BeginInvoke(CType(AddressOf AnonymousMethod2, MethodInvoker))
                SaveCalibrationData()
                UpdateTrackingUtilization()
            Case Else
        End Select
    End Sub


    Private Sub CloseForm()
        cf.Close()
        cbCursorControl.Checked = _cursorControl
    End Sub
```

The primary workhorse of the program is the event handler for parsing data from the Wii remote. This gets executed 100 times per second as new data arrives from the remote. Depending on the current state of the software, the data will be handled differently and trigger different behaviors. To simulate the mouse, we have to create a mapping between the IR light behavior and mouse events. The simplest mapping is to treat the behavior of the button on the IR pen similar to the mouse button. When we press the pen button, the LED illuminates, the camera acquires a new dot, and we generate a mouse down event at the calibrated location. When we release the pen button, the dot disappears corresponding to a mouse up event. If the IR dot moves, the pen is being moved with the button held down, which maps to a mouse drag behavior.

Parsing Data from the IR Camera

The Wii remote automatically enumerates up to four visible dots in the order in which they appeared. This program assumes that the only visible IR dot will be our pen. As a result, we only look at the dot that is enumerated as number one. If this dot is visible, then either we have just received a new dot or we are seeing the updated position of an existing dot. In either case, the program begins by warping the location data according to the calibration.

To determine whether the dot is new, we need to compare it to the previous state of the Wii remote held in the _lastWiiState variable. If we did not see it before, that means the dot has just appeared. If cursor control is enabled, we simulate pressing the mouse down. This is actually comprised of two events. First, we need to tell the mouse cursor to move to where the pen is, and then fire a mouse down event. If we don't do this, it will be interpreted as a very fast drag operation from the previous cursor location to the new one. To create these two events, we use our _buffer, which is large enough to hold two INPUT structures. We specify both as mouse events. The first event moves the mouse cursor to the absolute location on the screen that corresponds to the warped marker location. Microsoft Windows expects mouse coordinates to be normalized to 0–65535. The second event presses the left mouse button down at the current cursor location 10 milliseconds later. Once we have formatted our two event structures, SendInput inserts them into the event-processing queue of the operating system so any program will interpret these as normal mouse events.

If the program is in the midst of calibrating, we store these IR dot coordinates in our source points array (the camera pixels that correspond to the crosshair locations on the display) and increment the calibration state. If the dot is not new, we create a mouse move event. If the dot is not currently visible but was visible last time, the dot disappears and we generate a mouse left button up event. Some programs, particularly those written for tablet pens, expect a mouse move event after receiving the mouse up event to trigger their interface correctly. To make these programs happy, we throw in a mouse move event of zero distance.

When dragging, we also smooth the data coming from the Wiimote. By tracking the last five points of data from the Wiimote and then averaging their locations, we can create a much smoother line for things like drawing. When the virtual mouse button is released, the tracked IR data is reset for the next time.

Finally, we update the dot visibility in our stored Wii remote state for comparison the next time that this routine is called (see Examples 9-23 and 9-24).

C# Example 9-23. C# code for first half of the WiimoteChanged event handler

```
void wm_WiimoteChanged(object sender, WiimoteChangedEventArgs e)
{
    //extract the wiimote state
    WiimoteState ws = e.WiimoteState;
```

```
if (ws.IRState.IRSensors[0].Found)
{
    int x = ws.IRState.IRSensors[0].RawPosition.X;
    int y = ws.IRState.IRSensors[0].RawPosition.Y;
    float warpedX = x;
    float warpedY = y;

    _warper.Warp(x, y, ref warpedX, ref warpedY);

    if (!_lastWiiState.IRState.IRSensors[0].Found)//mouse down
    {
        _lastWiiState.IRState.IRSensors[0].Found = ws.IRState.IRSensors[0].Found;

        if (_cursorControl)
        {
            _buffer[0].type = INPUT_MOUSE;
            _buffer[0].mi.dx = (int)(warpedX * 65535.0f / _screenSize.Width);
            _buffer[0].mi.dy = (int)(warpedY * 65535.0f / _screenSize.Height);
            _buffer[0].mi.mouseData = 0;
            _buffer[0].mi.dwFlags = MOUSEEVENTF_ABSOLUTE | MOUSEEVENTF_MOVE;
            _buffer[0].mi.time = 0;
            _buffer[0].mi.dwExtraInfo = (IntPtr)0;

            _buffer[1].type = INPUT_MOUSE;
            _buffer[1].mi.dx = 0;
            _buffer[1].mi.dy = 0;
            _buffer[1].mi.mouseData = 0;
            _buffer[1].mi.dwFlags = MOUSEEVENTF_LEFTDOWN;
            _buffer[1].mi.time = 10;
            _buffer[1].mi.dwExtraInfo = (IntPtr)0;

            SendInput(2, _buffer, INPUT_SIZE);

        }//cusor control

        switch (_calibrationState)
        {
            case 1:
                _srcX[_calibrationState - 1] = x;
                _srcY[_calibrationState - 1] = y;
                _calibrationState = 2;
                DoCalibration();
                break;
            case 2:
                _srcX[_calibrationState - 1] = x;
```

```
                _srcY[_calibrationState - 1] = y;
                _calibrationState = 3;
                DoCalibration();
                break;
            case 3:
                _srcX[_calibrationState - 1] = x;
                _srcY[_calibrationState - 1] = y;
                _calibrationState = 4;
                DoCalibration();
                break;
            case 4:
                _srcX[_calibrationState - 1] = x;
                _srcY[_calibrationState - 1] = y;
                _calibrationState = 5;
                DoCalibration();
                break;
            default:
                break;
        }//calibtation state
    }//mouse down
    else
    {
        if (_cursorControl)//dragging
        {
            float sumX = warpedX, sumY = warpedY; //initialize the sum
            _smoothingCount += 1; //track number of stored values

            if (_smoothingCount > _smoothingPoints)
                _smoothingCount = _smoothingPoints;

            for (int i = 0; i < _smoothingPoints - 1; i++)
            {
                //shift stored points
                _smoothingX[i] = _smoothingX[i + 1];
                _smoothingY[i] = _smoothingY[i + 1];

                sumX += _smoothingX[i]; //adding sum
                sumY += _smoothingY[i];
            }

            //add new points to the last position
            _smoothingX[_smoothingPoints - 1] = warpedX;
            _smoothingY[_smoothingPoints - 1] = warpedY;
```

```
                //calculate the averaged values
                float smoothWarpedX = sumX / (_smoothingCount);
                float smoothWarpedY = sumY / (_smoothingCount);

                //mouse drag with the averaged coordinate
                _buffer[0].type = INPUT_MOUSE;
                _buffer[0].mi.dx = (int)(smoothWarpedX * 65535.0f /
                                        _screenSize.Width);
                _buffer[0].mi.dy = (int)(smoothWarpedY * 65535.0f /
                                        _screenSize.Height);
                _buffer[0].mi.mouseData = 0;
                _buffer[0].mi.dwFlags = MOUSEEVENTF_ABSOLUTE | MOUSEEVENTF_MOVE;
                _buffer[0].mi.time = 0;
                _buffer[0].mi.dwExtraInfo = (IntPtr)0;
                SendInput(1, _buffer, INPUT_SIZE);
            }
        }
    }//ir visible
    else
    {
        if (_lastWiiState.IRState.IRSensors[0].Found)//mouse up
        {
            if (_cursorControl)
            {
                _buffer[0].type = INPUT_MOUSE;
                _buffer[0].mi.dx = 0;
                _buffer[0].mi.dy = 0;
                _buffer[0].mi.mouseData = 0;
                _buffer[0].mi.dwFlags = MOUSEEVENTF_LEFTUP;
                _buffer[0].mi.time = 0;
                _buffer[0].mi.dwExtraInfo = (IntPtr)0;

                _buffer[1].type = INPUT_MOUSE;
                _buffer[1].mi.dx = 0;
                _buffer[1].mi.dy = 0;
                _buffer[1].mi.mouseData = 0;
                _buffer[1].mi.dwFlags = MOUSEEVENTF_MOVE;
                _buffer[1].mi.time = 0;
                _buffer[1].mi.dwExtraInfo = (IntPtr)0;
                SendInput(2, _buffer, INPUT_SIZE);

                //clear smoothing data when mouse up
                ResetCursorSmoothing();
            }
```

```
            }//ir lost
        }


        _lastWiiState.IRState.IRSensors[0].Found = ws.IRState.IRSensors[0].Found;
```

VB Example 9-24. *Visual Basic code for first half of the WiimoteChanged event handler*

```
    Private Sub wm_WiimoteChanged(ByVal sender As Object, _
                                  ByVal e As WiimoteChangedEventArgs)
        'extract the wiimote state
        Dim ws As WiimoteState = e.WiimoteState


        If ws.IRState.IRSensors(0).Found Then
            Dim x As Integer = ws.IRState.IRSensors(0).RawPosition.X
            Dim y As Integer = ws.IRState.IRSensors(0).RawPosition.Y
            Dim warpedX As Single = x
            Dim warpedY As Single = y


            _warper.Warp(x, y, warpedX, warpedY)


            If (Not _lastWiiState.IRState.IRSensors(0).Found) Then 'mouse down
                _lastWiiState.IRState.IRSensors(0).Found = ws.IRState.IRSensors(0).Found


                If _cursorControl Then
                    _buffer(0).type = INPUT_MOUSE
                    _buffer(0).mi.dx = CInt(Fix(warpedX * 65535.0f / _screenSize.Width))
                    _buffer(0).mi.dy = CInt(Fix(warpedY * 65535.0f / _screenSize.Height))
                    _buffer(0).mi.mouseData = 0
                    _buffer(0).mi.dwFlags = MOUSEEVENTF_ABSOLUTE Or MOUSEEVENTF_MOVE
                    _buffer(0).mi.time = 0
                    _buffer(0).mi.dwExtraInfo = CType(0, IntPtr)


                    _buffer(1).type = INPUT_MOUSE
                    _buffer(1).mi.dx = 0
                    _buffer(1).mi.dy = 0
                    _buffer(1).mi.mouseData = 0
                    _buffer(1).mi.dwFlags = MOUSEEVENTF_LEFTDOWN
                    _buffer(1).mi.time = 10
                    _buffer(1).mi.dwExtraInfo = CType(0, IntPtr)


                    SendInput(2, _buffer, INPUT_SIZE)


                End If 'cusor control
```

```vbnet
        Select Case _calibrationState
            Case 1
                _srcX(_calibrationState - 1) = x
                _srcY(_calibrationState - 1) = y
                _calibrationState = 2
                DoCalibration()
            Case 2
                _srcX(_calibrationState - 1) = x
                _srcY(_calibrationState - 1) = y
                _calibrationState = 3
                DoCalibration()
            Case 3
                _srcX(_calibrationState - 1) = x
                _srcY(_calibrationState - 1) = y
                _calibrationState = 4
                DoCalibration()
            Case 4
                _srcX(_calibrationState - 1) = x
                _srcY(_calibrationState - 1) = y
                _calibrationState = 5
                DoCalibration()
            Case Else
                Exit Select
        End Select 'calibtation state 'mouse down
    Else
        If _cursorControl Then 'dragging
            'initialize the sum
            Dim sumX As Single = warpedX, sumY As Single = warpedY
            _smoothingCount += 1 'track number of stored values

            If _smoothingCount > _smoothingPoints Then
                _smoothingCount = _smoothingPoints
            End If

            For i As Integer = 0 To _smoothingPoints - 2
                'shift stored points
                _smoothingX(i) = _smoothingX(i + 1)
                _smoothingY(i) = _smoothingY(i + 1)

                sumX += _smoothingX(i) 'adding sum
                sumY += _smoothingY(i)
            Next i

            'add new points to the last position
            _smoothingX(_smoothingPoints - 1) = warpedX
```

```
                    _smoothingY(_smoothingPoints - 1) = warpedY

                    'calculate the averaged values
                    Dim smoothWarpedX As Single = sumX / (_smoothingCount)
                    Dim smoothWarpedY As Single = sumY / (_smoothingCount)

                    'mouse drag with the averaged coordinate
                    _buffer(0).type = INPUT_MOUSE
                    _buffer(0).mi.dx = CInt(Fix(smoothWarpedX * 65535.0f / _
                                            _screenSize.Width))
                    _buffer(0).mi.dy = CInt(Fix(smoothWarpedY * 65535.0f / _
                                            _screenSize.Height))
                    _buffer(0).mi.mouseData = 0
                    _buffer(0).mi.dwFlags = MOUSEEVENTF_ABSOLUTE Or MOUSEEVENTF_MOVE
                    _buffer(0).mi.time = 0
                    _buffer(0).mi.dwExtraInfo = CType(0, IntPtr)
                    SendInput(1, _buffer, INPUT_SIZE)
                End If
            End If 'ir visible
        Else
            If _lastWiiState.IRState.IRSensors(0).Found Then 'mouse up
                If _cursorControl Then
                    _buffer(0).type = INPUT_MOUSE
                    _buffer(0).mi.dx = 0
                    _buffer(0).mi.dy = 0
                    _buffer(0).mi.mouseData = 0
                    _buffer(0).mi.dwFlags = MOUSEEVENTF_LEFTUP
                    _buffer(0).mi.time = 0
                    _buffer(0).mi.dwExtraInfo = CType(0, IntPtr)

                    _buffer(1).type = INPUT_MOUSE
                    _buffer(1).mi.dx = 0
                    _buffer(1).mi.dy = 0
                    _buffer(1).mi.mouseData = 0
                    _buffer(1).mi.dwFlags = MOUSEEVENTF_MOVE
                    _buffer(1).mi.time = 0
                    _buffer(1).mi.dwExtraInfo = CType(0, IntPtr)
                    SendInput(2, _buffer, INPUT_SIZE)

                    'clear smoothing data when mouse up
                    ResetCursorSmoothing()
                End If
            End If 'ir lost
        End If

    _lastWiiState.IRState.IRSensors(0).Found = ws.IRState.IRSensors(0).Found
```

The second half of the event handler adds some convenience by responding to button presses on the Wii remote, and updates the user interface. The "A" button on the remote will trigger the calibration process, so the user does not need to return to the computer after positioning the remote. Again, to detect new button presses, we compare the current button state against the previous button state. The directional pad is mapped to the arrow keys on the keyboard. The battery level meter is updated, and then the IR dot visibility is updated on the user interface. This visibility feedback is helpful in determining adequate placement of the Wii remote and the presence of IR interference. The ResetCursorSmoothing method is also included, which is used in the event handler to reset the smoothing data on the mouse up command (see Examples 9-25 and 9-26).

C#   **Example 9-25.** *C# code for the second half of the WiimoteChanged event handler*

```csharp
if (!_lastWiiState.ButtonState.A && ws.ButtonState.A)
    BeginInvoke((MethodInvoker)delegate() { btnCalibrate.PerformClick(); });

_lastWiiState.ButtonState.A = ws.ButtonState.A;

if (!_lastWiiState.ButtonState.Up && ws.ButtonState.Up)
    keybd_event(VK_UP, 0x45, 0, 0);
if (_lastWiiState.ButtonState.Up && !ws.ButtonState.Up)
    keybd_event(VK_UP, 0x45, KEYEVENTF_KEYUP, 0);
_lastWiiState.ButtonState.Up = ws.ButtonState.Up;

if (!_lastWiiState.ButtonState.Down && ws.ButtonState.Down)
    keybd_event(VK_DOWN, 0x45, 0, 0);
if (_lastWiiState.ButtonState.Down && !ws.ButtonState.Down)
    keybd_event(VK_DOWN, 0x45, KEYEVENTF_KEYUP, 0);
_lastWiiState.ButtonState.Down = ws.ButtonState.Down;

if (!_lastWiiState.ButtonState.Left && ws.ButtonState.Left)
    keybd_event(VK_LEFT, 0x45, 0, 0);
if (_lastWiiState.ButtonState.Left && !ws.ButtonState.Left)
    keybd_event(VK_LEFT, 0x45, KEYEVENTF_KEYUP, 0);
_lastWiiState.ButtonState.Left = ws.ButtonState.Left;

if (!_lastWiiState.ButtonState.Right && ws.ButtonState.Right)
    keybd_event(VK_RIGHT, 0x45, 0, 0);
if (_lastWiiState.ButtonState.Right && !ws.ButtonState.Right)
    keybd_event(VK_RIGHT, 0x45, KEYEVENTF_KEYUP, 0);
_lastWiiState.ButtonState.Right = ws.ButtonState.Right;
```

```
        BeginInvoke(new UpdateUIDelegate(UpdateUI), e.WiimoteState);
    }

    private void UpdateUI(WiimoteState ws)
    {
        //draw battery value on GUI
        pbBattery.Value = (ws.Battery > 0xc8 ? 0xc8 : (int)ws.Battery);
        float f = (((100.0f * 48.0f * (float)(ws.Battery / 48.0f))) / 192.0f);
        lblBattery.Text = f.ToString("F");

        //check the GUI check boxes if the IR dots are visible
        String irstatus = "Visible IR dots: ";
        if (ws.IRState.IRSensors[0].Found)
            irstatus += "1 ";
        if (ws.IRState.IRSensors[1].Found)
            irstatus += "2 ";
        if (ws.IRState.IRSensors[2].Found)
            irstatus += "3 ";
        if (ws.IRState.IRSensors[3].Found)
            irstatus += "4 ";

        lblIRVisible.Text = irstatus;
    }

    private void ResetCursorSmoothing() //reset smoothing data
    {
        _smoothingCount = 0;
        for (int i = 0; i < 10; i++)
        {
            _smoothingX[i] = 0;
            _smoothingY[i] = 0;
        }
    }
```

VB Example 9-26. *Visual Basic code for the second half of the WiimoteChanged event handler*

```
        If (Not _lastWiiState.ButtonState.A) AndAlso ws.ButtonState.A Then
            BeginInvoke(CType(AddressOf CalibrateClick, MethodInvoker))
        End If

        _lastWiiState.ButtonState.A = ws.ButtonState.A

        If (Not _lastWiiState.ButtonState.Up) AndAlso ws.ButtonState.Up Then
            keybd_event(VK_UP, &H45, 0, 0)
        End If
        If _lastWiiState.ButtonState.Up AndAlso (Not ws.ButtonState.Up) Then
```

```
            keybd_event(VK_UP, &H45, KEYEVENTF_KEYUP, 0)
        End If
        _lastWiiState.ButtonState.Up = ws.ButtonState.Up


        If (Not _lastWiiState.ButtonState.Down) AndAlso ws.ButtonState.Down Then
            keybd_event(VK_DOWN, &H45, 0, 0)
        End If
        If _lastWiiState.ButtonState.Down AndAlso (Not ws.ButtonState.Down) Then
            keybd_event(VK_DOWN, &H45, KEYEVENTF_KEYUP, 0)
        End If
        _lastWiiState.ButtonState.Down = ws.ButtonState.Down


        If (Not _lastWiiState.ButtonState.Left) AndAlso ws.ButtonState.Left Then
            keybd_event(VK_LEFT, &H45, 0, 0)
        End If
        If _lastWiiState.ButtonState.Left AndAlso (Not ws.ButtonState.Left) Then
            keybd_event(VK_LEFT, &H45, KEYEVENTF_KEYUP, 0)
        End If
        _lastWiiState.ButtonState.Left = ws.ButtonState.Left


        If (Not _lastWiiState.ButtonState.Right) AndAlso ws.ButtonState.Right Then
            keybd_event(VK_RIGHT, &H45, 0, 0)
        End If
        If _lastWiiState.ButtonState.Right AndAlso (Not ws.ButtonState.Right) Then
            keybd_event(VK_RIGHT, &H45, KEYEVENTF_KEYUP, 0)
        End If
        _lastWiiState.ButtonState.Right = ws.ButtonState.Right


        BeginInvoke(New UpdateUIDelegate(AddressOf UpdateUI), e.WiimoteState)
End Sub

Private Sub CalibrateClick()
    btnCalibrate.PerformClick()
End Sub

Private Sub UpdateUI(ByVal ws As WiimoteState)
    'draw battery value on GUI
    If ws.Battery > &Hc8 Then
        pbBattery.Value = (&Hc8)
    Else
        pbBattery.Value = (CInt(Fix(ws.Battery)))
    End If
    Dim f As Single = (((100.0f * 48.0f * CSng(ws.Battery / 48.0f))) / 192.0f)
    lblBattery.Text = f.ToString("F")
```

```
'check the GUI check boxes if the IR dots are visible
Dim irstatus As String = "Visible IR dots: "
If ws.IRState.IRSensors(0).Found Then
    irstatus &= "1 "
End If
If ws.IRState.IRSensors(1).Found Then
    irstatus &= "2 "
End If
If ws.IRState.IRSensors(2).Found Then
    irstatus &= "3 "
End If
If ws.IRState.IRSensors(3).Found Then
    irstatus &= "4 "
End If

    lblIRVisible.Text = irstatus
End Sub

Private Sub ResetCursorSmoothing() 'reset smoothing data
    _smoothingCount = 0
    For i As Integer = 0 To 9
        _smoothingX(i) = 0
        _smoothingY(i) = 0
    Next i
End Sub
```

We need a few utility methods for computing the tracking utilization and saving or loading the calibration data to and from a file. The tracking utilization computes the area of the quadrilateral defined by the source points divided by the ideal quadrilateral, which is the camera image size (1024x768) minus the specified margin on each side. This is the quadrilateral that would be defined if the Wii remote were placed directly in front of the display and aligned pixel to pixel.

The calibration file only holds the coordinates of the four source points obtained from the camera. This is because we already know the location of the destination points. They are the crosshair locations. When loading the file, we first check whether the file exists, and then compute the warp and enable cursor control (Examples 9-27 and 9-28).

C# | Example 9-27. *C# code for utility methods*

```
void UpdateTrackingUtilization()
{
    //area of ideal calibration coordinates (to match the screen)
    float idealArea = (1 - 2*_calibrationMargin) * 1024 *
                      (1 - 2*_calibrationMargin) * 768;
```

```
        //area of quadrliatera
        float actualArea = 0.5f * Math.Abs((_srcX[1] - _srcX[2]) *
                                            (_srcY[0] - _srcY[3]) -
                                            (_srcX[0] - _srcX[3]) *
                                            (_srcY[1] - _srcY[2]));

        float util = (actualArea / idealArea)*100;
        string utilstatus = "Tracking Utilization: " + util.ToString("f0")+"%";

        BeginInvoke(new UpdateTrackingUtilizationDelegate(UpdateTrackingUtilizationUI),
                                                          utilstatus);
    }

    private void UpdateTrackingUtilizationUI(string utilStatus)
    {
        lblTrackingUtil.Text = utilStatus;
    }

    public void LoadCalibrationData()
    {
        // create reader & open file
        try
        {
            TextReader tr = new StreamReader(CalibrationFilename);
            for (int i = 0; i < 4; i++)
            {
                _srcX[i] = float.Parse(tr.ReadLine());
                _srcY[i] = float.Parse(tr.ReadLine());
            }

            // close the stream
            tr.Close();
        }
        catch (FileNotFoundException)
        {
            //no preexisting calibration
            return;
        }

        _warper.SetDestination( _screenSize.Width  * _calibrationMargin,
                                _screenSize.Height * _calibrationMargin,
                                _screenSize.Width  * (1.0f-_calibrationMargin),
                                _screenSize.Height * _calibrationMargin,
                                _screenSize.Width  * _calibrationMargin,
                                _screenSize.Height * (1.0f - _calibrationMargin),
```

```
                    _screenSize.Width  * (1.0f - _calibrationMargin),
                    _screenSize.Height * (1.0f - _calibrationMargin));
    _warper.SetSource(_srcX[0], _srcY[0], _srcX[1], _srcY[1], _srcX[2], _srcY[2],
                    _srcX[3], _srcY[3]);

    _warper.ComputeWarp();
    _cursorControl = true;

    cbCursorControl.Checked = _cursorControl;

    UpdateTrackingUtilization();
}


public void SaveCalibrationData()
{
    TextWriter tw = new StreamWriter(CalibrationFilename);

    // write a line of text to the file
    for (int i = 0; i < 4; i++)
    {
        tw.WriteLine(_srcX[i]);
        tw.WriteLine(_srcY[i]);
    }

    // close the stream
    tw.Close();
}
```

VB Example 9-28. *Visual Basic code for utility methods*

```
Private Sub UpdateTrackingUtilization()
    'area of ideal calibration coordinates (to match the screen)
    Dim idealArea As Single = (1 - 2*_calibrationMargin) * 1024 * _
                            (1 - 2*_calibrationMargin) * 768

    'area of quadrliatera
    Dim actualArea As Single = 0.5f * Math.Abs((_srcX(1) - _srcX(2)) * _
                                            (_srcY(0) - _srcY(3)) - _
                                            (_srcX(0) - _srcX(3)) * _
                                            (_srcY(1) - _srcY(2)))

    Dim util As Single = (actualArea / idealArea)*100
    Dim utilstatus As String = "Tracking Utilization: " & util.ToString("f0") & "%"

    BeginInvoke(New UpdateTrackingUtilizationDelegate(AddressOf _
                                    UpdateTrackingUtilizationUI), utilstatus)
```

```vb
    End Sub

    Private Sub UpdateTrackingUtilizationUI(ByVal utilStatus As String)
        lblTrackingUtil.Text = utilStatus
    End Sub

    Public Sub LoadCalibrationData()
        ' create reader & open file
        Try
            Dim tr As TextReader = New StreamReader(CalibrationFilename)
            For i As Integer = 0 To 3
                _srcX(i) = Single.Parse(tr.ReadLine())
                _srcY(i) = Single.Parse(tr.ReadLine())
            Next i

            ' close the stream
            tr.Close()
        Catch e1 As FileNotFoundException
            'no prexsting calibration
            Return
        End Try

        _warper.SetDestination(_screenSize.Width * _calibrationMargin, _
                               _screenSize.Height * _calibrationMargin, _
                               _screenSize.Width * (1.0f-_calibrationMargin), _
                               _screenSize.Height * _calibrationMargin, _
                               _screenSize.Width * _calibrationMargin, _
                               _screenSize.Height * (1.0f - _calibrationMargin), _
                               _screenSize.Width * (1.0f - _calibrationMargin), _
                               _screenSize.Height * (1.0f - _calibrationMargin))
        _warper.SetSource(_srcX(0), _srcY(0), _srcX(1), _srcY(1), _srcX(2), _srcY(2), _
                          _srcX(3), _srcY(3))

        _warper.ComputeWarp()
        _cursorControl = True

        cbCursorControl.Checked = _cursorControl

        UpdateTrackingUtilization()
    End Sub

    Public Sub SaveCalibrationData()
        Dim tw As TextWriter = New StreamWriter(CalibrationFilename)

        ' write a line of text to the file
```

```
For i As Integer = 0 To 3
    tw.WriteLine(_srcX(i))
    tw.WriteLine(_srcY(i))
Next i

' close the stream
tw.Close()
End Sub
```

You're done! The program will connect to a Wii remote, present a calibration screen, acquire the calibration data, compute the warping homography to map the camera pixels to the display pixels, store the calibration data to a file, and simulate the mouse. Now you have your very own, reasonably effective, inexpensive interactive whiteboard system.

Using the Software

To use the software, find a place to mount your Wii remote so that the camera can see your display. The camera has a field of view of 45 degrees. Keep this mind and try to position the Wii remote as close as possible while keeping your entire screen in view of the camera. You can use the "Visible IR dots" feedback to test whether the Wiimote can see the whole display. Activate the marker around each corner of the display to check visibility. If it can see the dots, the diagnostic should respond. Start the calibration, and activate the LED at each crosshair location. It should automatically move to the next crosshair. Once you have done all four, the calibration screen should disappear, the IR pen should now control the mouse cursor, and you can start using your interactive whiteboard display.

The tracking quality is highly dependent on the placement of your Wii remote. If it is too far away from the screen or at too much of an angle, the camera does not have a good view and the tracking will be poor. You can use the Tracking Utilization diagnostic after each calibration to evaluate whether your Wii remote placement is good. The higher this number is, the better the tracking will be. Getting this value to be 100% is extremely difficult in any useful configuration since this would require that the Wii remote be directly in front of the screen. However, if utilization is below 50%, you should consider repositioning the remote. You will also need to be careful not to block the Wii remote's view of the IR tip. If you place your hand, arm, or body in front of the camera, it won't be able to see the dot and cannot track its movement. If you use the setup illustrated in Figure 9-6, you will achieve good tracking and will be less likely to block the camera. Holding the pen such that the tip is pointed out and away from you will also reduce accidental blocking.

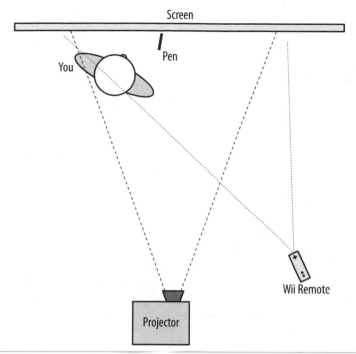

Figure 9-6. *A typical front-projected WiimoteWhiteboard setup*

If you are industrious enough to build a rear-projected screen, you can place the Wii remote behind the screen near the projector, obtaining very high-quality tracking without having to worry about blocking the camera. As mentioned before, if you do not have a projector, you can point the Wii remote at most flat displays and the tracking should still work, creating a tablet-PC-like display.

NOTE If you are using this with a projector, this combination will actually allow you to transform most flat surfaces into an interactive whiteboard. This could be your wall, your table, your floor, your ceiling, or even your shirt (so long as you don't move around too much). It's a fun and versatile little application.

Final Thoughts

Though multi-touch systems have existed since the 1970s in experimental form, they have only recently made their commercial debut. Multi-touch refers to interactive systems that are capable of detecting the location of more than one touch simultaneously. Since we have two hands and 10 fingers, and sometimes work simultaneously with other people, multi-touch systems provide a natural way of interacting with digital material that more closely resembles the way we interact with objects in the real world. Since the Wiimote Whiteboard application uses the Wii remote camera for tracking, it can see up to four dots simultaneously. This means you could potentially use four IR markers simultaneously. The data for those additional dots are readily accessible in the program you have already written. You simply read the other coordinate values from the WiimoteState variable in the WiimoteChanged event handler. However, what you do with those additional points is up to you. Since current versions of Microsoft Windows support only one mouse, there is no straightforward mapping between multiple markers and a single cursor. Multi-touch or multi-cursor applications have to be built from the ground up to support multiple simultaneous inputs and are currently rather rare. Of course, you could always start building your own multi-touch applications, building on what you have learned in this project. Enjoy!

Animated Musical Holiday Lights

AUTHOR	Brian Peek
DIFFICULTY	Medium
TIME REQUIRED	5 hours
COST	$80 per Phidget Interface Kit 0/0/4, plus the cost of extension cords, wire, and Christmas lights
SOFTWARE	Visual C# 2008 Express, Visual Basic 2008 Express, or any full edition of Visual Studio 2008
HARDWARE	Phidget Interface Kit 0/0/4 (one kit can control four separate strings of lights); five two-prong, outdoor use extension cords; 14–16 gauge wire; two wire nuts that can handle 14–16 gauge wire; a project box large enough to hold one or many Interface Kits (available at your local Radio Shack); holiday lights; and external speakers or FM transmitter so the music can be heard
DOWNLOAD	*http://www.c4fbook.com/HolidayLights*

At this point, practically everyone has seen a video of someone's house decked out in Christmas lights, all of which dance in synchronization to a musical score. In fact, Miller Brewing Company even had a television commercial showcasing a light show during the 2006 and 2007 holiday seasons.

Although these light shows may seem complex and appear to require a lot of knowledge to create, they can be built using nothing more than a Phidget Interface Kit, some extension cords, and a computer.

This project will show you how to use these items and some custom-built software to create your very own indoor or outdoor light show set to your favorite holiday music.

Overview

The overall architecture of this project is pretty simple. First, we will need to build some hardware to control switching the lights on and off. Then, we will write an application that will allow you to tap out the rhythm of the song being played to turn the different "channels" (i.e., strings of lights) on and off to design the show. Once the show is "recorded," the application will essentially play back the tapped-out rhythm at the same time periods that were synchronized to the songs. Additionally, we will add a MIDI library to the application, which will allow you to import a MIDI music file and use the data embedded in the file itself to drive the lights.

Building the Hardware

The hardware is based around the Phidget Interface Kit 0/0/4. This board contains four relay outputs that can switch (turn on or off at will) an AC or DC current. The instructions here will be for building a single unit light, which will drive four channels of lights, but you can build as many units as you'd like and use them all at once to create larger light shows.

Using the Interface Kit, we will build a device that can be plugged into a single AC outlet and will provide four output outlets that can be switched on and off by the Interface Kit's relays. With the light strings plugged into these four outlets, they can be turned on and off at will. The software that accompanies this chapter will allow you to build a "sequence" that will turn the lights on and off at specified times, usually in time to the music, creating an animated light show.

To start, we will prepare the extension cords. First, cut the female end (that's the one with the holes, not the plug) off of a single extension cord. Next, split the cord up the center about 2 inches. Strip a bit of insulation off of each wire to expose the ends, and then twist the ends with your fingers to create a neat, twisted wire, as shown in Figure 10-1. It is best to strip the wires using a pair of cutting pliers, which you can pick up at a local hardware store if you don't already have a set. Using a knife or scissors may work, but it will be a lot more difficult.

Figure 10-1. *Prepared female-ended extension cord*

Next, cut the male ends (the ends with the actual prongs on them) off the remaining four extension cords. As before, split the cord up the center a short distance, strip off the insulation from each wire, and twist the exposed ends to wind up with a cord like the one shown in Figure 10-2.

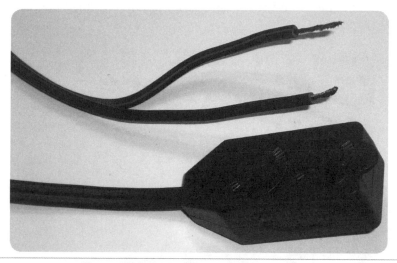

Figure 10-2. *Prepared male-ended extension cord*

Now, cut four equal lengths of the 14–16 gauge wire. These should be about two to four inches in length. Strip some insulation off of each end and twist up any loose wires as before.

This next step is critical. Each extension cord should have two different types of rubber insulation around the wires. One side should have a ribbed edge, and the other side should be smooth. The ribbed side, known as the neutral side, should be in line with the "fat" prong/receptacle; the smooth side, known as the active, or "hot," side, should be in line with the smaller prong/receptacle. The difference can be seen in Figure 10-3.

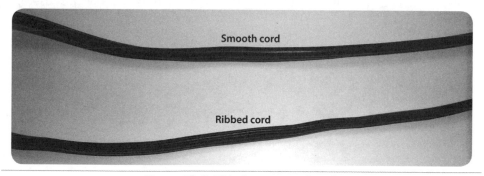

Figure 10-3. *Ribbed versus smooth cords*

You may wish to mark each wire with some masking tape and label them so you don't confuse them later on. It is important that the next steps be followed very carefully, using the exact wires that are referred to.

Take the four short wires cut earlier and twist one end from each all together along with the ribbed/neutral wire from the extension cord with the male end still attached, as shown in Figure 10-4.

Figure 10-4. *Four short wires and neutral wire twisted together*

Next, twist a wire nut over the exposed ends to keep them together and covered. Be sure you get all of the exposed wire under the cap so only the insulation is showing beneath the nut, as shown in Figure 10-5.

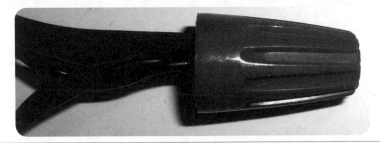

Figure 10-5. *Wires twisted together and secured with wire nut*

Next, twist the smooth/"hot" wires from the four extension cords with the female ends still attached together with the smooth/"hot" wire from the extension cord with the male end attached (that is, the other wire from the extension cord we just used), as shown in Figure 10-6.

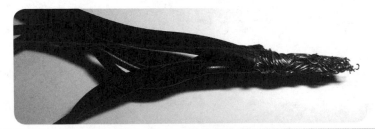

Figure 10-6. *Four "hot" wires twisted together with neutral wire*

Again, twist on a wire nut to keep things covered and safe, as shown in Figure 10-7.

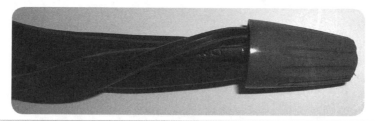

Figure 10-7. *Hot wires and neutral wire covered with wire nut*

After following all of these instructions, you should be left with the opposite ends of the four cut wires exposed, and the four ribbed/neutral wires of extension cord with the female end still attached. These will all be put into the screw terminals of the Phidget Interface Kit 0/0/4.

The Phidget Interface Kit 0/0/4 has four groups of screw terminals. Each terminal contains three connections: NO, NC, and XC, where *X* is the relay associated with the terminal. These stand for "Normally Open," "Normally Closed," and "Common," respectively. For this project, the lights should normally be off and switched on by our software, so the NO (Normally Open) and XC (Common) ports will be used.

Place one short wire and one extension cord wire from each exposed bundle into each NO and XC port on the Interface Kit. It doesn't matter which wire you plug into which terminal of each group, just that each group has only one short wire and one extension cord wire, as shown in Figure 10-8.

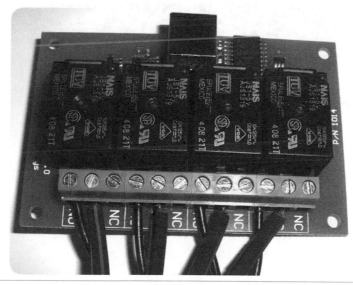

Figure 10-8. *Wires connected to the Phidget Interface Kit 0/0/4*

Figure 10-9 shows a very simple schematic of what was just wired.

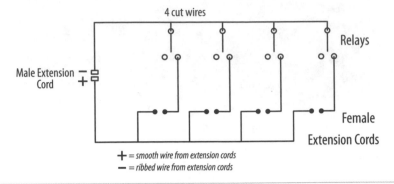

Figure 10-9. *Schematic of a single wired board*

To keep things neat and tidy, you should mount the Phidget Interface Kits into a project box of some sort. I created two boards for my project and placed them inside a single large project box. By drilling out holes in the short sides of the box, I could expose the USB jacks for each Interface Kit. I was also able to notch out the top edges of the longer sides so the extension cord bundles could pass through from each board. The boards were mounted inside the box with some carefully placed two-sided foam tape. Also note that if you plan on using these boxes outside for an outdoor show, be sure they are properly weatherproofed so the elements cannot get inside and damage the internals! The finished product can be seen in Figures 10-10 and 10-11.

Figure 10-10. *Inside the project box*

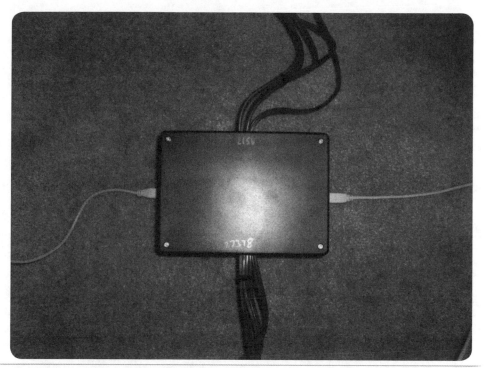

Figure 10-11. *The fully assembled project box containing two Interface Kits and exposing eight total channels*

Information on Amperages

Your individual strings of lights will be plugged into each extension cord outlet. An average strand of mini-lights draws about .3 amps. An average string of larger bulbs can draw as much as 1–2 amps. The relays on the Phidget board are rated at 10 amps for 250 volts of AC current, or approximately 20 amps for the standard 110-volt current found in your home.

That said, a standard house circuit will allow up to 15–20 amps before overloading. The circuit breaker in your own home should tell you what the allowed amperage is for the outlet you will be using. Keep in mind that any other devices that are plugged into that same circuit elsewhere will also be drawing power, which will count against that 15–20 amps.

So, in summary, be sure not to draw more than approximately 20 amps per channel on the Phidget Interface Kit, and no more than 15–20 amps in total per household circuit, including all additional devices plugged into that circuit.

Writing the Software

To drive the Interface Kits, we will build an application that will allow a user to record a sequence of key presses representing the timing of lights turning on and off, save that recording, and then play it back without user intervention.

Software Requirements

First, the Phidget API must be installed so the application can communicate with the attached Phidget Interface Kit. This library is updated frequently, and occasionally changes are made that break existing code. Therefore, the specific version used for this project, can be found at the book's website: *http://www.c4fbook.com/* or *http://www.oreilly.com/catalog/9780596520748*. If this isn't installed already, do this before continuing.

Software Implementation

As explained previously, the software that accompanies this project allows you to tap out a rhythm using the keyboard while the song is playing to turn individual strands of lights on and off to the music. To accomplish this, we need a way to record keystrokes and precise time intervals, a way to display that data, a way to save that data for later playback, and a way to play it back accurately so it matches the original timings. The next sections will talk about these important parts of the Light Sequencer application. The Light Sequencer software is far larger than what is contained in this chapter, but only the critical portions of the application will be discussed here. The full source code for the project can always be found on the book's website at *http://www.c4fbook.com/HolidayLights*.

Sequence

The main object used through the application is something we will call a Sequence. A sequence will contain a path to the music file we want to play (this application will support WAV, MP3, and MIDI files), some demographic information about the song (such as title and artist), the length of the song, the interval between ticks on the main grid (more on that soon), and a list of Channel objects. These channels represent a single output on a Phidget Interface Kit. The base object can be seen in Examples 10-1 and 10-2.

`C#` Example 10-1. *C# code for Sequence member variables and constructors*

```csharp
public enum MusicType
{
    Sample = 0,
    MIDI = 1
}
```

```csharp
public class Sequence
{
    private const string FILE_VERSION = "2";

    public string Title;
    public string Artist;
    public string MusicFile;
    public int MusicLength;
    public float Interval;      // in ms
    public int Version = int.Parse(FILE_VERSION);
    public List<Channel> Channels = new List<Channel>();
    public MusicType MusicType;

    public Sequence() : this(null)
    {
    }

    public Sequence(string filename)
    {
        if(!string.IsNullOrEmpty(filename))
            Load(filename);
    }
}
```

Example 10-2. *Visual Basic code for Sequence member variables and constructors*

```vb
Public Enum MusicType
    Sample = 0
    MIDI - 1
End Enum

Public Class Sequence
    Private Const FILE_VERSION As String = "2"

    Public Title As String
    Public Artist As String
    Public MusicFile As String
    Public MusicLength As Integer
    Public Interval As Single ' in ms
    Public Version As Integer = Integer.Parse(FILE_VERSION)
    Public Channels As List(Of Channel) = New List(Of Channel)()
    Public MusicType As MusicType

    Public Sub New()
        Me.New(Nothing)
    End Sub
```

```
    Public Sub New(ByVal filename As String)
        If (Not String.IsNullOrEmpty(filename)) Then
            Load(filename)
        End If
    End Sub
End Sequence
```

The Channel object contains the serial number of an individual Phidget Interface Kit (so it can be addressed directly), the output port on that Interface Kit the channel object maps to, an integer value that represents the channel as it stands in the entire sequence, an integer value that maps to a specific track in a MIDI file (more on that soon as well), and the actual tapped-out rhythm data for that channel. The code for the Channel object can be seen in Examples 10-3 and 10-4.

C# Example 10-3. C# code for the Channel object

```
public class Channel
{
    // serial number of the phidget device mapped to this channel
    private int _serialNumber;

    // index into output array of the phidget device mapped to this channel
    private int _outputIndex;

    // overall channel number
    private int _channelNumber;

    private int _MIDIChannel;

    // array of off/on states for each second tick
    private bool[] _data;

    public Channel(int channelNumber)
    {
        _channelNumber = channelNumber;
    }

    public Channel(int channelNumber, int serialNumber, int outputIndex)
    {
        _channelNumber = channelNumber;
        _serialNumber = serialNumber;
        _outputIndex = outputIndex;
    }

    public Channel(int channelNumber, int serialNumber, int outputIndex,
                int midiChannel, int dataLength)
    {
```

```
        _channelNumber = channelNumber;
        _serialNumber = serialNumber;
        _outputIndex = outputIndex;
        _MIDIChannel = midiChannel;
        _data = new bool[dataLength];
    }

    public Channel(int channelNumber, int serialNumber, int outputIndex,
                   int dataLength)
    {
        _channelNumber = channelNumber;
        _serialNumber = serialNumber;
        _outputIndex = outputIndex;
        _data = new bool[dataLength];
    }

    public int Number
    {
        get { return _channelNumber; }
        set { _channelNumber = value; }
    }

    public int SerialNumber
    {
        get { return _serialNumber; }
        set { _serialNumber = value; }
    }

    public int OutputIndex
    {
        get { return _outputIndex; }
        set { _outputIndex = value; }
    }

    public int MIDIChannel
    {
        get { return this._MIDIChannel; }
        set { this._MIDIChannel = value; }
    }

    public bool[] Data
    {
        get { return _data; }
        set { _data = value; }
    }
}
```

```vb
Public Class Channel
    ' serial number of the phidget device mapped to this channel
    Private _serialNumber As Integer

    ' index into output array of the phidget device mapped to this channel
    Private _outputIndex As Integer

    ' overall channel number
    Private _channelNumber As Integer

    Private _MIDIChannel As Integer

    ' array of off/on states for each second tick
    Private _data() As Boolean

    Public Sub New(ByVal channelNumber As Integer)
        _channelNumber = channelNumber
    End Sub

    Public Sub New(ByVal channelNumber As Integer, ByVal serialNumber As Integer, _
                ByVal outputIndex As Integer)
        _channelNumber = channelNumber
        _serialNumber = serialNumber
        _outputIndex = outputIndex
    End Sub

    Public Sub New(ByVal channelNumber As Integer, ByVal serialNumber As Integer, _
                ByVal outputIndex As Integer, ByVal midiChannel As Integer, _
                ByVal dataLength As Integer)
        _channelNumber = channelNumber
        _serialNumber = serialNumber
        _outputIndex = outputIndex
        _MIDIChannel = midiChannel
        _data = New Boolean(dataLength - 1){}
    End Sub

    Public Sub New(ByVal channelNumber As Integer, ByVal serialNumber As Integer, _
                ByVal outputIndex As Integer, ByVal dataLength As Integer)
        _channelNumber = channelNumber
        _serialNumber = serialNumber
        _outputIndex = outputIndex
        _data = New Boolean(dataLength - 1){}
    End Sub
```

```
    Public Property Number() As Integer
        Get
            Return _channelNumber
        End Get
        Set(ByVal value As Integer)
            _channelNumber = value
        End Set
    End Property

    Public Property SerialNumber() As Integer
        Get
            Return _serialNumber
        End Get
        Set(ByVal value As Integer)
            _serialNumber = value
        End Set
    End Property

    Public Property OutputIndex() As Integer
        Get
            Return _outputIndex
        End Get
        Set(ByVal value As Integer)
            _outputIndex = value
        End Set
    End Property

    Public Property MIDIChannel() As Integer
        Get
            Return Me._MIDIChannel
        End Get
        Set(ByVal value As Integer)
            Me._MIDIChannel = value
        End Set
    End Property

    Public Property Data() As Boolean()
        Get
            Return _data
        End Get
        Set(ByVal value As Boolean())
            _data = value
        End Set
    End Property
End Class
```

With these two objects, we can represent an entire sequence and all the data necessary to save it, load it, and play it back at any time.

When saved, the information is simply exported to an XML file. This can be seen in Examples 10-5 and 10-6.

C# Example 10-5. *C# code to save a Sequence object*

```csharp
public void Save(string filename)
{
    // indent our output file
    XmlWriterSettings settings = new XmlWriterSettings();
    settings.Indent = true;

    // create a new XML file
    XmlWriter xml = XmlWriter.Create(filename, settings);

    // write start tags
    xml.WriteStartDocument();

    SaveSequence(xml);

    // write end tags
    xml.WriteEndDocument();

    // close it up
    xml.Flush();
    xml.Close();
}

private void SaveSequence(XmlWriter xml)
{
    StringBuilder sb = new StringBuilder();

    xml.WriteComment("Sequence file for LightSequencer");

    xml.WriteStartElement("sequence");

        // write base config info
        xml.WriteStartElement("config");
            xml.WriteElementString("fileVersion", FILE_VERSION);
            xml.WriteElementString("musicFile", this.MusicFile);
            xml.WriteElementString("musicLength", this.MusicLength.ToString());
            xml.WriteElementString("numChannels", this.Channels.Count.ToString());
            xml.WriteElementString("interval", this.Interval.ToString());
        xml.WriteEndElement();
```

```
        // write music information
        xml.WriteStartElement("musicInfo");
            xml.WriteElementString("title", this.Title);
            xml.WriteElementString("artist", this.Artist);
        xml.WriteEndElement();

        // write channels
        xml.WriteStartElement("channels");

        foreach(Channel channel in this.Channels)
        {
            // 1==on, 0==off...lame, but it works. :)
            foreach(bool b in channel.Data)
                sb.Append((b ? "1" : "0"));

            // write channel specific info
            xml.WriteStartElement("channel");
                xml.WriteAttributeString("number", channel.Number.ToString());
                xml.WriteAttributeString("serialNumber",
                                        channel.SerialNumber.ToString());
                xml.WriteAttributeString("outputIndex",
                                        channel.OutputIndex.ToString());
                xml.WriteAttributeString("midiChannel",
                                        channel.MIDIChannel.ToString());
                xml.WriteString(sb.ToString());
            xml.WriteEndElement();

            sb.Remove(0, sb.Length);
        }
        xml.WriteEndElement();
    xml.WriteEndElement();
}
```

VB Example 10-6. *Visual Basic code to save a Sequence object*

```
Public Sub Save(ByVal filename As String)
    ' indent our output file
    Dim settings As New XmlWriterSettings()
    settings.Indent = True

    ' create a new XML file
    Dim xml As XmlWriter = XmlWriter.Create(filename, settings)

    ' write start tags
    xml.WriteStartDocument()
```

```vb
        SaveSequence(xml)

        ' write end tags
        xml.WriteEndDocument()

        ' close it up
        xml.Flush()
        xml.Close()
    End Sub

    Private Sub SaveSequence(ByVal xml As XmlWriter)
        Dim sb As New StringBuilder()

        xml.WriteComment("Sequence file for LightSequencer")

        xml.WriteStartElement("sequence")

            ' write base config info
            xml.WriteStartElement("config")
                xml.WriteElementString("fileVersion", FILE_VERSION)
                xml.WriteElementString("musicFile", Me.MusicFile)
                xml.WriteElementString("musicLength", Me.MusicLength.ToString())
                xml.WriteElementString("numChannels", Me.Channels.Count.ToString())
                xml.WriteElementString("interval", Me.Interval.ToString())
            xml.WriteEndElement()

            ' write music information
            xml.WriteStartElement("musicInfo")
                xml.WriteElementString("title", Me.Title)
                xml.WriteElementString("artist", Me.Artist)
            xml.WriteEndElement()

            ' write channels
            xml.WriteStartElement("channels")

            For Each channel As Channel In Me.Channels
                ' 1==on, 0==off...lame, but it works. :)
                For Each b As Boolean In channel.Data
                    If b Then
                        sb.Append(("1"))
                    Else
                        sb.Append(("0"))
                    End If
                Next b
```

```
            ' write channel specific info
            xml.WriteStartElement("channel")
                xml.WriteAttributeString("number", channel.Number.ToString())
                xml.WriteAttributeString("serialNumber", _
                                        channel.SerialNumber.ToString())
                xml.WriteAttributeString("outputIndex", _
                                        channel.OutputIndex.ToString())
                xml.WriteAttributeString("midiChannel", _
                                        channel.MIDIChannel.ToString())
                xml.WriteString(sb.ToString())
            xml.WriteEndElement()

            sb.Remove(0, sb.Length)
        Next channel
        xml.WriteEndElement()
    xml.WriteEndElement()
End Sub
```

When loaded, the XML data is parsed and the sequence is recreated in memory to be used by the application, as shown in Examples 10-7 and 10-8.

<u>C#</u>   **Example 10-7.** *C# code to load a Sequence object*

```csharp
public void Load(string filename)
{
    // load the XML file
    XmlDocument xmlDoc = new XmlDocument();
    xmlDoc.Load(filename);

    // grab the base config info
    this.Version =
        int.Parse(xmlDoc.SelectSingleNode("sequence/config/fileVersion").InnerText);
    switch(this.Version)
    {
        case 1:
            LoadV1Sequence(xmlDoc);
            break;
        default:
            LoadSequence(xmlDoc);
            break;
    }
}

public void LoadSequence(XmlDocument xmlDoc)
{
    XmlNode node;
```

```csharp
        // grab the base config info
        this.MusicFile = xmlDoc.SelectSingleNode("sequence/config/musicFile").InnerText;

        if(this.MusicFile.EndsWith(".mid"))
            this.MusicType = MusicType.MIDI;

        this.MusicLength =
            int.Parse(xmlDoc.SelectSingleNode("sequence/config/musicLength").InnerText);
        this.Interval =
            float.Parse(xmlDoc.SelectSingleNode("sequence/config/interval").InnerText);
        int numChannels =
            int.Parse(xmlDoc.SelectSingleNode("sequence/config/numChannels").InnerText);

        this.Title = xmlDoc.SelectSingleNode("sequence/musicInfo/title").InnerText;
        this.Artist = xmlDoc.SelectSingleNode("sequence/musicInfo/artist").InnerText;

        this.Channels.Clear();

        // add each channel to our internal list for easy tracking
        for(int i = 0; i < numChannels; i++)
        {
            node = xmlDoc.SelectSingleNode("sequence/channels/channel[@number='" +
                                    i.ToString() + "']");
            if(node != null)
            {
                int serial = int.Parse(node.Attributes["serialNumber"].Value);
                char[] data = node.InnerText.ToCharArray();

                // add the channel to the channel list
                this.Channels.Add(new Channel(i, serial,
                            int.Parse(node.Attributes["outputIndex"].Value),
                            int.Parse(node.Attributes["midiChannel"].Value),
                            data.Length));

                // read out the data
                for(int j = 0; j < data.Length; j++)
                    this.Channels[i].Data[j] = (data[j] == '1');
            }
            else
                this.Channels.Add(new Channel(i));
        }
    }
```

VB Example 10-8. *Visual Basic code to load a Sequence object*

```vb
Public Sub Load(ByVal filename As String)
    ' load the XML file
```

```
        Dim xmlDoc As New XmlDocument()
        xmlDoc.Load(filename)

        ' grab the base config info
        Me.Version = Integer.Parse( _
                        xmlDoc.SelectSingleNode("sequence/config/fileVersion").InnerText)
        Select Case Me.Version
            Case 1
                LoadV1Sequence(xmlDoc)
            Case Else
                LoadSequence(xmlDoc)
        End Select
    End Sub

    Public Sub LoadSequence(ByVal xmlDoc As XmlDocument)
        Dim node As XmlNode

        ' grab the base config info
        Me.MusicFile = xmlDoc.SelectSingleNode("sequence/config/musicFile").InnerText

        If Me.MusicFile.EndsWith(".mid") Then
            Me.MusicType = MusicType.MIDI
        End If

        Me.MusicLength = Integer.Parse( _
            xmlDoc.SelectSingleNode("sequence/config/musicLength").InnerText)
        Me.Interval = Single.Parse( _
            xmlDoc.SelectSingleNode("sequence/config/interval").InnerText)
        Dim numChannels As Integer = Integer.Parse( _
            xmlDoc.SelectSingleNode("sequence/config/numChannels").InnerText)

        Me.Title = xmlDoc.SelectSingleNode("sequence/musicInfo/title").InnerText
        Me.Artist = xmlDoc.SelectSingleNode("sequence/musicInfo/artist").InnerText

        Me.Channels.Clear()

        ' add each channel to our internal list for easy tracking
        For i As Integer = 0 To numChannels - 1
            node = xmlDoc.SelectSingleNode( _
                "sequence/channels/channel[@number='" & i.ToString() & "']")
            If node IsNot Nothing Then
                Dim serial As Integer = Integer.Parse( _
                    node.Attributes("serialNumber").Value)
                Dim data() As Char = node.InnerText.ToCharArray()

                ' add the channel to the channel list
```

```
            Me.Channels.Add(New Channel(i, serial, _
                        Integer.Parse(node.Attributes("outputIndex").Value), _
                        Integer.Parse(node.Attributes("midiChannel").Value), _
                        data.Length))

            ' read out the data
            For j As Integer = 0 To data.Length - 1
                Me.Channels(i).Data(j) = (data(j) = "1"c)
            Next j
        Else
            Me.Channels.Add(New Channel(i))
        End If
    Next i
End Sub
```

Grid display

Now that we can save and load a sequence, we need a way to display the recorded sequence data on the screen. The easiest way to represent the data is to use a grid view with each Phidget channel extending horizontally over time. When a rhythm sequence is recorded, the grid squares can be colored in where the buttons were pressed, representing the channel that should be turned on and off. An example screenshot can be seen in Figure 10-12.

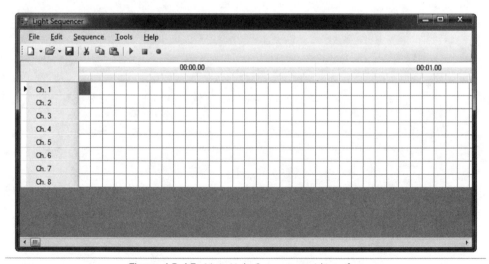

Figure 10-12. *Main Light Sequencer grid interface*

If you look closely, you can see that the grid contains two headers: one with a time display marked off at every second, and a second header with individual tick marks marking the grid squares at every 50 milliseconds (1 second / 20 squares = .05 seconds per square, or 50 milliseconds).

Along the left vertical axis, a text label appears denoting each channel from the Phidget Interface Kits, representing a strand of lights. When scrolling horizontally, this vertical column remains stationary, but the time headers on top move with the grid.

To create this view, two DataGridView objects can be dragged onto the main design surface of a form: one representing only the time header, the other being the entire grid. The DataGridView does not support multiple headers, which is why this "hack" is required.

After dropping the two grids on the surface, we can create the segmented timeline with the code shown in Examples 10-9 and 10-10.

C# Example 10-9. *C# code to draw the base sequence grid*

```csharp
private void CreateSequence()
{
    // clear out the current grids
    dgvHeader.Rows.Clear();
    dgvHeader.Columns.Clear();
    dgvMain.Rows.Clear();
    dgvMain.Columns.Clear();

    // make our grids invisible while drawing to speed it up
    dgvMain.Visible = false;
    dgvHeader.Visible = false;

    // columns per second = 1 second / length of time for each square
    _colsPerSec = 1000 / (int)_sequence.Interval;

    // draw the grid
    // for the length of the music track
    for(int sec = 0; sec < _sequence.MusicLength; sec++)
    {
        // for each second in the time specified, create a column in the header
        string header = "{0:0#}:{1:0#}.00";
        dgvHeader.Columns.Add(sec.ToString(), String.Format(header, sec/60, sec%60));

        // this value must be < 65535 for the entire grid (?)
        dgvHeader.Columns[sec].FillWeight = 0.0001f;

        // set the width to an appropriate size for display
        dgvHeader.Columns[sec].Width = _colsPerSec*COL_WIDTH;

        // now draw the squares contained within each second
        for(int partSec = 0; partSec < _colsPerSec; partSec++)
        {
```

```
                    // no name, FillWeight requirement, set the appropriate width
                    dgvMain.Columns.Add("", "");
                    dgvMain.Columns[(sec * _colsPerSec) + partSec].FillWeight = 0.0001f;
                    dgvMain.Columns[(sec * _colsPerSec) + partSec].Width = COL_WIDTH;
                }
            }

            // add the row headers (Ch. 1, Ch. 2, etc.)
            for(int channel = 0; channel < _sequence.Channels.Count; channel++)
            {
                // create the row and text
                DataGridViewRow dvr = new DataGridViewRow();
                dvr.HeaderCell.Value = "Ch. " + (channel+1);

                // store away the actual Channel object for later use
                dvr.Tag = _sequence.Channels[channel];

                // add the row
                dgvMain.Rows.Add(dvr);
            }

            // set the width of those row headers
            dgvMain.RowHeadersWidth = 100;
            dgvHeader.RowHeadersWidth = 100;

            // turn the grids back on
            dgvMain.Visible = true;
            dgvHeader.Visible = true;
        }
```

Example 10-10. *Visual Basic code to draw the base sequence grid*

```
    Private Sub CreateSequence()
        ' clear out the current grids
        dgvHeader.Rows.Clear()
        dgvHeader.Columns.Clear()
        dgvMain.Rows.Clear()
        dgvMain.Columns.Clear()

        ' make our grids invisible while drawing to speed it up
        dgvMain.Visible = False
        dgvHeader.Visible = False

        ' columns per second = 1 second / length of time for each square
        _colsPerSec = 1000 / CInt(Fix(_sequence.Interval))
```

```
            ' draw the grid
            ' for the length of the music track
            For sec As Integer = 0 To _sequence.MusicLength - 1
                ' for each second in the time specified, create a column in the header
                Dim header As String = "{0:0#}:{1:0#}.00"
                dgvHeader.Columns.Add(sec.ToString(), _
                                      String.Format(header, sec\60, sec Mod 60))
                ' this value must be < 65535 for the entire grid (?)
                dgvHeader.Columns(sec).FillWeight = 0.0001f
                ' set the width to an appropriate size for display
                dgvHeader.Columns(sec).Width = _colsPerSec*COL_WIDTH

                ' now draw the squares contained within each second
                For partSec As Integer = 0 To _colsPerSec - 1
                    ' no name, FillWeight requirement, set the appropriate width
                    dgvMain.Columns.Add("", "")
                    dgvMain.Columns((sec * _colsPerSec) + partSec).FillWeight = 0.0001f
                    dgvMain.Columns((sec * _colsPerSec) + partSec).Width = COL_WIDTH
                Next partSec
            Next sec

            ' add the row headers (Ch. 1, Ch. 2, etc.)
            For channel As Integer = 0 To _sequence.Channels.Count - 1
                ' create the row and text
                Dim dvr As New DataGridViewRow()
                dvr.HeaderCell.Value = "Ch. " & (channel+1)

                ' store away the actual Channel object for later use
                dvr.Tag = _sequence.Channels(channel)

                ' add the row
                dgvMain.Rows.Add(dvr)
            Next channel

            ' set the width of those row headers
            dgvMain.RowHeadersWidth = 100
            dgvHeader.RowHeadersWidth = 100

            ' turn the grids back on
            dgvMain.Visible = True
            dgvHeader.Visible = True
        End Sub
```

Now that the base grid is up on the screen, we need to turn individual squares on and off to represent the recorded sequence data. To do this, we simply enumerate through all channels and all intervals in each channel and turn the corresponding square blue to represent the channel (i.e., lights) being turned on at that time. The code for this can be found in Examples 10-11 and 10-12.

C#   Example 10-11. *C# code to draw sequence data on the grid*

```csharp
private void RedrawSequence()
{
    for(int i = 0; i < _sequence.Channels.Count; i++)
    {
        for(int j = 0; j < _sequence.Channels[i].Data.Length; j++)
            dgvMain.Rows[i].Cells[j].Style.BackColor =
                (_sequence.Channels[i].Data[j]) ? Color.Blue : Color.White;
    }
}
```

VB   Example 10-12. *Visual Basic code to draw sequence data on the grid*

```vb
Private Sub RedrawSequence()
    For i As Integer = 0 To _sequence.Channels.Count - 1
    For j As Integer = 0 To _sequence.Channels(i).Data.Length - 1
        If (_sequence.Channels(i).Data(j)) Then
            dgvMain.Rows(i).Cells(j).Style.BackColor = Color.Blue
        Else
            dgvMain.Rows(i).Cells(j).Style.BackColor = Color.White
        End If
    Next j
    Next i
End Sub
```

Playing music

Now that we can load, save, and display the sequence data, we need the ability to play the music for the sequence. Light Sequencer supports both WAV and MP3 files (i.e., sampled music) as well as MIDI files.

MIDI

MIDI stands for "Musical Instrument Digital Interface." Unlike an MP3 or WAV file, where the actual song is encoded in the data stream, a MIDI file contains data that tells various pieces of hardware how to play back music. Later, we will be able to use this data to automatically create a base sequence timed to the music, since we will know precisely when each instrument is playing a note.

Because we will be supporting these two types of files, we can create an interface that supports the various methods the application will need, and implement that interface in a class that handles WAV/MP3 and a class that handles MIDI. This also gives us the flexibility of easily adding a new playback type should the need arise.

The `IPlayback` interface can be seen in Examples 10-13 and 10-14.

`C#` Example 10-13. *C# code for the IPlayback interface*

```csharp
public interface IPlayback
{
    void Load(Sequence seq);
    void Unload();
    void Start();
    void Stop();
}
```

`VB` Example 10-14. *Visual Basic code for the IPlayback interface*

```vb
Public Interface IPlayback
    Sub Load(ByVal seq As Sequence)
    Sub Unload()
    Sub Start()
    Sub [Stop]()
End Interface
```

WAV/MP3 files can be played back easily using the Win32 API's MCI, or Media Control Interface. The MCI API allows you to send text-based commands to control multimedia devices. The commands we will be using are shown in Table 10-1.

Table 10-1. *MCI commands for load, unload, play, and stop*

COMMAND	STRING
Load media file	`open "filename.mp3" type mpegvideo alias MediaFile`
Unload media file	`close MediaFile`
Play media	`play MediaFile from 0`
Stop media	`stop MediaFile`

These commands can be sent to the multimedia hardware using the `mciSendString` Win32 API function. So, altogether, the `MCIPlayback` class to play WAV/MP3 files is shown in Examples 10-15 and 10-16.

`C#` Example 10-15. *C# code for the MCIPlayback class*

```csharp
public class MCIPlayback : IPlayback
{
```

```
    // dll export to MCI for playing music
    [DllImport("winmm.dll")]
    static extern Int32 mciSendString(String command, StringBuilder buffer,
                                      Int32 bufferSize, IntPtr hwndCallback);

    public void Load(Sequence seq)
    {
        string cmd = "open \"" + seq.MusicFile + "\" type mpegvideo alias MediaFile";
        mciSendString(cmd, null, 0, IntPtr.Zero);
    }

    public void Unload()
    {
        string cmd = "close MediaFile";
        mciSendString(cmd, null, 0, IntPtr.Zero);
    }

    public void Start()
    {
        string cmd = "play MediaFile from 0";
        mciSendString(cmd, null, 0, IntPtr.Zero);
    }

    public void Stop()
    {
        string cmd = "stop MediaFile";
        mciSendString(cmd, null, 0, IntPtr.Zero);
    }
}
```

VB Example 10-16. *Visual Basic code for the MCIPlayback class*

```
Public Class MCIPlayback
    Implements IPlayback
    ' dll export to MCI for playing music
    <DllImport("winmm.dll")> _
    Shared Function mciSendString(ByVal command As String, _
                        ByVal buffer As StringBuilder, _
                        ByVal bufferSize As Int32, _
                        ByVal hwndCallback As IntPtr) As Int32
    End Function

    Public Sub Load(ByVal seq As Sequence) Implements IPlayback.Load
        Dim cmd As String = "open """ & seq.MusicFile & _
                        """ type mpegvideo alias MediaFile"
        mciSendString(cmd, Nothing, 0, IntPtr.Zero)
    End Sub
```

```
        Public Sub Unload() Implements IPlayback.Unload
            Dim cmd As String = "close MediaFile"
            mciSendString(cmd, Nothing, 0, IntPtr.Zero)
        End Sub

        Public Sub Start() Implements IPlayback.Start
            Dim cmd As String = "play MediaFile from 0"
            mciSendString(cmd, Nothing, 0, IntPtr.Zero)
        End Sub

        Public Sub [Stop]() Implements IPlayback.Stop
            Dim cmd As String = "stop MediaFile"
            mciSendString(cmd, Nothing, 0, IntPtr.Zero)
        End Sub
    End Class
```

To play MIDI files, we will be using a third-party library named MIDI Toolkit, written by Leslie Sanford (*http://www.lesliesanford.com/*). This library allows us to very easily load a MIDI file and process its contents, both while loading and while playing back. The implementation of the IPlayback interface for the MIDIPlayback class looks like Examples 10-17 and 10-18.

C#   Example 10-17. *C# code for the MIDIPlayback class*

```csharp
public class MIDIPlayback : IPlayback
{
    private Midi.Sequencer _MIDISequencer;
    private Midi.Sequence _MIDISequence;
    private Midi.OutputDevice _MIDIOutDevice;

    public MIDIPlayback()
    {
        _MIDISequencer = new Midi.Sequencer();
        _MIDISequence = new Midi.Sequence();

        // event handlers for various message types
        _MIDISequencer.ChannelMessagePlayed += sequencer_ChannelMessagePlayed;
        _MIDISequencer.Chased += sequencer_Chased;
        _MIDISequencer.Stopped += sequencer_Stopped;
    }

    public void Start()
    {
        _MIDISequencer.Start();
    }
```

```csharp
public void Load(Sequence seq)
{
    // grab the first MIDI device
    if(_MIDIOutDevice == null)
        _MIDIOutDevice = new Midi.OutputDevice(0);

    // load the MIDI file
    _MIDISequence.Load(seq.MusicFile);
    _MIDISequencer.Sequence = _MIDISequence;
}

public void Unload()
{
    if(_MIDISequence != null)
        _MIDISequence.Clear();
    if(_MIDIOutDevice != null)
        _MIDIOutDevice.Close();
}

public void Stop()
{
    _MIDISequencer.Stop();
}

void sequencer_Stopped(object sender, StoppedEventArgs e)
{
    // send "stop" messages to the sound card
    foreach(ChannelMessage message in e.Messages)
    {
        if(!_MIDIOutDevice.IsDisposed)
            _MIDIOutDevice.Send(message);
    }
}

void sequencer_Chased(object sender, Sanford.Multimedia.Midi.ChasedEventArgs e)
{
    // send "chased" messages to the sound card
    foreach(ChannelMessage message in e.Messages)
    {
        if(!_MIDIOutDevice.IsDisposed)
            _MIDIOutDevice.Send(message);
    }
}
```

```
        void sequencer_ChannelMessagePlayed(object sender,
                              Sanford.Multimedia.Midi.ChannelMessageEventArgs e)
    {
        // send each MIDI command to the sound card
        if(!_MIDIOutDevice.IsDisposed)
            _MIDIOutDevice.Send(e.Message);
    }
}
```

Example 10-18. *Visual Basic code for the MIDIPlayback class*

```
Public Class MIDIPlayback
    Implements IPlayback
    Private _MIDISequencer As Midi.Sequencer
    Private _MIDISequence As Midi.Sequence
    Private _MIDIOutDevice As Midi.OutputDevice

    Public Sub New()
        _MIDISequencer = New Midi.Sequencer()
        _MIDISequence = New Midi.Sequence()

        ' event handlers for various message types
        AddHandler _MIDISequencer.ChannelMessagePlayed, _
                        AddressOf sequencer_ChannelMessagePlayed
        AddHandler _MIDISequencer.Chased, AddressOf sequencer_Chased
        AddHandler _MIDISequencer.Stopped, AddressOf sequencer_Stopped
    End Sub

    Public Sub Start() Implements IPlayback.Start
        _MIDISequencer.Start()
    End Sub

    Public Sub Load(ByVal seq As Sequence) Implements IPlayback.Load
        ' grab the first MIDI device
        If _MIDIOutDevice Is Nothing Then
            _MIDIOutDevice = New Midi.OutputDevice(0)
        End If

        ' load the MIDI file
        _MIDISequence.Load(seq.MusicFile)
        _MIDISequencer.Sequence = _MIDISequence
    End Sub

    Public Sub Unload() Implements IPlayback.Unload
        If _MIDISequence IsNot Nothing Then
            _MIDISequence.Clear()
```

```
        End If
        If _MIDIOutDevice IsNot Nothing Then
            _MIDIOutDevice.Close()
        End If
    End Sub

    Public Sub [Stop]() Implements IPlayback.Stop
        _MIDISequencer.Stop()
    End Sub

    Private Sub sequencer_Stopped(ByVal sender As Object, _
                                ByVal e As StoppedEventArgs)
        ' send "stop" messages to the sound card
        For Each message As ChannelMessage In e.Messages
            If (Not _MIDIOutDevice.IsDisposed) Then
                _MIDIOutDevice.Send(message)
            End If
        Next message
    End Sub

    Private Sub sequencer_Chased(ByVal sender As Object, _
                                ByVal e As Sanford.Multimedia.Midi.ChasedEventArgs)
        ' send "chased" messages to the sound card
        For Each message As ChannelMessage In e.Messages
            If (Not _MIDIOutDevice.IsDisposed) Then
                _MIDIOutDevice.Send(message)
            End If
        Next message
    End Sub

    Private Sub sequencer_ChannelMessagePlayed(ByVal sender As Object, _
                        ByVal e As Sanford.Multimedia.Midi.ChannelMessageEventArgs)
        ' send each MIDI command to the sound card
        If (Not _MIDIOutDevice.IsDisposed) Then
            _MIDIOutDevice.Send(e.Message)
        End If
    End Sub
End Class
```

This code sets up the MIDI hardware device, sets up event handlers to process specific MIDI messages, and then sends them to the sound card when they are encountered in real time.

Recording data

Now that we can play music and load, save, and display sequence data, we need a way to actually create the sequence data! When the record button is clicked in the main application, a separate form is displayed. When "Start recording" is clicked, a count-down timer begins. When the timer reaches 0, a new thread is created, the music starts to play, and a sequence can be created by tapping keys on the keyboard that correspond to the individual Phidget Interface Kit channels. Pressing the key turns the channel on, and releasing the key turns the channel off, which would, in turn, turn that specific string of lights on or off.

To accomplish this, a key map is set up. This maps an individual keyboard key to a single channel. This can be done by creating a Dictionary object that maps a Keys enum to an integer channel, and then assigning each keyboard key to a channel, as shown in Examples 10-19 and 10-20.

`C#` Example 10-19. *C# code to set up the key map*

```csharp
private Dictionary<Keys, int> _keyMap = new Dictionary<Keys,int>();

public RecordForm()
{
    InitializeComponent();

    // setup the key map
    _keyMap.Add(Keys.D1, 0);
    _keyMap.Add(Keys.D2, 1);
    _keyMap.Add(Keys.D3, 2);
    _keyMap.Add(Keys.D4, 3);
    _keyMap.Add(Keys.D5, 4);
    _keyMap.Add(Keys.D6, 5);
    _keyMap.Add(Keys.D7, 6);
    _keyMap.Add(Keys.D8, 7);
    _keyMap.Add(Keys.D9, 8);
    ...
    _keyMap.Add(Keys.OemQuestion, 39);
}
```

VB Example 10-20. *Visual Basic code to set up the key map*

```vbnet
Private _keyMap As Dictionary(Of Keys, Integer) = New Dictionary(Of Keys,Integer)()

Public Sub New()
    InitializeComponent()

    ' setup the key map
    _keyMap.Add(Keys.D1, 0)
```

```
_keyMap.Add(Keys.D2, 1)
_keyMap.Add(Keys.D3, 2)
_keyMap.Add(Keys.D4, 3)
_keyMap.Add(Keys.D5, 4)
_keyMap.Add(Keys.D6, 5)
_keyMap.Add(Keys.D7, 6)
_keyMap.Add(Keys.D8, 7)
_keyMap.Add(Keys.D9, 8)
...
_keyMap.Add(Keys.OemQuestion, 39)
End Sub
```

Now that we have a mapping from keyboard keys to channels, we need a way to record key presses at the appropriate intervals. First, KeyDown and KeyUp event handlers
are created to record which keys are pressed. An internal array maps a boolean to a
specific channel. When the key is down, the channel for that key is set to true, and vice
versa.

A separate thread also runs, and loops while the song is playing. In this loop, the current values of the previously mentioned array are assigned to the actual channel data
based on that "tick" we are at in the song. As discussed previously, the application
breaks the song into 50-millisecond chunks. Every 50 milliseconds, the state of the
keys is put into the channel data list, and the tick count is increased to the next position in the data. This can all be seen in Examples 10-21 and 10-22.

C# Example 10-21. *C# code to record the keypress sequences*

```
// list of all channels in sequence
private List<Channel> _channels;

// keypress data that will be copied out later if kept
private List<bool[]> _tempData = new List<bool[]>();

private Dictionary<Keys, int> _keyMap = new Dictionary<Keys,int>();
private Sequence _sequence;

// state of current channel
private bool[] _on;

// index into tempData array
private int _tickCount = 0;

// song still playing?
private bool _playing;

// MCIPlayback or MIDIPlayback
private IPlayback _playback;
```

```
private void RecordThread()
{
    float last = 0;
    Stopwatch s = new Stopwatch();

    _playback.Load(_sequence);

    s.Start();
    _playback.Start();

    _playing = true;

    while(_playing)
    {
        // if we've elapsed enough time, process keys
        if((s.ElapsedMilliseconds - last) > _sequence.Interval)
        {
            // if we're at the end, bail out
            if(_tickCount >= _channels[0].Data.Length)
                btnStart.PerformClick();

            // for each channel, set the ticks on and off as keys are pressed
            for(int i = 0; i < _channels.Count; i++)
            {
                if(_on[i])
                    _tempData[i][_tickCount] = _on[i];

                // every time we tick, set the output port for the current channel
                // on or off
                if(chkPlay.Checked && !_on[i])
                    PhidgetHandler.IFKits[_channels[i].SerialNumber]
                            .outputs[_channels[i].OutputIndex] =
                                _channels[i].Data[_tickCount];
            }
            _tickCount++;

            // maintain the last time we did this
            last = (s.ElapsedMilliseconds -
                    ((s.ElapsedMilliseconds - last) - _sequence.Interval));
        }
    }
    _playback.Stop();
}
```

```
' list of all channels in sequence
Private _channels As List(Of Channel)

' keypress data that will be copied out later if kept
Private _tempData As List(Of Boolean()) = New List(Of Boolean())()

Private _keyMap As Dictionary(Of Keys, Integer) = New Dictionary(Of Keys,Integer)()
Private _sequence As Sequence
Private _thread As Thread

' state of current channel
Private _on() As Boolean

' index into tempData array
Private _tickCount As Integer = 0

' song still playing?
Private _playing As Boolean

' MCIPlayback or MIDIPlayback
Private _playback As IPlayback

Private Sub RecordThread()
    Dim last As Single = 0
    Dim s As New Stopwatch()

    _playback.Load(_sequence)

    s.Start()
    _playback.Start()

    _playing = True

    Do While _playing
        ' if we've elapsed enough time, process keys
        If (s.ElapsedMilliseconds - last) > _sequence.Interval Then
            ' if we're at the end, bail out
            If _tickCount >= _channels(0).Data.Length Then
                btnStart.PerformClick()
            End If

            ' for each channel, set the ticks on and off as keys are pressed
            For i As Integer = 0 To _channels.Count - 1
```

```
        If _on(i) Then
            _tempData(i)(_tickCount) = _on(i)
        End If

        ' every time we tick, set the output port for the current channel
        ' on or off
        If chkPlay.Checked AndAlso (Not _on(i)) Then
            PhidgetHandler.IFKits(_channels(i).SerialNumber). _
                outputs(_channels(i).OutputIndex) = _
                    _channels(i).Data(_tickCount)
        End If
    Next i
    _tickCount += 1

    ' maintain the last time we did this
    last = (s.ElapsedMilliseconds - _
            ((s.ElapsedMilliseconds - last) - _sequence.Interval))
    End If
    Loop

    _playback.Stop()
End Sub
```

When recording is stopped and the user elects to keep the recorded data, the data from the _tempData array is copied out to the actual channel data of the sequence, as shown in Examples 10-23 and 10-24.

C#   Example 10-23. *C# code to copy temporary data to the sequence data*

```csharp
for(int i = 0; i < _tempData.Count; i++)
{
    for(int j = 0; j < _tempData[i].Length; j++)
    {
        if(_tempData[i][j])
            _channels[i].Data[j] = _tempData[i][j];
    }
}
```

VB   Example 10-24. *Visual Basic code to copy temporary data to the sequence data*

```vb
For i As Integer = 0 To _tempData.Count - 1
    For j As Integer = 0 To _tempData(i).Length - 1
        If _tempData(i)(j) Then
            _channels(i).Data(j) = _tempData(i)(j)
        End If
    Next j
Next i
```

In the case of MIDI files, we can use the data contained within the file to build a sequence automatically and use this as a base for creating a final show. MIDI files contain a series of messages that tell the sound hardware what to do. We will enumerate through these messages looking for specific types, and then use the time values for those messages to build our base sequence.

Playing a sequence

The code to play back a sequence is very similar to our recording code. The appropriate playback class is used to start the music and, once again, a thread is created that waits for the 50-millisecond interval to elapse. When it does, it checks to see whether each channel is on or off at that time, and then sets the Phidget Interface Kits appropriately. This is demonstrated in Examples 10-25 and 10-26.

C# Example 10-25. *C# code to play back a sequence*

```csharp
private void ThreadHandler()
{
    float last = 0;
    _tickCount = 0;

    _playback.Load(_sequence);

    _stopWatch = new Stopwatch();
    _stopWatch.Start();

    _playback.Start();

    _playing = true;

    while(_playing)
    {
        // if we hit our interval
        if((_stopWatch.ElapsedMilliseconds - last) >= _sequence.Interval)
        {
            // make sure we're still inside the bounds of the song
            if(_tickCount >= _sequence.Channels[0].Data.Length)
            {
                // dump out and let anyone listening know it's all over
                Thread.Sleep(100);
                _stopWatch.Stop();
                _playback.Stop();
                OnSequenceStopped(new EventArgs());
                return;
            }

            // every time we tick, set the output port for the current channel
```

```
        // on or off
        foreach(Channel c in _sequence.Channels)
        {
            if(PhidgetHandler.IFKits[c.SerialNumber].outputs[c.OutputIndex] !=
                    c.Data[_tickCount])
                PhidgetHandler.IFKits[c.SerialNumber].outputs[c.OutputIndex] =
                    c.Data[_tickCount];
        }

        _tickCount++;
        last = (_stopWatch.ElapsedMilliseconds -
                ((_stopWatch.ElapsedMilliseconds - last) - _sequence.Interval));
    }
    else
        // give the CPU a break until it's time to act again
        Thread.Sleep((int)(_stopWatch.ElapsedMilliseconds - last));
    }
    Thread.Sleep(100);
    _stopWatch.Stop();
    _playback.Stop();
}
```

VB Example 10-26. *Visual Basic code to play back a sequence*

```
Private Sub ThreadHandler()
    Dim last As Single = 0
    _tickCount = 0

    _playback.Load(_sequence)

    _stopWatch = New Stopwatch()
    _stopWatch.Start()

    _playback.Start()

    _playing = True

    Do While _playing
        ' if we hit our interval
        If (_stopWatch.ElapsedMilliseconds - last) >= _sequence.Interval Then
            ' make sure we're still inside the bounds of the song
            If _tickCount >= _sequence.Channels(0).Data.Length Then
                ' dump out and let anyone listening know it's all over
                Thread.Sleep(100)
                _stopWatch.Stop()
                _playback.Stop()
```

```
            OnSequenceStopped(New EventArgs())
            Return
        End If


        ' every time we tick, set the output port for the current channel
        ' on or off
        For Each c As Channel In _sequence.Channels
            If PhidgetHandler.IFKits(c.SerialNumber).outputs(c.OutputIndex) <> _
                    c.Data(_tickCount) Then
                PhidgetHandler.IFKits(c.SerialNumber).outputs(c.OutputIndex) = _
                    c.Data(_tickCount)
            End If
        Next c


        _tickCount += 1
        last = (_stopWatch.ElapsedMilliseconds - _
                ((_stopWatch.ElapsedMilliseconds - last) - _sequence.Interval))
    Else
        ' give the CPU a break until it's time to act again
        Thread.Sleep(CInt(Fix(_stopWatch.ElapsedMilliseconds - last)))
    End If
Loop
Thread.Sleep(100)
_stopWatch.Stop()
_playback.Stop()
End Sub
```

Creating a Show

Now that the hardware is built and the software is ready to run, it is time to create a
light sequence.

To begin, ensure that the Phidgets libraries are installed, as discussed previously. Next,
plug your Phidget boards into the USB ports on your computer. You do not need to
have the hardware fully built at this time, nor lights hooked up.

Start the Light Sequencer application and select File→New→Sequence. The window
shown in Figure 10-13 will appear.

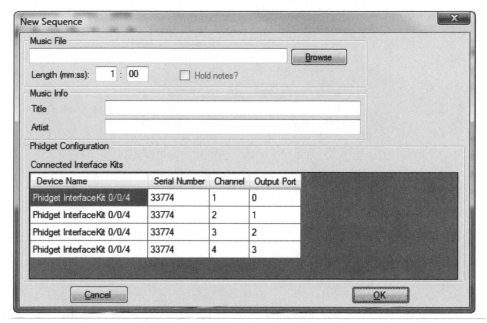

Figure 10-13. *New Sequence dialog box*

In the dialog that appears, select a WAV, MP3, or MIDI file. Then, enter the title, artist, and length of the song.

The grid at the bottom of the window will display all Phidget Interface Kits attached to the computer. You can add or remove these kits at any time from this screen.

In the Output Port column of the grid, map the Phidget Interface Kit output to the channel it should map to on the sequence grid. You can likely just leave these values as-is, unless you have a special need to place a certain channel on a certain output port.

If you are loading a MIDI file, you will see an additional column named MIDI Channel. This column will contain drop-down boxes that list each MIDI channel in the loaded MIDI file. Typically, a channel maps to a single instrument in a MIDI file and should be labeled as such, but not necessarily. From this column, select a MIDI channel to map to a Phidget output port, which maps to a channel on the grid.

Click OK, and a sequence grid will be created and displayed, as previously shown in Figure 10-12. If you loaded a WAV or MP3 file, the grid will be empty. If you loaded a MIDI file, the grid will be prefilled with some data that was processed from the MIDI file itself.

To start creating the light show for your song, select Sequence→Record Sequence, or press the Record button. A new window will appear, shown in Figure 10-14.

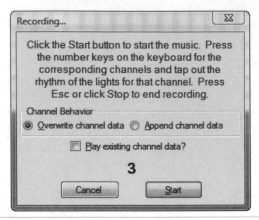

Figure 10-14. *Record Sequence window*

First, select how you want the recorded data to be put into the grid. If you want to overwrite all data on the grid, select the "Overwrite channel data" option. If you want to append your newly recorded data to the grid, select "Append channel data". Generally, you will append the data as you build your sequence out, unless you want to start over, in which case you can select the overwrite option.

When you are ready to start tapping out the rhythm for your light show, click the Start button. The window will count down from 3 to 0 to give you time to prepare, and then start the song. Using your keyboard, tap out the rhythm for each channel indicating how you want the lights to turn on and off to the music. The keyboard map is shown in Table 10-2.

Table 10-2. *Keyboard-to-channel map*

KEYBOARD KEYS	CHANNELS
1–0 (top row)	1–10
Q–P (second row)	11–19
A–; (third row)	20–29
Z–/ (fourth row)	30–39

When you are finished recording, click the Stop button or press Escape on the keyboard. Don't feel you have to sequence every channel for the entire song at once. This is what the append feature is for. For example, you may wish to tap out the background rhythm on channel 1. Once that is complete, you can start recording again and tap out the behavior for another channel or two, appending the data until you are finished. Additionally, the checkbox "Play existing channel data" will play back your channel data at the same time you are recording, so you can see your lights flash in real time as you record additional channels of data.

After clicking Stop, the application will ask you whether you want to save the data to the grid. Selecting Yes will add the data, and selecting No will throw away what you just tapped out and bring you back to the recording screen.

You can play your sequence back at any time by selecting Sequence→Play Sequence, or clicking the Play button. The music will be played and your Phidgets will run, turning the channels on and off as you originally recorded.

The other way to interact with sequence data is through the main grid itself. Individual squares can be turned on and off by clicking the square or dragging across a group of squares and pressing "O" to turn the squares on, or pressing "F" to turn the squares off. You can also right-click on the square and select On or Off from the context menu that appears. This is shown in Figure 10-15.

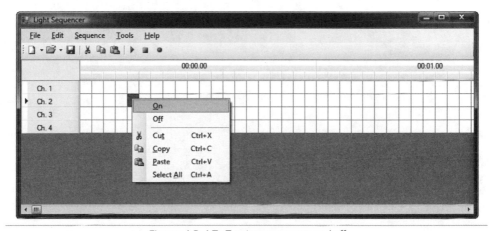

Figure 10-15. *Turning squares on and off*

This can be used to enter data from scratch, or clean up existing data where a button tap is too long or too short.

You can also cut, copy, and paste squares on the grid. This is great for repeating portions of sequences across the entire song. To do this, highlight a range of squares and select Cut or Copy from the Edit menu. Then, highlight the square where the paste should begin and select Paste from the Edit menu.

The final feature of the software is creating a playlist. If you want to record sequences for several songs and play them in a row, you can create a playlist of your sequences and play them back in order.

Select File→New→New Playlist to start. A new window will appear, as shown in Figure 10-16.

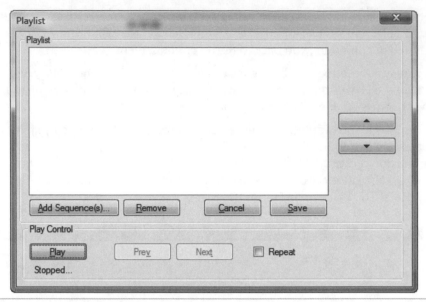

Figure 10-16. *New playlist window*

To add sequences to the list, click the "Add Sequence" button. This will bring up a standard Windows file locator dialog box where you can select one or many sequences to put in the list. Once they are added, you can use the arrow buttons to the right of the sequence list to rearrange the order of the items.

When you have finished adding all items to the list, click the Save button to save the playlist to a file that can be loaded later.

To play the playlist, click the Play button, and all songs will be played in order. Click the Repeat checkbox to have the sequences loop until you manually stop the show.

Final Thoughts

And there we have it: easy-to-build hardware and easy-to-run software to create your own holiday light show, or a light show for any occasion. This software has been used to create light shows, museum displays using robotics, and even a show driving an old Chuck E. Cheese singing robot!

We would love to see the sequences you come up with. Please contact us through our book's site at *http://www.c4fbook.com/* so we can promote your creativity!

Using the C4fStyle File for WPF Projects

C4fStyle Overview

Both the InnerTube and PeerCast Windows Presentation Foundation (WPF) projects use a set of predefined styles packaged in the *C4fStyle.xaml* file, which you can take and reuse to skin your WPF applications.

Adding the C4fStyle File to Your Application

To reuse the *C4fStyle.xaml* file, you will first need to add a reference to the *Presentation-Framework.Aero.dll* in your project, as shown in Figure A-1. This is required for the Button style, which uses a ButtonChrome defined in the Aero Presentation Framework.

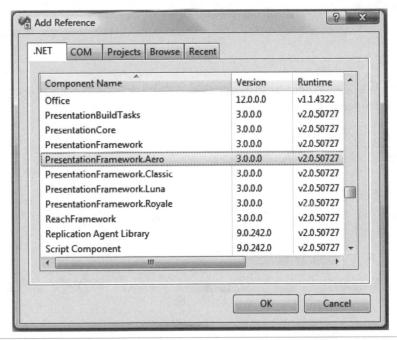

Figure A-1. *Referencing the Aero Presentation Framework library*

Next, add the *C4fStyle.xaml* file to your Visual Studio project. To apply *C4fStyles.xaml* at an application-level scope (meaning all button styles will inherit from *C4fStyles.xaml*), we simply add the XAML listed in Example 11-1 to our *App.xaml* (*Application.xaml* in VB) file.

```
<Application.Resources>
  <ResourceDictionary>
    <ResourceDictionary.MergedDictionaries>
      <ResourceDictionary Source="C4fStyles.xaml"/>
    </ResourceDictionary.MergedDictionaries>
  </ResourceDictionary>
</Application.Resources>
```

Generic and named styles

The *C4fStyles.xaml* file defines two kinds of styles: generic and named. Generic styles will automatically change the appearance of all buttons, labels, and listbox controls defined in the current scope. For example, the button style is a generic style that, when set to an application-level scope as shown in Example A-1, will change the styles of all buttons defined in your application.

 You can still manually edit the styles of controls that have a generic style by directly setting the control's **Style** property. Directly setting the style property will take precedence over a generic, application-level scoped style.

Named styles, on the other hand, require you to explicitly set the Style property of a control, as shown in Example A-2.

Example A-2. *Setting the HeaderStyle named style*

```
<Label Name="MyLabel" Style="{DynamicResource HeaderStyle}" >Hello</Label>
```

Style reference

Tables A-1 and A-2 contain a reference of the generic and named styles defined in the *C4fStyles.xaml* file.

Table A-1. *Generic styles in C4fStyles.xaml*

TARGETTYPE	DESCRIPTION
Label	Sets all labels to be bold and black
Button	Changes the button style to use a charcoal gradient and a click event animation
ListBox	Changes the ListBox borders, colors, scroll, etc.
ListBoxItem	Changes the ListBoxItem border, colors, background, etc.

Table A-2. *Named Styles in C4fStyles.xaml*

NAME	TARGETTYPE	USE FOR	DESCRIPTION
HeaderStyle	Label	Label controls	A large, bold, and orange label
SilverGradient	None	Window Background	A silver gradient radial (circular) brush
Orange	None	HeaderStyle	A custom orange color
AnimateMedia List	ListBox	Listbox	Animates a ListBox to shrink and grow

Before and after

By using *C4fSstyle.xaml*, we can change the default UI from the image in Figure A-2 to the image in Figure A-3.

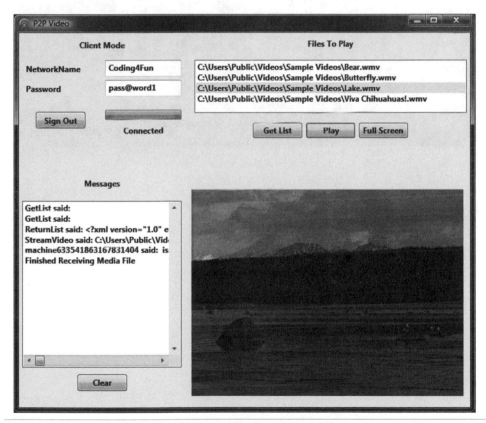

Figure A-2. *The PeerCast application using default styles*

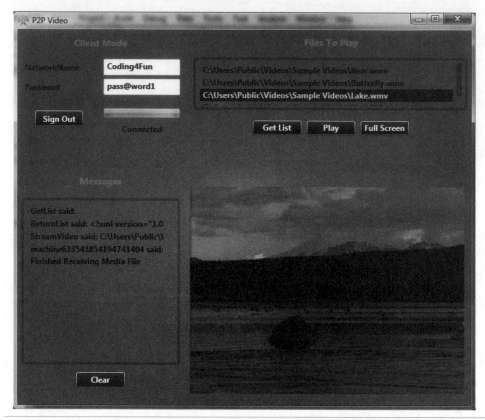

Figure A-3. *The PeerCast application after applying the C4fStyle*

Index

About the Authors

Dan Fernandez is an evangelism manager in the Developer and Platform Evangelism team at Microsoft. Dan has been with Microsoft since July 2001, working in multiple roles including the lead product manager for Visual Studio Express and Popfly, the Visual C# product manager, and as a developer evangelist in the Mid-Atlantic district. Prior to joining Microsoft, he worked as a developer at several consulting firms, including IBM Global Services, specializing in web-based and mobile application development. Dan is also the co-creator of Coding4Fun and works on fun open source projects in his spare time. You can read more about Dan on his blog at *http://blogs.msdn.com/danielfe/*.

Brian Peek is a senior developer at ASPSOFT, Inc., and a Microsoft C# MVP who has been actively developing in .NET since its early betas, but has been developing solutions using Microsoft technologies and platforms for even longer. Along with .NET, Brian is particularly skilled in the languages of C, C++ and assembly language for a variety of CPUs. He is also well versed in a wide variety of technologies, including web development, document imaging, GIS, graphics, game development, and hardware interfacing. Brian has a strong background in developing applications for the healthcare industry, as well as developing solutions for portable devices, such as tablet PCs and PDAs. Additionally, Brian previously co-authored the book *Debugging ASP.NET* (Sams) and currently writes for MSDN's Coding4Fun website. You can reach Brian via his blog at *http://www.brianpeek.com/*.

Colophon

The cover and heading font is Continuum; the text font is Myriad Pro; and the code font is TheSansMonoCondensed.